THE ARTS,
YOUNG CHILDREN,
AND LEARNING

SUSAN WRIGHT

Queensland University of Technology,
Australia

Boston   New York   San Francisco
Mexico City   Montreal   Toronto   London   Madrid   Munich   Paris
Hong Kong   Singapore   Tokyo   Cape Town   Sydney

Series Editor: *Traci Mueller*
Series Editorial Assistant: *Erica Tromblay*
Marketing Manager: *Elizabeth Fogarty*
Editorial-Production Administrator: *Beth Houston*
Editorial-Production Service: *Walsh & Associates, Inc.*
Composition and Prepress Buyer: *Linda Cox*
Manufacturing Buyer: *JoAnne Sweeney*
Cover Administrator: *Kristina Mose-Libon*
Electronic Composition: *Omegatype Typography, Inc.*

For related titles and support materials, visit our online catalog at www.ablongman.com.

Between the time Website information is gathered and then published, it is not unusual for some sites to have closed. Also, the transcription of URLs can result in typographical errors. The publisher would appreciate notification where these errors occur so that they may be corrected in subsequent editions.

Library of Congress Cataloging-in-Publication Data

Wright, Susan (Susan Kay)
    The arts, young children, and learning / Susan Wright.
        p.   cm.
    Includes bibliographical references (p.) and index.
    ISBN 0-205-19889-9
    1. Arts—Study and teaching (Early childhood)   2. Learning.   I. Title.

    LB1139.5.A78 W75 2002
    372.5—dc21

                                                        2002026141

Printed in the United States of America

10   9   8   7   6   5   4   3   2   1   06   05   04   03   02

This book is dedicated
to my father,
Hugh Wright

CONTENTS

CHAPTER SIX

Children's Artistic Development 102

CHAPTER SEVEN

Literacy in the Arts 126

CHAPTER EIGHT

The Visual Arts   151

CHAPTER THIRTEEN

Planning, Implementing, and Documenting the Curriculum   275

CHAPTER FOURTEEN

The Arts, Culture, and Schooling   298

PREFACE

The aim of this book is to provide an overview of current philosophies and practices in arts education in the early childhood years (birth to age eight). The content is geared toward the early childhood generalist teacher, but it is also applicable to arts specialists, other professionals, and parents who would like to learn more about the topic.

A number of books focus on early childhood education—the general curriculum, developmentally appropriate practice, young children's learning—or on specific arts disciplines, such as the visual arts, music, dance, and drama. However, there are very few examples in which the arts, young children, and learning are brought together into one book and where relevant topics are addressed in depth.

This book introduces and builds on key topics and systematically integrates theory and practice in a cumulative way through a range of topics:

Creativity
Approaches to arts education
Artistic learning and knowing
Socially constructed learning in early childhood arts education
The arts and intelligence
Children's artistic development
Literacy in the arts
The visual arts
Music
Enhancing dramatic activities in the early childhood years
Dance
The integration of the arts
Planning, implementing, and documenting the curriculum
The arts, culture, and schooling

ACKNOWLEDGMENTS

The photographs in the book were drawn from a number of observation-based and research-oriented projects over several years, including examples from the Queensland University of Technology Children's Art Archive (Barbara Piscitelli, Curator). Special acknowledgment is given to several centers that were supportive of this work and provided permission for their programs to be featured as examples of exemplary practice: Chistelhurst Kindergarten (Toowoomba), the Melbourne Lady Gowrie Child Centre, the Brisbane Lady

Gowrie Child Centre, and St. Martin's School, Carina. A special thank you is extended to several teachers for their input: Cynthia à Beckett; Ros Beeton; Lyn Bryant; Vivien Harris; Paula Melville-Clark; Raquel Redmond; Augene Nanning, for her story in Figure 5.5; Amy McKenzie, for compiling content for the glossary; Adrian Ashman, for formatting Figures 3.10 and 4.2 and for providing feedback in the early stages of the book; and Joachim Diederich, for his patience and support in the final stages of writing.

I would like to extend my sincere gratitude to Felicity McArdle and Julie Dunn, the authors of Chapters 8 and 10, for their significant contributions to this book. Both Felicity and Julie have had extensive experience working with young children and are well known for their exemplary practice in early childhood education, particularly in the disciplines of visual arts and drama respectively. Felicity currently is teaching and researching in the School of Early Childhood at the Queensland University of Technology, and Julie currently is an arts curriculum advisor with Education Queensland. I have worked and played with Felicity and Julie in a range of contexts over the years and am deeply indebted to them for sharing their richness of knowledge and experience through their chapter contributions.

Felicity McArdle, the author of Chapter 8, would like to thank Elisha Bertini and the children of room EB at St. Martin's School, Carina, for their example of good art practice in their involvement in the Wishing Tree experience.

The author would also like to thank reviewers Delia Richards, Prince George's Community College; Pat Hoebauer, Northwest State Community College; Nancy Baptiste, New Mexico State University; and Maria Runfola, State University of New York at Buffalo for their time and input.

CHAPTER ONE

CREATIVITY

I'd known Tony for about three years. He was a science teacher back in those days. If any word would describe Tony best, it was bizarre—at least, that's what I always told him. One day he arrived with a gift. It looked like an old-fashioned washstand (the sort our grandparents or great-grandparents might have had in their bedroom to compensate for a lack of a bathroom with hot and cold running water in the house). The base was made of old lumber with dowel legs, and it was liberally decorated with chocolate chip cookies and old teaspoons that had been stuck on with superglue and sealed with epoxy resin. An old sink rested in this decorated wooden frame, and around the edges of the sink were small rubber toy hippos and rhinos. A discarded mirror and a 1950s glass light shade were attached to the back of the washstand, and this was framed with bird feathers and Monopoly money.

The funny part of it all was that I immediately recognized the old sink, because Tony and I rescued after my husband threw it out during a big clean-up day. I thought the sink had rustic old-world qualities, and one day I would be disappointed if it had been dumped. Tony promised to store the sink at his place in case I ever wanted it. When Tony's wife complained about all the junk he stored for people under his own house, Tony began collecting objects to make his "functional garden sculpture," which included rooting around in the garages and under the houses of friends. When we "launched" the sculpture, there were cries of, "That's my toy hippo," "I wondered where my spoons had gone," and "I hope you realize that wood had been carefully measured and set aside for our bathroom renovations."

In spite of my friends' protests, I loved that sculpture, and it sat on our verandah for about two years until the ants discovered an unexpected source of nutrition as the epoxy began to wear off. We eventually had to dismantle the sculpture and put the old sink back under the house. I'm disappointed that I never took a photograph of it while it still looked good. I wonder where that sink is now.

Any book that deals with the arts would be incomplete if it did not address the realm of creativity. Creativity is so central to the visual and performing arts that they are frequently called the creative or expressive arts. Yet, while artistic activities involve creativity and expression, they are not the only components that make up the arts. All artistic endeavors do not require creativity—many people may not be creative but may still actively participate in and appreciate the arts.

When I reflect on my own early school years and university training, about 90 percent of my involvement in the arts—and music in particular—involved no creativity. Instead, the focus was on performance, interpretation, and analysis of the works of other visual and performing artists. While many arts students who excelled in the arts were highly proficient technicians who performed with sensitivity and stylistic accuracy, not all would have been described as creative. If they were creative, we wouldn't have known, since there were few opportunities to engage in musical improvisation, the spontaneous exploration of sound, or other creative experiences.

In contrast to my schooling experiences, my home and social interactions through music were spontaneous, responsive, personal, and interactive. My family harmonized while doing the dishes, traveling in the car, and during family picnics. We gathered around the piano in the evenings playing and singing while my father scratched on a fiddle, played the trombone, and fooled around with unconventional instruments like spoons or his favorite saw. My sisters and I improvised on the clarinet, French horn, piano, and trombone, while my mother encouraged, applauded, and kept us happily supplied with food and drinks.

Although the discrepancies in creative experiences that I experienced between my own home and schooling contexts may not be typical, the general issue of balancing creativity with mastery and analytical abilities is important for assisting artistry in all people. This chapter focuses on an understanding of creativity in relation to the development of knowledge and skills within the arts domain. It begins by defining creativity and creative products. This is followed by a discussion of creative individuals in relation to domains or disciplines and their ties with the field that judges the quality of their products. The third section focuses on resources that support the development of creativity; it concludes with a discussion of environmental contexts that support creativity and illustrates that neither creativity nor artistic competence can be developed in a vacuum.

CREATIVITY: WHAT IS IT?

Currently, there is an international trend for the educational policies of countries to place more emphasis on the development of creativity, partly in acknowledgment that creativity is essential to economic competitiveness (Design Council, 2000; Qualifications and Curriculum Authority and Arts Council of England, 2000; Seltzer & Bentley, 1999). In Hong Kong and Singapore, for example, the development of creativity within each area of the curriculum is now a national priority (International Review of Curriculum and

Assessment Frameworks Archive, 2000). The technological revolution has increased competition within and between countries and has placed a high value on intellectual capital. Because the rate of change within the world is escalating, employers now seek people who are able to produce creative and innovative ideas, so they can stay abreast with and hopefully surpass their competitors. In fact, many companies are now hiring arts graduates because of their specific training and experience in aspects of creativity.

Creativity is the process of generating ideas that are novel and bringing into existence a product that is appropriate and of high quality (Sternberg & Lubart, 1995). Novel products and ideas are unusual and original, but novelty alone does not equal creativity. Novelty must also be considered relative to other people's ideas and processes. Let us first consider novelty in relation to young children.

Many early childhood teachers consider children's ideas to be creative if they are novel for that individual child. For example, they consider the first "tadpole human" that a child creates to be justifiably classified as a *creative* act for that child, since it is the novelty of the first-time experience that counts, rather than any suggestion that this product will have profound cultural impact. To others, to elevate the first recognizable artwork of a child to the level of a truly creative act is considered to be romanticizing childhood and the process of creativity. Is the act of creating the first tadpole human similar to the first utterance of a recognizable word, like "mummy"? Is this utterance a truly creative act any more than, say, an adult making his or her first cheesecake?

No child would insist later, as an adult, that he or she could be classified as a creative prodigy by evidence of the act of learning to speak (brilliant as the achievement may be) because, unless impaired in some way, most children acquire this function almost "invisibly" through ordinary interactions with others. Similarly, most people, if they put their minds to it, could learn how to make a brilliant cheesecake by reading a good cookbook, but this may not be classified as a creative achievement. This is not to imply that children cannot be creative. Indeed, many have described early childhood as the peak of creativity and observed that, by middle childhood, creative tendencies seem to drop off. So what are truly creative acts, and how do they emerge?

Novel products are not predictable; they often provoke surprise in others because they go beyond the next logical step. What is creative is new and often brings positive changes. However, what is new is also strange, and what is strange can be threatening to others. In spite of the potential threat of creative ideas and products, it is important to accept them, because these new and challenging ideas and products will probably benefit others (Sternberg & Lubart, 1995).

Yet, to be deemed creative, novel products must also be appropriate and serve some useful function, rather than simply being bizarre or irrelevant.

Creative ideas and products must have quality and importance, be well executed, and be judged as showing a high level of skill (Sternberg & Lubart, 1995). I thought, for example, that Tony's chocolate-chip-cookie-covered garden sculpture was novel and creative. Others, who were not happy about Tony's chopping up lumber that had been set aside for bathroom renovations, or taking the 1950s glass light shade from their garage, might have had quite a different view! The relationship between creative ideas and products and the way ideas, products, and individuals are judged by others are discussed in the next segment.

Relationships between the Individual, Domain, and Field

Having the potential to be creative is different from actually being creative. While everyone has at least some creative potential, all differ widely in the extent to which they are able to realize that potential. The creative individual is a person who regularly solves problems, fashions products, or defines new questions in a way that is initially considered novel but that ultimately becomes accepted in a particular culture (Gardner, 1993a). In other words, an individual cannot be creative in the abstract.

Gardner (1993a, 1997) and Sternberg and Lubart (1995) have claimed that people tend to be creative in specific domains but not necessarily in others. For example, some business people may be creative in the area of marketing but not in finance, or vice versa. A person may be creative in the visual arts but not in music. Being creative in one domain, rather than across all domains, directly challenges the idea of an all-purpose creative trait that can be measured in a creativity test. Nonetheless, creativity within a domain can be enhanced, and the results can be considered in relation to a given time and place.

Nothing is, or is not, creative in and of itself. Creativity is inherently a communal or cultural judgment, and evaluation must be undertaken by a relevant portion of people from one's community or culture. The superstructure needed to account for creative activity has three core elements:

1. A creating human being
2. An object or project on which that individual is working
3. The other individuals who inhabit the world of the creative individual

Although creative individuals are often thought to work in isolation, the role of others is crucial throughout their development. These other individuals include families, teachers, and other supportive individuals. In addition to the family and local community, the wider society includes the field of surrounding people or institutions that render judgments about the quality of individuals and products.

Hence, creative activity grows out of the relationships between an *individual* person or talent, the objective world of work within a *domain* or discipline, and the ties between an individual and other human beings within the *field* that renders judgments about the quality of individuals and products. Creativity is best viewed as an interactive process in which these three elements participate (Csikszentmihalyi, 1988, 1996; Gardner, 1993a, 1997). It is possible, for example, that something that was considered creative at one period in history may not be considered creative at an earlier or later period of time.

Occasionally, an almost perfect fit among individual, domain, and field will exist, as in the case of exceptionally gifted young individuals, called prodigies. Mozart and Picasso are two prodigies who made the transition to the world of the creative adult. As adults, they continued the innovation and departure from the norm that few are able to make, and eventually became acknowledged masters within their domains. However, both men experienced anything but a smooth transition from youthful to adult practice (Gardner, 1993a).

Where there is pure synchrony, the individual, discipline, and field mesh perfectly. A modern example of synchrony resulted in Gary Wolf's development of the cartoon character Roger Rabbit. As a child, Wolf was engrossed by comic books and, after college, worked as a copywriter for an advertising agency while writing short stories in his spare time (often at 4 A.M.). During this period he became intrigued with TV commercials where cartoon characters, such as Snap, Crackle, and Pop, coexisted with real kids. For nine years, Wolf worked on a novel that combined real and animated characters, but his manuscript was rejected by more than one hundred publishers. Finally, his book was published by St. Martin's Press, during a period when Disney Studios was looking for a new animation script. The fit between individual, discipline, and field was right, and Wolf's novel eventually became the hit movie *Who Framed Roger Rabbit?* (D'Emidio, 1990).

While the successes of Mozart, Picasso, and Wolf apply to creative masters within the adult population, there are general issues of creativity that apply to adults and children in more ordinary circumstances. A focus on the types of personal and environmental conditions that can assist all individuals to acquire creativity in either a modest or grand way will be helpful in determining the educational conditions that can optimize creative development in teachers and children.

RESOURCES FOR DEVELOPING CREATIVITY

Creativity, at one level or another, can be found in most individuals and may be expressed in many different ways. Hence, creativity should not be regarded as "genius" behavior—the crown jewel of human achievement that most never experience. We need to demystify the notion of creativity so that it is seen as an obtainable goal for more individuals than at present.

A number of important resources come together to help people use and develop their creativity. These relate to personality, intelligence, thinking styles and processes, motivation and commitment to creative endeavors, and environmental contexts that support creativity.

Personality

Creativity is not just a cognitive or mental trait; it involves personality traits as well. Researchers interested in the development of creativity have identified the personality traits of creative people (Davis, 1992; Perkins, 1981; Sternberg & Lubart, 1995). These traits are not common to all creative people, and not all traits are found in one person, but the list can be a useful basis for understanding how we might enhance the creativity of young children. These traits are synthesized in Figure 1.1.

The links to childhood seem to run through the lives of highly creative people. Gardner (1993a) investigated case studies of Einstein, Picasso, Stravinsky, Graham, and Freud, and found that there was a similarity in the way in which each of these individuals searched for the most elemental forms within their domains. Gardner claimed that what may distinguish creative individuals is their ways of productively using the insights, feelings, and experiences of childhood. He described the creator as an individual who manages the formidable challenge of wedding the most advanced understandings achieved in a domain with the problems, questions, issues, and sensibilities that most characterized his or her life as a wonder-filled child. This special amalgam of the childlike and the adultlike behaviors occurs both in the sphere of personality and in the sphere of ideas. As Best (2000b, p. 4) described it:

> "Except you become as little children" is not a statement about childishness or regression but about an initial and already-awake entrance into the life of the mind that wonders, dreams, and figures out unrealistically. It is this unrealism, this desire for something out beyond, that marks a child's ways . . . the dayspring of that which only at a later time in a person's life dare we call intellect.

Einstein, for example, stood out among natural scientists in his abiding curiosity about children's minds. He once declared that we know all the physics we will ever need to know by the age of three. As Einstein often pointed out, the problems he pondered were those that children spontaneously raise but that most adults have long since stopped thinking about (Gardner, 1993a). It is interesting that it was Einstein who suggested to Piaget that he investigate children's intuitive notions of speed and time, thereby

FIGURE 1.1   Personality Traits of Creative People

Awareness of creativity. Creative people value originality and creativity in themselves and others and often seek friendships and experiences that enhance this. They want to be creative, enjoy the challenge of coming up with novel ideas, and believe they can make a contribution without necessarily knowing everything about a domain to work creatively within it. In fact, having too much knowledge can sometimes interfere with the creative process, as it can get in the way of seeing problems in a new light.

Originality. Creative people are often imaginative and enjoy pretending. They have flexible ideas, are nonconforming and unconventional, and can be bored by routine. Consequently, other people often see creative people as being irrational or even stupid.

Independence. People who are creative are individualistic, inner directed, self-confident, and self-accepting. They set their own rules, are uninhibited, and may not fit into some social contexts. While the pressure for conformity is often strong, to be creative one needs to take the risk of disagreeing with the crowd—to take a stance and stand up for beliefs, even in the face of objections and ridicule.

Risk-taking. Creative people generally accept the consequences of being different. They reject limits imposed by others and are optimistic and courageous. Such qualities involve persevering to overcome obstacles, continuing to generate ideas, being open to new experiences, and tolerating ambiguity.

Problem redefining. Creative people look through and around problems, not just directly at them. They do not accept what they are told about how to think or behave, but walk away from, and often ahead of, the crowd. They question traditional assumptions and have a positive attitude toward seeing problems in new ways.

Energy. Creative people are enthusiastic, alert, spontaneous, persistent, task-oriented, driven, committed, and ambitious. They can also be impulsive and excitable, and they enjoy telling others about their discoveries.

Curiosity. Because creative people are inquisitive, they often have wide interests, and are open to new experiences and growth.

Attraction to complexity. Creative people are attracted to the mysterious and asymmetrical. They are tolerant of ambiguity, disorder, and incongruity.

Artistic. Creative people are often artistic and have aesthetic interests.

Open-mindedness. Creative people are receptive to new ideas and other viewpoints. They are usually liberal and altruistic.

Need time alone. Creative people need time to be reflective and introspective, as they are often internally preoccupied.

Perceptiveness. Creative people are intuitive, using all senses in observing and responding. They make fine discriminations, fantasize, imagine, and mentally manipulate images and ideas. They can visualize actions and objects, hear music in their heads, and internalize movement without actions.

(continued)

FIGURE 1.1   Continued

Concentration. Creative people are able to focus their attention at a high level. They have a passionate attachment to their work that allows them to concentrate for long periods of time.

Humor and ability to regress. Creative people are usually playful, possess a freshness in their thinking and behavior, and enjoy regressing into childlike behavior: "fooling around," playing with ideas, projecting themselves into different roles, and using humor to break with conventions.

Childlike qualities. The creative adult is essentially a perpetual child. Adult artists and composers have described how they attempt to capture the freedom and grace of childhood, to open up new artistic possibilities, and to start afresh with images, sounds, and movements as if they had been discovered for the first time.

inspiring one of psychology's most illuminating lines of research (Gardner, 1993a).

Like Einstein, Picasso cultivated certain childlike personality features and demonstrated characteristics of young children in his artwork. He fragmented forms, searched for simple underlying shapes, and strove to capture on paper and canvas all aspects of a visual experience simultaneously. The composer Stravinsky anchored his work in the most basic elements of the medium—primitive rhythms and harmonies of the sort that had so impressed him when he was a young child. Martha Graham sought to remain forever young in her person and in her work, drawing on the child's imagination and the kinds of elemental expression that she favored through dance. Freud dealt with issues that are less likely to arise naturally in the minds of young children, yet they are just the ones that dominate the actual lives of children: dreaming, joking, and sexual play (Gardner, 1993a).

Intelligence and Knowledge

While personality is a significant influencing factor in creative individuals, it also links closely to the areas of intelligence and knowledge. Sternberg and Lubart (1995) described three key roles of intelligence in the development of creativity. *Synthetic intelligence* involves insightful information processes. It helps people see a problem in a new light, to redefine a problem altogether, and to turn things on their heads. *Analytical intelligence* involves recognizing which new ideas are good, and knowing how to structure ideas and problems appropriately. This involves allocating resources effectively and evaluating ideas objectively. *Practical intelligence* involves using the feedback from others in a positive way—knowing how to react to the feedback, deciding whether the criticism is worth considering, and deciding what changes will be optimal to meet the judgments of others.

When intelligence is coupled with having an appropriate body of knowledge, creative individuals can understand and apply basic principles, standards, and conventional notions of a society, but also can question or reject them. This involves toying imaginatively with combinations of ideas and not just accepting conventions. Too much knowledge can lead to entrenched thinking, when people become used to seeing things in one way and therefore have trouble seeing an alternative viewpoint. A person can become so accustomed to an accepted way of understanding something that it is difficult to go beyond it. Knowledge can "straitjacket" someone, making the person a slave rather than a master of his or her knowledge or point of view. For example, a psychologist who bases an understanding of a field in "truth" may have difficulty in accepting subjective reality (people interpret life through a blend of both *intuitive* beliefs and so-called *fact*).

Creative vision involves not only knowledge but also a willingness to see past it. There are a number of creative processes that can help individuals open their thinking to alternative viewpoints within their existing knowledge framework. These are described in Figure 1.2.

As illustrated in the creative processes in Figure 1.3, approaches to creativity involve a range of thinking and a variety of thinking styles.

Thinking Styles

Thinking styles are not abilities, but *how* individuals use their abilities and skills to learn and solve problems. Some people may have the ability to generate new ideas, but may prefer not to, or may not have the intellectual ability to do so effectively.

Almost fifty years ago, Apollinaire (1949) claimed that there were two kinds of artists: the "all-put-together" virtuoso, who draws on nature, and the "reflective cerebral structurer," who must draw from within the self. Mozart might serve as an example of the first, Beethoven the second. As a prodigy, Picasso could have been classified as a natural virtuoso, but changed into an analytical artist. Picasso's conflict during this period of change was reflected in his complaint to the famous philosopher Gertrude Stein, "If I can draw as well as Raphael, I have at least the right to choose my way and they should recognize that right, but no, they say no" (Stein, 1970, p. 23). Mozart, Beethoven, and Picasso drew on thinking styles that allowed them to forge new paths in history.

Yet many people are what Sternberg and Lubart (1995, p. 287) called "creative in the small." They may have new and useful ideas, but these ideas are at the level of detail. In contrast, creative people use a more global style of thinking, looking at the large picture rather than just the parts. Global

FIGURE 1.2   Creative Processes

Fluency. To produce many ideas for an open-ended problem or question (e.g., think of a hundred ways in which an old bicycle tire may be used). But fluency is not so much a matter of how numerous or diverse a person's ideas are or how quickly they come, but more about how flexibly and freely the ideas roam.

Flexibility. To take different approaches to a problem, think of ideas in different categories, or view a problem from different perspectives. This involves abandoning an old perspective if a new or more provocative idea suggests itself and redefining the problem entirely.

Elaboration. To add details to an idea, which includes developing, embellishing, improving, and implementing the idea (e.g., taking one of the hundred ideas on how to use an old bicycle tire and expanding on the idea).

Transformation. To change one object or idea into another by modifying, combining, or substituting. Transforming a problem involves making it more abstract, concrete, general, or specific (e.g., considering the bicycle tire as a huge eye within a wall sculpture).

Problem solving. To find problems and detect difficulties and missing information. A significant component of problem solving comes from defining or finding— exploring alternative goals and approaches. Creative individuals identify problem and solution "spaces" that appear promising and search within these spaces for approaches appropriate to the problem at hand and for leads that may pay off. This involves clarifying, simplifying, or defining a problem more broadly and evaluating alternative solutions to problems. Often, transforming problems involves working backward, imagining the result and then asking what would then lead up to it, as Sherlock Holmes did when approaching solutions to crimes.

Objectivity and selectivity. To distinguish between good and bad ideas and highly personal insights and commitments. Striving for objectivity prevents individuals from constructing a private world that has no testable reality for others. Hence, it is necessary to go beyond generating ideas to distinguishing which are the best, and whether these ideas have potential and are worth pursuing. It also involves setting aside final or intermediate products and coming back to them later so that they can be evaluated more distantly. Objectivity also involves reflecting on the critiques of others and seeking to improve.

Aesthetic and practical standards. To strive for something general, fundamental, and far-reaching. Attention is given to purposes, results, and high standards, and products that are elegant, beautiful, powerful, and original.

thinking increases the chance of finding a novel solution to a problem, particularly if this also includes shifting to the details when necessary, and using other styles of thinking that a task requires. Some qualities of thinking styles that are related to creativity are described in Figure 1.3.

FIGURE 1.3   Thinking Styles and Creativity

Visualization involves fantasizing, imagining, seeing things in the mind's eye, and mentally manipulating images and ideas. For example, daydreaming allows us the opportunity to reenact events and to play them out in our minds in a way we would wish them to have occurred or potentially to occur in the future.

Experimentation involves adopting a divergent way of thinking, experimenting, and going beyond the established practices in a discipline—for example, "decomposing" the music one is supposed to perform, rather than simply playing it as one is taught.

Analogical/metaphorical thinking involves borrowing ideas from one context and using them in another—for example, turning a functional object, such as a chair, into part of a backyard waterfall.

Logical thinking involves making reasonable decisions and deducing reasonable conclusions—for example, finding alternative ways to assemble pieces within a waterfall sculpture so that it won't fall apart or rust.

Predicting outcomes or consequences involves foreseeing the results of different solution alternatives and actions—for example, recognizing that the impact of a dance performance will be influenced by the surroundings in which it is presented, and choosing the best natural and technically produced lighting to enhance the movements of the dancers.

Analysis involves separating details and breaking down a whole into its parts. This involves practices such as working through segments of a musical piece that still need work and then rehearsing these in the context of the whole piece.

Synthesis involves seeing relationships and combining parts into a workable, creative whole. This could include issues such as considering props, costumes, sequences of events, positioning of characters, and staging in relation to a complete dramatic performance.

Evaluation involves separating the relevant from the irrelevant and thinking not only subjectively but critically and objectively. This involves determining when to probe further and when to cut losses and move on and, more generally, reflecting on one's own creating processes.

Motivation and Commitment

Creative people are driven to release their potential; they typically are task-focused, have high levels of energy, are more productive than many others, and pay more attention to the task than to the ultimate reward they may receive from it (Sternberg & Lubart, 1995). While they may receive extrinsic rewards, such as compliments, fame, or money, they generally are driven by personally set objectives and intrinsic goals and have a strong passion and love for their work, such as is illustrated in Figure 1.4.

Most inventive individuals find themselves enthralled by the quest itself—not just a means to some end, but an enjoyable activity. They believe that they, rather than other people or chance, are choosing what to do and how. Creative people are less likely to conform and more likely to follow their own judgment, even in the face of subtle social coercion. They are strong, independent, and unconventional, have autonomy, and are achievement-oriented.

The stereotype of a creative person is that of an isolate, needing no one or anything for inspiration. Perhaps the image is one of a windswept individual who lives alone on an island or in a mountain log cabin. Ideas come in the middle of the night, as bolts of energy from some unknown source, and the person is driven from bed to compose a symphony in two hours. Or perhaps there is a continuous pouring of creative energy that can be tapped at any time and, as a consequence, the person need not devote too much time to being exceptional. In reality, however, creative people—like all others—are most potent if they work in their area of interest in a committed, consistent fashion over a long period of time. Case studies of creative individuals, for example, reveal that "intellectual motifs" for symphonies, plays, or artworks do not appear in the minds of the creator, like energy from the fifth dimension, but can be traced through previous works over periods of time (Perkins, 1981). While some people may have a personality and tendency to be more creative than others—just as some people are naturally more perceptive or intellectually capable than others—most creative individuals just work at it. In many cases they have developed successful processes that they are able to transfer from one context to another.

FIGURE 1.4   **People with the Passion for Life**

People who are passionate about what they do seem to project an invisible energy. They might present as ordinary when in formal or conventional contexts, but when given free reign to expound about their work and how it energizes them, their whole bodies seem to come alive. Often I've seen their faces light up as their eyes dart from mental image to mental image; language is punctuated by sound effects and gesture, and you can almost "see" their stories—about what they do and believe in—like a film rolling across your own eyes. I think this depth of passion is something we all idolize, strive for. But like most things in life, passion has to be coupled with commitment, drive, and a lot of hard work—so long as you don't become possessed by work. These people I'm talking about don't just work hard, they also play hard. They "play around" with life and enjoy that. I suspect it's through this playing that they develop their passion.

Best (2000b, p. 3) described his creative process in the realm of musical composition:

> Virtually nothing of it is unearthly, otherworldly or daemonic . . . hard intellectual work is an abiding part of the compositional continuum (sketching, re-sketching and sketching some more; accepting, rejecting, erasing and doubting). But all along my mind is at work, gathering to itself a slowly acquired intellectual cabinet of knowledge, tools, structural options, procedural mechanisms. . . . Creativity is never done; the task is richly endless.

The commitment that creative people make to their field seems to be related to their work habits. They often are able to identify a situation in which, as young people, they fell in love with a specific material, situation, or person that continued to hold their attraction (Bloom & Sosniak, 1985). They speak of an initial romance, an intoxication, or a crystallizing experience (Feldman & Goldsmith, 1990). Yet no matter how potent their initial passion was with their field of pursuit, at least ten years of sustained activity and steady work at a discipline are required before creative individuals can attain significant breakthroughs. Gardner (1993a) argued, for example, that even Mozart had been composing for at least a decade before he could regularly produce works that are considered worthy of inclusion in the repertory. This is not to say that a person must be dedicated to a discipline for ten years before being able to demonstrate the *creative qualities* described above or to show *promise* within a discipline. In fact, Gardner contended that children who ultimately make creative breakthroughs often tend to show early signs of being explorers, innovators, and tinkerers, like Mozart.

In summary, it would be impossible for a single individual to possess all of the characteristics of personality, intelligence and knowledge, thinking style, and motivation and commitment described in this chapter. Some components of the lists presented earlier, however, are applicable to many creative people. Yet many personal characteristics and traits will be shaped by the creative person's environment. In other words, creativity is the product of an interaction between the individual and the context. Some environments encourage, nurture, and reward creativity while others inhibit it. The final segment focuses on ways in which an environment can support creativity within an early childhood context.

Environmental Support

The decision to encourage or limit creativity is often related to the attitudes of the significant people who shape the environment—whether they value creativity, and whether the creative products complement or challenge their own viewpoints. As mentioned earlier, any assessment of creativity should take into account the novelty, appropriateness, quality, and importance of a creative product. However, while risk taking is a quality considered to be relevant to creative productivity, the people who judge the products may not always be impartial, and their reactions may not be favorable if the product focuses on potentially controversial issues, such as organized religion or the way in which a nation is governed (Sternberg & Lubart, 1995).

Like judges of artistic products, teachers can be so focused on one goal that creativity is stifled. Children's products may be regarded as irrelevant, particularly if the product does not reflect the learning of the material presented in class. For example, a high school physics teacher who asks students to describe how they could measure the height of a tall building with a barometer might reject a student's response that proposes taking the barometer to the top of the building, dropping it, and measuring the time it takes before it smashes on the ground (Sternberg & Lubart, 1995). While the proposal is novel and would achieve the goal (perhaps even more accurately than the change in barometric pressure), the idea might not satisfy the teacher's view of appropriate uses of a barometer or the lesson objectives. Similarly, an early childhood teacher may overlook the feasibility of a young child's solution to a problem if it is outside the parameters of the specific content being taught.

Measurements of creativity are always considered in relation to the norms and expectations of a particular group in a specific time, place, and culture. In Western societies, we place a high level of importance on creativity in the artistic domains, provided the ideas and products also are appropriate and of high quality and importance. In China, by contrast, great emphasis is placed on quality and importance, with less emphasis on creativity. For example, kindergarten children are taught brush techniques and other skill-based methods during painting classes and, compared to their Western peers, have fewer opportunities to create their own images. Hence, the potential of the children from any culture to develop creatively is strongly associated with the support given within the school, home, and cultural contexts. This issue of the influence of culture and school will be discussed in greater detail in the final chapter and specifically in relation to music in Chapter 9.

Support systems are significant for all individuals and in all endeavors and are particularly relevant where thinking and behaving in contrary ways involves taking risks and overcoming obstacles. Support involves both affective and cognitive assistance from people who understand the nature of creativity. This supportive relationship in creative processes can occur between the child and adults and between the child and peers. There are intensive social and affective forces that surround individuals, and support is important in helping young children to generate new ideas and options and to have the motivation to pursue creative endeavors.

People who have studied the development of musical prodigies—young children who perform at the level of an adult—have discovered that their exceptional abilities are not associated only with talent or intelligence. Equally important is the role of parents in providing high levels of support by encouraging them to practice many hours per week, transporting them to music lessons and waiting to take them home again, providing emotional support before and after performances, and encouraging them to have social experiences on top of their incredible disruptions to schedules as a result of competitions, tours, and media exposure. This support is similar to that given to the young swimmer who is taken to the pool by admiring parents before and after school each day in the hope that, in years to come, an Olympic medal might result. In many ways, musical (and other) prodigies grow up very fast and, because of the pressure they sometimes encounter, many experience a "midlife crisis" at adolescence and often drop out of music and turn their talents and energies to other fields (Feldman & Goldsmith, 1990).

While most children do not experience life at such a rapid pace as that of the child prodigy, there are current changes in the educational system that influence the way in which children are taught and the support they receive. The expansion of early childhood programs in public schools enhances the likelihood that the curriculum will be vulnerable to the same social and political influences that affect elementary and high school curricula. These include the widespread focus on outcomes-based curricula and the increase in public pressure for accountability—especially in English and mathematics—which is evidenced by the increasing use of achievement testing and the current interest in the development of national goals and national student exams (Grieshaber & Ashby, 1997; Kessler, 1992).

The shifting emphasis toward accountability and achievement testing could tip the balance away from creative, child-centered experiences in learning toward more formal, teacher-oriented emphases. It seems that children learn attitudes toward work and play by the ways in which teachers structure the school day and the classroom environment. If an activity such as easel painting or making banana bread is assigned by the teacher and highly specified in terms of procedures and outcome, children often see it as work. However, if an activity such as alphabet bingo is freely chosen by the children, they think of it as play. In other words, whether an activity is thought of as work or play can depend not on the nature of the activity, but whether it is teacher- or child-initiated.

Learning environments typically contain elements that may not support creativity, such as task constraints or competitions. However, rather than being restricted by a stifling environment the creative person learns to adapt to it and to shape it into a preferred environment or even attempt to find another environment—another place to live, another place to go to school or work, or other relationships (Sternberg & Lubart, 1995). Yet potentially creative individuals may not have such opportunities to alter their environments and may never be recognized as creative. Young children, for example, are not free to choose where they live or perhaps even where they go to school. Some creative children may even encounter the low expectations reserved for the weakest of students because teachers and even parents may not recognize the special talents or gifts the children possess. Moreover, if young children express their creativity, they are often labeled as a problem rather than creative. Ultimately, as they are frustrated again and again in their attempts to realize their abilities, they may fulfill the problem-child prophesy (Sternberg & Lubart, 1995). Therefore, one of the aims of this book is to provide many examples of ways in which creativity can be enhanced within early childhood contexts.

SUMMARY

Creativity is the process of generating ideas that are relatively novel and bringing into existence a product that is appropriate and of high quality. Novel products and ideas are unusual and original, but novelty alone does not equal creativity. Novel products must also be appropriate, serve some useful function, and have quality and importance. To be fully appreciated, they should be judged as showing a high level of skill and be well executed.

Having the potential to be creative is different from actually being creative. While everyone has at least some potential to be creative, people differ widely in the extent to which they realize that potential. People tend to be creative in certain domains but not necessarily in others. Personal and environmental conditions can assist all individuals to acquire creativity in either a modest or grand way, and include:

- Personality
- Intelligence and knowledge
- Creative processes
- Thinking styles
- Motivation and commitment
- Environmental support

The decision to encourage or limit creativity is often related to the attitudes of the significant people who shape the environment: whether they value creativity and whether the creative products they judge complement or challenge their own viewpoints. Support systems are important for all individuals and in all endeavors and are particularly relevant in the area of creativity, where thinking and behaving in contrary ways involves taking risks and overcoming obstacles. However, learning environments typically contain elements that may not support creativity or creative children. It is important that teachers and parents recognize the special qualities of creative individuals, their processes and products, and provide supportive conditions for all children to develop to their full creative potential.

ADDITIONAL READINGS

Csikszentmihalyi, M. (1996). *Creativity: Flow and the psychology of discovery and invention.* New York: Harper Collins.

Davis, G. A. (1992). *Creativity is forever.* Dubuque, IA: Kendall/Hunt.

Feldman, D. H., & Goldsmith, L. T. (1990). *Nature's gambit: Child prodigies and the development of talent.* West Lafayette, IN: Purdue University.

Gardner, H. (1997). The key in the key slot: Creativity in a Chinese key. *Journal of Cognitive Education, 6* (1), 15–26.

Sternberg, R. J., & Lubart, T. I. (1995). *Defying the crowd: Cultivating creativity in a culture of conformity.* New York: Free Press.

PRACTICAL ACTIVITIES

1. Think of creative people you know. What are some of their characteristics or personality traits? How closely do these traits fit with those described in Figure 1.1? What other characteristics would you add to this list? Can you provide examples of how these people demonstrated creative characteristics?

2. Take a few minutes to jot down two or three experiences you have had that you think are creative. Look back over this chapter and identify the types of creative processes or thinking styles you used in these experiences. Then talk about these experiences with your friends or classmates. Consider these questions and think of other questions to discuss:
   - In what ways are these experiences similar or different? (Think in terms of creative processes, products, and thinking styles used.)
   - How have other people, such as past teachers, friends, or work mates, responded to your creative endeavors?
   - Have you felt supported in your attempts to be creative? (Describe this support.)
   - In what ways could your creative potential have been developed more?

3. Reflect on your experiences with young children in relation to their creative personalities and use of creative processes. (Refer to Figures 1.1 and 1.2 and think of examples of how children have demonstrated these personalities or processes.) What types of support have the children received from their parents, teachers, or other significant people? Have you observed situations in which young children's creative expression could have been more supported by their environment? What type of support do you think would be helpful?

4. Divergent learning usually involves multiple paths of inquiry, whereas convergent learning usually merges on one "correct" response (e.g., "2 + 2 = ?"). There are many enjoyable games you can try that apply to many age levels and enhance divergent learning. Try these two with your friends or children:

   What can you do with this chair? A chair is placed in the center of the room and, going around the circle, people think of ways of using the chair in a nonconventional way, such as pretending it is a TV, turning it on, and staring at it, or putting it on their back and pretending it is a backpack. Others in the group guess what the person is miming and identify the various roles given to the chair during the mime.

What's my name? Like in the previous example, people take turns miming something that also can be associated with a person's name. For example, if the mimer bounces up and down in one place, others guess that the name is Bob; if the mimer dances freely around the room, others guess the name Grace.

CHAPTER TWO

APPROACHES TO ARTS EDUCATION

One of my friends, Jane, has these to-die-for hands that I often say I wish she could transplant onto my arms. I fantasize that I might be able to play the piano better if I had her long, flexible fingers. Jane can reach well over an octave without effort, and I suspect she could handle the technical aspects of playing the piano with a lot more ease than I do. Yet she has no interest in playing, largely because when she was taking piano lessons as a kid, her teacher used to smack her hands with a ruler whenever she made a mistake. I have this image of a mean old biddy perched on the edge of the piano, ready to pounce at any musical inadequacies. We laugh about this now, but deep down that type of approach to teaching makes me feel sad, because I can't help but wonder if Jane might have been just as musical as she is artistic today if she'd had a more positive start in her music education.

But another thing that makes me sad is when friends tell me about how they really didn't have a chance to learn music, even if they wanted to, because their parents couldn't afford lessons, or their school didn't have music (or if it did, music was slotted in about one month before an end-of-year school concert, and the rest of the time it just didn't happen). It seems to me that people generally gravitate to their areas of interest and expertise as they go through life and often end up taking on a profession that lets them fulfill their special skills and talents. But I can't help but wonder as well whether some people might not know that they have a special interest or talent if they haven't had a chance to discover it, particularly early in life when there are more opportunities to express their talents freely and openly. I remember a twenty-year-old student commenting to me, after making a remarkable sketch of one of her friends, that she had no idea until then that she could draw. I was floored. I wondered how this amazing ability could have laid dormant within her for so many years and how life for her might have been different if she'd had the chance to develop her talent throughout her life.

The example above illustrates how our experiences in the arts can shape our later attitudes and potentials. Experiences are strongly influenced by the styles of teaching that are provided and the types of learning that particular approaches offer. This chapter provides a background on the origins and development of some basic beliefs about early childhood arts education and presents a rationale for a blend of approaches that allows young children freedom to express themselves within a context in which teachers are active participants and supporters of children's learning. It outlines principles of guided learning, the role of the adult in forming partnerships with young children, and strategies for an effective teaching-learning interface. The material is based upon the belief that teachers' philosophies about early childhood arts education will significantly influence the way in which they plan the curriculum, choose teaching strategies, and evaluate their programs. It begins by contrasting two relatively common approaches to arts education—the productive and reproductive—which sets the stage for a discussion of an alternative approach, guided learning.

BASIC APPROACHES

Quite a few years ago, the terms *productive* and *reproductive* were coined by Rosario and Collazo (1981) to describe two contrasting pedagogical beliefs and practices in early childhood arts education. In the *productive* approach:

- Arts experiences are child-centered and based upon children's personal criteria.
- The teacher facilitates and supports children's self-expression and creativity.
- Arts media are easily accessible to children so that they have opportunities to use them when they prefer.

In contrast, in the *reproductive* approach:

- Arts experiences are regulated by the teacher.
- The teacher didactically controls the arts process, where minimal value is assigned to children's spontaneous artistic activity.
- The teacher controls access to materials and how they are to be used.

In 1981, Rosario and Collazo indicated that there was more evidence of the reproductive approach used in early childhood education contexts than of the productive approach. Perhaps in some ways this situation has remained relatively unchanged in many early childhood contexts, even today. Let us examine some of the beliefs that are at the core of each of these two practices so that we can come to know how and why they have developed, and see the strengths and weaknesses inherent in each.

The Productive Approach

In a productive approach, the traditional beliefs and practices of early childhood arts education center on the spontaneous flourishing of children's self-expression. Through this child-centered approach, it is believed that children should be in charge of their own learning, in their own way, at their own pace. The ultimate goal is to provide learning opportunities that allow children to interact spontaneously with arts resources so that whatever talent, knowledge, and skills the child possesses can develop freely.

Those who believe in the productive philosophy stress freedom for the child within a supportive, safe, and secure learning environment—one in which children follow their instincts and interests and engage in activities of their own choice. The notion of *helping* children become artistic, either in terms of understanding or production, is seen as unimportant, if not inappropriate (Walsh, 1993). Through spontaneous, free, hands-on arts experiences, it is believed that children have endless opportunities to become involved in a number of processes and modes of expression, where the focus is generally on discovery, self-awareness, and personal communication. However, in reality, many opportunities for children to develop artistically can be overlooked. There is little or no attention given to social interaction, artistic perception, the mastery of technical skills, or the ability to analyze or to critique artistic experience.

The productive approach might be called *maturationist.* It is based on the belief that children should be allowed to mature or "unfold naturally," a term used over fifty years ago by one of the early advocates of arts education, Victor Lowenfeld (1947). From the maturationist's point of view, if children are not discovering particular concepts, it is because they cannot, or are not yet *ready* to do so. The arts are seen essentially as providing opportunities for self-expression of that which is hidden within the child, which surfaces when the child is ready (Walsh, 1993). Beyond the teachers' primary tasks of preparing and arranging classroom resources; providing space, time, and materials; and offering gentle nurturance, children's artistry is expected to develop spontaneously and independently. Any attempts to teach (e.g., extend, show, or explain) before a child is mentally ready, it is believed, will do little to foster development, may interfere with the child's own efforts to learn, and might even damage children's self-concept and creativity. Within the productive philosophy, intervention from the teacher is viewed as interference.

Yet, it is clear that learning needs a context in which to mature in the same way as a rose grows and unfolds when the optimum conditions exist. As a rose bush requires water, fertilizer, and shaping to develop to its full beauty, children also require instruction and feedback to function beyond their current level of understanding. An early childhood arts curriculum that is based on children's experiencing only their own art, dance, music, and play would be like expecting children to acquire language by talking only with their same-aged peers.

Children and adults do not construct an understanding of themselves and their world solely on the basis of private encounters. They need to interact with and see the perspectives of others if they are to learn. While perspective taking was once viewed as being beyond the abilities of young children, current views are now questioning this belief. Young children are not as self-centered or unable to take the perspectives of other people as once thought, yet the theory of egocentrism and the belief that children have no conception of other people's minds still endures (Bruner, 1986; Walsh, 1993).

We know, for example, that all people, regardless of age, learn easily when they acquire knowledge relevant to the task at hand. When we cannot connect new information to previous experiences, we cannot learn; it is as if the information were presented in a foreign language. It is true that children act more intelligently in familiar situations than in unfamiliar ones, and it is this familiarity that will most affect performance. However, to base an early childhood arts program solely on children's interests is a romantic and limiting perspective that the noted American educationalist John Dewey criticized over ninety years ago (Archambault, 1964). Children's interests also need to be mediated (i.e., guided and extended). The unfamiliar must be linked to their sense of the world and their place within it. In practice, this means elaborating what children already know and encouraging connections between existing knowledge and new knowledge and skills.

Current educational approaches, for example, now stress the need for teachers to be active mediators of children's social and general competence. However, there is a gap between the recommended teaching practices found in textbooks, teaching manuals, and journals when compared to observations of what actually occurs in the classroom. Researchers have demonstrated that, during free play experiences, many teachers often do little to help children during interactions with their peers, except to settle disputes or restore order or to intervene when unacceptable behavior threatens classroom decorum or children's safety (File, 1993).

In a similar way, teachers often do not appear to know how to mediate artistic processes such as painting, dancing, or music making. Teachers often adopt a noninterventionist approach to children's art, music, dance, and play. They often view these areas of learning as private, creative domains and avoid entering them. When they do enter into children's artistic domains, they often make comments that focus on pleasing the child (e.g., saying "Good boy"), or else give only a quick, positive, evaluative remark (e.g., "That's beautiful), or basic information about general technique (e.g., how to take a painting to a drying rack, fasten the back of a tutu, or shift musical instruments to a more convenient space in the play area). In such circumstances, children are not provided with opportunities to extend their talent, knowledge, and skills beyond what they already possess. Essentially, the children's artistic expression is expected to unfold naturally without nurturance, guidance, or support.

Unsupported arts learning in the classroom sometimes can lead to a laissez-faire ("anything goes") type of practice. In a laissez-faire approach, the attitude is held that whatever children do in the arts is valuable; for a teacher to interfere would be to stifle children's creativity. This attitude restricts the teachers' role to one of organizing the environment only and discourages them from suggesting ideas or processes that might mediate children's learning. Yet, with no input from others, children can sometimes become bored and even frustrated with experiences that invite only independent experimentation. Clearly, children cannot create or compose from nothing. They need background ideas and suggestions, and we have a central role to play in providing children with support and guidance.

It should be clear that I am not advocating a reproductive, teacher-directed approach, but rather one of educated guidance. To clarify the distinction between productive and reproductive approaches, a brief discussion of the latter will provide a rationale for a third alternative, one of guided learning, which is less laissez-faire than a productive approach, but more democratic than a purely reproductive one.

The Reproductive Approach

In reproductive, teacher-directed approaches to arts education, the emphasis often is on the acquisition of skills and behaviors that the teacher believes to be important for children's successful transition into academic settings. Skill-oriented activities center on children's learning, for example, how to color in shapes without going out of the lines, to raise their hands for permission to ask or answer questions, to wait their turn and follow directions, and to learn to count or name colors and geometric shapes. Materials, activities, and experiences are chosen that lead to desired outcomes or preestablished learning objectives.

Teacher-directed practices minimize the child's role in learning, while maximizing the role of the adult. While didactic, activities-based programs can involve children in a range of learning experiences, these activities do not feature the core business of the arts: using arts media and their inherent "grammars" to symbolize thoughts and emotions through action. Most importantly, the approach is unidirectional—from the adult to the child—with the teacher dictating the materials and the methods to be used.

The interactions that occur in teacher-directed activities are usually highly routinized and scripted, where children follow step-by-step instructions rather than discover personal meaning through self-directed involvement. In art, for example, children follow teacher-conceived processes and reproduce teacher-conceived products, such as Mother's Day cards, Christmas decorations, or egg-carton caterpillars. Other activities include painting with novel implements such as feather dusters, squirting paint from plastic bottles, blowing paint through straws, or rolling marbles around in a tray to trace patterns on paper. In music, dance, or play, reproductive approaches include teaching songs through rote learning only, directing instrumental experiences where children only play predetermined rhythmic patterns at specific points, systematically teaching structured dance steps, or rehearsing scripted roles or "lines" from children's rhymes or storybooks. While there may be some place for the occasional use of these activities within an early childhood arts program, these experiences alone do not provide opportunities for children to make many personal choices, experience a variety of learning modes and styles, or learn from a range of artistic processes.

Some reproductive activities can be intriguing and enjoyable for children, and sometimes the results can be quite aesthetic. But the processes generally involve direct imitation, rote learning, and random exploration. The products often carry no significance for personal communication, analytical thinking, or aesthetic decision making. In addition, when provided with an exclusive diet of reproductive activities, children begin to depend on the teacher for ideas rather than to identify or pursue their own directions or purposes. More seriously, because the content, resources, and processes are prescribed by the teacher, children develop the impression that their own ideas and ways of pursuing them are of little importance. The children wait for instructions instead of independently or collaboratively pursuing their own or their group's interests or setting and solving their own artistic challenges. Meanwhile, open-ended materials (those that can be used in a variety of ways), such as blank paper, blocks for building, collage resources for construction, or clay for sculpting, remain untouched while the children ask, "What are we going to do today?" Similarly, in other areas of the arts, there is less time to experiment with xylophones and percussion instruments, explore the variety of uses of dress-up and dance props, or experience the potential of open-ended materials that might be made into puppets, masks, or other drama resources.

Hence, programs in which general educational goals and specific objectives are established in advance, exclusively by the teacher, illustrate a lack of attention to children's efforts to construct meaning through the selection and use of arts materials and artistic ideas. Instead, educators employ a highly selective filter that sifts out children's interests and responses that might be considered controversial. The end result can be curriculum units or themes of study that focus on innocuous topics that often are far removed from the passions of the children (New, 1993). Perhaps the reason why teachers from a reproductive philosophy apply a "top-down" approach to the arts is based on a belief that young children are incapable of learning without a great deal of intervention. In contrast, the basis for a productive approach appears to stem from the belief that child art is precious and should remain within the realm of personal self-expression. These views may be consciously or unconsciously shaped by the values about arts education that have evolved throughout the history of Western art education.

Origins of Philosophical Beliefs in Arts Education

From the late nineteenth century to the present, two streams of interest evolved and became forces in the field of art education in particular: theorists of child and developmental psychology and artists and aestheticians (Leeds, 1989). Leeds outlined how psychologists in the late 1800s, such as Perez and Sully, described the manner in which young children drew, and they critiqued children's performance against implied adult standards of visual realism. Hence, they saw the child's method of logic in visual expression as "mistaken" (e.g., the development of the use of detail was seen to be as if by chance), and they distanced themselves from the childlike state of logic, or "otherness" of children, by measuring it against "civilized" adult standards.

Others disputed these views, arguing that, instead of teaching children advanced artistic concepts at too early an age, young children should be allowed to work freely on their own (Ruskin, 1891, in Leeds, 1989). Rather than confining the aesthetic experience of human thought to accepted classical styles and adult standards of realism, both the child and the "primitive" artist were seen to "draw the natural object not as a representation of itself envisaged as beautiful, but as a sign of intention . . . of an elementary beauty that may be rough and crude indeed but which issues at last absolutely and exclusively from the power of thought" (Töpffler, 1847, in Leeds, 1989). Such direct appreciation of primal and inventive modes of work emerged in the aesthetic revolution of modern art.

Young avant-garde artists of early modernism wanted to invent a new form of expression and began to study peasant art, tribal arts, and the art of children and the insane to take on aspects of "the primitive, the authentic, the expressive, and the inventive as measures of excellence" (Leeds, 1989, p. 99). Two of the modern schools of style that flourished during the first part of the century, the Secession art of Vienna and the Blue Rider group in Germany, used the children's art model as a means for inspiration and study. Klee used his own drawings, saved from childhood, as sources for his work, and Kandinsky viewed the child as being in touch with a spiritual reality that was no longer accessible to most adults, believing that the unconscious power in children placed their work at a *higher* level than that of the adult (Leeds, 1989).

Franz Cizek, a painter of the Secession group, collected a large number of children's drawings and displayed them at the group's own Viennese exhibition in 1908, out of respect for child art as a form of both human and aesthetic expression, on a par with their own. The qualities that Cizek and other early modern artists admired in children's art were the spirit and process by which they were created, "the openness of feeling, the directness of approach, [and] the imaginative plasticity of mind so natural to children, which had come to be recognised as characteristic of creativity in general" (Leeds, 1989, p. 100).

The interest in the creative powers of children inspired Cizek eventually to give up painting to devote his life to teaching. He opened a juvenile art class in Vienna in 1897 that existed for the next forty years and became an important model for progressive art education movements throughout the world. Artistic creativity became a key interest of progressive educators in the first three decades of this century and John Dewey, Viktor Lowenfeld, and others began to change the way in which art was taught to children. The old methods of copying were replaced by free exploration of materials, and beliefs in promoting inventiveness, authenticity, and expressive qualities in children's work.

The study of child art became an interest of a large number of twentieth-century psychologists, educators, and aestheticians. Lowenfeld (1947), Arnheim (1954), Kellogg (1969), Golomb (1992), Goodnow (1977), Gardner (1973, 1980) and others offered developmental theories based on their views and interpretations. Lowenfeld's typology of stages of primary school children's development in drawing, which emphasized the significance of changes in spatial relationships and form, became accepted as the norm for about three decades. This typology, along with Lowenfeld's genuine aesthetic appreciation for children's spontaneous and untutored artistic invention, encouraged adults not to intervene with children's learning in the arts in case this might interfere with their creative process.

More recently, arts educators have advocated for a less precious attitude toward children's artistic processes, believing that children can be analytical about their own and other's works of art, music, dance, and drama in relation to aesthetic criteria without violating their natural means of expression or creativity. Many early childhood arts educators now realize that young children are more competent than previously supposed, and that Piaget and other early developmental psychologists underestimated children's cognitive abilities (Bruner, 1986; Donaldson, 1978; Walsh, 1993). Consequently, neo-Piagetian thinking now emphasizes the cultural and social nature of learning and principles of an emergent curriculum in relation to social constructivism (Berk & Winsler, 1995; Bruner, 1996; Edwards, Gandini, & Forman, 1993; Malaguzzi, 1993; Rinaldi, 1993; Rogoff, 1990).

Such an emergent curriculum allows opportunities for children to explore their own ideas, set personal goals, choose how they will solve problems, and find solutions with the help of others. How can we encourage children's natural desire to explore and learn while expanding their knowledge of themselves and the world around them? The answer is to guide children in the delightful and compelling process of learning through discovery by enhancing their creativity while providing them with knowledge and skills to use it productively.

THE GUIDED LEARNING APPROACH

Providing arts activities alone is less than half the job of teaching. Teachers and parents must act as resources, not only to satisfy or answer children's questions, but also to help children ask themselves good questions and discover the answers (Rinaldi, 1993). Most early childhood teachers acknowledge that guidance is important in the beginning stages of reading and writing, to familiarize children with common words—such as their own names—and to recognize and name objects. We realize that children's attitudes toward reading are influenced by seeing other people reading and discussing books. We also observe children treasuring certain books and memorizing their texts and acknowledge that children can be advantaged when they have attractive, interesting books available to them to encourage them to read.

In a similar way, children are influenced by adults' positive attitudes toward the arts. Children will have favorite paintings, recordings, and dances, and they are enhanced through exposure to a range of arts-related experiences. Hence, we should make accessible to children appropriate examples of their own and other people's art, music, dances, and dramatic productions for them to view, listen to, talk about, and incorporate into their own artistic experiences. Through such exposure, education in the arts will involve a blend of both unfolding and training. Not only will there be free play for them to experience the arts through doing, but there also will be careful guiding, inspiration, and critical reflection—reflection not only on their own work, but on the work of others.

During early learning experiences, we should provide appropriate materials and resources and set the learning context so that the children's range and types of learning experiences can be extended. By observing them interact with the resources and each other, adults can decide how young children learn spontaneously. We might, at times, simply observe from a distance, offering moral support through comments such as "I see," or by simply nodding or smiling. At other times, we might describe the children's processes or products using simple words that act as a form of encouragement, letting them know that what they were doing is valued and should be continued. Still, at other times, we may need to take a more active role and suggest alternatives or initiate learning while trying to ensure that the child will then take the lead again. This form of encouragement is dependent upon a number of conditions associated with the teaching-learning interface.

Conditions for Guiding Learning in the Arts

Chapter 4 provides greater detail of how to "scaffold" children's learning in the arts; however, as a starting place for this discussion, some general principles are discussed here. Regardless of the art form, conditions that are favorable to stimulate artistry across all age levels include:

- Provision of personally relevant experiences (e.g., issues, approaches, and interactions that engage children's interest and draw on their previous knowledge and experiences)
- Appropriate materials and tools for each arts discipline (e.g., quality art supplies, musical instruments, dance props, and resources to enhance dramatic play)
- Sufficient time and opportunities for children to discover the expressive, physical, visual, and aural properties of various arts media (e.g., opportunities to use materials and tools over an extended period of time, so children become familiar with ways in which they can use these resources for artistic intent, and make progress through each repeated and varied experience)

However, these are necessary but not sufficient conditions. We must also:

- Guide children to move from basic manipulation of arts materials toward the infusion of *meaning* into their expressive products (e.g., help children progress beyond occasional, activities-based exposure to materials, where they might think "been there, done that," to using resources for personal and collaborative exploration of thoughts, ideas, feelings, and purpose)
- Provide opportunities for children to work with increasingly demanding materials (e.g., recognizing when children are ready to extend their current knowledge and skills and providing more challenging resources to enhance their abilities and means of expression)
- Give feedback to children about their artistic pursuits and provide opportunities for them to discuss their own and other's artistic processes and products (e.g., talking about what they achieved and how they did this and ways they could extend their processes in different ways to achieve different results)
- Demonstrate sensitivity to children and a willingness to assume their perspectives (e.g., get into the thoughts and feelings of the children and attempt to go with the flow to take them to the next step of learning)
- Provide assistance so that children can recognize the unique features of each arts discipline while finding connections across disciplines (e.g., help children recognize how their playing of musical instruments could enhance the mood of a dramatic play experience)
- Demonstrate that all phenomena in our environment have aesthetic qualities so that children increase their capacity to recognize, analyze, and experience these qualities (e.g., taking time to appreciate the shadows cast by a tree on the tiles of the classroom courtyard, listen to the

birds nearby, taste the rain on their tongues, feel the warm texture of a brick wall)

■ Model the importance of artistic and aesthetic values for individuals, society, and culture (e.g., appreciate the colors and textures of a mother's sari, share the tastes of foods from other cultures, listen to multicultural music, view videos of dances from across the world and try similar movements).

While teachers may acknowledge that these conditions are important for children's development in the arts, they sometimes believe that they lack the skills or background in the arts to provide appropriate support. As a consequence, they may hope that children will "pick up" artistic skills on their own. But as in all areas of education, there is the risk that children with advanced skills will succeed, leaving those with less developed skills increasingly disadvantaged. In other words, the rich get rich and the poor get poorer. In addition, children with special talents in the arts may begin to lose interest and turn their attention to other areas of learning if their artistic energies are not channeled in productive and positive ways.

Providing conditions that encourage artistic development is not as complex as it may seem. The beginning step is achieved simply by helping children to look, listen, move, think, and feel with increasing sensitivity (Derham, 1973). Derham, a prominent early advocate of arts education, once commented to me that the greatest compliment she received was when a child realized that mountains were not just brown; they were bluish, greenish, purplish, and reddish brown. Figure 2.1 on page 30 illustrates how we can help children not only see but also hear, through guided looking and listening experiences.

Such involvement with children reflects an awareness of our role in assisting creative processes through extending children's previous experiences and helping them create new artistic experiences and products. The interface between process and product involves finding a balance between experience and outcome.

Assisting Artistic Processes and Products

One of the accepted truths of early childhood arts education is that the process is more important than the product. It is thought that the products of children's efforts are representative of their understanding of a concept or experience, and this product mirrors their cognitive abilities. However, how children view the world appears to be far more sophisticated than we may sometimes think (Golomb, 1992; Kindler, 1993). To illustrate this point in the domain of the visual arts, children as young as three years of age seem to understand that, while art works can express meaning, there are limitations in what they can express purely through graphic means. Hence, there can be a

FIGURE 2.1   Examples of How to Enhance Aesthetic Sensitivity to Sound

As teachers, I think we need to take more time to appreciate beauty and pleasant sensory experiences with children, like sitting and watching and listening to the rain on the window. Probably because of the types of things we push in schools, children seem to be getting more and more focused on the sense of sight and less aware of the other senses, like taste, touch, and sound. I try to keep these other senses active by doing things like taking the kids on listen walks, with my portable tape recorder tucked in my bag. We try to capture all kinds of sounds on our recordings. The children hone in on everything from lizards rustling in the scrub, to coffee being ground in a nearby house, to traffic sounds. They often listen to their tape recordings of these sounds and try to mimic what they hear. They will make up words to describe what they hear, like "scloop" or "splup" for walking through mud. Sometimes they search through the tapes to find a special sound to use it in their play. The other day, a few boys were role playing cave men on a hunt for dinosaurs, and they wanted to capture a feeling that was like dinosaur walking sounds, so they could feel scared while stalking the dinosaurs. The boys went to the tape to find the scurrying sound of the lizard and then tried to imagine and make this sound, except ten times as loud and scary. Then they created a sound story, acting out the parts of the dinosaurs and hunters.

discrepancy between what the children can draw and what they wish to draw. By the age of six, or even earlier, some children may become dissatisfied when their drawings fail to meet their standards of what something should look like (Kindler, 1992). This dissatisfaction may contribute to the documented decline in artistic production when children reach school age, not only in art, but also in music, dance, and dramatic experiences (Gardner, 1982).

While the arts can often express what language cannot, language can also help us express what drawings, dances, music, and play cannot. Thus, what children say about their artistic creations is not an addition, but an integral part of an arts activity (Kindler, 1994; Wright, 2001b). Therefore, teachers' conversations with children should deal with the *intent* as well as the *outcome* of their activities. Talking to children about their artworks could be viewed as being in dramatic opposition to the practice of emphasizing only the process of the child's efforts.In a purely process-oriented approach, adults often dismiss the child's complaints that the finished drawing, for example, "doesn't look right." However, children can be encouraged and helped to rework their images if they fail to convey their intended purpose until they are satisfied that they have expressed themselves adequately (New, 1993). Such assistance also applies in the realms of music, dance, and drama.

To illustrate this issue in relation to the visual realm, traditionally, art experiences in early childhood have involved children in drawing, painting, and using other media through the use of imagination and memory only. Having children participate in drawing from observation, such as looking at and drawing an object or person, has been considered to be inappropriate, classified as "copying," or considered more relevant for older children than young children. However, observation-based drawing experiences do not inhibit young children's desire or ability to draw or paint from their imaginations. Instead, the observational and imaginative drawing experiences balance each other. Together, they encompass a variety of forms of visually symbolizing and expressing—representative and unrepresentative, realistic and abstract.

For example, preschool-aged children show evidence of increased skill in drawing self-portraits when given opportunities to engage in this activity throughout the year (Musatti, 1987). Though such experiences, children are provided with opportunities to extend their observational and drawing skills, reflect on their earlier interpretations and perceptions of themselves, and modify their previously held beliefs about how specific facial features can be rendered (New, 1993). This engages children in a range of forms of expression and complements their desires and competence. Drawing self-portraits or still lifes from observation can evolve naturally from a child's interest to explore an idea, technique, artistic concept, or an aspect of interpersonal behavior component (such as capturing facial expression, or the aesthetic qualities of a bouquet of flowers).

Assisting children to extend their interest and, in the process, develop artistic competence is applicable to all areas of the arts, not just the visual arts. In a program in which there is a great deal of interaction between the children and adults, the interest of one child can become infectious, and soon the teacher and a small group of other children can become involved in an extended learning project—an open-ended journey that has the potential to travel in a number of directions, involving a multitude of purposes. The story below (Figure 2.2 on page 32) was told to me by my close colleague Felicity McArdle, who is also the author of the visual arts chapter (Chapter 8) in this book. It illustrates how we can extend the interest of one child while providing opportunities for a range of artistic and general learning experiences for other individuals and groups of children.

Such educational journeys require a perceptiveness on the part of the adult, a willingness to attempt to "get into" the heads and hearts of the children and to follow their direction intuitively while gently taking them to the next step in their learning. Deciding on the most appropriate next step does not occur in a purely child-centered context in which children are encouraged to go it alone. Likewise, taking children to the next step is not the same as for-mal instruction designed to teach a specific skill or academic knowledge. The difference in approach is shown in how teachers engage children in the process, and the degree of control children have in pursuing their own interests and activities (Goldenberg & Gillamore, 1991; Stremmel & Fu, 1993).

Teaching does not require excessive demonstration, ready solutions, or increasing the demands on children. The teacher assesses the situation and decides whether the children could benefit from his or her assistance. In this

FIGURE 2.2   The Open-Ended Journey of Making a Movie

John, a five-year-old boy in my preschool, arrived one day with a movie camera he had made at home on the weekend—a cardboard box with a plastic-wrap cylinder attached to the front. Within a short while, he and few of the children were intent on developing a movie, with John as the producer. They began developing a script centered around a girl getting lost in a large supermarket, and this extended into children playing a number of roles, such as check-out clerks, a policeman, a lady at the lost-and-found office, and a frantic mother. For several days the children continued with this play, and the script and roles became more real as they added dress-up clothing and play props such as note pads for interviewing witnesses. They also developed clapboards to show the number of takes they were filming, and added paraphernalia to the cameras, like microphones and leads.

Because of the children's strong, continuing interest in the project, I got one of the school's video cameras and filmed and talked to the children as they developed their props, script, and roles. By this time, most of the children were involved in the movie in some way or another. They transformed the room into a shopping center with different departments. These were identified by large signs that the children made, and they clustered a number of items like clothing, food, toys, and furniture in different areas of the room. A few children had set up the lost-and-found department, others were the movie crew, and there were star roles such as the policeman, mother, child, shoppers, and shop assistants.

While the end result—the movie itself—was rather stilted, with the children acting camera shy and playing out their roles stiffly and self-consciously compared to how they had acted during free play, they learned a great deal about the process of piecing the film together and loved watching themselves on camera. An important gain from the project was that the parents, other staff, and the principal became very interested in the teaching-learning process that comes from an extended project originating from the children's interests. They appreciated how the project stimulated a range of learning, such as reading, writing, interviewing, role playing, filming, categorizing objects found in different departments, and appreciated the sense of what it would be like to be lost, learning what to do when you are lost, and understanding how others can help in the process.

I also learned a lot about what the children currently understood, how I could extend their understanding, and the value of going with the flow when children have a strong interest and commitment to an idea. In many ways, the movie-making project transformed my thinking about the power of an emergent curriculum—one that evolves out of the children's ideas and interests—and I have used many of the principles and processes I learned from this experience to apply them to other similar learning experiences with children. I am less inclined now to see myself as a teacher of children, but more as one who is learning *with* them and *from* them. The teaching-learning interaction between the children and me is like an interactive dance or a musical improvisation, where sometimes it can be difficult to tell who is doing the leading and who is following. I like it that way. The kids and I are partners in learning.

way, teaching and assessment are dynamically interrelated, particularly when both are child-sensitive and responsive. This requires a willingness and ability to interact with children on an equal partnership basis.

Forming Partnerships with Children

Determining how to give assistance is often difficult because children's minds work quickly. Particularly during free-play sessions, teachers often must make some split-second decisions to mediate and encourage learning. Rinaldi (1993), one of the key authors describing the Italian-based early childhood arts programs in the region of Reggio Emilia, suggested a number of roles we can adopt to facilitate children's discovery. These roles are described in Figure 2.3, along with a number of my own examples within each of the arts disciplines.

FIGURE 2.3   Adult Roles for the Facilitation of Learning Partnerships

Be present, without being intrusive, in order to sustain children's cognitive and social dynamics while they are in progress (e.g., place a large box near children during play if they require, for example, something to hide behind, "travel" from one place to another, or be a fantasy character, such as a robot or television monitor).

Actively foster productive debate, at times, by challenging the responses of one or several children (e.g., suggesting that there may be other ways to dance a mood while still capturing the essence of an idea).

Step in to revive a situation if children are losing interest because the work is beneath or beyond their capabilities (e.g., taking on a role, such as a traveling salesperson, to shift the children's play to a different context, where new opportunities might emerge).

Help children formulate hypotheses, asking them what they need in order to do experiments, even when you might know that a particular approach or hypothesis is not "correct" (e.g., trying out the use of a rubber band for supporting a heavy object and, when it breaks, helping the children think of other materials that are stretchy but stronger).

Become the children's partner, offering assistance, resources, and strategies when they are encountering difficulties (e.g., helping children play one of their rhythms on an instrument that is easier to use or that may produce a more appropriate sound for what is being captured).

Reflect on their own thoughts and hypothesize about the children and about how these influence their interactions with them (e.g., making notes of children's learning experiences and planning ways in which to encourage new knowledge, skills, concepts, feelings, and social interactions on different occasions).

Several of these practices may seem contradictory to traditional early childhood practices, many of which have stemmed from Piagetian principle. Piaget (1932, 1951) emphasized that children should construct their own knowledge largely through self-directed activities. Although social interaction with peers was thought to foster development by exposing children to other perspectives and conflicting ideas, it was the Piagetian belief that premature teaching by adults could not enhance understanding of certain tasks or concepts and could, in fact, interfere with children's creativity. It was believed that learning could be achieved only when the child constructed personal understanding through largely unassisted activity(Elkind, 1987; Stremmell & Fu, 1993).

More recently, philosophies of early childhood education acknowledge that children are active learners, but that their construction of knowledge is not achieved in isolation. Educational theorists now embrace the notion of a more active approach to facilitating learning in arts education by helping children to construct their own knowledge within a social context. More details of how to guide such learning are provided in Chapter 4.

SUMMARY

Productive and reproductive approaches to early childhood arts education have been common practices for quite some time. These positions have been examined to come to know how and why they have developed and to see the positive and negative aspects inherent in each. Many of the philosophical underpinnings for approaches to arts education have evolved from the studies of child art that occurred in the late nineteenth century by psychologists and aestheticians. In addition, developmental theories were offered in the early twentieth century, and stages of children's development in drawing became accepted as the norm for about three decades, based on the belief that children's spontaneous and untutored artistic inventions should occur without any intervention, as this might interfere with children's creative processes and self-esteem.

More recently, however, arts educators have advocated for a less precious attitude toward children's artistic processes, believing that young children are more competent than previously supposed and that early developmental psychologists underestimated children's cognitive and general artistic abilities. Children can be analytical about their own and other's works in relation to aesthetic criteria, without violating their natural means of expression or creativity. Current thinking now emphasizes the cultural and social nature of learning and principles of guiding children in their learning. A guided approach allows opportunities for children to explore their own ideas, set personal goals, choose how they will solve problems, and find solutions with the help of others. Teachers can be active mediators of children's social and general competence and assist them with their artistic process and products. By aiming to provide appropriate conditions for learning, we can help children value and understand both the processes and products of their artistic experiences.

Perceptiveness on the part of the adult is required, to "get into" the heads and hearts of the children, along with a willingness and ability to interact with children on an equal partnership basis. This involves intuitively following the children's direction, while gently taking them to the next step in their learning. Rather than learning in isolation, children should become active learners with guidance in the construction of learning within a collaborative, positive, and supportive learning context.

ADDITIONAL READINGS

File, N. (1993). The teacher as a guide of children's competence with peers. *Child and Youth Care Forum, 22* (5), 351–360.

Jalongo, M. R., & Stamp, L. N. (1997). *The arts in children's lives: Aesthetic education for early childhood education.* Boston: Allyn and Bacon.

Jones, E., & Nimmo, J. (1994). *The emergent curriculum.* Washington, DC: National Association for the Education of Young Children.

Seefeldt, C. (1999). The early childhood curriculum: Current findings in theory and practice. New York: Teachers College Press.

PRACTICAL ACTIVITIES

1. Reflect on your observations of teachers or your own interactions with children during art, music, dance, and dramatic play experiences. Do some of these interactions with children reflect either a productive or a reproductive approach to teaching? Discuss.

2. Role-play three situations, each of which includes a child and an adult in an early childhood context: (a) a reproductive approach, (b) a productive approach, and (c) a guided approach. Reflect on each of these role-play enactments in relation to the common early childhood "truth" that process is more important than product.

3. Is it possible that the interpretation of guided learning can go too far and begin to appear to be similar to a reproductive approach? Consider, for example, how you would respond to a child who asked you to assist him or her with drawing a horse. What are the distinguishing features that make guided, productive, and reproductive approaches different?

CHAPTER THREE

ARTISTIC LEARNING
AND KNOWING

I took Latin percussion lessons for a few years because I've always loved Latin rhythms, and I wanted to learn more about playing congas and hand-percussion, like the guiro, claves, and cowbells. My teacher was a spunky Bermudan with black skin and long, ornamented dreadlocks who used the traditional master-apprentice approach—he'd demonstrate the rhythm and I would imitate it. Sometimes he would call in all of his students, and we would have a group session with about ten drums going at once. Keith would play the guuuung-**doo**-da *bottom rhythm on a low-pitched bass drum, and periodically he would blow a whistle, using different rhythmic patterns that would let us know when we should either go into unison or break out into independent but combined parts.*

Having come from a classical kind of training, I often found it difficult to remember the rhythms later in the week because they weren't written down anywhere, at least as far as I could find. Keith didn't know how to use music notation, and my attempts at trying to write out the rhythms nearly sent me gaga. Although I could notate the overall rhythm, this was meaningless unless I also showed which syncopated beat landed on which of three congas, and the way in which each drum was to be struck—say with a slap, a tone, or flat-handed bounce—which made a lot of difference to the sound. So I ended up calling Keith on the phone sometimes to ask, "Hey, how does that such-and-such rhythm go again?" And he'd vocalize the sounds over the phone, using pops of his lips or tongue and voiced syllables, like dooka **chee**ga daka daka, dooka **chee**ga da (grunt). *This was helpful, but eventually I found videotaping him was the best way to pick up his technique and the expressive ways he got the drums to sing.*

He used to say, "You ain't got the feeeel yet, girl," and show me again. I'd join on another drum, copying his movements, trying to make my hands and body dance with the rhythm. Within a short time Keith would shift off into an improvisation while I carried the underpinning rhythm. Eyes closed, I'd go off into a kind of trance-like state—my body sort of went into automatic pilot, with the volume of my emotions turned way up to max. The pops, cracks, and rumbling sounds, and the little rhythmic surprises that Keith randomly inserted into his improvisation actually shot

36

my mind with images, and my voice would involuntarily respond, sometimes quite primally. I found out later that the neighbors, who used to sit on their fence and listen to us drumming our hands off, called me "the student who lets out little squeals of delight to go with the drums."

I think my whole concept of music changed dramatically through learning the congas. This totally oral, bodily-kinesthetic connection to music helped me identify with young children's music a lot more. It made me get away from the straitjacket of musical notation and into the raw energy of music—the guts of emotional response.

The way in which we learn and know through the arts can be dramatically different than learning and knowing in other disciplines. No longer are the traditional academic areas of literacy and numeracy—reading, writing, and arithmetic—adequate for engaging learners in all aspects of understanding that will be necessary for the careers of the next generation. In fact, many of the jobs and careers in which today's children will engage in the future have not even been created, because technology, industry, and resulting career options are evolving so quickly. This has profound implications for the field of education and the decisions to be made about which subjects and learning processes are considered important and which ones are not. Today it seems that many people are seeking an educational system where a balance is given to intellectual, interpersonal, social, emotional, and spiritual components of learning—knowledge that will help children acquire the holistic background necessary to cope with the demands of contemporary society. Educators are embodying the goal of educating for understanding, which includes more than just cognitive understanding.

Many authors today are now highlighting the significance of social and emotional factors of education at a time when the fabric of society seems to be unraveling our communal lives (Goleman, 1995; Malaguzzi, 1993). For example, Goleman's theory of intelligence puts emotions at the center of aptitudes for living, where self-restraint and compassion are central. He claimed that what we learn as children at home and at school shapes the emotional circuitry of the brain and establishes emotional habits that govern our lives. However, Goleman believes that we leave the emotional education of our children to chance rather than educating the whole child, bringing together mind and heart, emphasizing self-awareness, self-control, and empathy, and the skills of listening, resolving conflicts, and cooperating. In a similar vein, Zohar and Marshall (2000, p. 18), in a book called *Spiritual Intelligence: The Ultimate Intelligence,* describe the concept of "the spiritual" as being in touch with "some larger, deeper, richer whole that puts our present limited situation into a new perspective."

Within this broader definition of ways of knowing and learning, many educators are now emphasizing a need for the curriculum to address "multiliteracies"—new definitions of what it means to be literate within our contemporary society (Cazden et al., 1996; Wright, 2001b). They are seeking to find the connections between the changing social environment facing children and teachers and a new approach to literacy pedagogy that includes the integration of significant modes of meaning-making, where the textual is also related to the visual, the audio, the spatial, the multi-modal, the behavioral, and so on. Such literacy involves a range of representational forms, such as visual images, the written word, and the "grammars" of film, photography, gesture, dance, and music. Today's teachers need a new "meta-language" for talking about language, images, texts, and meaning-making interactions that describes meaning and human knowledge in many different forms. Such knowledge, which requires an immersion in meaningful practices within a community of learners, involves teachers assisting children to learn how to learn.

This chapter begins with a discussion of the importance of helping children learn how to learn. Learning how to learn is a fundamental feature of the arts because music, dance, drama/play, and the visual arts involve ways of knowing about the world unlike those emphasized in areas like science, mathematics, and technology. The second section deals with artistic ways of knowing through thought, emotion, and action, providing a window into the past and allowing young people to express views of the future. Finally, the significance of the arts in educating children for the future is discussed in relation to learning through personal and group discovery, in play and other forms of artistic learning.

LEARNING HOW TO LEARN IN ARTISTIC WAYS

Over sixty years ago, John Dewey, the founder of progressive education, spoke of learning how to learn. Defining the process of learning in today's world is becoming exceedingly complex; however, principles can help in developing effective educational programs. Many writers have emphasized the importance of teaching young children how to plan and solve problems, to enhance their control, imagination, and creative thinking (see, for example, Beane, 1997; Bruner, 1996; Eisner, 2001; Gardner, 1999a; Wright, 2001a). The importance of this form of learning lies in its emphasis on intellectual flexibility and lateral thinking, lifelong learning, whole-person and cross-disciplinary education, and a shift in emphasis from learning *content* to learning *processes.*

Focusing attention on the *how* rather than the *what* to learn will require some fundamental changes to educational practice—not only to our social values about education, but also to many of the learning activities that occur within our schools. Rather than being isolated, individual, and passive recipients of change, children and adults must work together as active creators of their futures, a term that is described in the plural because many futures are possible. Bruner (1986, p. 149) expressed "futures" well when he described the central concern of education as being one in which we:

> create in the young an appreciation of the fact that many worlds are possible, that meaning and reality are created and not discovered, that negotiation is the art of constructing new meanings by which individuals can regulate their relations with each other.

Central to the goal of collaboration within learning contexts is the belief that children learn through personally valued experiences—in other words, educational experiences must connect with children's existing knowledge through the integration of *feeling* (intuitive-artistic components) and *knowing* (discursive-scientific components). It is by promoting the interdependence of emotions and knowledge that education through the arts becomes important. The arts involve thinking, perceiving, and feeling processes that tap into unique ways of knowing ourselves and the world in which we live. In many ways, the arts incorporate aspects of learning that are closely linked to the ideals of education for the future: flexible thinking, whole-person education, and lifelong learning.

Anyone who has had intimate experiences with the arts (e.g., as a creator, performer, or teacher) would appreciate the special ways in which thinking and communicating occurs via multimodal information processing (Eisner, 1996). Participation in the arts provides numerous opportunities for the integration of thought, emotion, action; thinking through imagery and movement; turning action into representation; "reading" and "writing" using artistic symbols; and communicating via a unique language. Consequently, there is a growing body of evidence that the arts are essential for children (Snyder, 2001).

Learning through both *verbal* and *nonverbal* domains or modes enhances our understanding. Dual coding theory, which was posited nearly two decades ago, describes how the encoding of information in two ways is better comprehended, recalled, and elaborated (Sadoski, Paivio, & Goetz, 1991). Such cognition consists of two separate but interconnected systems—a *verbal* system that specializes in processing language and a *nonverbal* system for processing world knowledge of objects and events, such as images, music, and dance (Eisner, 2001; Sweet, 1996). Expression becomes a process of conveying ideas, feelings, and meanings through the selective use of multiple communicative possibilities, both verbally and nonverbally. In the arts, a great deal of what is learned is initiated by the nonverbal modes of understanding, which in turn are enriched by the verbal modes. These artistic ways of learning, which integrate both domains, are described in the following segments.

Thought, Emotion, and Action

Bruner (1986) described learning as a multifaceted process in which emotions, thoughts, and actions do not occur in isolation but are aspects of a larger, unified whole. He suggested that drawing heavy conceptual boundaries between thought, action, and emotion as regions of the mind would only require us to construct unrealistic conceptual bridges to connect what should never have been separated. He argued that people "perfink," that is, they perceive, feel, and think all at once, and act within the constraints of what they perfink (p. 118).

More recently, others have discussed how artistic mindedness has three sides or more: creativity, valuing, and "spirit." Each of these three modes participates with the other—contains the other as a whole—while still remaining distinct (Best, 2000b). Best described artistic mindedness as the *creative* aspect of intellect; *values* sort and sift issues in relation to personal taste; and the *spiritual* side includes heartfelt passion and intensity. The greatest arts occur when there is a near perfect balance among these three sides—where craft, taste, and expression consort together, and creative imagination takes up simultaneously with the lyrical and procedural. In "less than great" arts, there is intellect without expressiveness or expressiveness without the use of intellect. Integrative components, such as bringing together the modes of creativity, valuing, and spirit, are all key aspects of artistic learning. This is because the arts draw upon unique forms of cognition and communication, through the use of imagery and the movement of the body.

Thinking through Imagery with the Body

Arnheim (1969) coined the term *visual thinking* as a concept to challenge philosophers and psychologists who, at that time, did not acknowledge the intertwined connection between perceiving and thinking. He asserted that all truly productive thinking takes place in the realm of imagery, and that images underlie language (Becker, 1993; Wong, 2001). He provocatively described purely *verbal* thinking as "thoughtless thinking," saying that, although verbal thinking is useful for information retrieval, it is basically "sterile" thinking (Arnheim, 1969, pp. 231–232). Suzanne Langer also discussed the limitations of language in her classic text, *Philosophy in a New Key* (1924/1971). She described nondiscursive or visual forms of thinking as being particularly well suited to the expression of ideas—ideas that are *too subtle* for speech.

The link between image, thought, and action has been well documented for decades. More than fifty years ago, Piaget (1951) described sensorimotor intelligence as thinking with the body. Young children's body-based thinking involves *action*, which helps them develop *concepts*—general ideas that are learned through a number of instances or experiences. Currently, more attention is being given to the cognitive functions of *imagery* and the *body* as a source of order, which exceeds that of language and logic. In fact, the brain and the mechanics of cognition have become the focus of major scientific, medical, and education research on imagery and the body (Moen, 1991; Ross, 2000; Walker, 2000), and the implications of this research will be discussed in subsequent chapters.

Through the sensory experiences of the body, we form representational frameworks for thought, which Johnson (1991) calls *image schemata*. These image schemata are crucial to our ability to understand our experiences and to make sense of our environment; they form the basis of human reasoning, inference, logic, and meaning. Albert Einstein, for example, appeared to rely heavily on image schemata. He described his method of working as attempting to remain within the realm of images for as long as possible, postponing the expression of these ideas in words and actions. Ultimately, Einstein's theory of relatively seems to have been derived from visual/spatial concepts and modes rather than from purely mathematical lines of reasoning (Davis, 1992; Gardner, 1993a).

For people of all ages, the arts are rooted in the fundamental experience of *somatic* knowledge—the linking of the body, "soul," and mind/psyche (Best, 2000a, b). Ross (2000) described the "thinking body" as a cognitive process in which individuals gather information through exchanges between the psyche and soma (i.e., the mind and body) and where the five senses and emotions are the conduits of these experiences—the apertures or portals to the outside. The arts involve this type of "somatic" knowing. Through the arts, our emotions are fundamentally linked with our muscular activity. Figure 3.1 illustrates a young boy's vigorous pounding of clay as a beginning step in shaping his thoughts and feelings in this visual arts media. Music, for example, is based on motor patterns, spatial concepts, and movement metaphors (Carterette & Kendall, 1999; Walker, 2000).

Ethnomusicologists have taken a great interest in the musical and movement processes of audiences and performers and have discovered that many cultures use one word for both music and dance. In some cultures, body-percussion, costumes, and attachments, such as ankle bells, allow the dancing body itself to become a musical instrument (Baily, 1985). In community-based music, such as that found in sub-Saharan Africa, audience participation through movement and body-percussion is an integral part of musical events. Some ethnomusicologists claim that, if music and movement are so obviously and integrally related in some cultures, we cannot easily dismiss the possibility that they are equally related in all cultures, but perhaps just expressed in different ways (Walker, 2000).

Some ethnomusicologists claim that music and dance are part of a human *biogrammar* of communication. Music and dance provide unique insights into knowing that are not available through linguistic forms of communication (Baumann, 1995). In fact, there is ethnomusicological evidence

FIGURE 3.1   Pounding in Clay as a Somatic Form of Understanding.

From Wright, S. (Ed.). (1991). *The arts in early childhood*. Sydney: Prentice Hall. Reprinted with permission of Pearson Education.

that the cognitive link between music and movement is much closer than the connection between music and language (Walker, 2000). Brain research also shows evidence that the use of the biogrammar of music is a form of understanding that *precedes* speech. In other words, babies "communicate" via music before they can speak. This concept of *prelanguage* musical communication is discussed in greater detail in the chapter on music (Chapter 9).

All the arts involve somatic understanding, using a kind of "spatiomotor mode"—a side of thinking and understanding that connects the spatial and the physical (Baily, 1985; Gardner, 1983). Bodily-kinesthetic thinking is one of several intelligences described in Gardner's theory of multiple intelligence (discussed in more detail in Chapter 5). In music, for example, the spatiomotor mode or bodily-kinesthetic intelligence is used to activate and control musical performance, sometimes even in the absence of a musical instrument or sound. For example, musicians often think musical passages in their mind and simultaneously "play" these with their fingers, in the air, or on a table. There is a direct association between musicians' bodily-kinesthetic movements and the sounds they hear in their heads. Through physical-spatial knowing, musicians find ways to move on an instrument, which is guided by their aesthetic evaluation of sound and sound patterns.

When involved in the arts, our bodies are actively and intimately engaged in aesthetic thinking and sensitivity to beauty through perceiving, imagining, and moving/acting. This union of body and mind is most obviously demonstrated in dance and in musical performance, but is true also of the work of the painter, sculptor, potter, and actor; there comes a union between bodily-kinesthetic understanding and thinking, feeling, and doing. This is why the arts can engender a sense of freedom, release, fulfillment, and wholeness—sometimes to the "point of ecstasy" (Reid, 1983, p. 25). Through such integrated understanding, people of all ages are able to express and represent their knowledge.

Turning Action into Representation

There are three ways in which humans can represent the world or capture reality through experience: by enaction, with imagery, and through constructing symbols (Bruner, 1996). It is the *enactive* mode that blends thought, emotion, and action. Through action, we portray or depict thoughts and emotions by example. For instance, in pretend play, children represent ideas and feelings when capturing the feelings of, say, power and strength (e.g., superhero play) or nurturance (e.g., domestic play). Through movement and the use of props, such as capes, dolls, hats, and other resources, children enact or represent these thoughts and images through action (as in Figure 3.2).

The second mode involves *imagery*. Images can be thought as stopped action frames, or visual impressions of actions. Another way to think of imagery is "seeing in the mind's eye." For example, when we listen to music, such as a "rippling" piano concerto, we might image a glassy pond or a moonlit night. Indeed, it might have been the intention of the composer to conjure up such images in association with the music. Similarly, imagery can be involved in an expressive or abstract way in dance where we might, for example, image the delicate, random movements of a butterfly or the graceful, flowing movement of a swan (as in the ballet *Swan Lake*).

Young children also are able to engage in such imagery and have the power to render the world in terms of images. This provides them with a kind of preconceptual understanding of how they operate in the world. Capturing reality or representing the world through imagery is very much an aspect of artistic experience. Children use imagery in drama, for example, when they picture in their mind an image of a powerful figure, such as a sun god, and visualize the body stance and gesture of such a figure. Imagery can include a large range of instances, such as visualizing the movement of swirling, falling leaves, or the colors, emotions, and movement patterns of music. Such aspects of imagery are discussed in greater detail in Chapter 7 in relation to artistic literacy and synesthesia.

FIGURE 3.2   A Child Enacting through Play

Through imagery, action, and other forms of understanding, children participate in the third mode of representation, namely *symbolizing*. Symbolizing involves representing or showing a likeness between one thing and another. As in the examples above, children may symbolize falling leaves through dance, a sun god through drama, the feeling of gentleness through music, and a range of other forms of representing. When children symbolize, they turn image into action and action into representation.

It is the ability to symbolize that places humans above other living creatures. Human have invented symbol systems—such as numbers, words, and letters—that are used systematically to help us make ideas and experiences a public, shared form of communication. Such symbol systems include not only mathematics and language, but also art, music, dance, history, physics, and other invented forms of symbolizing and representing.

Of these symbol systems, the arts have their own *distinctive* ways of constructing and communicating symbols, so that the viewer or listener comes to understand what is being communicated. For example, Ross (2000) described dance as the construction of narrative through gesture. Dance involves using the body as an art medium that is as expressive as "composed sounds, chiselled marble, or the traces of a paint brush" (p. 29). The body as art illustrates the concept of "turning action into representation" quite clearly. But representing or symbolizing is part of all of the arts. In fact, it is significant that many forms of creating and interpreting meaning are found *only* in the arts.

In the arts, children engage in the processes of symbolizing through drawing (and other forms of graphic representation), through the expressive use of the voice and movement, and through gesturing, making music, dancing, and many other forms of knowing and communicating. Such artistic representation engages children in unique forms of cognition, where they depict objects, events, and images through symbols. In this way, children not only *make* representations, they also *manipulate* representations in abstract ways.

Perhaps the easiest way of understanding the process of symbolizing is to consider the field of study that focuses on symbolic forms of understanding, called *semiotics*. Semiotics involves the study of any medium (or genre) as a sign system. Signs may be words, images, gestures, numbers, or anything from which meaning may be generated. Semioticians commonly refer to films, television, art works, advertising posters, and so on as "texts" that are "read."

For example, interpretation of a "text" involves us in recognizing signs and then in elaborating and reflecting on the meaning of these signs. "Meaning" of an image of a racing car, for instance, is understood in the context of our culture and its conventions. In other words, the image of a car can often have significance quite other than what it means literally, as an object. The car can *stand for* virility or freedom, particularly if the way in which it is depicted in the photograph includes a muscle-bound driver and a blurred background to indicate the enormous power and speed of the vehicle. Often such means of communicating ideas are referred to as discourses. Discourses are not equivalent to language; they are language filled with values, messages, and histories. They "integrate words, acts, beliefs, attitudes and social identities as well as gestures, glances, body positions and clothes" (Gee, 1989, p. 517).

We use discourses to interpret signs or symbols by drawing on *world knowledge,* such as in the example of the powerful, free, fast car. We may not even be consciously aware of how we make these associations because our understanding has many layers of meaning, based on our personal experience. For example, our understanding of the symbols in the car advertisement involves a combination of: (1) focusing attention on the reference the signs make to an object (e.g., speed and muscles are associated with the car) and (2) making an interpretative response (e.g., car equals virility and power). In other words, our understanding of strength and energy and our values associated with these concepts are projected onto the car. When we recognize the subtle messages of the advertisement, we begin to understand how the advertisement for the car is specifically designed to appeal to a particular type of person, someone seeking a powerful and virile image. Because the emotional overtones and interpretations we associate with such a message are based on our learned personal values, various people's responses to the advertisement might range from "Yum, cool" to "Danger-ous, bad" to "Eek, macho."

So too, children's participation in the arts involves these types of mean-ing making and meaning interpretation. Whether painting a picture, com-posing music, refining a poem, or evolving a dance, representation involves a process of imitation, where children:

- Turn actions into images and/or sounds
- Turn images into actions and/or sounds
- Sequence actions, images, and sounds in relationships
- Work to a system of signs (e.g., words, gestures, images, sounds)
- Share the artwork with a community

It is child's ability to not only represent, but to *manipulate* representations, that leads to abstract thought. Representing or symbolizing gives children the ability to organize and make sense of their environment based on their bodily experience (Johnson, 1991; Walker, 2000).

Such forms of representation are strongly featured in the arts. In fact, many of the ways in which we create and interpret meaning through the arts cannot be found in other disciplines. The arts engage a unique form of cogni-tion. So, while we may all speak English, for example, we do not all speak the *discourse* of art, music, dance, or drama.

Children learn to speak the *discourse* of the arts by using sensory, tactile, aesthetic, expressive, and imaginative forms of understanding. This type of discourse involves visual, spatial, aural, and bodily-kinesthetic modes of knowing. As discussed in this section, it is the connection between the body, thought, imagery, emotion, action, and representation that makes the arts a highly important component of education for young children. Children learn such artistic discourse through learning how to "read" and "write" using artistic symbols.

"Reading" and "Writing" Using Artistic Symbols

Like all disciplines, the arts involve cognition and gaining insight and under-standing by all available means. Some of the mental activities involved in the arts are shared with other pursuits—like attending to detail—while others are unique to the arts, such as sensitivity to patterns in music (i.e., selectively perceiving qualitative relationships in sound, or silence, over time). There-fore, artistic cognition requires the ability to "read" and to "write" using arts symbol systems (Gardner, 1993a, c). In music, for example, an artistic *reader* can discriminate different styles, such as jazz, rock, or classical. An artistic *writer* can create sound abstractly to suggest different moods and represent impressions and effect psychological states. Most people, for example, can remember the sound tracks in particular films and how these effected them emotionally. Two classic examples are the sounds used in the shower scene of the movie *Psycho* and the music linked to the sharks in the movie *Jaws.* Music in movies, when coupled with the images, creates feelings, such as suspense, action, romance, space-ageness, loneliness, and a range of intensified associations. Yet our ability to interpret music and patterns of sound far exceeds our ability to describe them because we often have no words for what we are able to hear (Eisner, 2001).

Each of the art domains (art, music, dance, and play/drama) includes its own ways of reading and writing, using symbols. The specific way of symbolizing meaning through the arts is discussed in relation to young children's learning in much greater detail in Chapter 4. But, to establish a general background to understanding this content later in the book, let us begin by looking at how the arts involve communication through a unique form of language and how this may or may not be supported in school contexts.

Communicating via a Unique "Language"

Western cultures, in particular, seem to believe that the dominant means of communication and understanding in any form of life is through language, and that words (and numbers) are the primary, if not the only, means of doing intellectual work. In schools, for example, the curriculum is usually word-bound, and oral discourse becomes the key method that children use to make meaning, such as stating their understanding of content "in their own words." In fact, children are judged to be conversant with a subject if they have used oral or written language to demonstrate understanding (Marzano et al., 1988). With the exception of mathematics, some of the sciences, and the arts, all other academic disciplines rely almost exclusively on speech logic as their predominant discursive form (Best, 2000a, b). However, the valuing of *only* verbal competence within schools (or in life in general) diminishes the significance of nonverbal forms of understanding—spatial, visual, kinesthetic, and musical.

Malaguzzi (1987, p. 23) commented on the limits of words, particularly in relation to the education of young children:

> Today the spoken language is increasingly imposed on children through imitative mechanisms which are poor in, or devoid of, interchange, rather than through strong imaginative processes linked to experience and to the problems of experience.

Children's understanding, thinking, and learning through the "languages" of the arts are often based on nonverbal forms of meaning making and communication. The arts include the worlds of still and moving images, sounds, textures, gestures, and many other symbolic forms. These worlds are fertile areas for thinking, feeling, and expressing and are an intrinsic part of the visual and performing arts. Hence, the arts express and externalize ideas, and convey meanings that evoke responses in the child and in others. Like all areas of learning, the arts involve complex and high levels of information processing.

Playing and listening to music, for example, are as cognitively complex as speaking and reading. Both require rapid perceptual processing, quick sequential production, and enormous amounts of information. However, performing musicians must also translate this complex information into motor responses. Pianists, for example, can play fifteen to twenty notes per second, in the correct order, with feeling. Such musical perception involves the ability to monitor performance and to plan ahead (Azar, 1996). Because the arts involve the senses and motor responses, our perception, awareness, judgment, and the expression of ideas encompass "special" ways of knowing that are quite different from linguistic or scientific (Best 2000a, b; Eisner, 1978; Gardner, 1983).

Some writers, like Vygotsky (1962), have linked the term *cognition* with a kind of *inner speech*—thinking ideas in your head through the use of words. However, as was discussed earlier, a large part of thinking involves imagery and the body, not speech. When we try to remember where we may have lost our keys, for example, we often retrace our steps in our minds by imaging where we have been, and "feeling" the physical actions of holding or putting down our keys somewhere. This type of remembering may involve some language, such as, "OK, I remember I had my keys with me when I went to the grocery store, and then . . . " But often our thinking is more centered on images and bodily actions, similar in some ways to daydreaming.

There is danger in assuming that language is the *primary* means of communicating and representing. Language is inadequate for the expression of everything we feel and sense. Yet the underlying assumption of a "speech logic" viewpoint is that, if something is not expressed through language, it is considered to be outside *rational* thought, outside *articulate* feeling (Kress, 2000a). This assumption is not just anchored in popular common sense; it is also entrenched in cultural practices, such as valuing the school subjects of reading and arithmetic above the arts.

The process of taking in and understanding information nonverbally—through the senses and through movement—is more obvious in babies and very young children, who may not always be able to express themselves clearly through words. Sound is meaningful to infants long before they understand words. In fact, because babies cannot see very well, the "musical" characteristics of parents' infant-directed speech affect their emotion, attention, and development, more so than parents' facial expressions. The melody is the message (Adler, 1990). In addition, babies and infants use simple forms of communication before verbal language is developed. They request, indicate, and associate themselves with other people through gesture, vocalization, body language, and the regulation of gaze (see Figure 3.3).

FIGURE 3.3   Infants' Thought Characteristics

Infants have their own language of thought and use a kind of "mentalese" through which they understand their world (Gardner, 1991). Information is taken in and understood through the senses—sight, sound, touch, taste, and movement. For example, an infant can experience the aural and physical sensations of gentle music, communicate that he or she is ill, or identify objects long before this information can be expressed in words. Through the senses, the young child can understand many concepts—ideas, images, impression, and thoughts—without requiring words. Indeed, some abstract concepts, like freedom or love, are understood through sensations and other nonverbal means. This is the case even with adults.

Perhaps the best way to think of the arts is that they are not merely preverbal or subverbal, they are supraverbal. In other words, they involve symbolic modes of thinking, understanding, and knowing, and express ideas in a unique manner. Yet, in spite of the arts being essentially nonverbal, it is commonplace to hear the arts described as "languages" through which we discover, express, and exchange meanings that are otherwise unavailable (Plummeridge, 1991). This is because the arts enable us to "say" things to each other that cannot be expressed in any other way. But while we can enjoy and appreciate artistic experiences, it is often difficult to explain in words precisely what it is that we have come to know or understand as a result of such an experience. We can, for example, be emotionally moved to the point of tears in a concert, at the theater or ballet, or at an art exhibition, without being able to say exactly why, and different people will be moved in different ways at the same concert or exhibition. This may occur because the arts can mean many things to different people, at different times, and in varying contexts.

Our responses to artworks—where "artwork" is meant in the generic sense to include music, dance, art, or drama—are related to how artistic expression is communicated. Artworks communicate at least three forms of knowledge:

- *Information* (e.g., this is a picture of a lily pond, or a dance about spring)
- *Aesthetic appreciation* (e.g., it is visually/aurally pleasing)
- A *personal response* that relates solely to our experiences (e.g., it makes me feel calm because it reminds me of walking through autumn leaves)

In these ways, artworks have *suggestive* qualities to which we attach special meaning. Even when words are part of an artwork, their meaning may not be communicated literally, or exactly, but through devices such as metaphor and analogy. For example, red, orange, and yellow colors can create an *impression* of heat in a painting, and flowing movements in dance can establish a peaceful mood. Meaning that is derived is often grasped intuitively and evolves from our interpretation of the work's formal structure, our response to its emotional impact, and our inferences about the creator's intentions (e.g., the meaning of his or her symbolism and what it represents). Such interpretation of meaning occurs in a similar way, regardless of whether the artwork is created by an adult or a child. To illustrate how five- to eight-year-old children interpret and describe adult drawings/painting/illustrations, let me describe some of the responses of young children in one of my research projects currently in progress (Figure 3.4).

Children are able not only to interpret artworks of the adult world, they are also able to depict meaning in their own works. They use signs, sounds, gestures, and words as symbols to express thoughts and feelings through drawing, block building, dancing, play, musical experimentation, or clay

FIGURE 3.4   Five- to Eight-Year-Old Children's Cross-Modal Interpretation of Emotion

While looking at a range of art works that expressed four different emotions—happy, sad, angry, and peaceful—the children were asked (on a one-to-one basis) to say which art works were happy, sad, angry, or peaceful and also to indicate which artworks "went with" music that was one of these four emotions. Most children could select art works that depicted each of these four emotions and could also identify artworks that were "a bit sad, but also a bit peaceful." For example, they could see aspects in the images that could be interpreted in more than one way. Particularly when these artworks were coupled with music, the children would make a new and sometimes contradictory interpretation of the art. For example, a painting that a child may have identified as "angry" earlier (without music) could be seen later as being angry *and* sad when "sad" music was played.

Often children would make comments like "this is happy, because the person in the picture is springing into the air, being bouncy." Children seemed to participate in a kind of story making based on their life experiences, imagination, and fantasy to describe the works. When they did not have the vocabulary to express some ideas verbally, often they would show their understanding in nonverbal ways, cross-modally. For example, to describe the bouncy feeling of a character in a children's book illustration, or the feeling of the music, the child might get up and dance the concept, demonstrating bounciness through gesture and movement. In addition, children would made cross-modal connections when describing an image, such as a volcano, by using upward, eruption-type gestures with their arms and saying that the music goes with the picture because it "goes up," forcefully (like the volcano).

modeling. Current views of education describe these forms of symbolic communication as languages, each having the potential to be used in sophisticated ways (Malaguzzi, 1987, 1993; Plummeridge, 1991; Wright, 1994b, 2001b). Malaguzzi and other teachers in Reggio Emilia use the expression *the hundred languages of children* to illustrate that children express themselves in many spatial, visual, aural, and bodily-kinesthetic ways, and that every language has the right to realize itself fully and to enrich the other languages. Their metaphor of one hundred languages is meant to suggest that there are numerous ways to use gesture, for example, to communicate a range of meanings—waving hello, thumbs down for "no good," and many other, less conventional expressions of meaning. Likewise, there are numerous ways that children sing, dance, role-play, and express themselves using the grammars of the arts to communicate meaning.

Therefore, it is important that all expressive, cognitive, and communicative languages exist in equal dignity. Children must have opportunities to express ideas and feelings in both verbal and nonverbal, symbolic ways. They should engage in arts discourses through using the inherent symbols within the arts—images, sounds, movement—which may or may not include words. By participating in arts discourse, the child becomes the "author" of a range of languages. For the young child, the interfacing of these languages often occurs through discovery learning.

LEARNING THROUGH DISCOVERY

Learning in the arts involves a succession of discoveries linked to personal mastery. Children figure things out for themselves, but, as discussed in Chapter 2, such learning should also include the support of peers and adults. Learning through discovery should enlist children's natural energies that sustain their spontaneous learning, curiosity, and desire for competence. In the arts, children's self-understanding is enhanced when they have opportunities to gain a sense of personal achievement and worth through the exploration of objects and materials. This type of learning often takes place when children work and play alongside their peers, and in the process they become committed to learning through interaction with others (Edwards, 1993; New, 1993; Rinaldi, 1993). Peer interaction, or collaboration, also helps children become aware of their own artistic processes—they develop independence and gain a sense of ownership of their learning.

The process of children's owning their learning has been discussed in educational literature for decades. In the arts, it is easy to see children involved in independent decision making, collaborative learning, and problem solving. These processes can be enhanced when there are numerous solutions to a problem rather than one "correct" response. Open-ended learning (where many alternative processes and solutions can be found) provides children with opportunities to identify the:

- *Problem* (e.g., making a musical composition and expressive dance)
- *Subject matter* (e.g., calling the composition/dance "Scary Monsters")
- *Materials* (e.g., selecting drums, shakers, capes, and big boots to enact the composition/dance)
- *Direction* (e.g., beginning the dance in the mud patch but, as the ideas and expressive content evolve, shifting the enactment to behind the trees)
- *Means of evaluation* (e.g., deciding that the best part was when the monsters jumped out from behind the trees and beat their drums while roaring)

The general principles surrounding open-ended experiences are that they provide opportunities for children to: (1) define, explore, and refine multiple solutions and approaches (e.g., they determine the problem, subject matter, and materials to be used and how they will use them); (2) become analytical about the results of their efforts (e.g., they determine the direction and evaluate the end product); and (3) understand through exploring, enjoying, learning, and discovering through the process of play.

Discovery Learning through Play

The way that the arts and play are closely linked is reflected in the words that we use to describe them. For example, we talk about *playing* music, going to the theater to see a *play*, and even *playing* games that might involve a *play* on words. So, if there is a playful aspect to the arts, it may be that they are linked to creative dream worlds into which we can escape from reality (Swanwick, 1988). This dream world often involves a high level of imagination, which Vygotsky (1976) defined as *play without action*. Imagination can extend well beyond the period of early childhood, and, as described in the creativity chapter, childlike playfulness is a significant characteristic of many creative adults and a key component of working in music, dance, drama, and art at all ages.

For young children, imagination often is accompanied by action, partly because they are uninhibited about expressing their imagining, but also because their way of thinking with the body provides a natural means of integrating thought and emotion through action. As children participate in free-play activities, they are motivated by their own actions and go about their "work" making decisions about what they will do, how they will do it, and why. Such decisions involve a number of decision-making processes, a majority of which are shown in a variety of nonverbal, sensory, physical, and intuitive ways. Hence, the arts are like games, because they allow us to create other "worlds" that are dreamlike, or at least playlike—they are other-worldly (Swanwick, 1988). However, play seems to precede understanding and the use of various thinking skills. Much of the child's thinking is based on *doing* and then *understanding*. Let us turn our attention now to the ways in which the arts provide potential for children to *learn how to learn* through the processes of doing.

Engaging Artistic Processes

Children engage in artistic activities through several processes that include and go beyond that of discovery through play. Figure 3.5 on pages 54–55 describes how artistic processes are involved in educational experiences and how children's engagement in the arts enhances their self-awareness, communication, social interaction, perception, technique, and processes of analysis and critique. The processes apply to all arts domains (music, dance, play/drama, and visual arts). The key educational issue is to provide children with opportunities for meaning-making through hands-on experiences.

These eight general artistic processes are not hierarchical (i.e., one process is not more important than another), although some principles apply in relation to the how the processes may be learned:

- There is an implicit order of complexity in which the processes are presented. Critiquing, for example, is a higher-level skill than discovery, but even young children can evaluate their own and other people's efforts and products (Cole & Schaefer, 1990), and they also informally critique *during* processes of discovery.
- One process is not replaced by another when mastery is achieved. A child, for example, does not stop discovering once particular technical skills have been mastered, because there are always new techniques to discover.
- All processes are integrated and are part of a repeating spiral of learning, where each of the processes is revisited time and time again, depending upon the activity, regardless of developmental level.

While some of the processes described in Figure 3.5 may appear advanced for young children, each is appropriate if understood in relation to young children's developmental abilities. Exploring options, for example, will be shown differently by children of different ages: A two-year-old will chew on the crayon and make intermittent, physically driven marks on the paper; a three-year-old will discover more controlled ways to make marks; and a four-year-old will explore different techniques to achieve specific "recognizable" images. (Such developmental aspects are discussed in more detail in Chapter 6 in all areas of the arts.) Children will show different capabilities as a result of experience, yet within a supportive learning environment they will have a

FIGURE 3.5 General Artistic Processes Applicable to Each of the Arts Domains

Discovery and pursuit involves being open-minded, observing, comparing, exploring options from a variety of perspectives, reinterpreting, making associations, using the imagination and creativity, experimenting and taking risks with media, generating ideas, seeing possibilities, setting challenges, being goal directed, focusing on a specific area, finding alternatives, questioning, testing, finding purpose, taking initiative, planning, staying on task, making decisions, solving problems, showing care and attention to detail, developing works over time and around personal themes, and expressing ideas without conformity or competition.

Self-awareness involves working independently; tapping into personal feelings; recognizing and working within personal capabilities; making statements that reflect values, feelings, and ideas; developing individual identity, self-concept, self-esteem, confidence, and well-being; finding a sense of style; developing personal artistic visions; tolerating frustration; finding personal, cultural, or "spiritual" meaning; releasing emotions through socially acceptable and personally rewarding outlets; and developing feelings of assurance in one's own judgment, ability, and power.

Communication involves competencies in nonverbal and verbal art forms, choosing artistic materials and elements with communicative intent, using symbols to represent and express ideas or feelings (both literally and metaphorically), using the imagination, selecting resources with artistic purpose, creating stories or captions to artistic products, making statements about self and world, externalizing knowledge, and expressing impressions.

Social interaction involves learning to work in groups, developing interpersonal skills, interacting, cooperating, participating in preparation and clean-up, understanding various social roles, respecting the uniqueness of others, sharing discoveries, making suggestions, negotiating, empathizing, modeling, appreciating other people's contributions, understanding social roles, and developing cooperation and respect for others.

Perception involves showing awareness of sensory experience; illustrating sensitivity to physical properties and qualities of materials and the environment; responding aurally, visually, and kinesthetically; seeing mental pictures in the mind (visualizing); hearing "inside the head," internalizing movement; making fine discriminations; giving form to sensation, translating intention into action; evidencing sensitivity to and seeing connections across a variety of genres, cultures, and historical periods; being able to understand another person's perspective; and developing aesthetic and cultural sensitivities.

Technique involves manipulating materials; developing basic techniques; working to gain gross and fine motor control and eye, hand, and mind coordination; performing actions that often require practice, concentration, and repetition; developing competency, techniques, and mastery through experience and time; responding to different situations flexibly; understanding the limitations and potential of specific arts media; using materials inventively; developing qualities and abilities such as poise, grace, and coordination; and integrating bodily-kinesthetic, aural, visual, imaginative, and expressive dimensions.

FIGURE 3.5 Continued

Analysis involves making choices; describing to others what is seen, heard, felt, thought, or imagined; appreciating; reflecting on process and product; contributing personal opinions; relating learning to previous learning; changing attitudes and direction if necessary; developing sensitivity toward and awareness and knowledge of the natural and cultural environments; examining the role of the arts in different social and cultural contexts; and developing nonverbal literacies—aural, visual, verbal, bodily-kinesthetic, and symbolic.

Critique involves gaining insight and understanding through thoughtful observation; showing a sense of standards for quality; accepting and incorporating suggestions where appropriate; using the work of others for ideas and inspiration; articulating artistic goals; showing an interest in hearing and using arts terminology; talking about the works of peers and published artists of the past and present; developing aesthetic awareness and sensitivity, acquiring an artistic vocabulary through listening, speaking, reading, and writing in all arts areas; reflecting upon aesthetic traditions and value systems; and using aesthetic values as a basis for discriminating, selecting, responding to, enjoying, describing, interpreting, challenging, feeling, analyzing, valuing, evaluating, and questioning the ways in which values are formed.

chance to practice and develop all processes in a way that suits their developmental level and personal learning style.

The descriptions of the processes illustrate how young children engage in visual arts, music, dance, and drama/play experiences. These descriptions are valuable in a number of ways:

- They provide early childhood teachers with an open-ended rather than narrow perspective of artistic processes that are applicable to all arts areas (e.g., discovery and pursuit is involved in music just as it is in sociodramatic play, dance, and the visual arts).
- They assist early childhood educators in planning, implementing, and evaluating teaching and learning goals for the arts (e.g., by providing a framework for documenting children's progress, developing a profile of each child, and reflecting upon individual and group activities used in an arts program).
- They provide justifications for the place of the arts in the early childhood curriculum that can be helpful during discussions with parents, other teachers, educational administrators, and community members.
- They help early childhood educators see that, while each process has its own merit, individual children will become involved in the process, in different processes, in individualistic ways, partly as a result of their differing learning styles.

Figure 3.5 is not intended to be a checklist for teachers to monitor whether all children are receiving a "balanced diet" of artistic experiences. Rather, the processes should be viewed in relation to how children *participate* in the arts in individualistic and collaborative ways. Because of the broad, all-encompassing nature of these general artistic processes, they will be revisited several times throughout this book as an underpinning for understanding children's artistic participation. In Chapters 5 and 7, for example, children's artistic processes will be discussed in relation to the specific ways in which we can help children learn through modeling, describing, and discussing their artworks. Examples of how to apply these processes in the specific and integrated domains of art, music, play/drama, and dance are provided in Chapters 8 through 12, and ways to incorporate the general artistic processes into curriculum planning and documentation of children's learning are discussed in Chapter 13. For the remainder of this chapter, however, these general artistic processes will be described more universally in relation to how children enter into artistic activities and what they encounter and learn from these activities. The way a child enters into learning in the arts is largely dependent upon his or her preferred learning style and whether this learning style is honored and supported or disregarded and perhaps even thwarted.

Honoring Individual Learning Style

Children have different ways of dealing with the arts, and their use and understanding of the artistic processes described in Figure 3.5 will differ significantly across each of these domains or discipline. For example, how a young painter deals with shape and form will differ from how he or she uses these same artistic elements in music, dance, or dramatic play. In addition, each child will express these elements in an individual way according to his or her preferred learning style. Even four-year-old children show distinctive styles of thinking and learning (Gardner, 1991). Some children, for example, approach the world predominantly through the use of language; others through spatial, visual, aural, or physical means; and others through social relationships. Many early childhood teachers have informally confirmed Gardner's view, noting that some children steer away from certain visually oriented activities—such as block building or painting—but spend a great deal of time climbing or digging in the sand. Others enjoy creating musical compositions but may not be very good at telling stories or listening to them.

Another distinguishing feature of children's preferred style of thinking or learning relates to their overall interest in events and objects. For example, some children are interested in activities that focus on the unfolding of *events,* such as drawing a story-based picture, or acting out story through dance, drama, and music. Others may be more interested in *objects,* such as drawing an image, or an impression of an image, without necessarily telling a story, or building with blocks or digging in mud for the sheer pleasure of constructing a wooden structure or a mud sculpture. Similarly, their music, dance, and drama may feature the expressive, more abstract aspects of creating and communicating, such as the textures and sound qualities of music or the gestural and bodily-kinesthetic aspects of drama and dance. Of course, children may shift between a focus on events or objects, depending upon what they are wanting to achieve in their play and with whom they may be playing at the time. This issue of objects and events is discussed in greater detail in Chapter 6 along with many examples of how children use objects and events as a means of defining purpose and structure in their artistic play.

Generally, children who are events-oriented may show interest and ability in communicating with others, and create art works, dances, musical explorations, and play experiences that allow them to make statements about themselves. They may give titles to their works, such as "Cavemen Hunting for Dinosaurs," and can talk at length about the content of their creations or play experiences. Figure 3.6, for example, illustrates a four-year-old child's painting of her pregnant mother. The child has painted large red hands to highlight the mother's bulging belly. A sophisticated level of problem-solving

FIGURE 3.6 Event-Based Painting: "My Mommy Is Going to Have a Baby"

and technical skill were used to accomplish this. In addition, the discussion she had with her teacher about the painting showed a positive attitude about her mother's pregnancy and a confident understanding of herself in relation to her changing family situation.

In contrast, children who are more object-oriented may be less interested in the "story" aspects of the arts, but may be highly skilled in physical, technical, or analytical components. Their involvement often may center on activities such as making complex structures with blocks, Lego, or Mobilo, or making aesthetic arrangements with natural objects (see Figure 3.7). Their paintings can be highly detailed, patterned, and aesthetically pleasing, but may not necessarily involve an unfolding of events, such as in the painting by a three-year-old girl (see Figure 3.8).

When we recognize the intent of a child's artistic endeavors, we are able to be sensitive to ways in which to complement the learning style of the child.

FIGURE 3.7   Nonevent-Based Construction

FIGURE 3.8 Nonevent-Based Painting

An awareness of children's learning styles assists us to find an appropriate "entry point" for children's learning (Gardner, 1993b, 1999b). Entry points provide ways of thinking about how to engage children in an activity, or to extend an activity that has already began. Because individuals have different types of intelligence, cultural backgrounds, and values, a common entry point may not work for all learning experiences. Therefore, multiple entry points provide a means by which all children may become willing and interested participants in learning (see Figure 3.9 on page 60).

The use of these several ways of focusing attention on the purpose of an activity can help us understand and support children's different learning styles, concepts, beliefs, and values. Alternative entry points can encourage children to come to know a concept or skill in more than one way and to approach the task from a number of different angles, both verbally and nonverbally. A multifaceted approach helps children develop numerous representations and to understand these in relation to other children's perspectives. Children come to understand something in terms of something else that is both different and similar in certain respects. Given a variety of entry points and several routes to learning, it should be possible to find at least one route that is appropriate for each child. This should

FIGURE 3.9   Entry Points for Learning

An *aesthetic* approach emphasizes sensory features. This appeals to children who favor an artistic stance to the experiences of living. Experiences might include illustrating fantasy issues, such as trying to capture the beauty and delicacy of a fairy through drawing, music, dance, or dramatization.

In using a *narrative* entry point, a teacher might present a story or ask a question about a concept. For example, folk tales or legends can be used to understand moral issues, such as empathy for others, rights in relation to responsibilities, or spiritual values. Such issues might inspire an enactment of events through *dramatic* or *narrative* play, such as that illustrated in the example of children making a film about being lost in a supermarket (see Figure 2.2 in Chapter 2).

A *logical-quantitative* entry point centers on logical reasoning, making the connection between generic principles and specific examples of the principle (i.e., deductive reasoning). For example, understanding the gigantic proportion of the Diplodocus dinosaur (81 by 27 feet) could be approached by plotting a drawing of it on a playing field using yard-long paper rods as a measuring device (see Rankin, 1993). Such experiences are particularly appealing to children who are *numerically* inclined.

A *foundational* (or philosophical/existential) entry point is appropriate for children who like to pose fundamental questions of the sort that one associates with philosopher's debates. Such questions include issues that many adults may have difficulty answering, such as "Where did the stars come from?" or "Why did the dinosaurs disappear?" A foundational approach might consider, for example, the reasons for origins and changes and lead to searching for factual information in books to satisfy children's thirst for knowledge.

Finally, an *experiential* approach emphasizes hands-on participation. Through such experiences, children deal directly with the materials that embody or convey the idea or concept. For example, children might cluster into groups and make *interpersonal* decisions about which direction an unfinished story might take and how this will affect the characters.

Source: Adapted from Gardner, 1993b, 1999b.

increase the likelihood that every child can attain understanding of concepts and ideas across a variety of learning domains.

In addition, when children work together, collaboratively negotiating their learning with others, they develop new understandings of each other's perspectives and learning styles. Together, they socially construct their understanding. Within a mutually supportive environment, they assist and enhance each other's learning—they cooperate in the co-construction of understanding. Such co-constructed learning within social contexts is the focus of the next chapter.

SUMMARY

Educational systems are currently being challenged to address the balance given to intellectual, interpersonal, social, emotional, and spiritual components of learning. There is now an educational trend to promote the development of children's intellectual flexibility and lateral thinking through cross-disciplinary learning, using a range of "languages," many of which may be nonverbal. Rather than focusing on the teaching of traditional academic areas and the process of transmitting knowledge and values *from* the expert *to* the novice, contemporary educational practices must pass on knowledge about cultures in a way that encourages a variety of learning styles and processes. This will assist children to construct meaning through interaction and negotiation. To accommodate contemporary changes, education is not a matter of teaching *content* only or *processes* only, but emphasizing the interdependence of both; in other words, learning how to learn. In the context of the school curriculum, this occurs through immersion in the learning process and through a variety of social experiences.

In arts disciplines, the interconnectedness between content and process provides opportunities for children to articulate their understanding through spatial, visual, aural, bodily-kinesthetic, and inter- and intrapersonal knowing. Education through the arts involves thinking, perceiving, and feeling and provides numerous opportunities for the integration of thought, emotion, action; thinking with the body and through imagery; turning action into representation; "reading" and "writing" using artistic symbols; and communicating via a unique language. These are important media for learning how to learn, since they involve high levels of discovery-based processes and problem solving, where play is the primary vehicle for learning. Artistic processes provide various entry points for children who have different learning styles to understand themselves and their interactions with the world. Such understanding is achieved through the unfolding of events, and by depicting ideas in abstract and aesthetic ways. A graphic depiction of important concepts related to the arts is shown in Figure 3.10 on page 62. The metaphor of a chalice is used to summarize some of the key learning opportunities the arts offer.

ADDITIONAL READINGS

Edwards, C., Gandini, L., & Forman, G. (1993). Introduction. In C. Edwards, L. Gandini, & G. Forman (Eds.), *The hundred languages of children: The Reggio Emilia approach to early childhood education* (pp. 3–18). Norwood, NJ: Ablex.

Kress, G. (2000). Multimodality. In B. Cope & M. Kalantzis (Eds.), *Multiliteracies: Literacy learning and the design of social futures.* South Yarra, Victoria, Australia: Macmillan.

Leland, C. H., & Harste, J. D. (1996). Multiple ways of knowing: Curriculum in a new key. In J. Flood, S. Brice Heath, & D. Lapp (Eds.). *Handbook of research on teaching literacy*

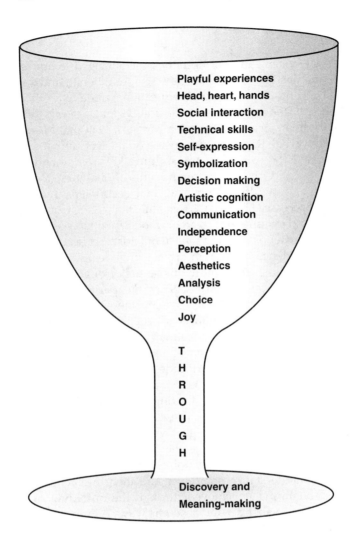

Playful experiences
Head, heart, hands
Social interaction
Technical skills
Self-expression
Symbolization
Decision making
Artistic cognition
Communication
Independence
Perception
Aesthetics
Analysis
Choice
Joy

T
H
R
O
U
G
H

Discovery and
Meaning-making

FIGURE 3.10   Core Experiences in the Arts

through the communicative and visual arts (pp. 167–180). New York: Simon & Schuster/ Macmillan.

Sweet, A. P. (1996). A national policy perspective on research intersections between literacy and the visual/communicative arts. In J. Flood, S. Brice Heath, & D. Lapp (Eds.). *Handbook of research on teaching literacy through the communicative and visual arts* (pp. 264–285). New York: Simon & Schuster/Macmillan.

PRACTICAL ACTIVITIES

1. What would the world be like without the arts? No movies, hit songs, sculptures in the park, people singing or dancing for pleasure, stilt walkers, jugglers, street musicians, rock concerts, musicals, ballerinas, laser-fireworks shows, cartoon characters, operas, or soap operas? Think of the many ways in which the arts are part of your life. This may range from responses to background music (while on telephone hold, while shopping, or when partying), to personal experiences (the joy of singing in the shower or doodling during lectures), to philosophical discussions about the role of the arts in society. Discuss mutual and individual activities that make up your artistic lives.

2. Observe children during play, particularly when they are involved in music, dance, art, or dramatic enactment. Make notes on the ways in which they use the supraverbal "languages" of the arts for meaning making and communicating (e.g., still and moving images, signs, sounds, gestures, bodily actions, expressive vocalization). What was the medium for this communication (e.g., drawing, painting, block building, clay modeling, collage construction, dance, sociodramatic play, music making, singing, role-playing)? What thoughts and feelings were being communicated?

3. Consider the various "entry points" through which children participate in the arts. (Refer to Figure 3.9.) Make a collection of examples of young children's art, musical improvisations, pretend play, or exploratory dance experiences that illustrate one or more of these types or styles of learning. You might collect art or take photos or sound or video recordings (with the children's and school's/center's consent). Discuss these examples with other students in relation to Figure 3.9.

4. Goodman (1984, p. 147) commented that "coming to understand a painting or a symphony in an unfamiliar style, to recognize the work of an artist or school, to see or to hear in new ways, is as cognitive an achievement as learning to read or write or add." Discuss examples of how you have been cognitive and emotional in relation to a painting, a play or movie, the lyrics of a song, or a musical performance. Describe your personal responses to the artwork in relation to its suggestive, symbolic qualities and the impression these made on you.

5. Through collaboration, there are many opportunities for children to become aware of their own artistic processes and to develop independence and a sense of "ownership" of their learning. Think of examples where you have observed children engrossed in problem solving through discovery learning. What did they do, make, discuss, pretend to be, or talk about? Do you remember doing similar things as a child? Discuss this with friends or classmates.

CHAPTER FOUR

SOCIALLY CONSTRUCTED LEARNING IN EARLY CHILDHOOD ARTS EDUCATION

I grew up in a small rural town in the midwestern United States. Many of the kids in the town would get together and play in vacant lots, and most parents knew most of the kids from around the neighborhood. When there was more than one family with the same last name in the town, many adults would refer to you as "so-and-so's kid."

One weekend I ended up playing in a vacant lot outside of my immediate neighborhood and discovered that these kids' parents had provided them with a large range of cardboard boxes of a variety of sizes—huge refrigerator and washing machine boxes and other, regular-sized boxes. There were kids from all ages—five to twelve or so—all going in and out of the miniature buildings that they had constructed from these boxes. I remember there was a jail made from a refrigerator box, turned on its side, with slats cut into the cardboard to look like jail bars. There was a church with a steeple, a grocery store, a bakery, an ice cream shop, and many other buildings. Some of the buildings had carpet pieces on the floors, shelving made out of smaller boxes, flat pieces of cardboard on the ground to connect the buildings, and other bits of furnishings like curtains, cushions to sit on, kids' chairs, and pictures hanging on the walls.

They must have been making these buildings for many days, and I guess there had been a lot of talk between the kids and the parents about types of buildings they could make, their locations within the miniature town, and things like furnishings that would make the buildings more real. Some of the older kids acted sort of like tour guides, showing me and other kids around the town, locking me up in the jail, taking me to the bakery, and stuff like that. In every building we went, all the kids just naturally went into some kind of role and played in that building before they went off to explore other buildings.

My experience in the miniature town is an example of how children of different ages (and often their parents and other adults as well) can become involved in socially constructed learning. Through interaction, people of various ages and experiences learn with and from each other through socializing in naturalistic contexts. Such progressive views of early childhood education are based on child-centered approaches to learning, where the emphasis is on creativity-oriented activities, naturalistic learning, and real-world outcomes. Since the time of Rousseau, progressives have consistently decried artificial learning conditions such as the dominance of outcomes-based objectives, the use of "measurable behavior" checklists, and, with older children, the overuse of textbooks and written exams (Ellis & Fouts, 2001).

The progressive Dewey (1913) described the policy of compulsory education as either rising or falling with our ability to make "school life an interesting and absorbing experience for the child," because the child may *attend* school, but may not be willing to be "present" or participate in activities that do not capture his or her interests, powers, and capabilities (p. ix). Stemming from the interest of the child, much of the learning in early childhood arts occurs through play-based interaction in which children are generally willing participants. Because play is an intrinsically interesting activity, the child generally will be very "present" and actually engaged with learning.

The early thinking of progressives is in harmony with the more recent constructivist thought. Constructivism is a theory of learning that is based on the premise that each person must construct his or her own reality and that such construction always precedes analysis. Experience is the key to meaningful learning—not the teacher's experience abstracted and condensed for children, but children's own direct experience. Constructivists argue that profound meaning can be found in all art forms and that individual children derive this meaning *for themselves,* based upon their background, interest, and artistic context. Social constructivists have extended this theory, stating that children's meaning can be *enhanced by others,* and the artistic context should involve interaction with arts mentors and peers. Through projects, devoted to intrinsically interesting topics or processes, children have opportunities to work together, where different kinds of intelligence and their combinations can be explored in an inquiry-generating atmosphere (Gardner, 1999a).

This chapter begins with the underpinning principles of socially constructed learning, followed by examples of specific ways adults can help children learn, and how children help each other learn through interaction. It also describes how children can become involved in special arts projects that are of mutual interest (such as the building of the miniature town). Within a school context, such arts projects should be part of a curriculum that is not necessarily firmly set, but evolves or emerges out of the interest of the learners.

UNDERPINNING PRINCIPLES
OF SOCIAL CONSTRUCTIVISM

Much of the current thinking in early childhood education has been influenced by the writings of the Russian education theorist Lev Vygotsky (1978) and his belief that learning occurs most effectively within social interactions. He claimed that mental functions occur first at a *social* level and then at an *individual* level. Thus, interaction between the child and more capable peers and adults is the first context for learning. Through interaction, children share the construction of understanding, and this shared learning provides guidance in skills and understanding that the child eventually internalizes (File, 1993). In other words, support from others is crucial for nurturing the skills that a child is developing.

Most early childhood educators understand how to support young children's knowledge and skills in language and social-based areas, and are relatively comfortable with enhancing mathematical, scientific, and interpersonal concepts with children. However, the arts can pose some philosophical dilemmas for teachers as they grapple with the issues discussed in Chapter 2. An adult with a "productive" philosophical framework, for example, might wonder how to socially construct children's learning in the arts if he or she views the arts as a discipline in which children should be left to unfold naturally in their own time, in their own way, without the "interference" of adults.

Yet, as described in Chapter 2, supporting children's learning in the arts is as important as supporting their learning in any other discipline. As in all disciplines, socially constructing learning in the arts requires a sensitivity to the children's areas of understanding that have not yet matured and working within these areas. This might involve, for example, noticing that a child may enjoy the challenge of painting with smaller brushes and experimenting with smaller images, finer details, and delicate technique. Vygotsky introduced the term *Zone of Proximal Development* (ZPD) to describe this sensitivity to children's "readiness" for new challenges (Figure 4.1).

FIGURE 4.1   **The Definition of the Zone of Proximal Development**

The distance between the child's actual developmental level	(as assessed by what the child can do on his or her own)
And the next, higher level of potential development	(as determined by what the child can do with the assistance of others who are more skilled in a certain domain of knowledge)

This ZDP is shown graphically in Figure 4.2. It is the area where teaching should be focused, by extending the knowledge that the child has already acquired. After learning has occurred, the ZPD—and the focus of teaching and learning—extends beyond the child's recently acquired knowledge. This cycle occurs over and over again as individual children build their knowledge bases.

When guiding learning in the arts, we facilitate learning by mediation, that is, by becoming a co-participant in the child's construction of knowledge. This shared construction of learning emerges in the arts through social processes that involve thinking, feeling, linguistic knowledge and skills, non-verbal symbolic communication (e.g., using imagery and the body and turning action into representation). When working in the ZPD, the teacher takes initial responsibility for the child's learning by focusing on aspects of tasks that are just beyond the child's capacity. (Examples of this are provided in the next segment.) As learning progresses, the balance shifts so that the child takes on more responsibility for independent problem solving and the application

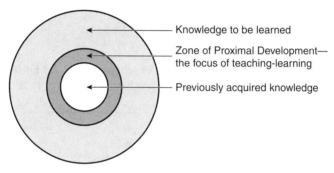

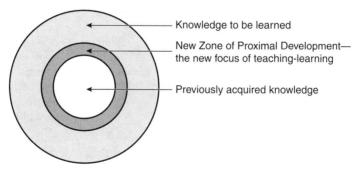

FIGURE 4.2   **A Graphic Representation of the Location of the Zone of Proximal Development**

of skills. Support from the adult is offered less often and less directly than before, as the child develops skill and gains understanding until he or she is able to assume autonomous control over the performance of a task. With each new arts learning experience, children will draw on their acquired knowledge, but this knowledge in itself may not be enough. And so the process begins again, with the teacher offering more support and the child developing a new set of autonomous skills.

Applying the techniques of social construction requires us to be aware of ways to help the child take the next step toward learning. In addition, determining which strategies work for whom under what circumstances is of primary concern. We can ask ourselves questions to organize our thinking and decision making so that we can be active agents in facilitating children's artistic learning (File, 1993). Figure 4.3 provides some examples of general questions we might ask ourselves to assist children's artistry.

Through such questions, teachers can plan activities that make sense from a child's perspective. In other words, we need to center on the child's meaning and intentions, rather than focusing on how to reach a predetermined goal. The *guided* approach to arts education, as discussed in Chapter 2, requires making on-the-spot decisions to capitalize on the child's involve-

FIGURE 4.3   Questions for Organizing Teachers' Decision Making

QUESTIONS	PURPOSE	PRACTICAL ACTIVITY
What have I seen the child do before in situations similar to this?	To assess the ability and skill of individuals; to assess growth; to assess the child's divergent reactions.	Observe children's expressive, technical, or cognitive processes and products in the arts.
How much help is required for the child to meet his or her goals and the goals I have for the classroom?	To determine the quantity and quality of support needed to individualize teaching interventions; to identify potential reactions to future teaching-learning events.	Think of the types of support you can provide to help children meet their goals in expressive, technical, or cognitive processes that are creating difficulties for them in specific arts disciplines.
How can I keep the children involved in interactions with peers rather than with me?	To prevent intrusion by the teacher; to stimulate peer-oriented learning and support.	Think of ways in which children can learn from each other through activities that are mutually constructed.

ment in an activity. A number of strategies for guiding learning were discussed in general:

- Modeling or demonstrating
- Providing descriptive feedback
- Explaining to help organize children's thought
- Asking questions to extend children's ideas and understanding

Let us now examine these four strategies in more detail, with specific application to early childhood arts education.

Modeling or Demonstrating

This teaching strategy can focus on social, physical, emotional, or cognitive aspects of the child's development. Showing by example allows the child to try the teacher's approach until he or she finds personal ways that work just as well. Demonstrating can be less threatening for the child if we phrase comments to highlight alternatives, rather than suggesting only one way—ours. The use of the word "sometimes" can be useful, as it suggests that there are alternative approaches to many things. For example, when modeling good mallet technique while playing a xylophone, a teacher might say, "Sometimes it's helpful to let the mallet bounce gently in the center of the bar, rather than on the outside, because the sound is clearer and lasts longer." When modeling movement while dancing, we might say, "Sometimes I like to just let my arms dangle freely by my sides, and other times I lift them up really high." "Sometimes" types of comments are likely to elicit other responses from the children, such as "Yes, I can dangle my arms too, and I can even wave them around." When children see other children's approaches, they are often inspired to try these alternatives, and in the process they are modeling movements from each other, rather than always taking the lead from us.

Once children have tried their new skill successfully—whether this is physically, visually, or through sound—they develop the confidence to apply this knowledge in new but different situations. Sensitive teaching involves demonstrating how the situations may be different but the processes are similar. For example, children might discover that the different qualities of sound they get when playing the bars of a xylophone is a general acoustical principle that is applicable also to tapping the skin of a drum or tamborine with the hand. When children grasp this principle, they are likely to show other children when using instruments during free play. Young children often adopt the role of the teacher, and less experienced children learn from more competent peers.

Providing Descriptive Feedback

Feedback can help children structure or organize their thoughts. Feedback might include supporting children who don't know how to get started on a task, or by helping them determine the most appropriate direction to take.

For example, we can help a child select the "best" or most appropriate musical instrument to use in a play encounter to support the mood or idea being explored (e.g., selecting bright, ringing sounds versus crisp, wooden sounds). We can also help children identify important cues, such as listening for when the music changes (e.g., gets faster), and altering their dance accordingly (e.g., using quicker movements). Such principles apply to all arts domains, and are valuable for helping children resume more responsibility when they are having success, but also to prevent children from becoming frustrated when more assistance would be helpful. To help a child find direction or identify important cues when sculpting with clay, for example, we might say, "You seem to be having fun working in the clay, but it looks like you're having some difficulty attaching the legs to your clay animal. Sometimes it helps if you scratch the tops of the legs with a fork and add a bit of water to help stick the legs to the body."

When accompanied with demonstration, our verbal descriptions or processes do more than simply indicate our pleasure with children's participation. They also provide specific feedback about the child's learning processes. Yet it is often common to hear very general feedback that is predominantly centered on a child's emotional engagement, or reinforce "good boy/girl" behavior, or to simply say, "You're doing a find job, keep it up." Such comments might be "You're having fun, aren't you?," "Well done," or "That sounds nice."

Through such comments, we communicate an appreciation of the aesthetic results of a child's work, but we do not affirm the positive aspect of the action and learning that is taking place. Examples of both pleasure and affirmation of learning, based on the previous examples, might be:

> "You're having fun, aren't you? I like the way you've used the blocks to make a long, winding pathway."
> "Well done! You danced along that narrow bridge by holding your arms out like airplane wings to help you balance."
> "That sounds nice. I especially liked how you ran up the piano keys two notes at a time."

Descriptive feedback provides a positive way of encouraging children to continue their explorations and extends their knowledge and skills beyond what they already possess. It helps children become metacognitive about their own learning. Often children are told what *not* to do, particularly when there is a dispute, or if unacceptable behavior is interrupting class decorum or threatens children's safety (e.g., "Don't throw blocks," "No running inside"). However, positive feedback that affirms children's *appropriate* behavior can help clarify what is not only acceptable, but ways in which children can take control of their own learning (socially, emotionally, and cognitively). As in all learning, the arts can be enhanced by positive feedback so that children not only feel *inspired* to participate, but also understand *how* to participate in many fulfilling ways.

Explaining to Organize Children's Thoughts

Comments and reflections can encourage children to respond and interact sensitively, while reinforcing specific knowledge and skills and helping them organize their ideas. These might include talking about the child's movement (e.g., while playing an instrument), feelings (e.g., emotional involvement with the dance), the way things sound, look, feel (e.g., soft, gentle, flowing), and by using arts-based language (e.g., fast/slow, smooth/jerky, bright/dark). Such comments might also involve providing examples of *strategies* for how the child might try something, such as suggesting alternative movements, sounds, or images to create contrast. In this way, we are providing visual, oral, movement, and verbal prompts.

The descriptions of each of the general artistic processes described in Figure 3.5 in Chapter 3 can provide a framework for teachers to focus their teaching strategies, such as the use of comments and prompts, and to help children organize their thoughts. For example, in the first of the general processes, discovery and pursuit, we might focus on the various subprocesses to encourage children's further learning, such as in Figure 4.4 on page 72.

Applying similar ways of explaining processes to children are equally applicable to each of the general artistic processes. Self-awareness, communication, social interaction, perception, technique, analysis, and critique are all important processes in arts education, and the subpoints within each of these areas can provide a means for thinking about how to give children descriptive feedback about their learning, beyond that of discovery and pursuit. The subpoints described in each of these artistic processes can be applied to asking a range of questions that will enhance children's learning in relation to an almost infinite number of artistic possibilities.

Asking Questions to Stimulate Children's Ideas and Understanding

In the examples in Figure 4.4, a number of questions were used to help children reflect on their work or their involvement in an arts process. These questions or comments were examples of open-ended leads, where the end point (i.e., the answer or behavior) can diverge in many directions, rather than converge on one "right" answer. Open-ended questions provide opportunities for children to initiate ideas, take the lead, and actively contribute to an activity. Such questions often involve the use of the words *who, when, why, where,* and *how.* For example:

> *What* other things could you use?
> *Why* is it hard to . . . [hear the wood block]?
> *What* happened when . . . [you tried the chiffon instead of the burlap]?
> *What* do you think you could do with these?
> *Where* will we get what we need?

FIGURE 4.4   Explaining to Assist Children's Discovery and Pursuit

Being open-minded. "You know, Jack, I'm with *you.* I can't see any reason why an elephant can't do a tap dance! Would you like to pretend to be a tap-dancing elephant?"

Observing. "Tricia, you've been looking at the spider's web for a long time. I really like the way the sun's making the threads look so shiny and white. What are you seeing?"

Comparing. "You two boys have been trying a lot of different rhythms on your drums. I wonder what the two rhythms would sound like together?"

Exploring options. "John has thought of an unusual way to make his puppet sing and dance. I wonder if there are other ways?"

Reinterpreting. "That's a good version of that song. You've changed the words to go with what you're doing here. How else do you think you could change your song to make even more versions?"

Making associations. "Hissss" (after a child has held up a long, snakelike coil of clay and hissed at the teacher). "I'd better slither back to my own house before I get too frightened!"

Finding alternatives. "There doesn't seem to be enough room in here to dance with those big capes. Perhaps if you went out under the tree you'd have more space, and the capes would look even nicer in the filtered sun."

Imagining. "You took your magic rug to the beach, did you? What happened then?"

Testing. "I don't know if that would work either. Why don't we try it out?"

Taking initiative. "That's great. I like it when someone can think of something interesting to play even when it's raining outside. Do you think Mary might like to join you?"

How do you plan to do it?
Where might you get some ideas for how to do it?
Who would be someone we could ask?
Where in the room would you like to work?
Why do you think this might happen?
How could we check this out?
When do you think we'll know?

Figure 4.5 is a reflection on an interaction I had with preschool children while they were enacting "Sandy Beach Fairies" through music and movement. The story illustrates ways in which children's ideas and approaches to dramatic play, dance, and music can be developed through discovery learning and extended through open-ended questions. Through a flexible approach to interacting with children, where they have ready access to a range of supportive resources, there will be many opportunities for children to learn from one another while developing independence.

FIGURE 4.5   Scaffolding during the Sandy Beach Fairies' Play

Last week, Mary and a couple of other girls were pretending to be Sandy Beach Fairies and had draped their bodies with colorful chiffon cloth. They were beginning to experiment with fairy-type dance movements, but Mary's body-language and occasional comments suggested that she was becoming frustrated with the other girls' input—the dance and play were not developing the way she would have liked. I thought I might be able to extend the play by helping the girls "believe" in their roles.

Through open-ended questions, I helped the girls select other props to make their play area more like a beach. They found a large piece of yellow burlap and laid it on the floor where the sun was streaming through the windows to make it feel like a sunny beach. Then they selected some shells, sticks, stones, and leaves from the nature collection and placed them around the edges of the beach. In the process of creating the beach, they also made garlands of flowers for their hair and tied ribbons around their wrists so the chiffon would flow when they moved their arms and twirled around. This also freed their hands to pick up shells during their dance.

One of the girls suggested that they find some music on a CD to accompany their dance, but Mary wanted them to make up their own music. I helped them think about the types of sounds they wanted (e.g., soft, ringing, bright), and they selected finger cymbals, a triangle, and some seedpods to rattle. However, playing the triangle while dancing soon became awkward. Through discussion, I helped them discover that they could tie the seedpods to their ankles, and these would rattle when they moved their legs and feet. They soon discovered that sleigh bells could also be attached to their ankles and wrists, and because these sounded bright, they made a good substitute for the triangle sound they had discarded.

Through a few open-ended questions, the girls selected movement and drama props and musical instruments and danced the Sandy Beach Fairies for quite some time. Other children gathered around for a little performance and commented about the clever ways the girls had created the chiffon fairy costumes and their burlap beach and how they used the instrumental sounds to accompany their movements. Later in the week, I found other children expressed an interest in using other types of props "like the fairies did," to support different play experiences, such as a large black curtain draped over some chairs to make a cave and drums and woodblocks to create spooky music. I'm finding that, while I am still nearby to make suggestions and ask questions during the children's play, it seems the children are beginning to help each other work out their own solutions with less and less help from me.

The strategies described in this segment—modeling, demonstrating, explaining, and asking questions—are intended to mediate children's behavior. They draw children's attention to alternative ways of thinking about the activity in which they are involved and help them find new problems they might address. Importantly, they subtly help children acquire ways to learn how to learn. In more formal language, children *internalize* (socially *reconstruct*) new strategies and ways of exploring their environment, and they *apply* their knowledge when participating in new but similar activities. Using newly learned strategies in new situations is called *transfer* of learning (or *generalization*): Children see the connection between one learning context and another, and transfer this learning to new situations. For example, the children who observed the fairies' play generalized that a variety of resources could be used to enhance their play, and they transferred this understanding to a new learning context—spooky cave play.

Our involvement in guiding children's learning is a continuous process of determining how and when to help children take the next step. Recognizing and working within the child's Zone of Proximal Development ultimately helps him or her internalize the learning processes that have been assisted, or "scaffolded." Then children are more able to apply these learning processes in different ways independently. As in all areas of the curriculum, there will always be another next step to take—new information and insights just beyond the learner's independent capabilities. Children and adults alike advance to the next level of understanding through constructing shared meaning through conversation and interaction with others. Such socially constructed learning becomes the basis of a curriculum that "emerges" through shared meaning making, and evolves from project-based encounters.

THE PROJECT-BASED, EMERGENT CURRICULUM

There are many lessons we can learn from the practices of the early childhood programs at Reggio Emilia. The arts are not taught as a subject, as a discipline, as a discrete set of skills, or treated in other ways as a focus of instruction for its own sake. Rather, they are integrated into the program via problem solving, centered around projects. The arts are simply additional "languages" available to young children who are not yet very competent in conventional symbol systems, such as writing and reading.

In the Reggio Emilia approach, the teachers set general educational objectives but do not formulate the specific goals for each project or activity in advance. Rather, they formulate hypotheses of what could happen on the basis of their knowledge of children, and objectives are then developed—objectives that are flexible and adapted to the needs and interests of the children (Rinaldi, 1993). These interests, which include those expressed by children at any time during the project, as well as those that the teachers infer from the work as it proceeds, form the basis of what is referred to as an emergent curriculum. This type of planning allows for exchange and communication between three inter-active partners (or what the Italians call protagonists)—the children, the educators, and the families—integrated into the larger social system.

As a project develops, "teachers reflect, explore, study, research, and plan together possible ways to elaborate and extend the theme by means of materials, activities, visits, use of tools" (Rinaldi, 1993, p. 156). Teachers work in co-teaching pairs, learning to cooperate and adapt, accommodating constantly. In the process, they value the social nature of intellectual growth and communicate with parents about the project, encouraging them to become involved in a number of ways: participating in the activities of their children, finding necessary materials (e.g., supplementary books, CDs, and resources for dance or dramatic play), and working with teachers on the physical environment. In this approach, parents are stimulated to revise their image of their children. They come to understand childhood in a more rich and complex way.

There are no formal prespecified lessons that all children must learn, and the full group is not subjected to instruction at the same time. Instead, work is done in small groups and the content of the teacher-child relationship is rich with problem setting and problem solving. In this way, teachers assist children in activities and help them develop a deeper understanding of a particular topic. "In Reggio, the teachers know how to listen to children, how to allow them to take the initiative, and yet how to guide them in productive ways" (Gardner, 1993b, p. xi). Being familiar with the children is foundational to such an approach. It requires us to be aware of children's individualistic learning styles, knowledge, and skills, and their abilities to collaborate with others. Such familiarity is largely based on our observations and interactions with children, and our reflections and documentations of the outcomes of co-constructed learning.

Reflection and the Role of Documentation

Reggio educators believe that "reciprocity, exchange, and dialogue lie at the heart of successful education" (Edwards, Gandini, & Forman, 1993, p. 7). The problem-setting/problem-solving experiences "provide ample texts, pretexts and contexts for extensive genuine conversations between the adults and the children, as well as among them" (Katz, 1993). The teachers act as participant observers, responding to what they see by asking questions, initiating face-to-face exchanges, redirecting activities, and modifying the way or the intensity of their interaction with particular children (Malaguzzi, 1993).

In addition to the participant-observer role, teachers are actively and systematically involved in the documentation of the process and results of their work with children, believing that such documentation serves three key functions (Edwards, Gandini, & Forman, 1993, p. 7):

- To provide the *children* with a concrete and visible "memory" of what they have said and done in order to serve as a jumping-off point for the next steps in learning
- To provide the *educators* with a tool for research and a key to continuous improvement and renewal
- To provide *parents* and the *public* with detailed information about what happens in the schools, which also is a means for eliciting their reactions and support

Parental and public involvement is stimulated through the display of such documentation, which in turn strengthens community understanding of young children's learning, while providing a rich basis for parent-child discussion. For example, alongside the children's work are photographs of the children actively involved in the processes of learning and transcriptions of the children's questions and comments that evolved throughout the work (Katz, 1993).

The use of the camera, tape recorder, slide projector, typewriter, video camera, computer, and photocopying machine are valuable instruments for capturing such experiences and for assisting teachers to reflect on the teaching-learning interface (Vecchi, 1993). Each child's characteristics, aptitude, needs, and interests are monitored and evaluated by this extensive and detailed record keeping, and the whole staff, including nonteaching members, meet on a weekly basis to discuss and plan the program based on this (Katz, 1993).

> Throughout the project, the teachers act as the group's "memory" and discuss with children the results of the documentation. This systematically allows children to revisit their own and others' feelings, perceptions, observations, reflections, and then reconstruct and reinterpret them in deeper ways. In reliving earlier moments via photography and tape-recording, children are deeply reinforced and validated for their efforts and provided with a boost to their memory that is critical at their young age (Edwards, 1993, p. 156).

For example, in a project in which children were exploring the shadows of their own bodies and of trees, a group of buildings, a cat, a swing, an iron gate, and so on, children explored a number of paradoxes, spontaneously offering the following theories about shadows at the beginning of their experiment (Petter, 1987, p. 70):

- It's there and you can't hold on to it.
- It has a shape but it has a hundred more.
- It seems like it's going to obey you and then it does what it wants.

- It comes and goes when it wants.
- It's part of the night but it's also part of the day.
- It's made of dark air and sky but also of wind and earth.
- It's light and fragile but also very strong because it stays where it is even if you squash it with a big stone.
- It doesn't drown if you pour water over it.
- It's something we carry inside ourselves and it comes out of our feet.
- The sun makes it be born in the morning and die at night.

Such statements "provide vivid testimony to the versatility of children's ideas" and of "their capacity to choose words and thoughts that give connotations and interpretations to a subtle phenomenon" (Petter, 1987, p. 70). The teacher's ability to act as the group's memory in the documentation of such experiments is critical for children at such a young age. The children revisit their own and others' feelings, perceptions, observations, and reflections. It also helps them reconstruct and reinterpret these feelings, perceptions, observations, and reflections in deeper ways.

Malaguzzi (1987, p. 23) encapsulated the philosophy and practices of Reggio in this statement:

> Is it possible to visualise a type of education which sees the child as a builder of images? We think it is. Children (like poets, writers, musicians, scientists) are fervent seekers and builders of images. Images can be used to make other images: by passing through sensations, emotions, relationships, problems, passing theories, ideas about the possible and the coherent and about what seems to be impossible and incoherent.

The notions of building images with children is relevant not only within the visual realm, such as in the graphic domains of painting or sculpting. Image building also applies to the aural, bodily-kinesthetic, and spatial domains of music, dance, and drama. All of these domains draw on imaginative, expressive, and technical dimensions of artistic expression. These forms of expression incorporate a number of higher cognitive skills such as those described in the first chapter, on creativity: fluency, flexibility, originality, elaboration, transformation, problem solving, objectivity and selectivity, and applying aesthetic and practical standards.

While this chapter centered predominantly on the origins of social constructivism and techniques for teaching within the Zone of Proximal Development (e.g., modeling, providing feedback, explaining, and asking questions), it also would be helpful to review this content in relation to content presented in Chapter 2—in particular, the conditions for guiding learning in the arts and the principles associated with forming partnerships with children. These key issues provide the significant underpinnings for an emergent curriculum that can evolve from projects where children and adults co-construct learning.

These educational initiatives offer a means of assisting children to cope with diversity and change and to develop the flexible skills, attitudes, and abilities necessary to function successfully as adults in the coming century. Education should provide a forum in which children and adults can affirm their connections with the world, culture, society, and the environment—bound together as active *creators* of their futures rather than as isolated, individual, and passive *recipients* of change.

SUMMARY

Current philosophies of early childhood education acknowledge that children are active learners, but that their construction of knowledge is not achieved in isolation. As discussed in Chapter 2 and in this chapter, educational theorists now embrace the notion of a more active approach to facilitating learning in arts education by helping children to construct their own knowledge within a social context. Through interaction, children share the construction of understanding, and this shared learning provides guidance in skills and understanding that the child eventually internalizes. We can help children learn if we are sensitive to the children's areas of understanding that have not yet matured and work within the Zone of Proximal Development. Our involvement in guiding children's learning is a continuous process of determining how and when to help children take the next step. This involves a number of teaching strategies: modeling or demonstrating, providing descriptive feedback, explaining to help organize children's thought, and asking questions to extend children's ideas and understanding. These strategies help teachers mediate children's behavior, by drawing children's attention to alternative ways of thinking about the activity in which they are involved, or new problems they might address. The descriptions of each of the general artistic processes provided in Figure 3.5 in Chapter 3 can provide a framework for how to focus our comments and reflections.

Teaching young children is a deliberate, reflective process involving action, analysis, and evaluation according to well-defined but flexible goals that stem from a project-based, emergent curriculum. Through the exchange between children, teachers, and families, all participants contribute to the understanding of a range of topics and interests. Through dialogue, these three participants engage in problem *setting* and problem *solving*. Teachers act as participant observers, actively and systematically documenting processes and results of their work with children. This documentation serves as a memory for children and helps them go to the next step of learning. It also acts as a tool for teachers' reflections on their own work and a means to share with the parents and community what children have learned in the early childhood setting. This can serve as an inspiration for parents to participate in their children's artistic learning, both in and out of school.

ADDITIONAL READINGS

Katz, L. G., & Chard, S. C. (1989). *Engaging children's minds: The project approach.* Norwood, NJ: Ablex.

Kessler, S. A. (1992). The social context of the early childhood curriculum. In S. Kessler & B. B. Swaderer (Eds.), *Reconceptualizing the early childhood curriculum: Beginning the dialogue* (pp. 21–42). New York: Teachers College Press.

Malaguzzi, L. (1993). History, ideas, and basic philosophy. In C. Edwards, L. Gandini, & G. Forman (Eds.), *The hundred languages of children* (pp. 41–90). Norwood, NJ: Ablex.

Rinaldi, C. (1993). The emergent curriculum and social constructivism: An interview with Lella Gandini. In C. Edwards, L. Gandini, & G. Forman (Eds.), *The hundred languages of children* (pp. 101–112). Norwood, NJ: Ablex.

Rogoff, B. (1990). *Apprenticeship in thinking: Cognitive development in social context.* New York: Oxford University Press.

Stremmel, A. J., & Fu, V. R. (1993). Teaching in the zone of proximal development: Implications for responsive teaching practice. *Child & Youth Care Forum, 22* (5), 337–350.

PRACTICAL ACTIVITIES

Teachers (and more capable peers) can assist children in learning how to structure and manage their own meaning. Responsive early childhood learning is a dynamic, interpersonal process, originating in communicative processes. Below are questions that focus on the social construction of learning between teachers and children and between children and more capable peers.

1. Observe children and teachers being co-partners in artistic processes, jot down your impressions of what you have observed, and discuss your responses to the following questions with your classmates:

   ■ What examples have you observed of children constructing shared meaning through interaction and conversation with other children? How have children helped other children learn through such interpersonal experiences?

   ■ In what ways have you observed children learning through observing other children? Did you notice if these children internalized this understanding and applied it in their own, independent activities?

   ■ How can children learn through activities that are mutually constructed, such as developing differing perspectives? Provide an example of a mutually constructed learning experience involving young children in the arts.

2. Provide some examples of the Zone of Proximal Development (ZPD) in learning experiences in painting, dancing, block construction, role play, or exploration with musical instruments.

   ■ What strategies did the teacher use to extend children's arts experiences to take them to the next step of understanding?

   ■ In what ways did the teacher act as a co-partner with children in arts activities to assess their meaning and intentions or to take them to the next step?

CHAPTER FIVE

THE ARTS AND INTELLIGENCE

Most people probably have friends or acquaintances who are very accomplished in some special way. We might know musicians or artists who regularly perform or sell their art, others who can design gorgeous gardens, others who are athletic even in to their middle or later years of life, and others who can spin a yarn or tell a joke that will have even strangers roaring with laughter.

Because of the amazingly diverse skills and personal histories of people, it is both a celebration and a mystery that some people can be exceptionally accomplished in some areas, but not necessarily in other areas. One person might have an astonishing knowledge of literature and a passion for science fiction, but have no interest in writing a sci-fi novel. Others may be excellent singers or instrumentalists, but not be able to read music. Some may have refined interpersonal skills and an ability to work positively with most people, but might feel extremely embarrassed about having to dance at a party.

I wouldn't hesitate, for example, to ask one of my artist friends to give me aesthetic advice, like about which of my paintings should be hung in which rooms, but I probably wouldn't ask her to help me hang the artworks because her carpentry skills and ability to locate struts in a wall aren't that hot. In return, she would probably want me to help her wire her stereo system, figuring out which lead should go where and, while I'm doing this, make me a great meal because I'm lazy when it comes to cooking.

Most of us probably value the extreme individual differences among our friends and realize that each of us manages to deal with our own characteristic weaknesses in relation to our strengths. We learn how to do this, partly through our general exposure to the world and certain people in it, but also because of our desires and interests to do well in highly specific areas of endeavor, or perhaps in broad general areas. How is it that people can be "intelligent" in such diverse ways?

For well over two thousand years, certain ideas have dominated discussions of the existence and importance of mental powers. Philosophers such as Plato, Socrates, Aristotle, Decartes, and many others have emphasized individual capabilities in relation to mental powers. Such notions have been debated through medieval, Renaissance, and other periods of time up to the present.

In postindustrial societies, the notion that intelligence is a characteristic or trait of individuals became tied to innovations in psychological testing that began in the early years of the twentieth century. Binet's (1905) intelligence scales were developed to identify children who were performing poorly in school and who might benefit from special education. Intelligence became defined operationally as the ability to answer items on tests of intelligence, which generally measured people's ability to solve linguistic and logical problems. Hence, a high value was placed on verbal and mathematical skills.

While Binet avoided using a single score to represent a child's performance on his intelligence test, those who translated and used the test later, however, were not reluctant to do so. This score became the Intelligence Quotient (IQ), and it is calculated on the norm for a population of children of a similar age. Intelligence was considered to be an inborn, underlying attribute or faculty situated in the heads of individuals. A single faculty of intelligence, described by Spearman (1927) as a general ability (or g), was believed not to change much with age, training, or experience. Although this perspective of g has remained a common view among many theorists of intelligence, others have proposed different "vectors of mind" or different "products, content, and operations" of intellect (Guilford, 1967; Thurstone, 1938) and different domains or "modules of the mind" (Carey & Gelman, 1991; Fodor, 1983; Keil, 1989).

Several contemporary theories of intelligence reflect a broader notion of intelligence to account for the diverse abilities of individuals to pursue various domains of knowledge and, indeed, to create new ones. Instead of there being one, general intelligence that governs all behavior, it is suggested that there are several specific aspects of thinking ability that relate to competence in various domains of intelligence. Each of the "multiple intelligences" perspectives suggests that the mind is organized into relatively independent realms of functioning. Instead of a single dimension, called intellect, on which individuals can be rank-ordered, there are vast differences among individuals in their mental strengths and weaknesses and also in their style of pursuing cognitive tasks.

Successful people, for example, are not necessarily good at everything; and people who are good at the same thing do not necessarily achieve it in the same way. Thus, intelligent people capitalize on their strengths and compensate for their weaknesses. This process involves a balance of analytical, creative, and practical components of intelligence, where successful people shape or change the environment to suit their conditions or escape from these conditions and find another alternative, if possible (Sternberg & Lubart, 1995).

There is evidence to suggest that intellectual differences (strengths and weaknesses) are apparent even before the years of formal schooling. Once

children reach formal schooling, however, we can predict that they will perform well on IQ tests and standard tests of achievement if they are good in
language and *logic,* because these are the two main areas that generally are
measured in these tests. But whether these children continue to do well later
in life will depend as much on the extent to which they possess and use *other*
types of intelligence. In fact, adult accomplishments after school are commonly contrary to IQ predictions. Goleman (1995), for example, commented
that, at best, IQ contributes about 20 percent to the factors that determine life
success. This leaves 80 percent to other forces, such as social class, emotional
characteristics, or luck. The emotional components include the ability to
motivate ourself, to persist in the face of frustrations, to control impulse and
delay gratification, to regulate moods, to empathize, and to hope. Let us consider the notion of multiple intelligences a little more closely.

MULTIPLE INTELLIGENCES

Two decades ago, Gardner (1983) suggested that there are several human
intelligences that are common to all cultures. His theory of multiple intelligences has provided a valuable alternative to the traditional notion of intelligence. Gardner stated that intelligence cannot be defined only by ability in
verbal communication or number, nor should children be classified as
"smart" or "dumb" based only on their capabilities in these two areas. A person can be considered to be intelligent because of competency in one or more
of several broadly defined areas.

Gardner described at least eight domains of intelligence—musical,
spatial, bodily-kinesthetic, interpersonal, intrapersonal, linguistic, logical-
mathematical, and naturalistic. More recently he has proposed that there
could be even more domains, such as existential intelligence, which has to
do with the human proclivity for raising and trying to answer very big questions (Gardner, 1999b). In addition, other authors have proposed two other
forms of intelligence—emotional and spiritual (Goleman, 1995; Zohar &
Marshall, 2000). Each of these intelligences has its own pattern of development and brain activity, each different in kind from the others, and each
existing autonomously from other intelligences. Anybody who is not completely brain dead will have the full set of intelligences.

Gardner's (1993a) definition of intelligence is the ability to solve problems or to fashion products that are valued in one or more cultural or community settings. The problems to be solved can range from creating an end
for a story to anticipating a mating move in chess to repairing a quilt. Products can range from scientific theories to musical compositions to successful
political campaigns.

Rather than reducing an individual's potential to an IQ score, Gardner
(1993b) suggested that we foster and educate all of these intelligences. He

makes the case that raw, biological potentials can be seen in a pure form only in individuals who are—in the technical sense—freaks. In almost everybody else, the intelligences work together, and the educational process should help people reach vocational and avocational goals that are appropriate to their particular spectrum of intelligences, so that people feel engaged and competent, and inclined to serve society in a constructive way.

He illustrated the distinctions in the domain of music, where musical intelligence is significant, but other intelligences are important as well, depending on which aspect of music is at issue. For example:

> A violinist must have bodily-kinesthetic intelligence; a conductor requires considerable interpersonal intelligence; the director of an opera requires spatial, personal, and linguistic as well as musical intelligences. Just as a domain may require more than one intelligence, so, too, an intelligence can be deployed in many domains (pp. 37–38).

Gardner established eight signs that provide evidence of independent aspects of intelligences and that help define the difference between an intelligence and a highly developed skill. As two of these signs have particular relevance to our discussion of the arts, these will be discussed briefly. One sign is the existence of people who have very low intellectual ability but an exceptional skill in an area like mathematical computations or musical skill. These individuals are called *idiot savants* (literally, "bright fools"). There are also other individuals who may have a single exceptional intelligence in the face of an otherwise meager array of abilities, such as highly proficient musicians with very poor social skills.

Another sign for the independent aspects of intelligence is available from analyzing the outcomes of people who have suffered from *specific brain damage* (Gardner, 1993b). A faculty such as linguistic or musical intelligence can be destroyed or spared in isolation as a result of brain damage, and this faculty remains relatively autonomous from other human faculties. For example, while linguistic abilities are lateralized almost exclusively to the left hemisphere by normally functioning right-handed individuals, the majority of musical capacities are localized in most individuals in the right hemisphere (Gardner, 1983). Thus, injury to the right frontal and temporal lobes causes pronounced difficulties in discriminating tones and in reproducing them correctly. However, injuries in similar areas in the left hemisphere—which causes devastating difficulties in language—generally leave musical abilities relatively unimpaired. For example, a professional musician who received left-hemispherical brain damage could recite words to songs but could not sing the melody; another musician with right-hemispherical brain damage could play music but could not name the work or remember the words (Wright, 1985). Several studies suggest that both sides of the brain have a role in perceiving music and that people process melody and rhythm separately. Researchers estimate that there may be up to twelve distinct regions in the auditory cortex that control musical perception on each side of the brain, although it remains unknown what musical roles these anatomical regions play (Azar, 1996).

These two signs illustrate the existence of different forms of intelligence in normal and exceptional cases. Let us now turn our attention to the various intelligences that are featured in the arts—musical, spatial, bodily-kinesthetic, and intra- and interpersonal intelligences—and the knowledge, skills, and abilities associated with young children's artistry.

Although Gardner's multiple intelligences are discussed quite frequently in the academic and popular literature, often this discussion does not receive the level of depth that his theory warrants, nor are there attempts to draw practical conclusions or to make recommendations for education. The next section provides a brief summary of the characteristics of the key intelligences that are central to the arts. This description of the intelligences is intended to serve as a framework to which the reader can return on many occasions to reflect on related content within this book, such as child development and curriculum planning. Then, the following sections of this chapter will illustrate how these key intelligences employ different types of communication (i.e., symbolizing) and how children often express themselves in these intelligences both literally and metaphorically.

It should be noted that the linguistic and logical-mathematical forms of intelligence are also components of artistry; however, these two areas will not be featured in this discussion, largely due to the emphasis already given to these within society in general. Rather, they will be discussed only in terms of how they relate to the artistic aspects of expression. Likewise, naturalistic, existential, emotional, and spiritual intelligences, which also are part of artistic learning, cannot be covered adequately within the length restrictions of this book, but aspects of these domains are illustrated at other times throughout the book.

Musical Intelligence

"Of all the gifts with which individuals may be endowed, none emerges earlier than musical talent" (Gardner, 1983, p. 99). Leonard Bernstein had lots of it; Mozart, presumably, had even more (Gardner, 1993b). Types of musical skills one might encounter in young, exceptionally talented individuals (called prodigies) might include playing a Bach suite for solo violin with technical accuracy as well as considerable feeling; performing a complete aria from a Mozart opera after hearing it sung but a single time; or playing on a piano a simple minuet the child has composed. There is a wide range of musical skills and abilities found in the human population and of ways in which people encounter music through the senses, media, and modalities. These abilities might be shown through singing, playing instruments by hand or with the mouth, writing or reading musical notation, listening to recordings, or moving to music.

Music has been described as the controlled movement of sound in time, and the "succession of tones and tone combinations so organized as to have an agreeable impression on the ear and its impression on the intelligence is comprehensible" (see Sessions, 1970). Composers, for example, work with tones, rhythms, and an overall sense of form and movement when deciding how much melodic, rhythmic, or harmonic *repetition* is appropriate and how much *variation* or elaboration is required to achieve their musical ideas (Gardner, 1983). These key components of music are discussed in greater detail in Chapter 9, particularly in relation to how young children perceive and apply patterning in music. Of the constituent elements of music, pitch and rhythm are central to the tonal and temporal aspects and provide the structural and organization components of the aural expression (Wright, 1985). While pitch and rhythm can exist independently, most often musical elements coexist.

Musical intelligence involves musical *memory,* a sensitivity to *sound,* and a responsiveness to sound *sequences and structures.* In addition, most people who have been involved intimately with music acknowledge the importance of emotions. Music conveys emotions or affects by capturing the *forms* of these feelings—it imitates the world around us and our human emotions (Worth, 2000). However, these emotions are more in the abstract than directly linked to events, objects, or persons. Music, which is perhaps the most abstract of the various art forms, is similar to abstract art—there is no object to which our emotions can be directed. In some ways, understanding music is a purer process than understanding language, because language is complicated with outside referents in order to determine meaning and to communicate. Music does not have easily detectable referents. Instead, it represents what is closest to us, too close to be put into words. It has the capacity not only to "go beyond words, but to exist only beyond words" (Worth, 2000, p. 105). Music is about "the experience that moves us, that reaches the deepest part of our interior world, that part in which the human spirit resides" (Eisner, 2001).

Spatial Intelligence

People who are generally considered to have highly developed spatial intelligence include sailors, engineers, surgeons, sculptors, and painters (Gardner, 1983). Their spatial intelligence involves the ability to perceive the visual world accurately. However, these abilities are not identical, and hence individuals may be good at visual perception while having little ability to draw or imagine. Nonetheless, just as rhythm and pitch work together in music, the following capacities typically occur together in the spatial realm, operating as a family and reinforcing one another. Spatial intelligence (Gardner, 1983) involves the ability to:

- Form a mental model of a spatial world and maneuver and operate using that model
- Create mental imagery and then transform that imagery and re-create visual experiences in the absence of relevant physical stimuli
- Produce graphic likenesses of spatial information

In normal human beings, spatial intelligence is tied to the ability to observe the visual world; however, spatial intelligence can develop in, and be extremely important for, individuals who are blind and have no direct access to the visual world. Indeed, many scientific theories have derived from "image" involving resemblances across remote domains—domains that could have been created, or at least appreciated, even by individuals who are blind (Gardner, 1983, p. 174). Such scientific conceptions include Darwin's theory of evolution as a vision of the "tree of life" (with each branch of the tree representing a different species), Freud's notion of the unconscious being submerged like an iceberg, and Dalton's view of the atom as a tiny solar system.

A number of writers have acknowledged the significance of visual and spatial imagery. Arnheim, one of the pioneers of visual thinking, viewed it as a primary source of thought, claiming that the most important operations of cognitive processes take place in the realm of imagery (Gardner, 1983, p. 177). Thurstone (1947) described spatial ability as being one of seven primary factors and divided it into three abilities: to recognize an object when seen from different angles, to imagine movement, and to think about spatial relations in terms of body orientation. Finally, Piaget described infant sensorimotor development as a precursor to the later capacity to make mental images of scenes or events and to transform or manipulate these images without having to be there. As adults, we perform similar mental operations, as discussed in Chapter 3, in relation to "thinking with imagery and the body" to remember where we have lost our keys to the car.

Spatial intelligence involves not only a combination of the abilities described above, but also other capabilities, such as creativity and control of fine motor movement. The essence of graphic artistry, for example, lies in the spatial realm. In fashioning a work of art, whether a painting or a sculpture, a high level of sensitivity to the visual and spatial world is required.

Bodily-Kinesthetic Intelligence

This is the ability to solve problems or fashion products using one's body. Highly developed bodily-kinesthetic intelligence is exhibited by people such as dancers, athletes, surgeons, artisans, and musicians. Gardner (1993b) defined characteristics of bodily-kinesthetic intelligence as including:

- Using one's body in highly differentiated and skilled ways, for expressive and goal-directed purposes
- Working skillfully with objects, both those that involve the fine motor movements of one's fingers and hands and those that exploit gross motor movements of the body
- Controlling bodily motions and the capacity to handle objects

Skilled performance includes characteristics, such as a sense of timing, sensitivity to points of repose or shifts of behavior, and a sense of direction. Fine motor abilities involve the ability to use one's hands and fingers to carry out delicate movements involving precise control. In music, for example, refined independent patterns of movement are involved when a pianist plays contrasting patterns of movement, simultaneously sustaining different rhythms or melodies. Our kinesthetic sense monitors the execution of motor actions, allowing us to judge the timing, force, and extent of our movements, and to make necessary adjustments.

The abilities to watch, observe keenly, imitate, and re-create are central to all performing arts. It is the capacity to involuntarily mimic and go through the experiences and feelings of others that allows us to understand and participate in the arts. We apprehend directly the actions or the dynamic abilities of other people or objects, as when we feel a lump in our throats when an actor cries.

Personal Intelligences

This domain is immensely important, although it is not well understood and is elusive to study. *Interpersonal* intelligence involves the development of the internal aspects of a person and the capacity to access one's feeling life and a range of affects or emotions (Gardner, 1983). It is the capacity to form an accurate and truthful model of oneself and to be able to use that model to operate effectively in life. This intelligence includes making discriminations among personal feelings and understanding and drawing on them to guide our behavior. The types of occupations that utilize this intelligence include the novelist, therapist, and wise elder.

In contrast, *intrapersonal intelligence* turns us outward to others, and involves the ability to notice and make distinctions among other individuals, particularly their moods, temperaments, motivations, and intentions. Gardner (1993b) suggested that this form of intelligence includes the ability to understand other people: what motivates them, how they work, and how to work cooperatively with them. Individuals likely to have high degrees of intrapersonal intelligence include successful salespeople, politicians, teachers, clinicians, religious leaders, and people involved in the helping professions, such as counselors and social workers.

Compared to other realms of intelligence, there are many forms of interpersonal and intrapersonal intelligence. Because of the distinct symbol systems found in each culture, meanings for interpreting experiences can be culturally distinctive and perhaps even unknowable to someone from an alien society. This is a main reason why intelligence of any form should be considered in relation to symbols and how they are created, communicated, and interpreted. Let us now consider symbol systems used in the arts.

INTELLIGENCE, SYMBOLS, AND SYMBOL SYSTEMS

In the twentieth century, trends in philosophy and psychology have shifted away from a focus on the external behavior of humans to an interest in the activities and products of the human mind. Inspired by influential thinkers in the early and middle part of the century, such as Alfred North Whitehead, Susanne Langer, and Ernst Cassier, interest increased in how people use symbols to express and communicate meanings and how this capacity distinguishes humans from other creatures. The ability to use symbols has been identified as central to evolution and the creative achievements of human beings. Through symbol use, people have devised myths, languages, arts, mathematics, sciences, and other symbol systems.

In the latter part of the twentieth century, others investigated the use of symbol systems as a distinctive feature of human cognition (Ashman & Wright, 1997; Feldman, 1980; Gardner & Wolf, 1982; Goodman, 1976; Wright, 2001b). What are the symbol systems and how do they influence creative and intelligent human behavior?

Symbols and Symbol Systems

A symbol is any element that calls to mind people, objects, or events that are not present. Vehicles of symbolization can be physical marks (e.g., drawings or other graphic images), but symbols can also be abstractions (e.g. gestures, play, visualization, fantasy, and dreams). When the physical quality of the symbol is similar in appearance to the real object it depicts, representation occurs. For example, a child's drawing of a circle with protruding arms and legs can stand for a person. When a visual symbol is represented abstractly, it can be shown through imitation and other means of expressive communication, such as through the use of textures, shapes, colors, or positioning on the page. Such abstract qualities of children's art were illustrated in Chapter 3 (Figures 3.7 and 3.8) as examples of non-event-based construction and painting. Similarly, abstract symbols are used in the performing arts through, for instance, sounds, images, gestures, and movements.

Painters, composers, dancers, or actors—whether they are publicly acclaimed geniuses or preschool-aged children—work with artistic materials or actions and turn them into representations. What is important to the observer is that these symbols are universally recognizable. For instance, children as young as seven years old are able to describe music in terms of weight, size, stiffness, outward or inward direction, and the degree of activity (Swanwick, 1988). Two- to four-month-old infants can match the pitch, loudness, melodic contour, and rhythmic structure of their mother's songs far more easily than they can respond to the core properties of their native language. What is more, they can engage in sound play that exhibits not only imitative but also creative properties (Papõsck & Papõsck, 1982). In other words, in addition to copying the parents' or caregivers' vocal sounds, infants throughout the world are able to initiate new pitch and vowel-consonant combinations in playful contexts, with the intention of this being copied by the adult (this is discussed in greater detail in Chapter 9).

For survival and productivity, humans have developed a number of symbol systems. Four symbol systems that are used almost worldwide but in differing ways, depending upon the culture, are language, mathematics, picturing/graphics, and music. Dance, drama, and art do not use such notational systems, but involve other forms of encoding systems that are described in greater detail in Chapter 7 in relation to artistic literacy. Some examples from each of the three most commonly used symbol systems are illustrated in Figure 5.1 on page 90.

Symbol systems are collections of symbols that have come to be used in organized and systematic ways through cultural practice. Not only do we communicate through and within a range of quite different modes (e.g., visual, aural, bodily-kinesthetic), each of these modes has regularities that are akin to (but not the same as) those of spoken or written language. Cultures differ in this respect. The Chinese culture, for example, has developed visual communication systems using pictographs or characters. Egyptian hieroglyphics and Australian Aboriginal iconographies are other instances of how symbols have been developed and conventionalized in other cultures. Other groups of people have developed bodily movement for communication and expression, such as in the hand-signing used by the speech- and hearing-impaired.

Just as children in different cultures learn different verbal languages, they also learn to value culturally specific art forms, accept specific styles of artistic expression, and learn what types of artistic forms and processes are accepted (or rejected) within their particular culture. For example, it is highly likely that Chinese children would be exposed to traditional art styles, such a brush and ink landscapes, more frequently than to abstract art; Greek children would more likely hear and dance to music with complex metric groupings, such as sevens, than would many American children; and it is likely that many European children would have more opportunities to view live opera than would children from Fiji.

FIGURE 5.1   Some Ways in Which Symbols Are Used

LANGUAGE

Graphemes   The letter symbols (e.g., a, b, c, and so on)
Syntax   The way in which words are formed into language
                             units (e.g., grammar)
Semantics   The meaning of language

MATHEMATICS

Number series   1, 2, 3 . . . 20, 21, 22, and so on
Operations $+ - \times /$
Algebra $a + b = c$

PICTURING OR GRAPHICS

Picturing   Drawings, maps, conventions such as Z Z z z zzz, or
                             an idea lightbulb
Diagrams   Bar charts, graphs, $\updownarrow$, $\rightarrow$, ■
Graphics   Commands (no smoking), ☺ ● ♀ ♂

MUSIC

Rhythm   ♪♫
Pitch   Notes on a staff, including ♭ ♮ ♯ .
Expression $<\ >$, *rit.*

Regardless of culture, there are a number of ways in which young children use symbols when they engage in artistic activities, which become evident in their artistic products. Children symbolize through the use of:

- *Images* (e.g., creating two-dimensional and three-dimensional works and interpreting images, such as illustrations in books or exit signs)
- *Sounds* (e.g., creating "sound stories" and using sound expressively in music)
- *Movement* (e.g., gesturing to communicate ideas or express emotions, creating "gentle" dances, rolling a toy truck across the floor)

While language is often used in combination with these visual, aural, and bodily-kinesthetic domains, the arts are not dependent upon language to create and communicate meaning. Each of the arts domains has its own symbols and grammars that young children acquire in their early years. As discussed in Chapter 3, the symbolic grammars of the arts have been described metaphorically as languages. Hence, children learn ways to use *verbal* language in face-to-face conversations, in arguments, telling jokes and singing songs, in poems and recipes, and in a number of other ways. They also learn how to use *nonverbal* language more abstractly when they read maps, use windows on a computer, interpret people's body language, and employ number, gesture, drawing, music, dance, dramatic play, and a range of other symbolic methods to understand and to communicate this understanding.

Learning to use the grammar of drawing, for example, involves showing how the full-sized, three-dimensional, moving, colored world can be translated into a set of marks on a flat surface. In this visual domain, where spatial aspects of intelligence are important, visual experiences can be captured through various processes. Let us consider a hypothetical situation to illustrate how the grammar of drawing might be used in an adult social gathering at a coffee shop in the center of a city. The range of spatial and visual symbol systems used by the individuals gathering for this event might include:

- Reading a city map to find the venue, coupled with recognizing and spatially orienting themselves to important landmarks and streets
- Sketching the avenue through the window of the shop, featuring a garden or interesting building, thus capturing the aesthetic aspects of the area of the city
- Recording the social dynamics of the venue, by devising graphic diagrams that illustrate clusterings of people and how these clusters shifted throughout the evening

Children are also able to use similar visual and spatial concepts symbolically, and often they blend these with other aspects, such as sound, movement, and language. For example, while drawing, they may start with the visual domain, such as drawing a person, but also use sound effects while dotting the spots on the person's dress, use squiggly lines to show the person's movements, or scribble out the image of the person to symbolize that it is now night time or that the person has gone somewhere else. Such symbolic depictions are discussed in greater details in Chapter 6 in relation to children's development in each of the domains.

Learning about one's culture involves learning how to gain, render, and communicate meaning in a number of symbolic ways. Because each symbolic domain has its own special qualities, problem solving in one domain may not necessarily be translated directly to another. For example, children's ability to handle space in drawing is not equivalent to their ability to master rhythm in music or to learn the rules of story telling. This is because symbols are subject to classification (Wolf & Davis Perry, 1988). Artworks, for instance, can be classified by:

- *Subject:* religious icons, medical bulletins
- *Style:* Impressionist paintings, rock music, contemporary theater
- *Genre:* still life, short stories, ballet

- *Medium:* watercolors, video clips
- *Creators:* Monets, Hemingways, Spielbergs
- *Historical and cultural milieu:* Renaissance or Victorian works

Such classifications are found in all art forms, and children are sensitive to such classifications (an aspect that will be discussed in Chapter 7 in relation to artistic literacy). The complex aspect of symbolism is that one individual symbol can be used and interpreted in many ways. It can belong to several systems at the same time and take on many meanings. For example, in a scene in the film *Jesus Christ Superstar,* Jesus and his disciples are walking through the desert—oddly, they are speaking modern-day language with European accents—when unexpectedly, a twentieth-century fighter plane streaks across the sky, temporarily drowning out the dialogue of the actors and shifting the context to the present. This anachronistic blend of historical periods, cultures, and events was one of a number of symbolic ploys used throughout the film as a constant reminder that the *medium* of film provided the *creators* with opportunities to interpret the *subject* of a *historical event* in a modern *style.* When we watch a film such as this, we need to known how the symbols are operating to understand what and how they represent, otherwise we would not grasp the humor of that particular segment of the film.

Our knowledge of a representation and its context enhance our understanding of it. However, the issue of sorting between symbols and what they mean becomes complicated because the symbols can have both *literal* meanings (i.e., factual), as well as *figurative* meaning (i.e., expressive). In the example above, the viewer is subconsciously invited to wonder how Jesus and what he represented would have managed in modern society. This message was communicated through our ability to go beyond the literal scene of the disciples walking through the desert and accepting the irony of the out-of-context modern symbols. Such knowledge of both the literal and expressive symbols is key to intelligence in the arts.

Literal and Expressive Symbolizing

Some symbol systems, like numerical notation, scientific symbols, and representational drawings or diagrams, highlight denotational elements while having little or no expressive potential. In a *denotational* or *literal* application, where a specific meaning is communicated directly, the symbolic element expresses or represents an item or object as it exists. A three-year-old child, for example, might select a block of wood and represent the domestic duty of ironing. In contrast, *figurative* or *expressive* representations capture a property of human experience without designating a specific object. Poetry, modern dance, improvised jazz, and abstract art exhibit a wide range of

FIGURE 5.2   A Child's Expressive Drawing of the Forest at Night

expressive reference. In Figure 5.2, a six-year-old child uses figural symbols to depict a forest at night by applying expressive lines, contrasting black and white images, and foregrounding the stars as if we have a bird's-eye view of the scene.

Hence, symbols can vary from instances where denotation is the key characteristic (such as in "ironing") to instances where expressive properties are intended (such as in expressing "sadness" through the use of color and line). Intelligences function artistically in the extent that they exploit the literal/denotational or figurative/expressive properties of a symbols. When language is used in an ordinary, expository way—such as the way in which this chapter is presented—the linguistic intelligence generally is not used in an aesthetic manner. However, if language is used metaphorically or expressively, it will call attention to sound or structural properties—such as that found in poetry—and have artistic appeal. Similarly, spatial intelligence may be exploited aesthetically by a sculptor or nonartistically by a surgeon or a cartographer. Even music can function nonartistically, as when continuous background music becomes the "aural wallpaper" of an early childhood environment, or when we encounter "canned" music when we are put on hold during a telephone conversation.

In addition, patterned artworks or computer-generated musical compositions can be derived from mathematical formulas and still be classified as aesthetic, suitable for display in art galleries or for presentation in performance halls. Even commercial products can have artistic value. For example, a section of the Museum of Modern Art in New York contains a collection of functional objects (lamps, kitchen utensils, even a very early Macintosh computer) that could be considered art.

When exploiting the expressive aspects, a symbol refers to another idea *metaphorically* and is capable of expressing a mood or sentiment, where an impression is conveyed that is not literally part of the work. Generally, we think of metaphor as a language-based concept. We define it as a figure of speech in which a word or phrase literally denoting one kind of object or idea is applied to another, to suggest a likeness or analogy between them. Common language-based metaphors are "Her eyes *drank* in the scenery" or "The ship *plows* the sea." However, metaphor is not restricted only to literature, and can be a powerful component in all artworks. Figure 5.3 shows an example of an eight-year-old boy's visual metaphor of a lost boy crying puddles of tears. As adults, we regard these types of artistic symbols as relatively common in children's artworks. Yet in our adult "wisdom" we often classify such images as quaint but lacking in realism, since we know that it is impossible to cry puddles.

Is this child's image a conscious application of visual metaphor or an accidental result of immature cognition? Common examples of children's visual metaphors include the ubiquitous sun, personified by human features, who "beams" down from the top corner of most preschool-aged children's artworks. Does the child see the sun as a real, living entity with human qualities? Piaget's daughter claimed the sun was alive because it followed her wherever she went, but does that mean that her drawings of the sun are a representation of it as being humanlike (Piaget, 1955)?

Metaphors are used in the drawing in Figure 5.4, which illustrates a seven-year-old child's depiction of sadness. The artwork shows a small figure walking in the distance, with a large amount of foreground space with swirling lines to lead the eye to the figure. The red sun draws the viewer's eye upward and back to the lone figure. The expressive qualities of this and of other artworks may communicate psychological moods (such as depression or loneliness) or sensory qualities (such as the heat of the desert sand and the burning sun). The viewer of the artwork gains a subjective impression through the artist's expressive use of artistic elements, such as color, shape, style, and composition.

Language can help us understand an artistic work, but it cannot fully explain or replace the work; it must be interpreted (Simpson, 1988). A piece of music, for example, is a series of sounds that has the power to communicate ideas or feelings through analogy—it can metaphorically express or stand for other concepts, such as liveliness, patriotism, tranquility, or fear. Metaphor is used extensively in all art forms across all spoken languages. For example, music can be as light as air or ponderous, and an artwork can give the impression of being heavy or dynamic. Such properties are associated with our per-

FIGURE 5.3 Crying Puddles of Tears

sonal experiences that have been re-created and implied by the composer or painter, and interpreted by the listener and viewer. Artistic re-creation is achieved in a number of ways, such as through color and brush stroke and through the use of selected musical instruments and expressive musical controls such as speed or dynamics.

FIGURE 5.4   Metaphors Used in a "Sad" Drawing

Music cannot express fear, but its movement, in tones, accents, and rhythmic design, can be restless, sharply agitated, violent, and even suspenseful. . . . It cannot express despair, but it can move slowly, in a prevailing downward direction; its texture can become heavy and, as we are wont to say, dark—or it can vanish entirely (Sessions, 1970, p. 101).

Several authors have argued that, although children use metaphor in their early years, during their elementary school years they reject metaphor in their quest for technical accomplishment (Wolf & Gardner, 1980). The well-known art educator Victor Lowenfeld (1947) described the elementary school period of development as dawning realism. Is this rejection of metaphor a function of development and genetic programming, or is it, as Fielding (1993) suggested, a product of socialization and learning based on the expectations of parents, schools, and the culture?

It is clear that, although school-aged children have a desire to acquire the technical skills and knowledge to master sophisticated levels of expression in each of the arts domain, they also are able to retain and extend their ability to use expressive components of symbolizing if given the opportunity.

Figure 5.5 is an example of an eight-year-old girl's metaphoric expression of her feelings about herself and her world during a period in which she was undergoing cortisone treatment associated with her failing kidney. The author was a secure, independent, and confident girl who was comfortable with her close friendship with an unpopular, overweight boy in the class, even though this cross-gender relationship often elicited teasing from her classmates. As a result of gaining weight through the administered drugs and developing what she called a chipmunk face, her sense of self is personified in her story through the depiction of a tired, weak bird, living in a context where no one understood the value of the sensitive support she received from her friend—whom she metaphorically depicts as a sad, ugly tree. (The original language, spelling, and punctuation are retained.)

This child's story provides an opportunity to summarize how symbols can be used to make links to the earlier segment of this chapter in relation to forms of intelligence and how they are expressed. The young author used *symbols* to represent people, objects, and events. Her communication was

FIGURE 5.5   Metaphoric Story about Friendship

Once there was a ugly droopy tree. Nobuty liked him, so that made him very unhappy. You see it's because all these trees were very beautiful, there were little creeks running in and out with the most beautiful tinkering sound, but when it came to the droop tree as they called him, the creek would make a most awful grunting crackling noise. That would make poordroopy more unhappy for he couldn't help being ugly, just as we can't help breathing. But one day ther was a bird all gray and week. It couldn't hardly fly and was very scard to be in this very bright forest, because if you had seen him which you haven't so I'll tell you.

He had just been in a storm with lots of dark misty clouds, roars of crashes and all kinds of things that can scar a little tiny bird. So the bird wanted a kind of hom that's not noisy or anything like that. In this forst it was quite hard to, everthing was bright and cheerful which didn't sound good to this bird. But just as the bird was to give up and die it faited. As it was faiting droopytree saw it fall and clang out to save it, for if this tree would have any friends it would surly be a beetin up bird. The droopy tree made a comfort little bed for the bird so when it woke up it didn't want to leave though the tree was ugly, it never mattred. Just the way the trees friendly actions does matter, not the looks!

> THIS story may be able to
> teach you something,
> That being beautiful is
> not always the most
> important it's how you
> ACT!!!!!!

through linguistic means, using the *genre* of story with a moral (i.e., "actions are more important than beauty"). On this occasion, the creator chose to use written language, but she might also have used drawing, painting, sculpture, or some other visual medium, or expressed these ideas through dramatization, dance, or music (as she did on other occasions with other topics).

The key emphasis of the story was not communicated literally but through *metaphor,* drawing on other forms of expression and intelligences—bodily-kinesthetic, musical, spatial, and personal. The metaphors used in the story are illustrated within each of the areas of intelligence (the key words are highlighted in italics). (The author's spelling is "corrected" to assist clarity and to help illustrate how the concepts are clustered.)

Bodily-kinesthetic (posture, movement). There was an ugly *droopy* tree, a little creek *running in and out,* and a bird all gray and *weak,* who could *hardly fly* and was very scared because it had just been in a *storm.* Just as the bird was to give up and die it *fainted.* Droopytree *clang out* to save it.

Musical (aural, sounds). The creek had the most *beautiful tinkering sound* when it ran past the beautiful trees, but when it came to the droop tree it would make the most *awful grunting crackling noise.* The storm had *roars of crashes,* and the bird wanted a place that's not *noisy* or anything like that.

Spatial (visual). The storm had lots of *dark misty clouds.* The bird was scared to be in this *very bright forest.* As the bird was *fainting,* droopytree *saw it fall.*

Interpersonal (personal emotions). Nobody *liked* the droopy tree, so that made him very *unhappy.* He *couldn't help* being ugly, just as we can't help breathing. The bird was all *gray, scared* and about to *give up and die* It *wanted* a kind of *home.*

Intrapersonal (understanding others and their actions). The *other* trees were very *beautiful. When the creek made awful noises* as it passed him, that would make poor droopy more unhappy. In this forest it was quite hard to find a home that's not noisy because everything was *bright and cheerful* which didn't *sound good* to this bird. If droopy tree would have any *friends* it would surely be a *beaten-up* bird. The droopy tree *made a comfortable little bed* for the bird so when it woke up it didn't want to leave. Although the tree was ugly, it didn't matter. Just the way the tree's *friendly actions* does matter, not the *looks*!

It is somewhat surprising that a child of a relatively young age could express such abstract concepts. This was probably due largely to her interpersonal and intrapersonal maturity as a result of reflecting on her long-term illness and potential early death. Her family also played a significant role in her maturity through their actions, open discussions, support, and positive attitudes. It was also significant that her mother was a practicing artist who regularly expressed concepts through visual symbols that included metaphors. This child's development (and that of all children) is significantly influenced not only by the type and level of support they receive from others, but also by their exposure to, and experience with, literal and metaphoric symbols. These issues are discussed in greater detail in the next chapter.

SUMMARY

The notion of intelligence as a trait of individuals originated through psychological testing, where a high value was placed on verbal and mathematical skills, but where other areas, such as intelligence related to in the disciplines of the arts—musical, spatial, bodily-kinesthetic, and personal—were overlooked. We now realize that there are relationships between intelligence and processes that are inherent across all domains of learning, such as personality, motivation, knowledge, learning style, and environmental conditions. Gardner described several human intelligences that are common to all cultures, each existing autonomously and with its own pattern of development. Although each of these intelligences can exist independently, as in the case with *idiot savants* and brain-damaged people, there usually is a crossover of domains.

Musical intelligence involves musical memory, a sensitivity to sound, a responsiveness to sound sequences and structures, and a range of skills (singing, playing instruments, reading and writing music, and listening and moving to music). *Spatial* intelligence involves forming spatial models of the world, creating and transforming mental images, producing graphic likenesses of spatial information, and special abilities (to recognize objects from different angles, imagine movement, and think of spatial relations in terms of body orientation). *Bodily-kinesthetic* intelligence involves using the body for expressive and goal-directed purposes, using fine and gross motor movements, controlling body motions and handling objects, and using skills, such as timing, direction, and feeling the actions of other people. *Personal* intelligence involves the ability to access our emotions, form an accurate model of ourselves, use this model to operate effectively in life, and draw on our emotions to guide our behavior. *Intrapersonal* intelligence involves making distinctions among other people's moods, temperaments, motivations and intentions, and understanding and working collaboratively with others.

In each of these intelligences, the use of symbols is a distinctive feature of human cognition. Many forms of problem solving involve working with materials or actions and turning them into representations using *symbols*. Vehicles of symbolization can be physical marks (e.g., drawings and maps), but can also be abstractions (e.g., gestures, play, visualization, fantasy, and dreams). For survival and productivity, humans have developed a number of *symbol systems* that have come to be used in organized and systematic ways through cultural practice. Each of these symbol systems has special qualities and "grammars," depending upon the domain that is involved (e.g., visual, aural, bodily-kinesthetic). Learning about one's culture involves learning how to acquire, use, and communicate meaning by representing objects and events either *literally* (communicating specific meaning directly) or *expressively* (conveying an idea, impression, mood or sentiment metaphorically). Much of young children's symbolic communication is nonverbal and occurs through playful experiences that alternate between reality and fantasy—they depict meaning and represent reality using symbols as tools of thought.

ADDITIONAL READINGS

Haas Dyson, A. (1992). Symbol makers, symbol weavers: How children link play, pictures, and print, *Young Children, 45* (2), 50–57.

Walsh, D. J. (1993). Art as socially constructed narrative: Implications for early childhood education. *Arts Education Policy Review, 94* (6), 18–23.

Wright, S. (1995). Children's musical composition and information processing style. *Journal of Cognitive Education, 4* (2–3), 103–111.

Wright, S. (2001). Drawing and storytelling as a means for understanding children's concepts of the future. *Futures, 6*(2), 1–20.

PRACTICAL ACTIVITIES

1. Think of people whom you know (which can include yourself) who have high levels of ability in one of the "intelligences" listed below:
   - Musical
   - Spatial
   - Bodily-kinesthetic
   - Interpersonal
   - Intrapersonal

   In what ways do these individuals demonstrate their special abilities? Discuss some of these characteristics and ways of expressing and showing special skills. The examples below (and others discussed in this chapter) might provide a helpful starting point.

   - Knowing a large amount of information about music (history, composers)
   - Navigating through an unfamiliar city without a map
   - Showing coordination, agility, and confidence in a variety of sports and in dance
   - Having a deep knowledge of self in relation to others (almost a sixth sense)
   - Fitting into any social situation with ease while making people feel good

2. Do you know people who are highly gifted in one or these intelligences but may not show evidence of such a high level of ability in other areas? In what ways do you think the multiple intelligences cross over? Can you provide examples?

3. Some of the geniuses of the world might not have scored very well if measured on standard IQ tests. Picasso, for example, had a great deal of difficulty in his early schooling, and Einstein had difficulty learning to read. Yet each reached outstanding achievements later in life.
   - Do you think IQ scores could have a negative influence on teachers' expectations of the intellectual abilities of children within their classrooms?
   - Is it possible that you might have a young Picasso or Einstein in your classroom one day? What types of education experiences would you provide them?

4. Discuss art, music, dance, and dramatic play experiences of young children in relation to the literal and expressive symbols they use.

5. Using a plain white piece of paper and a pencil, make a sad drawing (either in class or in your own time). Share your drawing with other classmates or friends. Discuss specific aspects of the drawings that make them sad (e.g., the content or subject; the use of artistic aspects such as line, texture, or composition). Were expressive qualities and/or symbols used in the drawings that communicated the emotion of sadness? If so, discuss these and how they were communicated.

CHAPTER SIX

CHILDREN'S ARTISTIC DEVELOPMENT

When I was in first grade, I remember begging my teacher for art lessons. I found most of the other lessons boring and frustrating because I had difficulties learning how to read, and just about everything you did at school involved reading. But I was good at drawing and would have liked to show my teacher and the other kids that, even though I couldn't read very well, I could make great pictures. After school hours, I spent much of my time at home engaged in art activities and in fantasy play, and I enjoyed building with blocks and creating imaginary worlds. When I asked why we didn't have art at school, I remember my teacher telling us we were "big children now." I guess she thought drawing was just for preschool kids and that there were more important things to do at school than making pretty pictures.

Eventually, we did have a few lessons in "art," if you could call it that. In one lesson, we stood in line to wait for our turn to have a two-minute experience with finger painting. In the second lesson, we all colored in a stencil of an apple (everyone was told to use red and to not go outside the lines). Finally, we did a group mural, where we each cut something out of a magazine and stuck it on a large piece of paper. I hated these lessons and wanted the chance to make my own pictures, instead of just following the rules of the teacher and making junk. I couldn't even identify my own red apple when all of them were put up on the windows for the parent-teacher's night. I suppose it's not surprising that I stopped asking for art lessons.

From that point on in my elementary school years, I can only remember being given the chance to color in the illustrations on our worksheets—but only after we had done our "work." Although our school had a music specialist, the teaching of art was left up to the classroom teachers. It seems none of them had any interest in art or a willingness to let us make our own. So I took to hoarding blank sheets of paper and doing sneak drawings whenever there were gaps in the daily timetable, and I would take these drawings home to work on later. Once my teacher caught me drawing on a picture I had been working on for days and ripped it up in front of all the other kids.

With time, I overcame some of the difficulties I had with learning how to read. By about third grade, I was on track with the other kids. I can't help but think, though, that if art had been a more important part of my early schooling—where I could have made my own images and told my own stories—I would have overcome some of the reading difficulties I was having. My attitude toward school would have been a lot more positive, too. I know it was quite a while ago when I was in elementary school, so things have probably changed since then. But when I pass by schools, even today, I still see twenty identical apples in some of the windows.

As illustrated in the story above, some children can find school unfulfilling if there are not opportunities for them to learn in domains that complement their learning styles and ways of thinking. Creating and communicating concepts and emotions, not only through art but also through dance, drama/ play, and music, provide opportunities for children to understand themselves and their worlds and make connections with other areas of learning. There is evidence that the visual, aural, and bodily-kinesthetic domains of learning are important avenues for young children's development, and this will be discussed in this chapter.

To explore an understanding of children's artistic development, we must acknowledge a number of key issues. This analysis should be based upon children's:

- Participation in artistic activity
- Evidence of self-expression and communication skills
- Use of symbols and materials
- Emergence of perception and critical thinking skills

In all areas of study, children learn to acquire and apply the "grammars" and rules specific to the symbol systems of a particular discipline. A "snapshot" of the development of artistic symbol systems is provided here, followed by a more detailed account of key structural components that shape young children's thinking and feelings while working in arts domains.

Typically, one-year-old children know a number of objects and people through direct, sensorimotor experiences. They know the touch of their mother, the sound of rattles, the coolness of the breeze, and many other things. In a general sense, the shape (or trajectory) of development in each area of intelligence begins with patterning, such as being able to discriminate tones or rhythms in music, verbal and gestural sequences in social interchanges, and movement patterns in music. It also involves realizing that objects can be represented two-dimensionally on paper and three-dimensionally through construction with blocks, clay, Legos, and other materials. While these early developing capabilities appear universally, they may be advanced in those infants and young children who appear to have promise in a particular domain (musical, spatial, bodily-kinesthetic or inter- and intrapersonal intelligence). Advanced ability will be shown in particular ways, such as exceptional skill in exploring sounds and movements, or using imagination during sociodramatic play.

By their fifth year of life, children's actions usually include generating a song, painting a picture, creating a dance, and dramatizing through play. Within a relatively short period, their art, songs, dances, and play show a development of themes, and children begin to take an interest in using notational systems, such a writing down basic symbols to help them remember versions of their music or dance. Increasingly, development becomes dependent upon the use of symbols in a variety of domains. Hence, when children are older, they demonstrate their abilities in the various intelligences through their grasp of symbols, their accompanying notational components, and ways to represent ideas and concepts through these systems. In most Western cultures, notational systems are typically mastered in elementary educational settings, although some children independently acquire the ability to use symbol systems, such as learning to read written words or music, prior to elementary school.

This chapter will focus on specific ways in which children of various ages typically develop in and through the arts. However, it should be noted that any content that focuses on developmental principles must acknowledge the difficulty of attempting to describe *typicality*. From the outset, I would like to state that I do not believe it is possible to describe universal stages and ages of artistic development and then to prescribe developmentally appropriate practice accordingly. There are far too many variations of typicality to make generalizations about children's development or to make recommendations for an arts education for all children from all cultural backgrounds. However, there are some general developmental characteristics that seem to be broadly applicable, and an awareness of these can provide a helpful framework for early childhood arts education.

In particular, there are a number of general artistic processes that appear to be almost universal and seem to apply to all developmental levels, from infants and toddlers to old age. These were described in Chapter 3 (Figure 3.5) and discussed in relation to various entry points for learning, which are influenced by children's personalities, learning styles, and preferences for certain symbolic domains or arts activities (Figure 3.9). Hence, from the perspective of general artistic processes and individual differences, children's development should be viewed in relation to their learning styles and experience. We can observe, for example, many occasions in which children return to previously learned artistic processes, knowledge, and skills when they encounter new challenges. For instance, when presented with an electronic keyboard for the first time, children (and people of all ages for that matter) generally are interested in exploring the various sound options provided by the instrument. In the process, they might engage in trial-and-error behavior, such as repeating the same musical pattern with each newly explored sound. Such repetitive behavior is not an indication of immaturity or regression, but more a reflection of the need to explore the unfamiliar and discover options (cognitive, affective, technical) before applying higher levels of knowledge and skills. In other words, artistic behavior does not seem to evolve in set stages without variation but instead is influenced by previous experience, opportunities, and exposure. Examples of such characteristics are discussed in relation to each of the arts disciplines in Chapters 8 to 11. In addition, recommendations for providing adequate experience and time for children to experiment and develop the necessary knowledge and skills to work successfully in each of the arts disciplines is discussed in Chapter 13 in relation to curriculum.

Consequently, this chapter begins with a more general focus on children's learning in and through the arts and the importance of learning objects and scripts in the artistic expression of thoughts and feelings. It should be noted that many of the photographs provided in this section are related to art, largely because it is easier in a book format to illustrate children's ideas through visual examples. Although photography can capture children's dances, songs, movement, and gesture, it is more difficult to grasp the context of these art forms through still, soundless images. Nonetheless, discussion of the characteristics of children's artistic development in spatial, aural, and bodily-kinesthetic domains will attempt to provide a "picture" of children's artistic participation.

This chapter is intended to provide a general overview of artistic development, by illustrating broad, developmental milestones, from very early childhood to the early elementary school period. It illustrates how development is domain specific and how even young children may show a specific ability in one or more domains, but probably not in all domains. More specific details of development are found in Chapters 8 through 11, which focus on each of these disciplines, with specific guidelines for how to nurture young children's development in each of these domains.

OBJECTS AND EVENTS

Two important thinking skills seem to influence the way in which children represent and communicate meaning in their day-to-day interactions, and through the use of symbols and symbols systems: (1) They learn to mentally cluster objects that are similar, and (2) they recognize familiar events or sequences that occur on a regular basis. Categorizing objects and events helps children understand themselves in relation to their world. It should be noted, however, that not all artistic processes and products involve the use of objects and events, as in the case where children are representing their thoughts and feelings abstractly (e.g., using color and texture in painting purely for aesthetic purposes, rather than to tell a story or depict something specifically). As was discussed in the previous chapter in relation to expressive and metaphoric aspects, all art is not literal. Similarly, dance, music, and dramatic play frequently embrace the expressive and metaphoric components of depicting, and some children can be more inclined toward the expressive than the literal. (See Chapter 3 in relation to individual learning styles and entry points.) Nonetheless, a discussion of objects and events is a valuable framework for understanding young children's thinking, representing, and artistic communication in a general sense. It is related to how the brain or mind searches for and uses structure to help organize thoughts and feelings in relation to experience (an aspect that is discussed in greater detail in Chapter 12, on integration).

Because understanding of the self and the world is soundly rooted in artistic expression, the next two segments focus on children's general use of objects and scripts through artistic processes and products. This content should be coupled with the understanding that individual learning styles and literal/metaphoric forms of expression can create exceptions to these general principles.

Categorizing Objects

When children categorize objects—just as adults do—they base their categories on a representational example. In other words, they think of good versions of something, create a *prototype* or model, and then see if other objects are like or unlike that version. For example, children recognize a dog as a four-legged hairy pet with a tail (of some description) and with ears that are located on top of the head. When they encounter other dogs that are not exactly like their original mental image, they must decide whether the features are sufficiently similar to place it in the category "dog" or into a different category, say "horse." Sometimes it is difficult to place an object into an existing category, and this leads to the development of other categories. For example, Australian marsupials, such as kangaroos and wombats, are mammals. But instead of giving birth to a baby connected to a placenta, the fetuses of these animals must crawl into the pouch of the female when they are only about an inch long. The Australian platypus is a strange case of a small aquatic mammal that lays eggs, has a fleshy bill resembling that of a duck, webbed feet, and a broad, flattened tail. In unusual cases such as these, children learn to classify information about animals in relation to already learned categories.

We can see many examples of children applying their understanding of categories in a range of areas, not just with animals. But for the sake of example, let's stay in domain of animals for the moment. When a child learns a new category, he or she will create delightful errors, such as mistaking a horse for a cow. Often this misunderstanding will be expressed through sound and gesture associated with the image of the animal. "Moo," the child might say, and this will be accompanied with a pointing finger directed at the animal, indicating that the horse will sound the same way as a cow, an animal that was previously classified in the child's mind. In time the child will learn that there are larger (i.e., superordinate) categories that can contain cows and horses, dogs and cats, in fact anything that is called animal. There are also smaller, subordinate categories that he or she will learn that refine the categories of cow even further, such as gender (bull), age (calf), or type (Jersey).

Even during infancy, children categorize, although they often use senses other than sight, such as recognizing Mommy by her perfume or knowing Daddy is home from the sound of his footsteps. Similarly, three-year-olds draw pictures that demonstrate their use of prototypes in a graphic way—they illustrate the typical features of an image. The commonly drawn circle-and-stick-legs human (see Figure 6.1) is a prototype that is thought to be from a midlevel category (e.g., a lady or a boy) rather than from a superordinate category (e.g., a human) or a subordinate category (e.g., mommy).

This use of midlevel categories is applicable to a range of images, such as a house, a tree, a dog, and numerous other concepts. Such objects, depicted in drawings, paintings, clay, or construction, generally do not stand for, say, Grandma's house or the tree in the child's backyard, but houses and trees generally. This is because the child is representing events in a symbolic and

FIGURE 6.1   Prototype of a Human Form

often quite universal way. If asked a specific question, the child might oblige with a statement such as, "Yes, this is my mommy and my house," but this description could easily change five minutes later, depending upon how the drawing is developing—the house might evolve into a greenhouse, and the person might become a gardener. Consequently, there should be opportunities to discuss the child's artwork in an open-ended way, rather than through direct questions.

The graphic prototypes that a child uses—in other words, the "model" examples of house, tree, or other things—often look very similar in the beginning stages of development. Figure 6.1 illustrates the prototypes of a lady or man (or "person") that one three-year-old child, Tommy, used in his drawings. On the basis of several drawings of Tommy's, his prototype of a person usually has a straight vertical stroke for a nose, a belly button, and squiggles for hair, regardless of the subject of the drawing. In contrast, Mary generally draws her people with straight hair framing the sides of the face, a triangular body (like a skirt) with legs that come off the points of the triangle, and rounded hands with several fingers. Mary's prototype of a person is repeated for each example in one drawing, such as, "This is me, my mommy, my daddy, and my brother in the garden"—each person has the same prototypic triangular body and straight hair (Figure 6.2).

Over time, Tommy's and Mary's prototypes began to show more variation in size, gender, and shape and included more details (eyelashes, teeth, dimples, hair styles, or various details for clothing). By around age five, Mary discovered that the people in her drawings could not possibly stand with legs so far apart and still have them be attached to the hips. Even if someone might have told her that her drawing was unrealistic at the time when she was drawing these people, she would have preferred her standard prototype until she was ready to change. When Mary eventually discovered her repeated "error," she shunned many of her earlier drawings as immature and stupid.

Again, over time, the houses or trees that had once suited a number of different drawings of Tommy also began to contain more details and variation. Rather than continuing with his prototype of a house, which was a rectangle for the main part of the building and a triangle for the roof, at around age five, Tommy started to draw homes built on stumps (long wooden poles), with fencelike wooden boards between the stumps, as found in many of the Australian houses in Queensland, where he lived (Figure 6.3). Mary also began to spend time and care representing special events like "A Day at the Beach" and took a particular interest in including dogs and cats in her drawings (see Figure 6.4).

At first, Mary's drawings of animals included several legs, just as the hands on her drawings of people had included several fingers and toes. Eventually, her dogs and cats had four legs and the hands and feet of people had five fingers and toes. At around the age of four years, children seem to

FIGURE 6.2   A Standard Prototype for Both Genders and Many Ages

take an interest in capturing number and numerical relations, not only in their drawings but also in music, play, and story telling. This tendency, which Gardner and Wolf (1982) called digital mapping, can be found in all arts areas. In music, for example, children become more sensitive to the number of tones in a melody and can sing them more accurately. However, because of their limited vocal range (i.e., the span of high and low pitches) and their inconsistent ability to match pitch with others (i.e., sing the same note as those who are also singing), young children's early versions of the ABC (alphabet) song and other learned songs often only approximate the tune. As their singing range and vocal control develop, they are able to come closer to the recognized melody. Similarly, in their play they get a general or specific impression of which pirate has the most jewels or which string of blocks reaches furthest. In dance they are able to re-create a number of steps and put these into sequences. In their storytelling and dramatic play, they establish and maintain a number of characters and develop these characters and their roles in relation to particular events.

FIGURE 6.3   A Modified Prototype of a House

FIGURE 6.4   Animal Prototype

Categorizing Events

This form of categorizing is related to familiar sequences of events and is sometimes called the use of scripts (see Gardner, 1991). Scripts involve identifying and ordering aspects that children (and adults) come to associate with events that occur regularly. For example, children learn to recognize the event, or script, of going to the movies as involving:

- Entering a building that is recognizable from the outside because of, for example, its billboard displaying the various movies' titles, actors, and scenes
- Buying a ticket (and possibly popcorn or other things to eat and drink)
- Sitting in a tiered theater facing a large screen
- Anticipating the lowering of the lights when the feature begins
- Knowing the film has ended when the credits begin to roll

Like category labels, scripts help children compare familiar sequences of events with those that are newly encountered. To use a Piagetian term, children learn to "assimilate" going to a movie as being different from going to the art gallery, based on information such as the appearance of the building, whether you can or cannot eat food there, whether you stand quietly, walk around, or sit, and how you know when it is time to go home.

We commonly see children role playing the scripts of life through sociodramatic or pretend play. At times it can be surprising just how set young children's scripts of life can be. In *Frogs and Snails and Feminist Tales* (1988), Bronwyn Davies described how some preschool children's scripts associated with male-female roles were so strong that, after having been read feminist fairy tales, their play behavior and values showed they could not accept reversals of traditional roles, such as a female hero or a boy who preferred to dance rather than play football. While Davies's research was conducted quite some time ago, where there were fewer examples of girl heroes and boy dancers in children's books, movies, and other media, it illustrates the importance of children's having exposure to a range of examples and experiences so that their scripts of life are less stereotypic and more versatile.

Throughout our lives, scripts continue to help us assimilate new experiences into new sets of scripts (e.g., the script of attending preschool, then school and possibly college, then employment, then old age). Scripts also play an important part in our emotional and interpersonal lives. Sometimes, as in senility, the rehearsal of familiar scripts continues out of context. My eighty-eight-year-old mother-in-law, who suffered from Alzheimer's disease, daily insisted that she was visiting briefly for the Christmas holidays even though she had lived with me for five years, it was July, and there were no signs of a Christmas tree, presents, or decorations.

Scripts, like category labels, can be found in all areas of young children's artistic development. An infant who has learned the script of a song while being bounced on an adult's knee, such as "This is the way the ladies ride," will show through facial expression and body language that she knows the very point in the rhyme when Grandpa is about to "drop" her off his knee. Furthermore, preschool children experiment with behaviors that they have observed in real life or the media, such as being Batman or a shop attendant, and they can imagine and play as if they are flying or counting out imaginary money.

The way children represent events of life, however, may not necessarily focus on the temporal sequence of the actions or events as they might, say, in telling or writing a story about an experience. In telling a story about an event, children generally will refer to what was done, what is to be done, what might happen in such-and-such a case (Kress, 2000a). A typical example of a young child's story might be:

> On Sunday I went to my grandma's house. She gave us apple pie and then we went for a walk in the park. She showed me how to make a kind of whistle by blowing on a leaf. We fed some ducks and then we went home.

The syntax of speech derives from the logic of sequence and of its potentials. Earlier and later events are described in a temporal sequence through grammatical meanings such as the *subject* of an action (my grandma), followed by the resultant *action* (and then she gave us pie), followed by the *participant* affected by the action (and then we went home), and so on (Kress, 2000a). Yet when children represent events through drawing, these events often are not depicted in such a clear sequence or the sequence may flit from one event to another and then back to an earlier event (Wright, 2001b). The child's representation often transforms and condenses these experiences into a number of salient events, where people, objects, and actions are depicted simultaneously (see Figure 6.5).

Figure 6.5 illustrates an eight-year-old boy's concept of a solar-energized truck that cruises the highways providing opportunities for tired drivers to enter the back and then hook up to a roof hanger and have a *snoozzze* for a while. Marc provided many details about the interactive nature of each of the various energy lines and made sound effects and gestured as he showed these relationships. There was an involved story behind the collision between a helicopter and a plane during a Sky Patrol hookup and the important role of the underground surveillance cameras in monitoring each of these and other details. Marc depicted and described all of these concepts in interactive ways, and often one event affected another. Because the artist wanted to show the total event and the relevant content within it, he presented the full image as if it were a still photograph. However, "behind the scenes" he gestures to show explosions, makes action sounds with his voice, and flits from one event to another as the story unfolds. When children depict such action-based events, often one component of their artwork will be depicted followed by another, and then they may return again to the original component to add more details or to make qualifying statements. This, in turn, may affect

**FIGURE 6.5   Multisequential Events Unfolding within
a Multimodal Drawing Experience**

the development of another image, and an interactive interplay between several images in relation to the events being depicted continues throughout the full drawing experience (Wright, 2001b).

As illustrated in the above segment, objects and events provide important frameworks for children's artistic expression of thoughts and feelings. Objects and events offer a foundation upon which children may develop other artistic abilities, particularly meaning-making, the symbolizing of ideas, and the crafting of communication skills in increasingly sophisticated ways. These developmental characteristics of children are described in the next section.

CHARACTERISTICS OF YOUNG CHILDREN'S DEVELOPMENT

As mentioned earlier in this chapter, attempting to describe the typicality of young children's expression in the arts is a difficult and, perhaps in the opinion of some, an inappropriate topic to address, because there are so many variations in the capabilities of young children of a similar age, due to their individual learning styles, previous experiences and culture backgrounds. Nonetheless, having a general overview of characteristic development can be helpful as a guideline to assist teachers who may be just beginning their careers or who may not have had much experience in early childhood settings. In other words, the following breakdown of artistic development across the toddler, three-to-five-, and five-to-eight year age ranges should be seen only as a generic overview based on observational studies of children in Western, middle-class early childhood contexts. Such a description cannot necessarily be generalized to all racial, social, and economic groups within a diverse culture.

It should also be noted that the remainder of this chapter begins with older toddlers (eighteen months to three years), largely because the ability to walk and to use language are key components of dance and dramatic play. However, babies and fetuses are discussed in the context of other chapters (e.g., the chapters on literacy and music include sections that focus on prelanguage knowledge).

Toddlers: Meaning-Making

Between approximately eighteen months and three years of age, nearly everything assumes meaning to the child. Wolf and Gardner (1980) referred to this as a stage of meaning-making, because much of the learning that takes place consists of constructing meaning through interaction with others, and through the exploration of objects and events. The dominant activity of the very young child involves emotional contact, the manipulation of objects, the development of basic forms of communication, and a simple knowledge of the world. Gradually the child's "egocentric" view is replaced by an increased ability to distinguish between self, others, and objects. Their *actions* become the basis for beginning forms of aesthetic judging and performing, and their artistic *products* reflect direct, physical communication; generally these products are spirited, original, and aesthetically appealing.

Toddlers can relate personal experiences to others, such as telling Grandma about learning how to float a "leaf boat" in the puddle in the backyard. As language becomes more fluent and articulate, young children will enthusiastically include gesture as they speak. Listening to stories becomes an enjoyable pastime for toddlers, they enjoy humming simple melodies, and the expressiveness of dance is explored with delight. In drawing, young children will attempt to depict a person or an object, but many of the salient features may not be recognizable to an adult. In music, they will have a notion of whether a song gets louder or softer, faster or slower, or higher or lower, but may not always capture the exact pitch or dynamic features. When building with blocks, they may be aware of the general size and volume ratios of the blocks, but not be concerned about precise quantities.

This is a period of symbolic play, where objects are treated representationally. A clump of mud may be used as a cookie, a block of wood as a horse, or a pillow as a doll. The symbolic play of toddlers, like their language, often is related to specific events and includes statements such as "go swimming," or "want ice cream." They will use dramatic props such as bottles, blankets, and tea sets to play with their teddy bears or with others. For many, favorite events and situations often are replayed over and over again, such as suppertime, building a road in the sand, or bathing a baby. In addition, their use of language to structure events can be activated by other intellectual domains, such as spatial, musical, or bodily-kinesthetic forms of expression. For example, a child involved in block play may be reminded of a gas station by the shape of the structure. Soon, toys nearby might be incorporated into imaginary play built around a gas station, and the child's body and voice will represent the movements and sounds of cars and trucks, and include song or sound effects, accompanied with action.

Compared to symbolic play, in the visual realm of learning, young children's drawings often are not so obviously representational. They are developing a vocabulary of lines and shapes, and discrete forms or enclosures, such as, squares, circles, and crosses (Kellogg, 1969; Matthews, 1994a, b, 1997). By the end of their third year, various "aggregations"—combined forms—often appear, like sun shapes, or circles divided into quarters or eighths, like a pie, which is called a mandala. Eventually these symbols will relate to real things with which children are already familiar, as in Figure 6.3, in which Tommy used mandalas in the windows of his house. In the meantime, nonrepresentational visual forms will be driven more by young children's desires to work out *graphic language* than to depict an object or event.

Naming of drawings, termed proto-symbolism, is often prompted by the appearance of the finished product. In other words, a child might draw something that looks like something he or she might recognize, such as a window, and the child might then announce "look, window." Names for two- and three-dimensional art works often reflect the child's interpretations of properties in the material. For example, the color and texture of paint might suggest to a child smoke, rain, or fire, whereas clay might suggest food or animal figures; blocks might represent dishes or tools and, later, buildings.

Toddlers use art materials in a way that often combines creating marks on paper with creating sound and making gestures. They derive pleasure from making marks that seem to represent paths on a page, like footprints (Matthews, 1997; Winner, 1986). Many parents and teachers have watched a toddler use a crayon to draw a squiggly line on a piece of paper while making "vrooom vrooom" sounds. Through such experiences, the *pathway* of the car itself and the mark it makes on the paper becomes the symbol, similar to the way in which the child would move a toy car across the floor during a play experience. However, the final, visual result or mark on the paper—which the child might even call "car"—looks simply like a squiggly line on a piece of paper. To the adult who has not seen the toddler drawing and creating sound effects, the name or title will make little sense. We must recognize that, in this case, the *movement* of the crayon is the meaningful experience for the toddler.

Similarly, young children begin to learn how to "read" pictures in books, on the walls of the child-care center, at the supermarket, and in basic symbolic letters or icons (e.g., the golden arches of McDonalds). When listening to an adult reading a story, young children often become engrossed with the pictures, point to them, and name them as enthusiastically as if they were real objects. For example, a child might point to a picture of a bottle, hold an imaginary bottle near the mouth, and pretend to suck. Musically, young children seem to focus predominantly on the quality and impressiveness of the sound of an instrument. Their musical creations are unpredictable sound explorations, and the elements of music, such as a steady underlying pulse, melodic structure (e.g., a tune), or rhythmic pattern—are not easy to recognize. Nonetheless, while their musical productions may appear random, often their musical explorations are purposeful, focused, and aesthetic. In similar ways, there dances and dramatic play often involve repetition of movement and exploration of thoughts and feelings that may be on a different plane from that of the adult's mind, but often involve a great deal of purpose and pleasure.

Three- to Five-Year-Olds: Playful Symbol Use

Between the ages of about three to five years of age, children learn to use symbols through play and fantasy. During this period—which Gardner (1991) called the symbolic period—children learn to understand and use language to ask for things, to tell others what they want, and to request information. They also use language for more expressive purposes, such as telling jokes, teasing, making up or retelling stories, role-playing, or developing friendships. In addition to words, children communicate in a number of other ways:

- *Graphically,* for example, through drawing or painting (such as the tadpole humans, houses, and trees described earlier), through using other two-dimensional media (e.g., collages, printmaking), or through working with three-dimensional art forms (such as sculpting with clay, constructing with boxes, or building with blocks)
- *Dramatically,* for example, through role play (taking on a role, such as pouring imaginary tea and eating imaginary biscuits while talking on the phone); body expression and gesture (movements of the hands, arms, shoulders, or full body that express or emphasize an idea or attitude); facial expressions (such as a grimace or frown); language (such as developing play characters and "scripts" of events); and the use of open-ended resources (such as placing a towel on the head to represent long hair, or wearing hat, caps, and other dressup props)
- *Musically,* for example, through composing or improvising (e.g., creating "soundscapes") using vocal effects and the timbre of musical instru-

ments and uncoventional sound sources (e.g., shrill, fluid, hollow) and the expressive properties of singing and playing styles (e.g., flowing, calm, jerky, or energetic)

- *Through movement and dance,* for example, depicting a character, object, or scene from their imaginations or stimulated by another source, such as a story or book (e.g. "The Monster Romp" from *Where the Wild Things Are),* moving expressively to music, working out a set of movements for a dance, or using their bodies to represent an idea or feeling

Ability in visual media has now caught up to preschool/kindergarten children's capacity to tell a story, sing a song, create a dance, role play, and "read" a picture. They can use lines, space, shape, and color to construct a variety of visual concepts and create complex designs, and they understand that lines can stand for the edges of objects. They can draw, sculpt, and model recognizable forms and label their products accordingly. While drawing, painting, building with blocks or cardboard boxes, shaping clay, or creating collages, young children use visual images to symbolize objects and events. They imagine, fantasize, and act out thoughts and feelings while fashioning their worlds in the plastic domain. Gardner (1980), Golomb (1992), Goodnow (1977), Kellogg (1969), Matthews (1994a, b, 1997), Smith (1993), and Wright (2001b) provide a comprehensive description of the presymbolic and symbolic drawings that young children produce when becoming users of visual symbols. By the end of the third year, their prototypes of houses, animals, and people are now recognizable to adults. In addition, the "aggregates" (combinations of shapes) that were rehearsed when they were toddlers, such as the mandala, may be used for windows of a house or the eyes of a person.

The ability to represent objects and events visually releases a universe of graphic possibilities. However, for a number of years, children's visual depictions generally will remain schematic; in other words, children will incorporate the generic prototypical forms learned earlier and apply them to a range of instances. This is economical because these forms can represent members of a number of categories (e.g., the schema of a face can be incorporated into the "face" of a flower, the sun in the sky, or the head of an animal). With drawing experience and opportunities to view examples in the real or pictorial worlds, children begin to make discriminations within their schemata, such as in Figure 6.6 on page 118.

In musical composition, children in their preschool years are involved in personal modes of expression. Their increasing ability to make sound and develop technical skills using their voices and musical instruments allows them to explore and repeat long passages of music (e.g., steady pulse notes, scales, trills, and tremolos). These repeated musical passages are also forms of prototypes—they become their favorite or best examples of how to use sound for expressive and communicative purposes. For example, a child's use of the pitches in the first phrase of "Three Blind Mice" may be applied to

FIGURE 6.6   Differentiated Prototypes in One Drawing

a range of musical explorations, played at various speeds and volumes, for a range of expressive purposes and applications (e.g., slow and suspenseful, increasing in speed and volume as the emotion builds). Such sound explorations can also be inspired by or stimulate an encounter with other children who are dancing nearby and lead to music and dance play, where both aural and bodily-kinesthetic dimensions become integrated through group interaction. One child, for instance, who may be practicing a movement prototype of whirling in a circle, may ask another child to play "whirling" music, and a delightful music-dance "conversation" may develop.

Three- to five-year-old children do not always require realistic dramatic props to stimulate imaginative play. They often pretend that something is other than it actually is. For example, a length of white satin can be wrapped around the body to serve as a shawl, draped across a table to serve as a tablecloth, or spread across the floor to represent a stream. Similarly, a block of wood might represent a portable telephone or a miniature car, and a table might stand for a desk, a display counter for fruit, a garage, or a cage for an animal in a zoo.

The table, when used as a cage in a zoo, might unleash other symbolic forms of expression. For example, using their voices, musical instruments, and dance/movement, children might create sound stories that aurally depict a sequence of real or imaginary events, such as "going to the zoo." They might symbolize such an event through vocal effects, body movements, and gesture, becoming characters such as a tiger or other animals at the zoo. Often they use instruments for dramatic effect, like crashing cymbals and rumbling on a drum when a surprising moment occurs, like the unexpected roar of the *ferocious* tiger. Leading up to this surprise, they will build the suspense by crouching and creeping slowly and then suddenly stretch up on their toes with their arms raised above their heads and fingers rigid, as they prepare to pounce. Often they will repeat this episode several times, perfecting the effect and possibly modifying it to link with other components of the "going to the zoo" enactment, such as a "prowling growling tiger's dance."

Practice in both producing and perceiving symbols provides young children with the awareness that *meaning* and *revealing* may be derived from form. In other words, what children produce in the arts can help them make meaning about their thoughts, feelings, and problem-solving solutions that can be revealed to others. The young artists' products reflect self-expression, and often group expression, through the use of symbols—expressed visually, aurally, and bodily-kinesthetically—through thought, emotion, and action. As with toddlers, preschool children's artistic products are original, expressive, and aesthetically appealing.

Six- to Eight-Year-Olds: Crafting

From approximately age six to about eight years, children become focused on being efficient *senders* of messages, using the symbol systems of art, music, dance, and drama. Products become as important to children as the process, and they want their artistic expression to be competent, comprehensive, and to "speak" even to strangers. Because of this desire for artistic competence, Wolf and Gardner (1980) referred to this period as the craftsperson stage. "Craftspersons" have a desire to adopt methods by which their messages and meanings can as clear as possible. Such messages/meanings usually hold fast to culturally determined forms of expression. Within one culture, for example, the diversity of forms can range from a child illustrating the traditional Hungarian costume she might wear at a folk festival to depicting a space-age craft inspired by a modern film.

Children's desire to produce competent, comprehensible products inspires an interest in mastering skills. However, depending upon their experiences with each of the arts domains, such as taking dance or drama classes outside school hours, learning the piano, or attending art studio lessons, children's abilities can range from childlike schematic symbolization (e.g., a prototypical house and tree drawn from memory) to highly competent works (e.g., a still life of a plant drawn from observation). Children often seek aid to improve their skills, benefit from direction and educational guidance, and can make significant artistic progress in a relatively short period (as in the example in Chapter 2 of children drawing self-portraits through observation).

However, if children have few or no opportunities to receive artistic guidance through the support of teachers and arts mentors, their artistic products can become predictable and conventional or centered on being as "realistic" as possible, with less regard for the expressive components of art making. Figures 6.7 and 6.8 illustrate the difference in visual art works between two six-year-old children from diverse artistic backgrounds. The child who drew the still life from observation (Figure 6.7) had weekly art lessons with an art specialist, whereas the imagination-based artwork (Figure 6.8) was created by a child with minimal opportunities for artistic guidance.

With increased understanding of the adult world, school-aged children begin to adopt the attitudes and values of "grown-ups" in many areas, including the arts, but they also develop their own values and tastes. School children influence one another's tastes about which CDs should be coveted, which actor or rock star is the best, whether it is cool for boys to dance, and what types of clothes suit the image they want to present. Effectiveness

FIGURE 6.7   Six-Year-Old Child's Drawing from Observation

FIGURE 6.8   Six-Year-Old Child's Drawing from Imagination

within the group can become more important than personal belief systems and, consequently, fantasy often becomes internalized if there are not opportunities for externalized, symbolic forms of expression. In other words, the dramatic play and spoken narratives of their previous stage of development may be replaced with contemplative thought and daydreaming if opportunities are not provided for imaginative and expressive outlets, through music, dance, drama, and art.

Peer pressure and concern about being shunned from the group can cause children's personal efforts to become less accessible to their audience. However, with sensitive guidance from teachers, exposure to the world of the arts and the creators and performers within it, and processes where children can feel competent through making, presenting, and responding to the arts, they can feel comfortable about the expressive aspects of their personal artistry. A general goal is to lead children to proficiency, but to ensure that their craftsperson behavior becomes a *vehicle* for expression rather than an *end in itself.* In other words, we can help children find a balance between technical skill and personal expression in the arts by demonstrating that both components are important and that finding an aesthetic balance between technique and expression is what makes good works of art, music, drama, and dance.

As discussed in Chapters 2 and 5, the intelligences generally work together in development, and one domain often complements and enhances another—the visual, aural, bodily-kinesthetic, and personal domains often interface. Consequently, educational processes should help children reach personal goals that are appropriate to their particular spectrum of intelligences, learning styles, and preferred domains of learning, so that they feel engaged and competent and inclined to participate in school, and in life in general, in positive and constructive ways. The final segment discusses how domain-specific intelligence has implications for early childhood arts education in relation to young children's development.

DOMAIN-SPECIFIC INTELLIGENCE IN RELATION TO DEVELOPMENT

In optimal situations, people tend to gravitate toward work and leisure experiences that use symbolic domains in which they feel comfortable and competent—they maximize their intelligences, if possible, in what they choose to do. Throughout life, an individual's intelligences often are expressed through leisure pursuits; a young child who enjoys bodily-kinesthetic experiences, such as dancing and climbing, might find a similar outlet later in life, such as through cycling or skiing and through employment in which he or she can be physically active. Similarly, children with high levels of interest in spatial domains, such as drawing or constructing, may, as adults, prefer leisure activities such as playing chess or pursuing landscape gardening and might select an occupation in which spatial domains are featured, such as architecture, topology, or theatrical set designing (Gardner, 1983, 1993a, c).

The symbol systems that are inherent in the different domains of intelligence, and the ways in which individuals develop within these domains, can vary greatly. In exceptional cases, such as Picasso or Einstein, evidence of their special intelligences was clear even at an early age. Gardner (1993b) illustrated exceptionally through case studies of seven individuals working within each of the domains of intelligence: Einstein (logical-spatial), Eliot (linguistic), Freud (linguistic/personal), Gandhi (personal/linguistic), Graham (bodily/linguistic), Picasso (spatial/personal/bodily), and Stravinsky (musical/other artistic). While these individuals possessed the full range of intelligences and drew on these in their work, their exceptional development stemmed from their use of the symbol systems and operations associated with a particular intelligence, operating in a particular discipline or domain.

Gardner described these individuals as differing from one another, not only in terms of their different *dominant* intelligences, but also in terms of their *breadth* and *combination* of intelligences. Although Albert Einstein, for example, might have made Freud's discoveries, or Freud might have elaborated a theory of relativity, this is unlikely, because Einstein and Freud had different minds that operated with different kinds of symbol systems. Einstein, for example, thought in complex spatial schemes, bodily imagery, and mathematical formulas, with words entering as afterthoughts. His thinking was rich with visual-spatial images within a confined logical-mathematical structure, and he had limited interest in the personal sphere—the sphere in which Freud operated (Gardner, 1993a).

Brief descriptions of Pablo Picasso, Igor Stravinsky, and Martha Graham may be helpful to illustrate the potential endpoint of artistic development within the three key areas of intelligence discussed in this book—spatial-visual, musical, and bodily-kinesthetic. Although few children will reach the level of attainment achieved by these exceptional individuals, illustrations of how these individuals worked within these three domains may clarify issues of artistry in relation to the general development of young children.

Picasso dealt with colors, textures, lines, and forms as they related to objects in the world, and he demonstrated excellent manual dexterity. He had outstanding perceptual skill with visual details and arrangements and in thinking in spatial configurations. But Picasso was also gifted across visual-spatial, bodily-kinesthetic, and interpersonal areas, which he used systematically to advance his artistic career. The Russian composer Stravinsky, in contrast, worked in the world of sound (rhythm, pitch, tone color, and musical structure). He treated these elements analogously, through intramusical associations and relations with other aspects of the world of experience. Finally, Martha Graham worked chiefly with the materials of the human body through dance. She attempted to capture plot, emotion, and formal relations through gestures and by integrating these components with the accompanying music and decor (Gardner, 1993a).

Similarly, young children may show early signs of specific interest and developmental capabilities within one or more of the domains. We can assist all children to utilize their individual proclivities and special talents by opening up opportunities for them to work *within* and *across* domains. Through socially constructed learning, children will be enabled to increase their prospects to develop in all areas, experience numerous ways of learning and knowing, and apply general artistic processes in relation to their own specific learning styles. Aiming for the enhancement of all children's development within multiple areas of intelligence should be a primary goal of education. Education must acknowledge and honor the special and important role of the arts in the development of young children and place the arts in a core position within the curriculum. Then there probably would be fewer templates of red apples displayed in the windows of schools and more children enjoying learning how to learn with the support of adult mentors.

SUMMARY

Specific development in the arts occurs within the visual, aural, and bodily-kinesthetic domains and in related areas such as linguistics and interpersonal and intrapersonal domains. Understanding children's artistic development requires an awareness of how young children participate in artistic activity and, in the process, develop self-expression, communication, symbol use, and critical thinking/feeling skills. Two important thinking/feeling skills—categorizing objects and events—influence the way in which children learn to establish meaning in their day-to-day interactions and use symbols to create and refine this meaning. Children learn to categorize objects and to make graphic, musical, and movement *prototypes*. With time, children's prototypes become more varied and elaborate and can be applied in multiple ways in numerous contexts; this develops in tandem with their knowledge of the world and domains of expression. Children also learn to categorize events, and *scripts*, by identifying and ordering familiar sequences that occur regularly (these are commonly enacted through musical, graphic, and movement play). Scripts help children assimilate familiar sequences of events with newly encountered experiences.

Between approximately eighteen months and three years of age, toddlers and young children are involved in emotional contact, the manipulation of objects, the development of meaning, and beginning forms of aesthetic judgment. By around three to five years of age, children become playful symbol users. From approximately age six to about eight years, children have a desire to be competent artists and senders of clear messages. Educational processes should help children reach goals in all spectrums of intelligence, so that children feel engaged and competent and are stimulated to learn using all domains of knowing. Individual children may show early signs of a preference for particular symbol systems and operations and may excel in particular domains, such as spatial, bodily-kinesthetic, or aural. We can assist all children to utilize their individual interests and ways of knowing, while opening up opportunities for them to work both within their preferred domains and across a range of domains.

ADDITIONAL READINGS

Fowler, C. (1996). *Strong arts, strong schools: The promising potential and shortsighted disregard for the arts in American schooling.* New York: Oxford University Press.

Gardner, H. (1999). *The disciplined mind: What all students should understand.* New York: Simon & Schuster.

Golomb, C. (1992). *The child's creation of a pictorial world.* Los Angeles: University of California Press.

Kindler, A. M. (1996, March–April). Myths, habits, research and policy: The four pillars of early childhood art education. *Arts Education Policy Review, 97*(4).

Matthews, J. (1999). *The art of childhood and adolescence. The construction of meaning.* London: Falmer Press.

Seefeldt, C. (1995). Art: A serious work. *Young Children, 50*(3), 39–45.

Spodek, B. (1993). Selecting activities in the arts for early childhood education. *Arts Education Policy Review, 94* (6), 11–17.

Wright, S. (1991). *The arts in early childhood.* Sydney: Prentice Hall.

PRACTICAL ACTIVITIES

1. Observe children between three to five years of age during play, particularly if this includes one of the arts disciplines. How do young children use symbols and materials to:
   - Communicate nonverbally
   - Depict meaning
   - Represent reality
   - Use fantasy
   - Categorize objects
   - Categorize events

2. Identify some scripts that you have seen children use in one or more of the artistic domains.
   - Analyze the ways in which the children enact these scripts.
   - Discuss your analyses with friends and colleagues to discover similarities and differences in script use in children of different ages and in various environmental settings.
   - In what ways do you think playing out scripts of life helps children assimilate familiar sequences of events with newly encountered experiences?

3. Review the content in this chapter that describes the development characteristics of toddler, three- to five-year-olds, and five- to eight-year-olds.
   - Discuss examples of children's development that you have observed that would illustrate these characteristics and the ways in which children of particular age groups participated in one or more or the artistic disciplines.
   - Bring examples of children's artistic products or anecdotes of your observations of children to class to discuss with other students.

CHAPTER SEVEN

LITERACY IN THE ARTS

Most people are amazed at how some musicians are able to play music by ear. Some people can just "pick up" a song by listening to it and, within a relatively brief period, play it, capturing the melody, rhythm, harmony, and expression. They can create their own rendition of what they have heard and add their own personal interpretation to the song. As remarkable as this achievement may be, however, others who are classically trained in music often refer to people who play by ear as being musically illiterate because they are not able to read and write music.

Many self-taught musicians find their own way to perceive, interpret, and communicate music, and they often do this at an intuitive level, through processes of trial and error. Although they might jot down their own personal forms of notation to help remember patterns and complex musical sequences, they often acknowledge that they may not have the "proper" vocabulary to describe their systems of remembering musical information. They might describe a chord, for example, as a "sort of C chord, with B and a D at the top end of it." I've known some self-taught musicians who say that they can generally grasp the overall framework of the music by looking at a score, and they can see some advantages in being able to read music. But often they have almost a disdain for having to rely on music notation, believing that it inhibits the ability to improvise and to respond aesthetically. One friend used to refer to musical notation as "a bunch of fly [spots] on paper"—it had very little relevance to him or his music making.

Although a concert pianist and a rock musician may both be equally intelligent, talented, and successful, they often come from completely different musical perspectives and use very different processes to achieve their musicianship. To me, both are musically literate, just in different ways.

As discussed in Chapter 3, our cultural concept of what it means to be literate, or educated, can be narrowly equated with the ability to read and write words. Recently, however, people have been advocating for literacy learning that is more broadly defined. They refer to a new term, *multiliteracies*, and criticize our current theories of meaning-making and communication as being too heavily based on language. The new concept of multiliteracy acknowledges *multimodal* ways of thinking and working (Cope & Kalantzis, 2000; Kress, 2000a, b; Walker, 2000; Wright, 2001b). A multimodal framework for thinking about education and the processes of learning makes important inroads into dissolving many of the dichotomies that exist today; divisions of ideas that are seen to be contradictory, such as individual-society, subject-object, and mind-body. Yet, as described in Chapter 3, such divisions are unreal, and indeed there is increasing evidence that learning involves the *integration,* rather than segregation of parts. Consequently, a multiliteracy approach to education positions children as remakers, transformers, and reshapers of knowledge, and users of a range of representational resources and multiple modes of thinking, which include visual, aural, and bodily-kinesthetic.

A multimodal perspective of what it means to be "literate" acknowledges multiple ways of knowing—learning through thought, emotion, and action; thinking through imagery and the body; and using representational forms of communication. Young children combine these ways of knowing regularly, which is reflected in how they verbally describe their experiences. Kress (2000b, p. 155), for example, provided an example of a three-year-old using a physically based metaphor while attempting to clamber up a very steep, grassy slope. The young boy said, "This is a heavy hill," using a bodily-kinesthetic kind of system to express something like "It is really hard, really heavy work for me to climb this hill." Because the child didn't have the word "steep" as an available resource in his vocabulary, he used the term "heavy"—he chose the most apt form within his existing knowledge to represent and communicate his meaning, which, in his case, most easily matched his physical understanding. Children make similar multimodal associations when they describe a jet's streak across the sky by saying, "Look, the sky has a scar."

These types of expressions of children are part of the process of *synesthesia*—the transduction of meaning from one semiotic mode to another, such as seeing a jet stream in the sky and associating it with a scar on our body. For example, we often visualize a thought before the words come or hear a word that evokes many visual and audio senses. One mode of meaning slips over to describe meaning processes in another mode. So common is this experience that we often use metaphors to describe our meaning, such as when we talk about "imagery" in written text, or "perspective" and "points of view" in oral arguments (Johnson, 1991; Kress, 2000b). We represent physical reality through metaphor in thought and imagination (Dretske, 1994).

There is experimental evidence to show that music, for example, can be described in terms of weight, size, stiffness, outward or inward direction, and the degree of activity (Swanwick, 1999). Such descriptions were given at a statistically significant level by children as young as seven in response to simple musical phrases. Correlations were found between crude emotional labels, for instance, sadness, and the more subtle postural qualities of heaviness, passivity, and inward-lookingness. This is hardly surprising. We inevitably use postural metaphors to communicate the qualities of affective states. We all know what is meant when someone says that they were made to feel "small," or were "weighed down" with care, "stiff" with fright, "heavy" with apprehension, "light" as air, "depressed," and so on. The use of such expressions is not unique to the English language. Across cultures and across language barriers, we consistently use metaphors to describe sound qualities, such as dark, light, warm, lilting, or sprightly (Worth, 2000).

The expressive character of a musical passage is thus determined by our perception of its apparent weight, size, forward impulse, and manner of movement, all of which are components of posture and gesture. The metaphorical nature of such meanings may account for the power of music to stir and move people, even when there may be no words, no "program" (i.e., story), and no obvious associations with particular cultural values. Metaphorical richness accounts for much of the affective charge of not just music, but also poetry, drama, dance, literature, and in many cases, art. These forms of expression are free from literalness of representation; they are fluently *expressive* but not naturally *descriptive.*

Yet, "synesthetic" activity (i.e., metaphoric understanding and expression) has been suppressed in institutionalized education, largely due to the social and cultural dominance of literal language and written modes of expression (Kress, 2000b). Consequently, a multimodal, multiliteracy approach to education would open the doors to a range of expressions involving a variety of symbols and symbol systems, including gesture, graphic representation, play, music, mime, and dance. If we leave the artistic modes of learning outside the realm of meaning-making and communication, the arts become relegated to minor roles in the school curriculum. They are treated as specialist activities rather than significant modes for knowing and understanding.

As discussed throughout this book, the arts deal with objects and events that exist in modes other than language. They involve bodily kinesthetic, aural, visual, spatial, tactile, aesthetic, expressive, and imaginative forms of understanding. Just as in any area of learning, these forms of understanding require years of exposure to develop and understand and involve high levels of cognition and sophisticated forms of social, physical, and emotional involvement. Such involvement encompasses learning that develops a different type of literacy—artistic literacy—which is highly multimodal.

This chapter begins with a description of artistic literacy in relation to multiliteracy and describes processes for enhancing literacy through making, presenting, and responding to artworks—artistic products from all arts disciplines. It illustrates ways to understand how children use artistic elements within each of the arts domains, and how we can help them make multimodal connections across these domains, to become multiliterate.

MULTILITERACY

For decades, key authors of journal articles and textbooks on the arts (e.g., artistic development, arts education) have discussed multimodal processing and artistic forms of literacy (e.g., Abbs, 1987; Eisner, 1985; Gardner, 1973, 1980, 1982; Hausman, 1980). It is ironic that, only relatively recently, writers from the field of literacy (as traditionally defined as hearing sounds of speech and graphically representing sounds by letters on flat surfaces) have begun to acknowledge a broader definition of literacy as encompassing all forms of multimodal texts (see the discussion in Chapter 3 on semiotics and the interpretation of text).

Perhaps a main reason for a shift of thinking toward a more liberal interpretation of text has resulted from the necessity to assist children to learn to conceptualize, think, and communicate in new ways, using newly emerging communications environments: technologies (e.g., computers, the internet, digital media) and cross-world contexts (e.g., hypertext, web pages, e-mail messages). Through these new forms of text, we participate in a kind of vernacular republic. In other words, the dialect or language used in these communication environments is universal and resides with all the people, kind of like an "Infobahn" (Cope & Kalantzis, 2000). Children's views of the world are influenced by the new abilities offered through these technologies and cross-world modes of communication, and they can interact instantly with others from any part of the world or find information about different cultures, which is offered in many forms. For example, through the Internet, they can view the artworks of children from around the world.

Although we think of new technologies as being virtual—in other words, they are in essence and sort of "unreal"—older forms of virtual reality have been available for decades, such as photographs, telegraphs, newspapers, novels, telephones, radios, and televisions. Today's children accept all formats for communication as being commonplace, similar to the way they expect that, when they flick the light switch in their bedrooms, they will have instant electric lighting. Although adults refer to mass communication, such as teleconferences or videotelecasts, as taken-for-granted commodities in our modern society, these media possibilities can cause some confusion for children in relation to the ways in which such communication is transmitted, as is illustrated in Figure 7.1.

Whether the girl in Figure 7.1 was inquiring about when the people at the other end would begin to hear the teacher, and how this would occur, is hard to know. Perhaps she thought Sue's voice would simply stop working or maybe even be "transported" away, into some other dimension. As in the case of the boy who bodily-kinesthetically described the hill as being heavy, this girl's comment provides another example of a child's multimodal perspective of thinking—she made an association between the aural aspect of the teacher's voice with that of the technical aspect of televised media, and imaged the teacher's voice as going somewhere else. Such cross-domain ways of thinking are part of knowing and understanding associated with artistic literacy.

FIGURE 7.1   A Preschool Child's Confusion about a Videotelecast Transmission

Our college teaching team was eager to expose our early childhood students to an excellent preschool on campus. However, because we had such a large group of students and didn't want to interrupt the program by having a number of seminar groups traipsing through the center or being cramming together in the observation booth, we decided to film the program and have it telecast to the lecture theater, where 150 students could all view the preschool program at the same time. That way, we could talk to the teacher live and get more information about what was happening in the program.

Sue, the preschool teacher, explained to the children what was about to happen and told them that, in a few minutes, her "voice would go to a lecture theater somewhere else on campus." About twenty minutes later, when the program was in full swing and children were involved in a variety of learning experiences, a four-year-old girl went up to Sue and asked, "When is your voice going?"

Artistic Literacy

The concept of visual literacy originally referred to communication through film and the electronic media of television and computers (Curtiss, 1987). Today the term is adopted by educators and artists as well to refer to the ability to understand and use the fine arts (Rice, 1990). Literacy within the fine arts is now seen to encompass several domains—not only visual, but also aural, spatial, bodily-kinesthetic, and aesthetic domains (Gardner, 1983; Wright, 1994a, 1997b, 2001a).

In the broad sense, literacy means well educated. To be literate means being able to participate in rich personal experiences and to use written signs or symbols, such as music notation, as a way to encode a variety of events. But notating in the arts is not the same as sign recognition. Some aspects of the arts have no notation, such as painting. So, what would it mean for a person to be literate in the abstract, two-dimensional art form of painting? Because painting requires no intermediary signs, we get its experience directly from the art itself. Hence, literacy in painting is developed indirectly, with no need for a functional sign-decoding type of literacy (Reimer, 1989). This is true as well for other visual art forms such as sculpture, photography, and textile art.

However, other domains, such as architecture, theater, film, dance, and music all use some form of encoding system—architects' plans, theatrical and films scripts, choreographic notation, and musical scores are examples of such systems. Yet, in spite of the presence of these systems, we seldom need to draw upon them to appreciate architecture, theater, film, or dance. In other words, we do not need to study architectural renderings, film and theater scripts, various dance notations, or opera scores to be educated about those arts (although knowledge might be assisted by including some acquaintance with these special notational systems). Nonetheless, a comprehensive curriculum should include some attention to notations as a helpful way for children to explore the nature of these art forms, even if their personally generated notations may be rudimentary (e.g., squiggly lines to show the contour of a melody). However, having knowledge of artistic notations in and of themselves would be a restrictive and narrow interpretation of the term *artistic literacy,* as notation is only one component of knowing in the arts (Reimer, 1989).

Let me illustrate how a person can be literate in a non-notational domain. While there are no notational equivalents for a painting, a person would be considered literate about painting who understood a great deal about the art of painting—how to respond to it appropriately and sensitively; how to make discerning judgments about it; how to understand the history, techniques, and many styles of painting; its major practitioners; and where to go to see good examples of paintings. Such a person would be literate, educated, perceptive, and knowledgeable about painting. While his or her literacy would be enhanced through personal experiences with the act of painting, many serious painting lovers—and even professional curators and dealers—do not paint themselves.

Complete artistic literacy, therefore, is not just a set of isolated analytical and verbal-based skills associated with describing the formal elements of the arts. Purely descriptive forms of analysis do not adequately provide a *sense* of artworks. We cannot simply *see* paintings, sculptures, and other art works, or *view* theater or dance, or *hear* musical performances and describe these through words alone. In making sense of performances or art exhibitions, people can only fully understand and appreciate the importance of artworks if they have the necessary schema or knowledge not only to see, view, and hear, but also *interpret* artworks—interpret the diverse subject matter and the abstracted function of the work (Rice, 1990).

For people with little background or previous exposure to art, associative experiences play a key role in the aesthetic interpretation of a work of art (Csikszentmihalyi & Rochbert-Halton, 1985; Parsons, 1987). Through association, people are reminded of pleasant events, such as a special social experience, or of special places, such as a beautiful lake. Thus, those who have only minimal exposure to art often appreciate paintings if they "tell a story," such as Breugel's *Children's Games,* where the viewer can identify a number of outdoor activities that children are playing. Paintings that tell an easily recognizable story do not seem as abstract, because they appear to have a specific use. They are similar to illustrations in a book or magazine. Similar associative responses can occur in music, dance, and drama.

Yet artistic literacy involves more than just associating a work with personal experiences or stories. Full appreciation involves an awareness that comes from direct viewing and listening. This helps us to think critically or evaluatively about the arts, to communicate subtle aesthetic impressions and feelings, and to expand our vocabulary so we can talk about the formal elements of the arts. In addition, the process of artistic appreciation requires an understanding of the cultural framework in which an artwork was created. Hence, it is closely connected to cultural literacy (Rice, 1990). Someone who can make sense of artworks—such as plays, musicals, films, or contemporary dance—can do this by knowing how these works fit into a historical context, having the skills to analyze them, and having sufficient understanding of the relevant culture from which they originated. But, while an artistically literate person is by definition also culturally literate, a culturally literate person is not necessarily artistically literate. It is possible for a person to have a great deal of cultural knowledge, for example, about literature or history, but still not know how to understand the arts (although this is likely to be a rare occurrence).

Children's cultural and artistic literacy develops from a very early age, and can be enhanced in a number of ways:

- By providing opportunities for them to create and present artworks
- By viewing, listening, and speaking, and in the case of older children, reading and writing in the artistic domains

Through describing, analyzing, interpreting, and judging artworks, children acquire an artistic vocabulary that enables them not only to take part in artistic practice, but also to participate in the discourse of arts criticism, arts history, and aesthetic judgment. It is through competency in nonverbal arts forms, and through discussing them verbally, that young children engage in potent forms of communication and expression. Regular exposure to the arts is critical in children's education, because aesthetic delight in the arts comes more naturally to children who already have a great deal of comfort and familiarity with artworks. This familiarity is generally achieved through repeated exposure to artistic objects and performances, which often involves "just looking" or "just listening."

Yet passive looking and listening is difficult for young children, because touching is a way of making contact with the physical world, and is as—or more—basic than looking. It is understandable but perhaps disappointing that art museums have to post signs asking people not to touch the exhibits. Therefore, children need to understand why they should not touch works of art, in the same way that they generally are discouraged from calling out responses to actors during live professional performances, or singing along with the music, or emulating the movements of dancers. Of course, many children's programs encourage them to interact with the actors or musicians, but in formal, adult-oriented performance, children are encouraged to listen quietly and watch live music, dance, and drama.

Sensitive viewing and listening is one of a number of literacy skills that can and should be taught to children. Young children are capable of learning the type of analytical looking and listening involved in appreciating the arts, as they begin to use their visual, aural, and kinesthetic senses contemplatively and analytically. However, the less active form of analytical looking and listening need not be a dreary experience. Indeed, understanding through seeing and hearing can be positively encouraged in young children with enjoyable results. Of course, a balance needs to be achieved between listening and looking, and *doing*. It is predominantly through the tangible, hands-on aspect of doing that children come to appreciate and become literate in the arts. Let us turn our attention now to ways in which children *interact* with the arts and processes that can help them become artistically literate.

PROCESSES TOWARD ARTISTIC LITERACY

Figure 3.5 (Chapter 3) outlined a range of general processes that are involved in learning in the artistic disciplines of music, dance, play/drama, and the visual arts. These processes are key components in the experience of meaning-making and expression. In addition to these generic processes, meaning-making and expression must also be understood in relation to how children learn *in* the arts through the integrated processes of making, presenting, and responding.

To separate *performance in* from *thoughts about* the arts would be tragically missing the point of arts education. Great art, and all experiences of it, are brought about by the experiences of making (creating), presenting (performing or displaying artworks), and responding (perceiving). These three artistic processes cannot be duplicated, yet there are many aspects that they share in common—they are bound together in a mutual exercise of "bringing each other out, as deeply as possible" (Best, 2000b). Sophisticated words about the arts are not the artistic experiences itself; they are only *about* the experience. Likewise, having an artistic experience without engaging the mind and emotions is only partial. Therefore, it is necessary for children to *participate in* the arts, not simply learn *through* them.

Given the information that has been discussed in relation to artistic learning and knowing (Chapter 3), multiple intelligences (Chapter 4), and children's artistic development and learning styles (Chapter 5), there is increasing evidence that the average baby is born with the ability to think *in* the arts before thinking *about* them. Therefore, education must begin with and expand from the process of making as the originating source for learning. For young children, the process of making is most intimately connected with using the primary "language" of the arts. Making "unites the contemplation of something with the very doing of it" (Best, 2000b).

Making

Making refers to the full range of ways in which children generate and experiment with ideas, bring a new product into existence, and rework and transform existing works or ideas. Making involves experimentation, risk-taking, and uncertainty—the elements of flexibility and other creative components described in Chapter 1. For an individual to be flexible, options must be available; hence, decision making revolves around making artistic choices and solving artistic problems. Artistic problem solving is addressed best in the context of artistic making. Making is vitally important in promoting forms of thinking that demand attention to the ways in which sounds, images, and movement are created and organized. Making is a way of grappling with relationships, imaging new artistic possibilities, and pursuing new artistic ideas, regardless of the arts medium being used.

We can inspire children to participate in solving both structured and open-ended arts problems. Such challenges should invite multiple modes and strategies for their solution. A *structured* problem, for example, is one in which all the information and resources are available to complete the task, for example, setting the challenge of making a three-dimensional structure using sculptural wire, yarn, and objects from nature. It should be noted that this type of structured problem is different from a reproductive learning experience, as described in Chapter 2. An *open-ended* problem is one in which all the information and resources are not specified, for example, when a child spontaneously decides to draw a picture of what it might be like on Earth in the year 5000. In both types of learning, however, children have opportunities to work on ideas by selecting, refining, and making decisions.

"Real" artistic engagement—where the encounter is *relevant* to the individual—demands a sense of purpose and application. In other words, the child should *feel* like developing an idea in a committed manner. Clearly, commitment involves practice and the development of skills and techniques in the arts requires perseverance, just as it does in any area of learning. This does not imply that the arts are only for those who have been fully initiated into its mysteries through hours of toil and drudgery. However, unless children experience the arts as relevant and rigorous forms of study, their understanding and enjoyment of the discipline will be superficial, at best.

We must make conscious instructional efforts to turn arts experiences into *active* learning situations that encourage children to make decisions and develop their artistic thinking processes. Students studying the arts at college, for example, make choices and evaluate the results of an improvisation or a learned performance before they can talk about it. Young children engage in similar analytical processes, albeit at a less advanced level. When children are actively *doing* music, dance, drama, or art, they experience what it means to act and think like musicians, dancers, actors, and artists. Acting as artists challenges children to think and feel musically, spatially, kinesthetically, and visually and to develop intuition about the value of the learning event. The key to artistic independence lies in learning how to be metacognitive—being aware of the cognitive (and affective and social) processes being used.

Consequently, teachers of young children also require artistic and metacognitive strategies within themselves, so they can assist children in acquiring these (Pautz, 1989, p. 102). When we have such skills, we can help children tap into their own existing artistic ideas and processes. We can assist children to express and reflect on their own thoughts and feelings and to take pleasure in the end result or product. Helping children enjoy both artistic processes and products gives them an appreciation of how the arts are a significant part of life, not simply an enhancement or embellishment of it. We are essentially "training" children's eyes to see and observe better and their ears and bodies to hear and move in aesthetic ways. Through the arts, children engage in multimodal connections between visual, aural, spatial, bodily-kinesthetic, and imaginative and expressive dimensions.

Yet much of the criticism about arts education in schools has been that children do not have the knowledge and techniques to be involved in the arts at a "proficient" level—presumably at the level of established composers, choreographers, actors, or artists. Setting such high benchmarks is not only unrealistic, but overlooks the value of children's developing insights into the techniques, structures, and grammars of the arts, using processes similar to those used by professionals, albeit at a less advanced level. A more accurate criticism of school arts education might be that many art, music, dance, or drama experiences have limited opportunities for children to express their artistic ideas or discoveries in developmentally *meaningful* ways, *artistic independence*, because the content and processes of many arts experiences in schools are often provided for the children. Yet independent, supported, and child-initiated learning is vitally important for development in the arts, just as it is in any area of disciplined activity. Consequently, all encounters with the arts should include an element of discovery that enlists the natural energies that sustain spontaneous learning through curiosity. Effective teaching requires us to maximize the potential for artistic encounters in the classroom, and to structure these encounters in a purposeful rather than aimless or careless way.

Presenting

The second form of learning that enhances children's artistic literacy is through presenting their work to others. While we normally think of presenting as being part of the performing arts, we also engage in the process of presenting in the visual arts through the mounting of artworks, either informally in the classroom, or through exhibitions. Through presenting the completed artwork or performing a dance, play enactment, or musical piece, the artistic end results may be shared with others.

As in the case of adult artists, some of the works of children may be private—not meant to be shared. But in many cases, children enjoy presenting their artistic processes and products to others. When professional artists, musicians, actors, and dancers present their works, sometimes the audiences who attend art galleries, concert halls, or theaters are almost limitless, whereas at other times there might be only a small social group who are viewing and listening. In school contexts, children's presentations usually occur informally, where children share their artistic endeavors with their peers and reflect on their own works as well as respond to the works of others (see Figure 7.2).

Some teachers might question whether presenting and performing might put more emphasis on the product than the process. However, a balance can be found for process and product if discussions with children about their presentations emphasize their thoughts, ideas, perceptions, concepts, techniques, inspirations, and ideas that stimulated the end result. Sometimes we may wish to compare and contrast the processes of a few children's performances or products. This is not a matter of rating or ranking children's works, but describing the artistic, technical, imaginative, expressive, or emotive aspects of each work. This requires us to apply flexible teaching strategies, an intuitive ability to understand children's artistic expression from their viewpoint, a respect for children's personal endeavors, and sensitive guidance in helping children make their personal expression more successful. When children present their works to others, however elementary the resources or techniques may be, we must be receptive and alert—really listening and responding—and modeling this attentiveness to the child audience at the same time. Through such modeling, young children can learn to make fine discriminations, recognize different artistic approaches, and make sensitive responses and evaluations.

Responding

The arts satisfy a basic human need to make sense of life and to engage in rich experiences. The role of adults is to develop in children the ability not only to participate in the arts, but also to respond to the arts in the fullest way possible, across the widest range of experiences. While the image of child-as-artist is important because it lays the foundations for creating and performing in artistic media, children should also come in contact with not only their own artworks, but the examples of outstanding works from the adult world (Gardner, 1999a). For this reason, the third process, which enhances artistic literacy in children, is that of responding.

Kindler (1993) demonstrated that, early in life, children engage in activities that involve description, analysis, interpretation, and critical appraisal of their own and their peers' work. She noted that, during informal performances for each other, children's comments to each other about their artworks quite consistently employed a positive strategy rather than the direct negative-feedback approach so common among adult critics. It seems as though young children's responding is contextualized, but also involves consideration of the artist who produced it. In some remarks, children were more precise, direct, and constructive than many professional

FIGURE 7.2   A Preschool Boy's Performance of a Sound Story

Lyn was interested in helping a five-year-old boy, Reygan, develop a story around a topic of interest he had been exploring with her for several days, which involved the association of sounds with "metamorphosizing" characters of a pinball game. (The character changed his head to become others things, ranging from a dragon to a banana). Lyn and Reygan sat together at the Sound Wall, a structure that held various instruments or component parts of instruments for the children to play. On this day, the Sound Wall consisted of three guitar strings strung across bridges to make sounds of a wide range of pitch. A triangle and a bell were also available near the Sound Wall.

As Reygan told the story, Lyn kept notes to assist their memory, and she helped Reygan select which string and how to play it to depict the character's metamorphizing or other story events. She asked Reygan questions centered on character development: what each character did and what its relationship was with other characters. The sounds Reygan created generally depicted the movement of the various characters. Lyn then spent considerable time helping Reygan construct a sequence, and she recorded his ideas on paper.

She encouraged Reygan to perform his sound composition for the rest of the preschool group, and she invited the children to congregate on the mat around the Sound Wall. Lyn described the composition as a "listening story" and encouraged children to sit and listen. Lyn told the story while Reygan performed on the strings, coupling the sounds with the text (events, characters). The various metamorphoses included the following images and sounds:

head with a horn on it	bass guitar string on the sound wall
handbag	triangle
spiders	bouncing a stick on the strings
bananas	hitting a bell five times
losing time	faster bells
boulders	drum
objects rolling down hills	fast tapping on drum

Reygan enjoyed performing his story for the other children and waited for cues in the storyline to play the instruments in specific ways. Sometimes Lyn had to remind him of the sounds he used (e.g., "remember, you played the triangle"), but generally Reygan remembered the sound sequences as they had been practiced and reproduced these within the story. The other children remarked on the unique ideas of the story and the way it was represented through sound.

critics, while still maintaining a sensitive and kind attitude. This ability to provide constructive feedback is an aspect that we should model in our approaches to enhance children's sensitive responsiveness and appreciation of the arts.

Through reflecting on and responding to their own arts works and the works of others, children develop the skills of talking and thinking (and later, reading and writing) about the arts. When they engage in arts criticism, children describe, analyze, interpret, judge, challenge, and value artworks and artistic ideas. Through these experiences, they develop aesthetic values of their own, and learn how aesthetic values are constructed in a wide range of contexts. Children begin to understand that, in a broader sense, social and cultural values and meanings are constructed, challenged, and reconstructed through the arts. They learn that the arts convey the ideas and feelings of different times and places, express a range of emotions, and employ a sense of beauty and harmony that enriches the experiences of all who can appreciate them (Gardner, 1999a). Therefore, exposure to the masterworks throughout history—the great works of civilization that we, as a culture over the centuries, have made our own—is giving children contact to the best that's been created.

By reflecting on historical masterworks and their own artworks, children's vocabularies and concepts about the arts allow them to make explicit their understandings, and for the teacher to enhance this understanding through the introduction of related vocabularies and concepts. There are many excellent resources for children that focus on the enhancement of observational, reflective, and analytical processes of engaging in the arts. One of the activities at the end of this chapter centers on resources to enhance visual thinking through exposure to masterworks in the visual arts. We can enhance children's artistic literacy in each of the arts areas by exposing them to recordings of music, photographs, and videos of musicians, dancers, artists, and actors and through attendance at live performances and art exhibitions.

Contextual information about the works is valuable, such as information about the creators, the development of the artworks, and the cultural/historical fabric of the period in which the artworks were created. We should aim to find ways in which to present such content to young children in interesting and enjoyable ways. However, children should also have opportunities to appreciate and interpret the arts in their own way, through direct perceiving of what is going on in the music, the art, or the dance and drama, and responding to it with enjoyment and possibly delight. Arts appreciation can help develop children's sense of the value of music, art, dance, and drama, and provide a glimpse of the power that these art forms have in engaging us, speaking to us, and, at the highest level, moving us profoundly.

ASSISTING CHILDREN'S THINKING ABOUT ARTISTIC LEARNING

There are many ways in which we can enhance children's awareness of their own thinking about learning before, during, and after artistic learning experiences. The following examples are framed within a context in which children are engaged in learning within small groups, where problem solving is sparked by the interest of the group.

Before an Arts Experience

The teacher may have observed a group of children pursuing a particular artistic idea within one of the arts domains. For example, they might be enacting their own version of the film *Jurassic Park,* or making up a musical composition to accompany others' dancing, or building box constructions for toy-motorcyclists' stunt show. At the beginning of such artistic experiences, the teacher and children might try an idea or a technique and then evaluate it in terms of what aural, visual, dramatic, or movement treatments could make the ideas or the work more interesting. A series of "Who knows how . . . " questions can invite children to demonstrate some examples of how they might approach a musical, movement, visual, or dramatic idea. Below is an example of how a teacher assisted children to get started in sandpit play:

> **Teacher:** "OK, why don't you guys have a think about what you're going to do."
>
> **James:** "We're going to build a dry river."
>
> **Mark:** "Yeah, and this one's [points to a truck] bogged."
>
> **Teacher:** "Are you going to have enough room? [unheard response] Where does the river go?"
>
> **James:** "I'll make a path with my foot to show where the river should go."
>
> **Mark:** [begins pushing his tractor around the river that James is drawing in the sand]

If such questions are followed with "what" and "why" questions, a number of ideas can be generated to help children plan their works.

During an Arts Experience

While children are involved in their works, we can circulate among the groups and informally invite children to talk about their progress, thought processes, and perceptions. Such discussions might be sparked by asking children to indicate how far they are into their works, to describe their line of thinking up to that point, or to describe how they intend to pursue the remainder of the work. Talking to children about their perceptions, progress, and processes not only helps children become aware of their own thinking and behavior, it also helps us understand the children's thinking and directions. When we understand the children's goals and processes, we can use the information to give children individualized assistance.

The most noteworthy elements of the musical, art, dance, or drama work in which the children are engaged can be labeled and attention drawn to these elements. For example, we might highlight a catchy rhythmic pattern that a child is using and suggest ways in which it could be developed with different instruments. A number of alternatives could also be provided, for example, on how to stabilize a fragile box construction, how a child might demonstrate flow in his movement, or how the child's selection of a dramatic prop has made her appear powerful and strong.

By labeling what children are exploring in their works, we help children focus their attention on specific processes and concepts. This helps them recall or retrieve their ideas so they can work on and develop them. Extending children's ideas can be enhanced if they are directed to sections of works by musical, visual, spatial, and dramatic aspects rather than more obvious aspects, such as subject content. For example, in a group-conceived dance, musical composition, or sociodramatic play experience, we can prompt children to focus on thinking about how to get through areas in which they are having mental blocks or on aspects of a work that are creating difficulties for them. A helpful comment might be, "Rather than going all the way back to the beginning again, let's start where we're having difficulties—the section where there is a shift in mood."

After an Arts Experience

Children can become involved in the knowledge about, and assessment of, the content and processes they have explored. As children listen to and look at each other's works, they should be encouraged to verbalize what they hear and see. Analytical listening, looking, and talking can focus on:

- The artistic ideas, techniques, and aesthetic qualities they think were particularly effective
- Their knowledge and control of the process they used
- Their work patterns and utilization of time and resources
- Their cooperation within the group
- Their ability to stay focused and on task
- Ideas they might have for future projects

While formal discussion should be short, perhaps about five minutes or so, we can arouse children's curiosity by using processes similar to those described in Chapter 4 in relation to guided learning, such as:

- Posing questions
- Summarizing information
- Clarifying unclear responses
- Acting as a resource

■ Praising astute observations
■ Providing a model of enjoyment, discovery, and inquiry

Learning in the arts should enable children to consider the social, cultural, and historical contexts in which the arts are produced and valued and to recognize how societies construct and record knowledge about the arts. This involves understanding how culture influences what we see and how we judge the quality of objects or performances and how this is conditioned by cultural conventions, methods, and techniques that have evolved among artists over hundreds and in some cases thousands of years. Ways in which children can learn to appreciate the cultural aspects of the arts are described in greater detail in the last segment of this chapter. For the moment, however, let us shift our attention to how artistic literacy is enhanced through an understanding of artistic concepts, through the use of the grammars of artistic expression—the artistic elements—and the forms of expression and symbolic domains that are used during the development of these grammars.

ARTISTIC ELEMENTS, FORMS OF EXPRESSION, AND SYMBOLIC DOMAINS

Much of what has been discussed so far in this book has centered on the generic aspects of artistic learning. Broad issues have been outlined in relation to creativity, approaches to arts education, artistic learning and knowing, socially constructed learning, and artistic intelligence, development, and literacy. The next segment draws together many of the key issues discussed so far, and describes them within a framework that illustrates the multimodal nature of artistic expression. It allows for a way of understanding the interface of the various symbol systems that are used in the arts and how this leads to artistic literacy.

Artistic literacy is expressed or shown through a variety of ways within each of the disciplines, through various forms of expression, such as painting, singing, choreographing, or role playing. Through such expression, literacy in the arts is developed through our involvement in the use and analysis of artistic concepts. A *concept* is a generic idea abstracted from particular instances. We often use the term *concept* to refer to people's ability to understand abstract issues based on their personal experience. For example, we might say, "She has no concept of what it is like to be a mother," implying that, unless someone has had the experience of waking at 2 A.M. to breast feed and deal with numerous other day-to-day experiences, she has no right to offer opinions about how to be a good mother.

Conceptual development in the arts involves regular experiences with artistic elements and understanding ideas abstracted from particular instances while using these elements. *Elements* are constituent parts or simplest principles of a subject of study. For example, in the visual arts, some elements are color, line, and shape. To understand color concepts, for example, some experiential knowledge might include:

- Colors change when you blend them.
- The choice of side-by-side colors can be striking if they are contrasting or subtle if they are similar.
- Some colors can be "bright" or "warm," whereas others are "dark" or "cool."

Our conceptual knowledge develops in all arts disciplines through our exposure to the arts and through our experiences in making, presenting, and responding to the arts. Through experience, we have direct contact with the core grammar of the arts as we make use of the elements. Each of the arts disciplines includes its own special elements, such as melody and rhythm in music, space and time in dance, and character and movement in drama. In addition, each arts discipline uses specific media and utilizes special ways of expressing thoughts, feelings, and concepts. The main elements and forms of expression that are involved in each discipline are summarized in Figure 7.3. This figures presents the *predominant* symbolic domains that are used in each of the disciplines and the means through which each domain is channeled (i.e., transmitted or communicated). Each of these categories and terms will be clarified and extended through examples in Chapters 8 through 11, but for the moment, let us begin by obtaining an overall understanding of the unique and shared components of each of the arts disciplines.

One of the difficulties of presenting a summary of artistic elements, media, processes, and domains, such as in Figure 7.3, is that there is no consensus in the professional literature about how each of these components should be defined or subdivided. In music, for example, a considerably smaller or larger list of elements could be included than that presented in the figure, yet this alternative list could still be considered an accurate description of the component elements of music. One variation to that presented below, for example, could center around five main music categories and related subcategories: tonal (pitch, melody, harmony), temporal (beat, rhythm, meter), acoustic (timbre, texture), expressive (tempo, dynamics, articulation), and structural (form). Similarly, it could be argued that the elements described for the visual arts, dance, and drama could be listed and structured in many alternative ways, depending upon one's philosophical, experiential, or pedagogical position. Criticism could also be made that the areas of literature and media are not included as arts disciplines.

Therefore, it should be stressed that the terminology presented in Figure 7.3 is not intended to be an *exhaustive* list but rather a way of succinctly presenting examples of the *types* of content and structures that fall within each of the arts disciplines. The intent is to assist the reader to recognize sim-

FIGURE 7.3   Elements and Forms of Expression in the Arts Disciplines

ARTS DISCIPLINES	VISUAL ARTS	MUSIC	DANCE	DRAMA
Elements	Line, shape, color, texture, form, composition, and expression	Rhythm, melody, harmony, form, tone quality, texture, and expressive controls	Body, space, time, effort, form, mood, function, and style	Tension, symbol, roles, relationships, language, movement, time, space, focus, and metaxis
Forms of expression (media and processes)	Drawing, painting, printing, constructing, modeling, and sculpting	Listening, singing/playing instruments, composing, notating, and conducting	Expressing and structuring (e.g., choreographing) through movement	Enrolling, enacting, improvising, miming, and story-building, using language and props
Predominant symbolic domain used	Visual, spatial	Aural	Bodily-kinesthetic	Inter- and intrapersonal
How each domain is channeled (transmitted or communicated)	Object-related (physical structure and the functions of objects)	Object-free (structures of auditory and oral systems)	Object-related (structures involving the body in skilled and expressive ways)	Person-related (structures involving one's self in relation to other persons)

ilarities and differences across the arts disciplines in order to understand not only their separate or independent functions, but also their potential overlaps, connections, and prospects for integration. For example, the use of symbols and improvisation are processes that are applicable to all arts disciplines.

Similarly, the symbolic domains (i.e., visual, spatial, aural, bodily-kinesthetic, and inter- and intrapersonal) also overlap across the arts disciplines. As discussed earlier in this chapter, all texts are multimodal—no text can exist in a single mode. However, one modality among these can be *predominant* within one arts domain. In other words, many of the arts draw on a number of symbolic domains, but specific modes are featured more in certain arts disciplines than in others. While dance, for example, is predominantly connected with bodily-kinesthetic knowledge and skills, the bodily-kinesthetic domain is also activated in the visual arts, music, and drama. The underlying component of "thinking with the body" or *somatic* knowing and the multimodal aspects of learning and knowing through *meaning-making* in the arts were issues discussed in great detail in Chapter 2. However, it will be helpful to briefly review this earlier content in relation to the issue of artistic literacy.

Somatic knowing, or thinking and feeling with the body, is part of all forms of artistic expression, to a greater or lesser extent. It involves using one's body to fashion artistic products and to make artistic responses. For example, there is a close link between musical response and the use of the body to communicate and express music, and the use of fine-motor coordination to accomplish technically complex material. Similarly, in the visual arts, bodily-kinesthetic forms of symbolizing are involved in technical skills and in capturing the emotional and expressive aspects of objects, events, and concepts. To capture the feeling of energy in a clay sculpture, for example, children must feel this energy within themselves to represent it in a three-dimensional form. Similarly, in drama and dance, the body is a vehicle for expressing and communicating through gesture and movement and through interpersonal and intrapersonal interactions. To express emotions through gesture and movement the child must feel these through the body.

The process of *meaning-making* is a second feature of the arts that is common to all arts domains; however, the uniqueness of each domain's symbols and symbol systems requires an understanding of the special ways in which each of the arts are depicted and interpreted. Children make meaning from their involvement in the predominant modes of each of the domains, but often there is also a crossover of domains and the use of many modes simultaneously—visual, spatial, aural, bodily-kinesthetic, and inter- and intrapersonal. We know, for instance, that meaning in relation to rhythm can be found not only in music, but also in the ways in which lines are used in a drawing, the way movements are used in dance, and how content unfolds within drama. How we learn such concepts can be best appreciated through first-hand experiences rather than through a theoretical exposition of this fact. Such understanding often occurs through our direct experience with artistic elements in relation to subject matter and our emotional associations with the subject matter. These components are illustrated in more detail in Chapter 12 in relation to integration of the arts.

The process of analysis in the arts cannot be removed from the issue of meaning any more than can the history of art, music, dance, or drama be taught as a set of facts and figures. However, in an attempt to give children skills for appreciating the arts, educators have sometimes stressed only the formal elements of the arts, such as focusing on an understanding of concepts associated with pattern, texture, style, or rhythm. But a purely analytical analysis of elements can result in a very dry description of content and in a purely intellectual study of the elements in relation to one another. The next segment attempts to illustrate how to enhance artistic literacy through a balanced relationship between, and *understanding* of, arts elements, and the intuitive, expressive, and metaphoric *responses* to the arts.

Expressive, Metaphoric, and Stylistic Facets

Artistic literacy can be enhanced when arts elements are considered in the context of the subject matter and the emotional effect they communicate—in other words, the expressive components of the works. In art, for example, when bold diagonal lines communicate motion in a painting, it is important to know why and also how that dynamism is communicated. The power of an image or particular subject that is being depicted might be enhanced, for instance, through energy lines projecting out from the arms of marching military men. It is not enough merely to identify and notice such lines—we should also try to understand them in relation to what is being expressed in the artwork, such as power, force, or uniformity (Rice, 1990; Wright, 1993). Understanding such expressive qualities in relation to other artistic, historical, and cultural aspects of artworks is an important dimension of artistic literacy that is achievable even with young children, as is illustrated in Figure 7.4 on page 146.

When children are involved in the arts and engaging in analysis, they are using the same kinds of thinking as that of the professional artist. They are using and thinking about subject matter, the processes they use to create and communicate ideas, and ways to reflect on and express thoughts and feelings. Therefore, the primary focus within arts education should be on learning artistic *behavior* rather than learning *about* things peripheral to the art, such as the date of Picasso's birth. Likewise, musical fluency should take precedence over the musical reading or writing of music notation. It is the aural ability to image music coupled with the skill of handling an instrument or the voice that characterizes jazz and folk music from all cultures, where musicians play "by ear." The amazing possibilities of memory and collective improvisation that these musicians use are similar to how children respond to music. Therefore, the learning environment in the arts must include opportunities for children to receive a balanced involvement in all three artistic processes—making, presenting, and responding—and to engage in the expressive aspects of artistic meaning making and communication. Again, these expressive components are featured more specifically in the chapter on integration.

BALANCING THE ARTS PROCESSES AND CONNECTING THE ARTS DOMAINS

Some of the practices in arts education do not provide a balanced emphasis on making, presenting, and responding. Instead, the arts are taught in a partial or lopsided manner. Music instruction, for example, can often exclude imaginative play, such as composing or improvising, if the program is too centered on "group time" music lessons. With older children, the learning of music can focus almost predominantly on performance skills and appreciation, or on aspects such as the history of music, acoustics, the biographies of

FIGURE 7.4　Preschool Children's Ability to Recognize Artists

I have been exposing my preschool children to the works of professional artists through the use of posters and postcards I've picked up from the art gallery and through books on art. We talk about how artists develop their own personal style—which, of course, can change throughout their lifetimes—and how you start to recognize the artist's works after you have looked at a number of examples, particularly from certain periods of his or her life. It's pretty amazing how quickly kids pick up on characteristics of artworks from particular periods of history and can even make fine discriminations between artists of the same period. Right now they are particularly interested in the Impressionist and Neo-Impressionist artists, like Monet, van Gogh, Seurat, and Cézanne.

Often the children will spontaneously point out something in an artwork that tells me that they are picking up on key things, like style. The other day, for instance, we were looking at Seurat's *A Sunday Afternoon on the Island of La Grande Jatte,* and they said things like, "That's like Monet, like when he painted those waterlilies with all the different colored dots. This one uses dots too, but they're all over her dress and umbrella and on the grass and trees too." When we talk about the medium of an artwork, many of the kids energetically inform me about the difference between things like watercolor and oil paintings, collage, sculpture, or an installation, and they even use words related to genre, like "still lifes" or "portraits." Sure, we've talked about these formal elements; I've given them the vocabulary, I guess, but I suppose that's what it's all about. That's the way they pick up the lingo. But the interesting thing is that they can transfer their understanding of art to works that they have never seen before and can sometimes even pick the right artist, historical period, or medium.

What I enjoy most about my talks with kids about art is that they are so open to the expressive elements—they pick up on the artist's meaning almost intuitively. This intuitive stuff seems almost part of being a child, because nonverbal communication, for them, is used in so many subtle ways. Compared to adults, children seem to be very aware of things like body language, facial expression, and other nonverbal messages. They pick up on the shifting of the psychological feel within a classroom environment throughout the day. But still, sometimes I'm floored by some of the astute comments kids make about art. They often grasp expressive characteristics of a work, such as anger or loneliness, not just from the stance or expression of the person in the artwork, but also by the artists' use of expressive things, like somber colors, lilting lines, or the placement of objects within the full space. In many ways I learn as much from them as they learn from me when we talk about art.

composers, or the sociology of rock and pop, without opportunities for children to participate in the actual *making* of music (Swanwick, 1988). Because music has a specific notation system, where musical symbols such as notes, staves, and expressive marks are used, it can be possible to come to believe that "musical literacy" is equivalent solely to the ability to read and write music using notation. However, studies of children's musical ability have shown that, when they have learned to notate music, there can be a loss—at least temporarily—of important expressive qualities or details (Bamberger, 1991). In the school years, there must be a balance between the scholastic aspects of musical and other forms of artistic literacy that are linked to creative and expressive aspects. While notation can be an excellent aid for understanding music, we must *use it* rather than be *used by it*. Music reading and writing is not the ultimate aim of music education; it is simply a means to an end in some music and is often unnecessary (Swanwick, 1999). We can help children to find their own ways to symbolize their understanding of sound and how it is expressed and, when they are ready, assist them in using the standard music notation system.

In contrast to the discipline of music, the visual arts have traditionally emphasized the artistic behavior of *making*, which usually has involved free expression, imaginative play, and creativity, while sometimes neglecting the technical or analytical components of art or the processes of responding to one's own works or the works of others. In dance and drama, there can be an imbalanced emphasis on *performance,* often through the systematic learning of set movements or specific character roles in plays, while neglecting the processes of making and responding. Therefore, the goal of arts education should be to help children grasp the meaning and structure of the arts so they can use the arts as a metaphor of reality. Drilling rhythm patterns in music, such as "Ta Ta Ti-Ti Ta," recalling color names in art, or practicing dance technique such as bending or stretching may be necessary at times, but only if the learner sees how it leads to a more complete sensitivity to the whole artistic process or artistic result. In most cases, it is the teacher who mediates such connections.

If, for example, children are painting with bold colors, we might show them examples of other art that uses bold colors. If the children are improvising a dramatic episode about a futuristic planet, we might look at futuristic illustrations of what might be found on such a planet, to stimulate ideas associated with their dramatic enactments. If children's dance improvisations appear to be leaning toward a specific style of movement, we might look for videotapes of dances from different cultures, where similar styles are used. When composing or performing contrasting elements in music (e.g., loud and soft), we might play pieces of music that embody that contrast, and invite children to illustrate these contrasts through movement, or through painting. Such examples are not intended to say, "This is how it should be done," but to show the children what others have done.

Making connections for young children can be enhanced through direct relationships between making, presenting, and responding. The process of making should be the beginning point as children learn through doing and through hands-on participation. However, making often is the *only* focus in early childhood arts education. Yet performing and responding, which help contextualize the arts, are also important for children's education in the arts.

As in elementary and secondary education, early childhood teachers can nurture analytical abilities in young children, but this is generally achieved by responding to and extending young children's initiatives rather than by *didactically teaching* the arts.

It is a challenging task for teachers to blend the processes of making, presenting, and responding. It requires helping children make connections across the visual, spatial, aural, and kinesthetic domains and assisting them to use the symbol systems and artistic elements and modes of expression unique to each of the arts disciplines. We must start by thinking about what we do as teachers, and what affect this has on children, to enable us to achieve our objectives with as many children as possible, as often as possible.

SUMMARY

Multiliteracy encompasses a range of expressions and a variety of symbols and symbol systems, not just words, but also gesture, play, music, mime, and dance. In the broad sense, to be literate means to be well educated: being able to participate in rich, personal experiences and use signs or symbols to encode a variety of meanings. Artistic literacy is not just about using a set of isolated analytical skills linked to artistic elements; nor is it simply about associating artworks with personal experiences or stories. Full appreciation involves an awareness that comes from participating, *as artists,* in creative making and analytical viewing and listening—by communicating subtle aesthetic impressions and feelings, by thinking analytically about artistic processes and products, and by expanding our vocabulary to talk about the structural and expressive components of the arts. Regular exposure to the arts is critical in children's education, because aesthetic delight in the arts is a natural byproduct of comfort and familiarity with artworks.

The tangible, hands-on experience of making can be enhanced through the processes of presenting and responding. Indeed, these three processes are highly interconnected. Through making, children learn how to work within specific arts disciplines—they experience what it means to act and think like musicians, dancers, actors, and artists. Presenting works to others, through informal performances or exhibitions, provides opportunities for children to reflect on their own works as well as respond to the works of others. By responding to their own works and the masterworks of many cultures throughout history, children develop the skills of talking and thinking about the arts; they describe, analyze, interpret, judge, challenge, and value artworks and arts ideas and, in the process, develop aesthetic values of their own, along with an awareness that aesthetic values are culturally constructed.

Development of artistic literacy involves the ability to understand, use, and reflect on the elements within each discipline, such as color and shape in the visual arts, melody and rhythm in music, space and time in dance, and character and movement in drama. Artistic literacy is expressed through a variety of forms of expression within each of the disciplines (e.g., painting, singing, choreographing, and role play). There are similarities and differences in forms of expression, largely because they each draw upon different symbolic domains or modalities—visual, spatial, aural, bodily-kinesthetic, and inter- and intrapersonal. Yet there are many multimodal overlaps or connections within and across the arts disciplines, which help children make and interpret meaning through multimodal involvement in the arts. Artistic literacy involves grasping the meaning and structure of the arts, communicating meaning, and developing knowledge that stems from current knowledge, and leads to new knowledge. Making connections for young children can be enhanced through providing a balanced emphasis on the processes of making, presenting, and responding and assisting children to participate in all forms of artistic expression and symbolic domains, thus grasping the elements and concepts associated with the arts.

ADDITIONAL READINGS

Kindler, A. M., & Darras, B. (1994). Artistic development in context: Emergence and development of pictorial imagery in early childhood. *Visual Arts Research, 20* (2), 1–13.

Parsons, M. J. (1987). *How we understand art: A cognitive developmental account of the aesthetic experience.* Cambridge, UK: University Press.

Plummeridge, C. (1991). *Music education in theory and practice.* London: Falmer.

Wright, S. (1997). Learning how to learn: The arts as core in an emergent curriculum. *Childhood Education, 73* (6), 361–365.

PRACTICAL ACTIVITIES

1. Observe children making art, creating music, or engaging in dance or sociodramatic play. Make a list of the ways in which these arts experiences provided opportunities for children to:
   - Use their imagination and curiosity
   - Express their artistic ideas or discoveries
   - Demonstrate independent decision making
   - Bring a new product into existence
   - Become involved in experimentation, risk-taking, and flexibility

   Observe the teacher interacting with children while they are in the artistic process of *making.* Think about the ways in which the teacher:

   - Provided opportunities for the children to solve problems
   - Inspired children to develop an idea
   - Helped children make choices
   - Gave models and strategies to help children
   - Helped children practice and develop skills and techniques

- Assisted children to make decisions
- Developed children's artistic thinking processes
- Discussed artistic processes and products with the children

2. Observe children informally *presenting* their artworks, musical compositions, dances, or play experiences to other children. Make a list of the ways in which the children, with the assistance of the teacher, had opportunities to:
   - Participate in and respond to the presentation with enjoyment
   - Talk about what was going on in the music, artwork, dance, or drama
   - Talk about the technical, imaginative, and expressive processes of making
   - Talk about the aesthetic qualities of the end result (the product)
   - Support and praise the creative endeavor
   - Discuss ways of extending the ideas and approaches in further experiences

3. There are a number of excellent books designed to help children learn about the elements of the arts. Below is a list of some books pertaining to the visual arts. Compile as many of these books as possible and, alone or with classmates or friends, become familiar with their content.

   Blizzard, G. (1992). *Animals in art.* Charlottesville, VA: Thomasson-Grant.

   Blizzard, G. (1992). *Come look with me: Enjoying art with children.* Charlottesville, VA: Thomasson-Grant.

   Delafoss, C., & Jeunesse, G. (1993). *Portraits.* London: Moonlight.

   Fairclough, C. (1990). *What made this mark.* London: Franklin Watts.

   Micklethwait, L. (1994). *I spy: Animals in art.* New York: Collins.

   Wick, W. (1992). *I spy: A book of picture riddles.* New York: Scholastic.

   Woolf, F. (1989). *Picture this: The first introduction to paintings.* London: Doubleday.

   Yenawine, P. (1991). *Colors.* New York: Museum of Modern Art.

   List ways in which these books provide opportunities for children to directly view images and artworks, discuss what they see, and enhance literacy in the visual arts through:

   - Participating in rich, personal experiences that assist them to become well educated
   - Developing a vocabulary to engage in arts criticism and aesthetic judgment
   - Making links with other domains of understanding (aural, spatial, bodily-kinesthetic)
   - Enhancing children's understanding of cultural and historical aspects of art

   Reflect on what you have learned by looking at and reading these art books. Make a list of the following:

   - The visual arts elements that are featured
   - The language and examples used to describe and illustrate these elements to children
   - Practical ideas of ways to use these books with children to extend their learning through the processes of making, presenting, and responding

CHAPTER EIGHT

THE VISUAL ARTS

BY FELICITY McARDLE

Our father Adam sat under the tree and scratched with a stick in the mould;
And the first rude sketch that the world had seen was joy to his mighty heart.
Til the devil whispered behind the leaves, "It's pretty, but is it Art?"

—Rudyard Kipling, 1940, "The Conundrum of the Workshops"

The idea of teaching art with young children can evoke much discussion and debate about the value of art and its place in society and schools. Some people think that to teach art "properly," all you need to do is provide an attractive array of materials, a safe environment, and be a warm and loving person. Why would they think that, and how would you respond to such a claim? In this chapter, more encompassing concepts of teaching the visual arts will be considered in the light of theories and research that suggest that teachers' work is shaped by our ways of thinking and speaking about it—the ways we see, think, and speak about children, art, and teaching all contribute to the choices and decisions we make about how to teach art "properly" with young children.

Many exemplary teachers and artists insist that they do not *teach* art with young children—that it comes from the children, that the children simply explore, experiment, and express themselves. However, a close examination of these teachers' and artists' practices invariably shows them guiding, modeling, demonstrating skills and techniques, providing children with opportunities to practice and master skills, organizing, and enacting teaching in any number of ways. They just don't like to think or speak of their work as teaching! The work of these teachers and artists is described ironically as teaching without teaching (McArdle, 2001).

Questions about the nature and purpose of art have been vigorously addressed in many forums. As with all discourses, a conversation about what counts as art is informed by a number of views that have emerged or reappeared at different times, in different cultures and contexts. In some cultures, art is part of everyday life. In other cultures, art is viewed as a trim; it is seen as nonessential or even elitist. Yet art also can be considered a valuable commodity, attracting large amounts of money; to others, art is thought to be above commercial interests. Such differing views of the nature and purpose of art shape our beliefs about the place of art in the education of children.

In schools, art can be sidelined, left to Friday afternoons, or called upon only for special occasions, such as festivals or school celebrations. In addition, school art often can involve children in activities in which they are more acted upon, rather than being active participants in artistic processes. The message of such didactic approaches to the arts is that adults make the rules about how art should be done, and that young children are incompetent or incapable of making such artistic decisions themselves (Fucigna, Ives, & Ives, 1982). Ideally, children should be encouraged to be active participants in shaping their own directions while engaging in art—to take risks, explore, and create—while also learning to master artistic media and develop competence with the support of adults. Or is this what Valerie Walkerdine (1992, p. 16) refers to as an "impossible fiction"?

How much teaching should the teacher do in the arts? Should the children be left to express themselves without interference from the teacher? When is it right for the teacher to intervene? What is the best way for the teacher to help the child's developing artistry? Will too much interference damage children's artistry, or worse, damage their self-esteem? These are the types of questions that this chapter addresses.

The chapter begins by discussing current thinking of *why* we teach art in early childhood and *how* we can do this effectively. This segment focuses on ways in which teachers and children can work together to construct knowledge by creating, reading, and appreciating art. It focuses on ways in which the art program can be meaningful to children, while at the same time meet the expectations of the school, the parents, and the community. Practical strategies are provided for ways of setting up supportive learning environments and for assisting children to develop and extend their skills and ideas through multiple learning processes. Finally, methods for evaluating teaching and learning in art will be discussed.

WHY ART IS IMPORTANT FOR YOUNG CHILDREN

Before making decisions about *what* to include in our arts programs and *how* we will go about our work with the children, it is important to give some thought to *why* we make such decisions. Without some strong philosophical underpinnings, our visual arts programs could be simply a series of ad hoc activities or the slavish following of a formula.

Research in early childhood art education has enjoyed an increased amount of attention over the recent years (e.g., Bresler, 1994; Kindler, 1996; Matthews, 1999; Piscitelli, 1996; Thompson, 1995; Wright, 2000). A review of the literature shows multiple forces pulling in different directions, with policy statements emerging from the field of early childhood *and* the field of art education. Uncertainties are perpetuated in a number of common beliefs or myths about the nature of art, development, and creativity of young children (Kindler, 1996).

The complexity and diversity of influences that have shaped views on the teaching of art can be understood as a *palimpsest,* a term that describes the way in which the ancient parchments used for writing were written over, but new messages only partially obliterated the original message beneath. Both the new and the original messages still stand, albeit partially erased and interrupted (Davies, 1993). The next section of this chapter uses a palimpsest as a metaphor to uncover some of the ideas and influences that have shaped our taken-for-granted practices in art education. A reading of the numerous philosophies and practices of art education throughout our relatively recent history allows us to see familiar things in new ways. This new way of seeing enables the continuous exploration of new ideas in bids to improve practice, while recognizing that traces of previous thinking are not always completely obliterated but instead recur, shape, and interact with new developments.

At the site where a young child is learning about art, there are points where ideas about the child, art, and teaching meet, sometimes connecting, sometimes colliding, sometimes competing. The next segment of this chapter looks at the beliefs that have shaped our ways of seeing the child, art, and teaching. It will set the context for the discussion of the core areas of art—drawing, painting, and clay—how these media can enhance our understanding of children and the art media themselves and how we can scaffold young children's learning within these media.

Ways of Seeing the Child

Commonly held images or constructions of the young child shape and inform all aspects of early childhood—policy, practice, institutions—as well as relationships between teacher and child, parent and child, and child and child (Dahlberg, Moss, & Pence, 1999). Some possible readings of why we do what we do in our work with young children can be explained by examining different constructions of childhood (Dahlberg et al., 1999; James, Jenks, & Prout, 1998; Jenks, 1996; Stainton Rogers, 1992).

To reiterate some content discussed earlier in this book in relation to the arts in general, let us go a bit more deeply into how children have been viewed throughout time, particularly in relation to the visual arts. Early views of the child as *tabula rasa* or an *empty vessel* shape the belief that children's early artworks are fairly worthless scribbles. With this view, teaching art is seen to lead the children on a path of progress toward realism and representation. In contrast, the view of the child as *natural*—as inherently innocent and uncorrupted by the world—shapes the notion of precious childhood and the idea that this should be preserved at all costs. From this perspective, teaching art requires preserving child innocence and spontaneity and avoiding any form of intervention that might corrupt spontaneous creativity.

Other views are that children are *capricious,* with innate propensities to the wild and savage. The work of teaching is seen to be one of "civilizing" the child, and art activities are extremely teacher-directed, leaving no room for error, experimentation, or accidents. *Developmental theory* also frames childhood as universal stages of development, and the teaching of art is seen in relation to developmental continua, ages, and stages, and the provision of developmentally appropriate activities. In addition, the view of childhood as a supply factor in determining the future *labor force* causes art to become marginalized in the curriculum, so that a greater emphasis can be placed on the "basics" of literacy and numeracy. Art is validated largely on the basis of how well it can integrate with or enhance these "more important" curriculum areas.

More recent views of the child center on democratic principles, where children are seen to be *freely choosing individuals.* However, if *freedom* and *fun* are viewed as the essence of childhood, it is possible that teaching art will be considered useful only if it ensures that children are busy, happy, spontaneous, and free, rather than bored. The notion of children's working at skills and techniques in art may be seen as inconsistent with a philosophy of democratic freedom. Some contemporary early childhood educators advocate the view of children as *competent beings,* co-constructors of knowledge, and art can be taught as one of the multiple languages available to children without destroying the children's sense of freedom; in fact, such co-construction can enhance children's enjoyment of learning (Dahlberg et al., 1999; Edwards, Gandini, & Forman, 1994; Malaguzzi, 1993).

When we realize that many positions have appeared, remained, or disappeared, only to reappear in a different time or place throughout our history, we come to understand that we also participate in the shaping of current and future views of art education. Evolution of ideas requires us to adapt to change—to recognize the influence of current, modern influences on children's lives and how we can incorporate some of these positively into an art program. Childhood cultures, for example, are made up of interwoven narratives and commodities that cross TV, toys, fast-food packaging, video games, T-shirts, shoes, bed linen, pencil cases, and lunch boxes (Luke, 1995). Teachers and parents can often find their own cultural and linguistic messages losing power as they compete with global narratives—the passing phases of pop culture fashions. Pokemon replaced Power Rangers, which replaced Ninja Turtles, which replaced something else. Yet popular culture and the media are a part of children's cultures, and we need to depart from the idea that cultures and languages other than those of the mainstream are *deficit.* To be relevant, teachers and parents need to *recruit,* rather than ignore or erase the different interests, intentions, commitments, and purposes that children bring to learning (Cazden, Cope, Fairclough, et al., 1996). One example of such recruitment of the pop culture of childhood into the classroom is expressed in Figure 8.1.

FIGURE 8.1   Popular Culture and the Arts

Some years ago, a colleague saw an opportunity in the local craze for Teenage Mutant Ninja Turtles, when many around her were banning them from the classrooms. Rather than choosing to see the negative commercial effects on the children in her class and shaking her head over the violence, which purportedly had made its way into the children's play, she watched the show herself. All the turtles were named after famous artists (Michelangelo, Leonardo, Donatello, and Raphael), so she introduced the children to the artworks and life stories of these classical artists. The children were thus introduced to the language and literacy of the arts through their involvement with popular culture.

As discussed in this segment, how we see children will affect the way we teach. We may view children as empty vessels, natural, capricious, developing, or competent. At times, some or all of these views may exist simultaneously; at other times, one view may seem more relevant in certain circumstances or for particular reasons. Not only is our teaching affected by our views of childhood, it is also influenced by our views on art.

Ways of Seeing Art

There is a great deal of confusion currently about where art fits into society and what function it serves beyond that of a salable commodity. Teachers need to consider what it is we are referring to when we speak of art and whether our art programs are designed to produce a certain type of art (e.g., self-expressive, representational, experimental, skilled). As discussed in the previous section, the ways of seeing the child might lead us to provide children with art activities that are, for example, fun, busy, exploratory, messy, highly structured, or completely child-centered—*but is it art?*

Here is another opportunity for another palimpsest to assist a reflecting on the value of art in young children's lives. As with our views of childhood, some ideas about art persist, some disappear, and others reappear to find favor in a different place or a different time. As has been discussed throughout this book, there are many reasons why art should be a core of the curriculum for young children.

Art is considered by some a *fundamental biological* need, a need that defines our existence and the human condition (Dissanayake, 1992). Those who hold this view will encourage children to appreciate beauty and aesthetics within their surroundings. Art should be valued "for art's sake" because it is considered an important means for *self-expression*—spontaneity, imagination, play, experimentation, and lack of inhibition are desirable components of making artworks—and for freedom of expression. Art is also valued as an *emotional* mode for communicating unconscious things otherwise unsayable (Feldman, 1996) and for enhancing "healthy" personalities. Art also enhances children's *cognitive* processes, involving children in problem solving, thinking, and using symbol systems to record their thoughts, ideas, and feelings. In many ways, art offers a form of *spiritual* awareness as well, revealing itself through the heart and intuition (Barthes, 1972) and embodied or somatic ways of learning.

When we view art as a distinct *discipline,* with a distinct body of knowledge that must be taught and mastered, we are not frightened to teach skills and techniques, as well as appreciation and art history. We will see art as an important discourse that should not be offered only to the special or talented, but as a universal and special way of making and communicating meaning, both at a personal level and in a broader sense as well. Art is viewed by others as an expression of *culture,* and a means of communicating about and between *cultures,* through links with the community. Opportunities to read and appreciate the lives of others are possible through art. Some consider art a conduit for *understanding self in relation to others,* a means for recognizing our interdependence as peoples, and a way for global unity and understanding (Eckersley, 1992). One aspect of teaching art is to bring the child's view, as depicted through their art, to a wider audience.

Our view of teaching art involves applying critical lenses to our ideas of art and teaching. In many ways, the application of critical analysis is similar to coming to grips with postmodern art. Postmodern art depicts life's confusions and fragmentations and subverts our *ways of seeing*—it makes us look again, to make the familiar appear strange. Our work with young children is about ways of seeing as well. It requires us to recognize how many influences have shaped our views of art, such as whether we consider art to be therapy, spirituality, a form of individual self-expression, a language, a cultural artifact, a discipline to be mastered, an expression of freedom, and an essential part of being human. Like the numerous views of childhood, each view of art holds truths, and each has implications for how art is best taught. Consequently, the teaching of art should also be viewed in relation to our ways of seeing the teacher and the meaning of teaching.

Ways of Seeing the Teacher

What we decide to say to a child about his or her art, or what we choose to provide in the environment, will be contingent to some extent on a view of teaching and learning—a view of the role of the teacher in the education of children in and through art. What is considered "proper" art teaching is contingent on a number of factors, including our experience, our training, and the discourse of education (McArdle, 2001).

Current discourses of art education have been influenced by *progressivism* and democratic ideals, which include notions of child-centered and hands-on learning and freedom for the individual (Dewey, 1902, 1916; Tyler, 1993). *Creativity and problem-solving skills* are currently favored in the education discourse in many countries (Eckersley, 1992; Fowler, 1996). Active *discovery* has become closely linked with play, and one of the enduring mantras in early childhood literature is that children learn through play (Berk, 1997; Katz, 1996; Perry & Irwin, 2000). Multiple intelligences (Gardner, 1983) have become an accepted conceptual framework for teachers' work, and many believe art should hold a privileged position within the curriculum. Current notions of a *master/apprentice* model of teaching position the teacher as *protagonist,* working alongside children who are pursuing self-determined projects (Malaguzzi, 1993).

Currently, art is seen as a language, a symbol system, a literacy (Gardner, 1983). The Reggio Emilia schools, where children's symbolic representations are read as "visible thinking," have become world renowned as a model for early childhood education (Edwards et al., 1994). In addition, influences of discipline-based art education (Eisner, 1988) outline a curriculum approach made up of four components: art history, art criticism, aesthetics, and art production. This takes art education beyond an ad hoc approach to the learning of a discrete discipline. The push for *national standardization* in countries such as the United States, the United Kingdom, and Australia has placed art within one of the key learning areas, and syllabus documents for art provide a framework for planning and enacting the art program. Within such frameworks, teaching and learning are seen to occur not only in schools, but also in galleries, museums, and other *informal places* of learning as sites for assisting young children's developing artistry. Here, learning occurs through interactions between children and objects, children and their teachers, and children and other children.

In spite of all of these influencing factors on our beliefs about art teaching, it is interesting that the issue of "freedom above discipline" remains a dominant discourse of art when compared to other curriculum areas such as literacy or numeracy. How is it that freedom of the individual is equated with noninterventive practices in art, but not in learning areas such as literacy or numeracy? For example, teachers place great importance on the child's acquisition of reading and mathematics skills, but are frightened to offer learning activities that enhance children's competencies in artistic areas (Spodek & Saracho, 1992). While most early childhood educators believe it is the right of every child to be taught literacy and numeracy skills, they may not be as concerned about the right of every child to be visually literate. Can a child have fun while learning the skills and techniques necessary to developing artistry? Can children be free to express their own thoughts and feelings through drawing, painting, or modeling with clay, if they have no artistic skills to enable them to articulate this?

Faced with such inconsistencies and contradictions in the field of art education, teachers can be excused for throwing their arms in the air and sticking to the "tried and true" practices they have come to know and with which they feel a degree of certainty (Kindler, 1996). Yet in our work with young children, we have a responsibility to consider, reflect, and live with the multiplicities of planning a visual arts program. It is part of our work to be informed about current thinking and make informed decisions about quality art programs. A recent study of exemplary art teachers showed that these teachers find ways to combine seemingly opposing messages about "proper" teaching—they blur the boundaries between natural unfolding and guided learning and between creativity and the training of skills and techniques (McArdle, 2001).

The following section describes how individual children can be viewed as competent beings who know lots of things already and are wondering about lots of other new things. Through art, children invite us into their thoughts by communicating through words, drawing, painting, clay, and a number of related "languages" to express these (Edwards et al., 1994). It is our role to provide children with rich experiences, good-quality materials, and skills that will help them be lifelong learners and lifelong thinkers. Such art experiences are *not* about: "Follow the directions, stick this on here and that on there, now color it in, and now doesn't that look pretty?" Children should be encouraged to be thinkers and theorists, not merely learn to follow directions. Based on the children's ideas, we can prepare a structured art program that allows for the sharing of the power and responsibility and positions the *children as artists* and all that this view of children, art, and art teaching entails.

How We Can Assist Children's Learning in and through Art

It is quite appropriate to assist children's learning in and through art and to ensure that children are equipped with the skills and techniques to enable them to express their own ideas better than they might do on their own. When we have a sound theoretical background and philosophical foundation for art education, we will be continually reflecting and revising what we do with young children. We will bring expertise to our work, provide plentiful and good quality resources, and plan the learning environment so that children will be enabled to learn within it. While syllabus documents can provide guidelines for content, skills, knowledge, techniques, and outcomes, we must ensure that the children remain at the center of the curriculum and that exploration, discovery, and play remain central to the child's experience.

Symbol making and symbol understanding are central to the program. Product-centered craft activities that use adult-designed templates will not allow children to develop and use symbolic representations. Likewise, art activities that change daily or weekly do not provide opportunities for children to consistently use core art media and processes for the purposes of symbolic development and meaning making. Hence, drawing, painting, and working with clay should be the core areas of our art programs and be

FIGURE 8.2   The Elements and Principles of the Visual Arts

Line: Thick, thin, wavy, straight, soft, hard, vertical, horizontal, diagonal, radiating, jagged, parallel, angry, calm, happy, sad

Shape: Geometric, organic, rectangle, square, circle, round, angular, curvy, fluid, symmetrical, spiral

Color: Primary, secondary, complementary, warm, cool, light, dark, bright

Texture: Rough, smooth, bumpy, fuzzy, prickly, slippery

Space: Two-dimensional, three-dimensional, real, illusions, foreground, middle ground, background, overlap. Space is related to *compositional* aspects within two-dimensional work, and *form* within three-dimensional work

Structural Principles: Unity, rhythm, proportion, design, balance, harmony, contrast, repetition

offered daily, so that children come to understand and use these media for cognitive and expressive purposes. Other art media or forms of expression, such as collage, construction, printmaking, constructing, and textiles, also can enrich the program, but painting, drawing and claywork should be offered daily.

Learning in and through the visual arts involves participating with and understanding basic elements and principles of art. These provide a vocabulary for teachers and children and a way of helping both to talk about their own processes, products, and the works of other artists. To review content from Chapter 7, children's engagement with the forms of learning in art—drawing, painting, printing, constructing, modeling, and sculpting—all involve the use and understanding of the following elements and principles within the visual-spatial domain of artistic learning (Figure 8.2).

The first segment of this chapter provided a framework for understanding the *why* aspects of art education in relation to our views of children, art, and teaching. This framework will now be applied in a deeper discussion of the three core media of the art program.

DRAWING

The Child

Children's discovery that they have the power to make marks is a significant point in their developing communication. For toddlers, making marks is an extension of their hand and arm movements, and they gradually learn to

FIGURE 8.3   Noah's Ark by Greta Smart, Age Four, Using Campfire Charcoal

have some control over where these marks occur, what shape they take, and the subtle and significant differences that they can control (Matthews, 1994a). Drawing is the easiest medium for children to master and quickly enables children to explain things with precision and detail. Children can make their thinking visible through drawing, and use it to make plans, theorize, and tell stories (see Figure 8.3).

The age of children can sometimes be a guide to their drawing capabilities, although children vary greatly, and their artistry is contingent on a number of other factors as well, such as the particular art medium being used, their personal experience with this medium, their family and cultural background, and their preferred style of learning. Making their own marks can be an empowering experience for children, and they rejoice in the beauty and uniqueness of their own art. In addition, children want to improve but, as has been discussed, their improvement will not occur "naturally," in a vacuum, or on its own.

Various researchers have observed developmental stages in children's drawing, through close scrutiny of children's work. Generally, continua move through age and stage benchmarks, beginning with scribbles and progressing to representation and realism (Kellogg, 1969; Matthews, 1994a). Other researchers have challenged the developmental assumptions and practices that have evolved from existing age-related frameworks. Ashton (1997), for instance, proposed new terms for describing changes in drawings in terms of *styles*, based on her observations that young artists return to different styles, such as scribbling, when their art calls for it.

Drawing is a cognitive process, and the mind is connected to the mark. The process of drawing requires concentration and problem solving. Although the symbol systems in drawing are not clear cut as they are, say, in music, where a specific notation system is available, nevertheless, when a child draws a house or a princess, he or she uses symbols to represent. Yet children are not always aiming to achieve realism when they draw. As Kolbe points out, the drawing is only part of the activity (Kolbe, 2001, p. 43). She insists that children know far more than they can represent in their drawing. If, for example, we are not present for the gestures, words, and sounds, we can miss much of the meaning of the child's art.

Respect for children means allowing them time to grow and explore and experiment with materials; in the case of drawing, this includes paper, pencils, felt-tip pens, crayons, chalk, and other mark-making materials (Seefeldt, 1995). Children should not be hurried or pressured into representing ideas or feelings through art. Toddlers will want to explore materials; to enjoy feeling, tasting, and playing with crayons; to scribble and mess around; to discover their power to make marks. Older children will also need time to explore various prototypes and to problem solve in relation to their depiction of objects and events, both literally and metaphorically (see Chapter 6).

We should not expect children to be immediately interested in what they produce (Seefeldt, 1995). When they have had the time to explore and gain control over the tools, they will use them to express ideas and feelings. If preschoolers or even older children (beginners of any age) have not been allowed the time to explore and experiment, they will need time to play with the materials before they can be expected to represent their ideas and feelings through art.

Respect for children also applies when providing them with materials. Which would you prefer to draw with: old motley crayons, or new, brightly colored felt-tip pens? Used paper with print on one side, or large, clean, good-quality paper? We should aim to provide the best that our budget can afford.

The Art

Lines are one of the basic elements of drawing. Lines can be thick or thin, jagged, smooth, sharp, soft, twirling, feathery, short, or long. Different drawing tools allow different lines. Lines can intersect, radiate, run parallel, or wander, and when they join up, they form shapes. Lines can also create texture through the use of techniques such as dotting, rubbing with the side of a crayon, or contrasting different marks through the use of different art tools—crayons, chalk, felt-tip pens, or charcoal.

Drawing and painting are often connected, although they are also very different. But many painters do preliminary drawings as studies for their paintings, and many artists keep visual diaries and draw every day as part of their discipline and craft. Drawing allows people of all ages opportunities to capture and record details. Young children engage in problem solving that often requires enormous concentration as they draw. They first think of something that is not present, devise a means of representing it through a symbol system, and often work out how to depict a three-dimensional object on a flat piece of paper. Such drawing involves imagination and visual memory and the ability to symbolize ideas and feelings.

But visual stimulation can also occur through drawing from observation. Observation-based drawing once was thought too difficult for young children and was considered possibly stifling for young children's self-expression and creativity. Drawing through observation was considered the reserve of serious art students. However, many early-childhood educators now offer this activity regularly to young children. Children learn to look closely at things, and these drawings are very different from those that children do from memory or imagination. Even for a skilled drawer, observation drawing is much more than copying what we see. The choice is in the detail, in what each person "sees."

While the holistic nature of children's learning is reason for integrating the arts with other curriculum areas, there are those who argue for "Art for art's sake" and call for art to be preserved as a distinct discipline, with a unique body of knowledge, skills, techniques, and attitudes. For instance, an appreciation for the art of drawing can begin with a look at the earliest cave drawings. In addition, using contemporary examples of drawing as a source for children's learning, we can draw upon artists such as Picasso, who was prolific in the media of drawing. The class library could include art books with reproductions of his and other artists' drawings, such as Beardsley and Matisse. Children will also be interested in Leonardo da Vinci's notebooks and inventions, architects' drawings, botanists' drawings, and medical drawings. All of these provide windows into the artists' thinking, planning, and ways of seeing. Children's picture books about drawing or those that contain quality drawings as illustrations within the book can also be useful additions on the bookshelf (see examples at the end of Chapter 7).

Teaching

When children say they don't know how to draw something, they often mean "I don't know where to start" (Kolbe, 2001). Talking with children about what they wish to draw, looking at photographs, or looking at how other artists have attempted to solve similar visual problems will often be enough to get children started.

To take the alternative route of asking children to complete patterned artwork or to color in adult models of shapes shows no respect for children's ideas and capabilities. It also gives children a message that their own art is inadequate. This is not to say that children require no intervention in their developing artistry. Teachers have an active role to play here. Children always want to improve their drawing skills, and they recognize and admire those among them who they consider "good drawers." To ignore or refuse their requests for help goes against the work of teaching in any curriculum area, including art.

There are a number of strategies for assisting children with their drawing, without drawing for them, or feeding their insecurity about believing they cannot draw. Talking them through the steps of drawing might be enough. With other children, sometimes it is not necessary to talk with them as they draw; our presence, appreciation, listening, and watching may be enough encouragement. Modeling is another effective strategy for assisting children to draw. This will involve drawing with the children, talking about what we are seeing and thinking, and using the vocabulary of art, such as "Now this leaf goes out to the side, so I need a long line going across the page here. The line for the stem joins the leaf here. I can use short, sharp little lines to show that the leaf is furry." Through such processes, we show children our concentration, our attempts, our mistakes, and our willingness to try again. Drawing should not be a one-time, succeed-or-fail exercise. We all learn to draw by drawing, and the more we draw, the better we get.

One teacher, Bob Steele (Steele, 2002), devised a program of daily drawing, over a thirty-day period, to illustrate to children how their drawing can improve with practice. At a regular time, say, mornings or after lunch, the young children drew for ten minutes, nominating whether they would be doing a drawing from imagination, memory, or observation. They began by all talking as a group about what they were going to draw. At the end of each session, they looked at each other's drawings, kept them in a folder, and nominated what they would be drawing the next day. At the end of the thirty days, the children were delighted with their own progress and development. In addition, they learned the pleasures and rewards of practice, and they learned about critique and appreciation of their own and others' work. As teachers, we might try this ourselves. By drawing every day for ten or fifteen minutes, we can observe our own development over thirty days and, in the process, learn a variety of techniques and skills that will enhance our aesthetic visual-spatial expression through a fulfilling and reinforcing experience.

The thirty-days-of-drawing program also illustrates another point. Children do not get bored with using the same material over and over again. Indeed, some adult artists use the same materials for decades; what changes is their ways of seeing. Children have an endless supply of exciting ideas, interests, thoughts, feelings, and things to say. They take great pleasure and satisfaction in refining their skills and in communicating their ideas and feelings. In fact, if there were absolutely no other resources available, we could still provide children with a dynamic art program through drawing alone.

We must make a space for drawing within the daily early childhood curriculum, where children know they can go regularly for pens, pencils, crayons, paper, scissors, tape, and glue, and master the use of the resources through regular exposure and practice. It is best to begin with only a small choice of drawing materials so that children are not overwhelmed. Quality is important, and the materials should be attractive. Throw out dried pens and dirty crayons. Collect photographs, postcards, books, and found objects for inspiration. Provide magnifying glasses for curious observers. Take children on drawing excursions. Use charcoal from a campfire for variety in drawing. Play art games, such as going for a line walk, looking for the lines all around us in the garden, on the street, and in many areas of the community. Take photos and make a line book. Figure 8.4 provides an example of how one artist who works with children, both in schools and in private studio classes outside school hours, introduces children to drawing. Raquel Redmond takes a pen and a large sheet of paper, and as she draws she tells the story of Mr. Line.

FIGURE 8.4   An Example of How to Introduce Children to Drawing

Mr. Line goes out for a walk. First, he walks across the road and straight to the corner (lines can be straight and diagonal). Then he has to turn the corner and go up the hill (lines can go up the page). Now Mr. Line is feeling a little dizzy, and goes around in a circle (a line encloses a shape). This makes Mr. Line very angry (lines can convey emotion) . . . and so on.

The syllabus documents summarize the requirements of the educational institution and generally include sections on content, product, outcomes, skills, resources, and evaluation. Reflective art teachers refer to these documents and use them as guideposts for their curriculum planning and for their own accountability, all the while ensuring that the child is at the center of the emergent curriculum. For instance, the early expectations will be that children explore line and shape through drawing, and then transfer this understanding of familiar lines and shapes to experiments with different drawing materials. Using the syllabus as a guide can be helpful as a checking device, ensuring that our program is focused on specific skills, techniques, processes, and content. The syllabus documents are also valuable in assisting us in evaluation and assessment, providing signposts for focussed observations.

PAINTING

The Child

Just as children discover the power in making their own marks through drawing, they also are enthralled by the transformation that paint can make on a piece of paper. They delight in discovering color, texture, and properties of paint, how it spreads across the page, how it drips off the brush and can be transferred from the pot to the paper, and many other techniques (see Figures 8.5 and 8.6). The sensuous experience of paint is the first pleasure children derive from their earliest experiences with painting. This mark-making capacity is similar to drawing in that it is two-dimensional and connects seeing and moving. But children's paintings rarely show the same detail as their drawings. Working with a paintbrush is very different from working with a pen, and painting involves a different kind of thinking (Kolbe, 2001, p. 53).

Children take great delight in paint, in its feel and its color. Toddlers even need to taste it. Hence it is important to use nontoxic products! Finger painting is often a child's first introduction to painting, although it offers less scope for creating images and exploring ideas (Kolbe, 2001, p. 53). While drawing begins as an easy extension of the hand and arm movements, painting adds another dimension. The child needs to develop a concept of tools and tool use (Smith, 1993). At first, learning to hold a brush, dip it into a pot of paint, take it out, and transfer the paint onto paper is an exciting challenge for children. Later, they recognize that the marks they make can carry meaning, make shapes, and represent thoughts and ideas. But sometimes, children might just be playing with the paint and see their work and the work of others as essentially being about the use of paint, as illustrated in Figure 8.7.

The properties of paint mean that the space on the paper can be transformed through color. New colors can appear as paint is blended, and patterns

FIGURE 8.5   Painting of a Digger in the Sandpit, Four-Year-Old Artist

can be made by techniques such as repeating marks in rows or circles. Young children often paint a rainbow, for example, or a series of identical objects or figures side by side, when they try out all the colors on offer.

Developmental stages provide a broad picture of children's development in painting (Smith, 1993). Toddlers, for example, are more likely to be absorbed in the process itself, and gradually discover they can make shapes, add dots, dabs, extra colors, and fill in spaces inside or between shapes. As with drawing, older children will use the medium of painting as a means for

FIGURE 8.6   Painting after Talking about Shape, Color, and Positioning

FIGURE 8.7   Painting Is about Using Paint

We once took a group of five-year-olds on a visit to the art gallery, where an exhibition of the works of Emily Kngwarreye was showing. She is a renowned indigenous Australian artist, whose prolific works featured thick application of paint, sometimes with traditional dot painting, sometimes with swirling and intersecting lines, sometimes with vibrant patterns and shapes. The children were delighted by Emily's paintings and talked excitedly about the features that caught their attention and imagination. We asked one of our visitors, Isaac, what he thought the exhibition was about, and he replied, "It's about paint" (Piscitelli, McArdle, & Weier, 1999).

expressing and interpreting objects and events literally and metaphorically, through symbolic representation. A familiarity with these developmental stages can provide a useful framework for observations of children, although always with the awareness that all children are different and their previous use of and experience with particular media will influence how they capture their thoughts and feelings.

For example, it was once thought that the best practice was to give only large brushes to toddlers, because of their limited motor skill development. However, anyone who has observed a baby picking up a tiny crumb or a stray Lego piece from the floor will know that "the younger the child, the larger the brush" dictum does not hold. Children should be provided with a variety of materials and tools that will enable them to communicate in a variety of ways. Sometimes children enjoy working on miniature pictures. Consequently, they should not be restricted always to working big and bold.

The Art

Van Gogh is always a favorite artist with the first-grade children I teach. They are delighted with his thick paint, the brush lines, and the bright yellows. But I suspect that a lot of Van Gogh's appeal comes also from the colorful story of his life. Whenever we talk about the paintings of Van Gogh, somebody invariably comes up with the story of him cutting off his ear, and from that point on, children become fascinated with his paintings. Patrick, a first-grade boy, looked at Van Gogh's painting of the bedroom and commented, "It looks like a cartoon." When asked to explain further, he pointed out the black lines around the edge of the chair and bed and then said that he thought the chair looked "wonky"—he was able to express that the image of the chair was affected by its position in space relative to its negative or background space.

Picasso is another favorite with children, and they often laugh with delight when they first see one of his paintings. I feel certain that this would make Picasso happy to see the children's reactions to some of his works. Children are capable and confident when it comes to reading paintings and are fascinated to see how other artists have tackled the task. Sometimes it is the techniques that interest them; at other times it is the subject matter or the story. They will easily talk about how a painting makes them feel and will frequently make a profound statements about what they see in a work. Bianca, another six-year-old child, reacted to a painting of a farmyard produced by the artist Edward Hicks (c. 1846), which featured predominantly sepia tones, by saying that it "was an olden days painting." I asked her what made her think that, and she replied, "Because it's got olden days colors." Isobel looked at a painting of David Hockney's that is mostly the blue water of a swimming pool. She said, "When I look at that, I think that if I had a headache, which I do have right now, well, when I jumped into that pool, my headache would go away."

There is much that children can learn about color and its expressive potential through painting. Young children learn through making paintings, but also by looking, talking, and appreciating their own and other children's and adult's paintings. The color wheel is a useful tool for helping us understand how to assist children's learning about color through painting. Color theory is about primary, secondary, and complementary colors, and the psychological-emotional associations with the warm/cool, bright/dark, and contrasting/complementary effects that are achieved through the placement of colors in relation to each other. Colors can be descriptive, as when representing the features of a landscape. They also can be expressive and metaphoric when used to evoke feelings and emotions. Colors also can be symbolic when they involve "stand for" concepts that are linked to our own and other cultures, such as when purple is used to symbolize royalty. For a comprehensive description of color theory, see Itten (1973).

Texture, pattern, line, shape, balance, and composition can all be explored through painting. In addition, children can learn an appreciation of other cultures, through studying their art. The ritual of body painting, for instance, fascinates young children. The traditional forms of painting of indigenous Australians, or works from China, Japan, and Africa, or the religious icons from Eastern European countries, can all have much to say about culture, and can teach children about difference, style, and the power of art to convey more than a literal story.

Teaching

Children need time to master the use of the paintbrush, which will enable them to communicate ideas, thoughts, and feelings. With all this to learn in and through painting, there is no need to offer gimmicks, such as painting with novel implements. Lyn Bryant works with early childhood professionals and suggests that to replace the brushes with straws, dish mops, balloons, marbles, or string is like saying, "I'm teaching you to read, but I think you might be a bit bored with letters and words now, so this week, you cannot use letters and words. I want you to use only kitchen utensils to help you learn to read." As ridiculous as this analogy seems, it points out the children's need for time and repeated opportunities to work with brushes. It is also important that they use quality brushes of various sizes.

When painting is offered every day, very young children can learn how to care for the resources. Provide paints in pots, paint trays with separate compartments, or on lids (solid tempera paint blocks also can be provided for fine detail work using small brushes). Make sure there is clean water available for rinsing brushes, and teach children about using palettes for mixing, and about keeping the paint clean for future use. Easel painting can be set up each day, and alternatives can include table painting or floor setup. Cover surrounding areas with plastic if cleaners are likely to be concerned (but cleaners should not dictate your arts program). Some teachers like the children to wear protective smocks; others leave it to the child to choose. Children need to learn the routines of cleaning up, caring for brushes, and drying their works—this is all part of understanding the artistic process. If they do not learn to do this, we will find ourself cleaning up long after we should have finished for the day, and we will incur the wrath of the cleaner. Endless cleaning up has every possibility of leading us to think twice about offering painting as a daily part of our program.

As mentioned earlier in relation to drawing, watching children as they paint can reveal many aspects of children's art that would not be communicated through the painting alone. To illustrate that children draw on knowledge that they incorporate into their own work, one observation of a child after the first-grade class had been talking about the Impressionists' paintings revealed how Stephen drew upon aspects of Impressionism while painting collaboratively with two other children on a large piece of paper on the floor. He was about to finish when he exclaimed, "Oooh, I forgot to do my dots!" and then began singing, "Put a dot over here and a dot over there," as he dotted color in different places on the painting. As this example illustrates, sometimes the subject of children's work can be easily read or can be discovered through dialogue about the work after it has been completed. However, our *presence* is often necessary to understanding the child's intent, processes, and thoughts.

As another example of this, Cameron was carefully exploring color and shape, gradually covering one layer of color with another, until he had built a painting that had all the appearances of a dark, meaningless blob. In the afternoon, his mother had no way of reading this painting, until the teacher was able to share her observations of the process. For Cameron, the moment had passed and asking him about his painting would possibly have not elicited much of a response. In fact, he might have felt obliged to make up a story about his learning process or product. As in Cameron's artwork, it is important to remember that not all paintings tell stories; sometimes they are just "about paint," about the sensory and aesthetic aspects of working in color, texture, line, and composition.

To give children permission to explore such abstract, expressive, and nonstory based forms of creating, we can play movement games about paint, where the focus may be simply on dripping, spreading, dabbing, swirling, and building up layers. There are other techniques we can use to help children become aware of spatial aspects of their visual communication. Raquel Redmond, for example, has children get up and move under the table, around the table, and between two tables to discover spatial relationships between objects and how these can be perceived from different perspectives. She draws the children's attention to the space they have moved in and then points out how artists attempt to represent that space, using overlap and the principles of perspective. Before trying to represent space on paper, the children have felt and experienced that space. Such respect for children involves aiming to see their art from their perspective and to give them new perspectives of seeing.

Respect also involves taking care with children's paintings. A drying rack is best for their wet paintings, as it prevents drips. But drying racks can be expensive. Alternatives may include indoor laundry lines, flat bench spaces, or pegging paintings on a line strung across a part of the room. Adequate space should be available for the children to manage the care of their own work. In addition, thoughtful display of children's paintings gives them the message that their work is valued. We can enlist parents' help in preparing cardboard frames to enhance the visual display of children's paintings. We should aim to avoid haphazard hanging of their work in a clutter all over the room. In addition, names or titles that children give their works should be provided on separate labels, and the name of the artist should be written on the back of the painting. If the child wants you to scribe a story about his or her work, we should think of this as the artist's statement and write it on a separate piece of paper. Writing words on children's paintings, drawings, or other artworks ruins the aesthetic and can give the message that pictures are all well and good, but *real* communication and shared meaning occurs best through words. Consequently, techniques such as those described above should be used, or alternatively, we might use overhead transparencies as overlays on the children's work and write words on these if the children request. This way, the paintings and drawings have not been written on, and the overlay can be removed to retain the unblemished state of the original work.

If children say they don't know what to paint, rather than telling them what to paint, we might suggest that they just play with the paint and see what ideas come into their heads. We might also ask if they would like to do another painting to discover different ideas. Repetition often provides valuable learning opportunities and can be very satisfying.

We should also aim to collect postcards, prints (old calendars are a good source for these), and books about artists and ensure that children have easy access to these stimulating resources as sources of inspiration for their own works. In addition, we can plan visits to the art gallery and invite artists to come and work with the children. When children study the illustrations in picture books and discuss the techniques used by the illustrator, they are using the vocabulary of art. The work of Eric Carle, for instance, provides a starting point for much discussion about his use of paint, texture, overlap, and shape (Weier, 2000; Wolf, 1990). Figure 8.8 illustrates how a first-grade child's painting was influenced by the traditional painting styles of indigenous Australian artists, after visiting the art gallery and viewing a variety of such works.

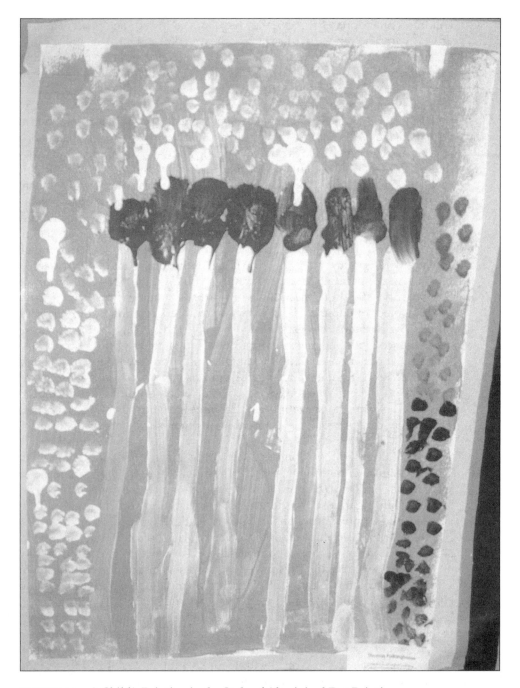

FIGURE 8.8   A Child's Painting in the Style of Aboriginal Dot Painting

CLAY

The Child

Like drawing and painting, claywork enables children to make their ideas visible. But with clay, they can make three-dimensional images. Clay interests and absorbs children, and they show unflagging desire to work with clay as a material for three-dimensional forms and, if relevant, to tell stories about objects and events (Kolbe, 1993). Very young children's first experience of clay is sensory, like their first finger-painting experiences. They delight in the process and the feeling of working with clay and discover its properties and how these can be used for expressive purposes. Children learn that they can put their mark on clay, making it change (Clemens, 1991).

Children begin by touching, poking, pinching, squeezing, rolling, patting, and pulling. Eventually they learn how to roll balls and make coils. They do this over and over again (Kolbe, 1993, p. 66). They may make stories with clay, make patterns and arrangements, or pile pieces on top of each other. The properties of clay allow children to make objects that stand alone, while sculpting, molding, and pulling shapes out of the clay itself.

Children who worry that they don't know what to make can be encouraged to play with the clay and discover its possibilities. Someone invariably makes a nest with eggs, and then all the children will make the ubiquitous nests and eggs for a while. But if the children learn to experience the touching and squeezing, patting and feeling, then ideas will emerge, and it can be exciting for children to discover that they can extend their symbol-making and visual language into three-dimensional form.

The Art

Clay is a material fundamental to the human species (Clemens, 1991). It is not the same as play dough or plasticine, which have similar qualities, but are less basic to people, historically and functionally. Clay has additional qualities and can be worked on a bigger or smaller scale. Humans have used clay for thousands of years to make utensils for eating and vessels for holding liquids. It is easy to show children examples of beautiful earthenware pieces (Koster, 1999). We can collect and display pieces from various countries and cultures and bring in dishes, cups, and bowls for use in dramatic play. Providing children with opportunities to see, touch, and appreciate collections of exquisite bowls, plates, and other pieces of pottery helps them become sensitive to the forms, colors, patterns, and textures of these artworks.

While children are creating clayworks and telling stories with clay, they are learning about form: mass, size, height, weight, texture, and shape, as well as structure and balance. They learn to make balls, coils, bridges, columns, and flat slabs. If they are not distracted too early by the use of clay tools and cutters, they quickly acquire skills of twisting, rolling, squeezing, bending, and flattening. They acquire a language of hands (Kolbe, 2001, p. 22).

Clay is a natural material and is an ideal entry into appreciation and the aesthetics of the natural world. Such appreciation can be enhanced by displaying collections of pebbles, shells, twigs, and seeds, and by viewing and appreciating other interesting shapes and patterns from nature. These materials will stimulate curiosity and provide endless inspiration for children. It is not necessary to make something with found materials—often it is enough simply to display, view, and appreciate them (Kolbe, 2001, p. 23). However, there may be times in which children will want to incorporate such objects into other artworks, such as collages and constructions.

Sculptures and carved forms may tell stories that can be simple or complex. The works of artists such as Henry Moore, which often incorporate objects from nature to depict fantasy creatures or characters, can appeal to children's imaginations and add to their knowledge and appreciation of form. Many indigenous cultures used clay and other sculpting materials, often as totems or religious symbols of great significance. An appreciation of these artworks can be an entry into the understanding of these and other cultures.

Teaching

If possible, we should help children find clay in the garden or in other sites nearby and dig it out so that children can see that clay is a natural resource in our environment. In addition, commercially available clay, which is inexpensive and usually prepared for adult artists, should be provided for children, as it has a pleasing texture and provides many opportunities for artistic exploration. Varieties of clay, such as terra cotta or buff raku, are appropriate for young children's use. Some teachers prefer a mixture of clay and paper pulp. This paper clay earthenware has all the qualities of clay, can be fired, but dries without the brittleness of terra-cotta clays. It can be coated with a layer of PVA glue and children can decorate their pieces with paint or pens. Their objects will keep without the need for glazes and firing.

Occasionally, some children will be reluctant to explore clay if they do not know what to do or what to explore. We can assist children by suggesting that they take a piece and squeeze it, and then ask them "Look at the shape. Does it remind you of anything? How could you change it?" Work on a flat, nonabsorbent surface, like laminate, cloth-covered boards, or plastic. If the weather is suitable, work outside on boards, trays, or a table. Have children work in smocks or protective shirts if they seem to be inhibited by the thought of getting dirty. Provide a bucket of warm, soapy water for children to wash their hands if they have an adverse response to dry clay on their skin or under their fingernails.

Children need to learn to care for and store the clay. Begin by putting out fist-sized balls and teach children to return the clay to this size when they have finished. The clay should be stored in an airtight container and kept moist with a damp cloth. When clay appears to be turning a bit dry and hard, which makes it difficult for children to use, make a small indentation in the clay ball and add water to the hole before storing it in the airtight container. Provide a small dish of water at the table, but teach the children that too much water makes the clay unworkable. A damp cloth is useful for wiping fingers. The routine for cleaning up should include sweeping the dry clay crumbs to the middle of the table and then sweeping them up. Remember, never flush clay particles down the sink. When the table is relatively free of dry clay, children can then wipe over the work surface with a wet cloth or sponge.

Clay is inexpensive, and once children learn the routines of cleaning up both the area and themselves, it is a simple matter for the teacher to make this experience available daily. Make an area for drying pieces and also for storing unfinished pieces (cover these with plastic wrap to prevent drying). Clay works that have been displayed and dried can be reconstituted if the children desire, by breaking the pieces up on a dry cloth and pouring the dried pieces and clay powder into a bucket, adding water, and allowing the dry clay to absorb the water over time.

Watch and listen as the children work the clay and talk with them about the qualities of the clay and the processes these use as they work with the medium. Use words such as pinch, pat, pound, roll, squeeze, shape, and mold. Use arts vocabulary and talk about the elements of line, shape, texture, size, and form. Sometimes we will need to teach children some skills and techniques to ensure satisfaction with their efforts. For instance, they will need to learn about pinching pieces together to make joins and using slip.

The science of clay and its changes in form is fascinating to young children. They will be interested in understanding the process of firing and the importance of working the clay and ensuring that no pockets of air remain, which will lead to explosions in the kiln. If possible, take children to a local potter and let them see the kiln firing their pieces. In addition, the local high school may have a kiln in its art department that they might let you use occasionally. Children also enjoy the process of recycling reconstituted dry clay works that have not been fired.

Take photographs of both the children's processes and their products. Documenting the children's work in this way shows the children and their parents that this work is valued. In addition, if children understand that they don't have to keep every piece for drying, they may feel more inclined to experiment with less regard for always making an end product. They will delight in the process of making an object, returning the clay to a formless lump, and making something completely different. This is not only a part of the artistic process, but is also early exploration of the mathematical concept of conservation.

OTHER ART MEDIA

In addition to drawing, painting, and clay, children should be given opportunities to express their thoughts and feelings through other visual arts media, such as textiles, blocks, woodwork, collage, and box construction. If we have a particular interest or passion for any one medium, we should teach this. Ultimately, teachers teach about passion and interest. Whatever the medium, three principles are applicable to learning in and through art (Schiller, 1995):

1. Children need many opportunities to create art.
2. Children need many opportunities to look at and talk about art.
3. Children need to become aware of art in their everyday lives.

Just as with other areas of the art curriculum, experiences with textiles and other art media requires careful planning. Raquel Redmond is an artist who regularly works as an artist-in-residence in lower primary classes. She describes her planning with textiles, for example, in the following way:

> The children are going to be working with textiles, and we are going to make windsocks for an upcoming festival. First, I think the activity through, and I try it out myself. That way, I can anticipate a number of problems that may arise. For instance, I have to cut the base cloth that each of the children will be starting with to fit the size of their individual desks in the classroom. If I don't do this, and their pieces are too big, it will just end up in a mess. The children will not be able to manage, and it will not work out. The experience will end in failure, and there is no pleasure for the children. You must be prepared and know how to solve problems that will arise. If you don't have the materials, and if you haven't prepared them, your art experience will not be a success. It is a waste of everyone's time.

What will this look like in practice? The next segment provides an example of many of the principles discussed in the chapter in relation to good practice.

AN EXAMPLE OF GOOD ART PRACTICE

First-grade children were required in the syllabus to work with the concept of the environment, and they had been addressing issues of pollution and care for the environment in social studies and science. The arts seemed a perfect integrating device, and we began by making a mind map of their thoughts about the environment. A number of areas of the environment emerged as special interests from this exercise, such as their own classroom, secret spots they knew of in the schoolyard, their own favorite places, bedrooms, and making houses for their Barbie dolls.

We did some research on each of these areas within the discipline of art, by looking through artists' books, as well as architects' magazines, and *National Geographic* magazines. One particular artist who interested the children was Andy Goldsworthy, whom we had accessed through a large book in the library, *Wood* (1996). The children were amazed by Goldsworthy's works, and we talked about his techniques and his use of lines, shapes, colors, and textures. We also talked about how he used natural materials that were not meant to last, and how the artist knew that nature would reclaim his work. This stimulated a discussion about how he must feel about nature. We read how he wanted to make people look again at the beauty around them, but that it did not matter to him that some of his work only lasted a very short time. The children found this a new and fascinating way to think of art. They were used to their works going up on walls or the refrigerator at home, rather than seeing art as something for the moment.

One day when the children arrived at school, there was a letter from the fairies, complaining about how the older children were running through the garden and asking if the children could please help to look after the place where they lived. We went looking for the fairies' houses and decided that they must live in the Wishing Tree, a special tree on the school grounds. This tree had been struck by lightning some years ago, and a new fig tree grew up from the middle of the old trunk.

We went down to the Wishing Tree, and the children did drawings from observation. They walked around the tree and touched its bark, putting fingers in the deep ruts that had formed in the old trunk. We talked about how the tree felt, the holes in the trunk, the shape at the base of the tree, the shape of the top of the tree, and its colors. Children sat around the tree with drawing boards and worked on their drawings for well over twenty minutes. Then we talked about what Andy Goldsworthy might have done with this tree. This inspired the children to work further on their drawings of the Wishing Tree, adding imaginary features and special decorations.

The children spent the next couple of days collecting items to incorporate into the decorating of the Wishing Tree, such as leaves, twigs, grass, and flowers, and we devised ways of sorting these objects by color, size, texture, and other properties. Then on Friday we all went down to the tree, and the children started their decorating. In the course of this, they encountered problems: The children who were putting large pieces of wood on top to make a structure were damaging the work of those decorating the crevices around the bottom of the tree. We stopped occasionally and problem-solved these dilemmas.

Eventually, the tree had a large pyramid structure on the top. Some of the large holes had beds of grass and leaves. One boy built a little bridge structure across one of the gaps, using thin twigs. The tiny cracks in the tree were filled with brightly colored flowers and leaves. Then we stood back, made a circle around the tree holding hands, and walked around the tree. Helen said it looked like a birthday tree and felt the urge to sing, so we all sang "Happy Birthday" to the tree. We took photographs of the tree and the various little special spots in the tree and then went back to the room. That day, in the play breaks, other children from the school visited the tree. The children who had decorated the tree took great delight and pride in telling the others about their special treatment for the tree.

ASSESSMENT

The notion that art is so personal and exclusive that individuals should be left to figure it out for themselves has a powerful and persistent influence on the shaping of practice in many early childhood settings. Yet evaluating and assessing progress is something that happens at every stage of the artistic process and at every stage of teaching art. While the children and teacher are engaged in discovering, planning, designing, and doing, the teacher can also be observing and assessing the children's progress and evaluating his or her own teaching methods, programs, and organization. As discussed earlier in this chapter, teachers need to interact with children, talking, watching, listening, appraising their needs and modeling, demonstrating, and teaching when appropriate. All these processes are a part of the ongoing work of the teacher as researcher who is constantly observing, questioning, reflecting, evaluating, and assessing. Children, too, are researching their artistic processes, and also engage in the processes of evaluation, assessment and critique. Therefore, the following section offers some thoughts on systematic means of assessment, which are useful for accountability, advocacy, reporting, and record keeping. In some cases, assessment also may be a requirement of educational institutions.

Interpreting children's artistry is a value-based process (MacNaughton & Williams, 2000). There are many contingencies that might add extra dimensions to any judgments we make about children's behaviors and achievements. Cultural differences can shape children, and this includes the different family cultures that exist even within one ethnic group. For instance, some children are taught to be clean at all times, so for them playing in the sandpit or with clay might be quite distressing. Teachers need to be sensitive to different cultural practices and see these as sources of strength for the child and the group.

Getting to know each child will assist us in understanding children's capabilities and needs. To become confident in assisting children's developing artistry, it is important to watch children and learn about them while sharing the art-making processes with them. One of the pleasures of working with young children is being privy to their rich conversations as we sit with them while they are drawing, painting, working clay, or being engaged in other art experiences.

Children's progress should be assessed in relation to their own previous work, not in comparison to the work of others. Information we observe can be recorded through the use of checklists, anecdotal records, work samples, and photographs. Displaying children's work is the best way for them to learn to appreciate their own and others' work. It provides a means for them to learn from one another and for us to assess the needs of the group. Exhibitions are also wonderful for advocacy, and parents and others in the community can learn to see what young children think and do. The teachers of

Reggio Emilia developed their own version of the process of documentation that not only forms an integral part of their reflective teaching process, but ultimately also communicated a powerful, worldwide message about children as competent beings.

Keeping track of children's learning can be assisted by the use of syllabus documents. They are useful for articulating outcomes and for focusing observations on the key learning experiences. For example, standards documents often emphasize core content related to forms, materials, processes, elements, concepts, display, functions, and contexts. These can be referred to as guidelines for the building and assessing of individual children's portfolios.

Assessment in the arts also calls for reflection and judgment of the effectiveness of the classroom environment, both emotional and physical. A checklist of criteria for quality in the environment should include questions such as:

- Do the children feel free to experiment and take risks?
- Are they provided with support and guidance?
- Can the children feel confident that their attempts and ideas will be respected?
- Is the furniture arrangement flexible, to suit the needs of different activities?
- Are there objects and pictures displayed aesthetically for children to view and appreciate?
- Do the children contribute to the arrangement and decoration of their environment?
- Is their work displayed around the room?

Other elements of teaching that should be subjected to regular scrutiny include classroom procedures, routines, selection of resources, use of time, effectiveness of the program, and teaching methods. Reflective teachers are constantly researching their work and ask themselves questions, such as:

- What did I do?
- Why did I do it?
- How would I do it next time?
- Did I help children generate their own ideas and solutions?
- Am I able to give individualized guidance as well as instruct the whole group?
- Do I make children aware of my expectations about their working habits?

Finally, critique is a valuable tool for assessment and evaluation, both for the artist and the viewer. Feldman's (1972) basic framework is a useful starting point for critique and can be adapted for use by teachers and young children, as they learn to read and appreciate their own visual images and the works of other artists. This formula for critique has four steps: describe (what do you see?); analyze (elements, techniques); interpret (the meaning of the work); judge (what do you think of this work, based on the previous three steps?). Rather than remaining at a superficial level using statements such as "I don't know much about art, but I know what I like," a firm understanding of the place of assessment and evaluation in the arts can assist in the acquisition of visual literacy, and enable viewers to make judgments and express opinions.

SUMMARY

Children wonder at the world, and they look and touch and listen as they learn more about their surroundings. Visual arts experiences empower them to make images, to explore their thoughts and ideas, and to communicate their thinking to themselves and others. Their ways of seeing can teach us new things, and our ways of seeing, as we watch children, can shape our work.

It is important that we are able to read and interpret the visual images that surround us, without feeling that visual literacy is the domain of the elite, the arty, or the curators of galleries. With more information, even the most obscure pieces of art can take on new meaning. When we learn of Van Gogh's life, we return to his paintings with new knowledge and a new way of seeing, and we can express an opinion. Art as symbolic representation, as a language, can communicate across cultures, move us above the mundane, make thinking visible, create new possibilities, touch the heart, and stretch the mind. Art is a cognitive experience, a sensory experience, an aesthetic experience. Art is all of these things.

Teaching and learning should not be confined to classrooms and early childhood centers. Galleries, homes, gardens, families, the community, and arts festivals all provide opportunities for children to learn about themselves and their world, through the arts. A quality visual arts program attends to processes, products, skills, creativity, aesthetics, the environment, art appreciation, critique, and evaluation. The work of the teacher is to watch children, learn about them, interact with them, and be co-players, co-artists, and co-constructors of knowledge.

This chapter was about quality art programs. It began with a discussion of important *why* questions. It is not enough to advocate for the arts. It is not enough to provide children with an attractive array of materials and opportunities to engage in play using these materials. Instead of looking for formulas and recipes, we can develop confidence through watching the children, and understanding the dilemmas and problems they encounter as they engage in artmaking. If space, time, light, resources, knowledge, skills, or confidence are limited, we can see these as challenges, not barriers. We need to find solutions, not excuses. Where possible, we can enlist the help of the experts. We should ensure that children are exposed to the artworks of adults, through photographs, posters, postcards, visits to galleries, and opportunities to see artists at work. We should also place importance on the aesthetics of children's surroundings and teach them to appreciate beauty, both in artistic experiences and in the world around them. Then we can make informed decisions about art teaching, maintain a continuing interest in researching our own practice, and learn to live with multiplicities and uncertainties.

ADDITIONAL READINGS

Ashton, L. (1997). Repositioning children's drawing development: From rungs to rings. *Australian Art Education, 20* (3), 3–16.

Kolbe, U. (2001). *Rapunzel's supermarket: All about young children and their art.* Sydney: Peppinot Press.

Kindler, A. (1996). Myths, habits, research and policy: The four pillars of early childhood art education. *Arts Education Policy Review, 97*(4, March–April), 24–29.

Smith, N. (1993). *Experience and art: Teaching children to paint* (2nd ed.). New York: Teachers College Press.

PRACTICAL ACTIVITIES

1. Research your own practice. How do you see children? How do you see art? How do you see the work of teaching?

2. Develop a plan of action for difficult situations, such as when:
   - There is no water faucet in your classroom.
   - Your center has no easels and no paint.
   - A parent volunteers to come and make Mother's Day cards or some other step-by-step didactic craft experience with the children.

3. Keep a personal visual diary and make an entry every day. Draw in it for thirty days.

4. What are the characteristics of a rich environment in an early childhood program?

5. Describe three sources of inspiration for drawing. Give an example of each.

CHAPTER NINE

MUSIC

Most of the local folks' occupations in the small country town I grew up in were associated with small business or farming. My dad's job was to deliver gasoline to the farms in our region. So, during the summer holidays, particularly when there wasn't much happening (or when Mom wanted to "get the kids out of her hair"), we three girls got loaded into the big red gas truck and would ride along with Dad to the farms, bip-bopping down the narrow dirt roads, leaving heaps of dust behind us while singing up a storm inside the cab. I was so little then I used to stand on the seat to see out the window and hold onto the dash to keep from falling over, but I was still singing along as much as they were.

The cornier the song the better—Dad was a sucker for romance. We liked stuff like "Oh, Give Me a Home Where the Buffalo Roam," or "Show Me the Way to Go Home," probably because they were nice and slow and gave us a chance to work out some good harmonies. The older we got, Dad seemed to find ways to challenge us, particularly with barbershop-type harmonies. Dad liked to keep the harmony close, so he always shot for the seventh or ninth notes in the chord. His voice wasn't great but he knew about singing, and because he had to be the most versatile, sometimes he'd be singing the bass and at other times he'd go into falsetto and squeak out one of these really "special close notes," as he called them. I remember his face when he did. His eyebrows would lift into his hairline and he stretched up the crown of his head toward the roof of the cab. He'd hold up one of his hands (while hanging onto the steering wheel with the other, mostly) in a lifting sort of way—wrist high, thumb and first finger lightly touching.

This would happen in special places in the song, like in the last note of "Where seldom is heard, a discouraging woooorrrrrd," and we'd all hang on, looking at each other in anticipation for the beginning of the last phrase. But Dad would get so moved by the sound of that "woooorrrrrd," he'd sort of sigh and slowly say, "Damn, that seventh is nice," and then there would be total silence. And then on cue—from his sudden upward eyebrow movement and his little sniff of breath—we'd all join in on the last line.

It took me a while to figure out why his special close notes were called sevenths, but I certainly knew how they sounded, long before I could count. Pretty soon I learned to find places in the songs for my own sevenths. In fact, eventually my sisters and I began to "elbow our way in" to come up with unusual harmonies. Sometimes we'd all stop and someone would say, "Hey, somebody's gotta sing the melody."

Most children entering an early childhood program come with some kind of background in music and sometimes will have well-defined musical preferences. Children's introduction to music usually occurs in a social context, singing with family and family friends. This social context widens even further when the early childhood teacher enters their young lives. During the process of enculturation (i.e., learning the values and practices of a particular culture), children develop their personal tastes in many things, including music. The music that they hear the most is likely to become what they like the best. So it follows that what the teachers and parents listen to the most will probably also become the children's favorites.

Yet research into preschool children's musical preferences has shown that they are open to *all* kinds of music, from classical to rap (Scott, 1989). Consequently, young children should be introduced to a diverse range of musical styles and periods and to the music of other cultures, so they can develop eclectic taste. Such variety will provide contrast, sustain children's interest, and stimulate comparisons between musical scales, rhythms, harmonies, the timbre of different instruments and voices, and the playing and singing characteristics of different musical styles, periods, and cultures. Preschool children, for example, respond readily to the syncopated rhythms of music from the medieval period, to the "grounded" feeling of African music, and to the "lifting" sense associated with Mozart's music. An eclectic listening and movement program, therefore, could include English country dances, bluegrass, reggae, European brass bands, African drums, avant-garde electronic sounds, 1920s American jazz, Aboriginal song, Gregorian chant, Latin American rhythms, and a range of music from all periods, styles, and cultures.

THE INFLUENCE OF CULTURE, FAMILY, AND SCHOOLING ON YOUNG CHILDREN'S MUSICAL DEVELOPMENT

It is fascinating that musical behaviors are revealed very early in life—even at prenatal, neonatal, and infant stages—before cultural factors achieve a strong influence. For example, when music is played through the abdomen of a pregnant mother, the physical responses of the baby in utero show sharp, rapid, or agitated movement to "stimulative" music, and rolling or soft, muted motor movement to "sedative" music (Shetler, 1989). There also is evidence that babies in utero actually attend and learn while listening to music. Some remarkable findings of research with two- to four-day-old babies show that those who had been exposed to the theme tune of a popular TV program while still *in the womb* exhibited changes in heart-rate and movements when the same tune was presented to them *after birth*. Even more amazingly, *fetuses* of 29–37 weeks gestational age also showed specific behavioral responses to tunes played earlier in pregnancy (Hepper, 1991). Infants who receive systematic prenatal musical stimulation are more advanced in attention and vocalization than those whose musical stimulation comes later (LaFuente et al., 1997; Lamb & Gregory, 1993). For example, in utero infants, programmed with music, poetry, and hearing *The Cat in the Hat* read to them by their parents, showed dramatic developmental differences when compared to their other siblings who had not experienced this systematic stimulation (Van de Carr, 1986).

Many of these types of studies are based on the premise that humans are born with certain brain cell groups that respond to patterns, whether in numbers, musical notes, or moves on a chessboard. Leng and Shaw (1991) described response to pattern as a kind of prelanguage, which exists in the brain even before verbal language skills have developed (see Figure 9.1). Infants as young as two months, for example, have been found capable of matching the pitch, loudness, and melodic contour of their mother's songs, and at four months they can match rhythmic structure as well (Papõsck & Papõsck, 1982). Infants seem to be predisposed to pick up these aspects of music far more than they are sensitive to the core properties of speech. For example:

- At four months they can tell when the musical ending of a segment of Mozart's music has been altered from its original (Kramhansl & Jusczyk, 1990).
- At seven to nine months they can recognize melodies independently of tempo and can detect changes in rhythm (Trehub & Thorpe, 1989).

FIGURE 9.1   **Singing and Infant-Directed Speech Are Forms of a Prelanguage**

- At eight to eleven months they can perceive and remember melodic contour and relationships between notes (Olsho, 1984; Reis, 1987; Trehub, Bull, & Thorpe, 1984).
- They use auditory memory to "chunk" sequences of sounds similar to how adults chunk numbers when memorizing lengthy telephone numbers (Thorpe & Trehub, 1989).

That infants can make such remarkable discriminations and perceive musical patterns at such an early age has implications for how teachers and parents enhance infants' and young children's musical abilities. The musical environment in early childhood is roughly equal to that of the linguistic environment. Depending on the musical tradition of a culture, children grow to expect certain musical sounds and patterns to go together, in a similar way to how they expect certain sounds and patterns within the spoken language of their culture (Azar, 1996). The cues in music are similar to cues in language. When people speak, for example, they slow down when they come to the end of a sentence. In similar ways, children know the end of a musical phrase is coming when some aspect of the notes within the phrase slows down (Azar, 1996). So, just as talking to babies and young children enhances their linguistic skills, singing and otherwise exposing children to music will enhance their musicianship, and more than likely, it could also enhance their cognitive development in ways described earlier.

In fact, acquiring musical skills *before* language skills seems to affect the way a child will approach music. Not surprisingly, the most tuneful young singers are those who grow up with the most opportunities for singing and listening to music and have had parents who sang a great deal to them (McDonald, 1979; Scott, 1989). In one study, Kelly and Sutton-Smith (1987) compared the learning contexts of homes in which there was a professional music orientation, a nonprofessional music orientation, and no music orientation at all. It was found that children from homes in which music was an important part of life approached singing from a musical base, whereas children from less-musical backgrounds approached singing via the words and adopted a language-based approach to music.

The value placed on music by those who are most loved and respected by the child cannot be overlooked. An infant's early experience of the love that parents express in their songs imbues music with an emotional association, and the child's own music may rekindle a similar feeling of connection (Rogers, 1990). Polynesian family and community life, for example, is filled with experiences of singing in harmony; consequently, six-year-old Polynesian children sing more accurately than children of European descent (Buckton, 1983). The home and cultural environment had a significant influence on the lives of two exceptional individuals in the history of music, Haydn and Mozart, whose early signs of talent were nurtured by their families and other significant people.

The ethnomusicologist Blacking (1990) described how children who grow up in Nigeria come to understand that *egwu,* the Nigerian word for music, encompasses a whole nexus of activities—it is costume, dance, drama, and ritual. In fact, in African performances, one hardly finds a "pure" art form (Nettl et al., 1997). Blacking relates a story from the African republic of Venda, where a potter's child was playing around and "drumming" with one of the seed pods the parent was using to create pots. As is typical in Venda, when infants start making sounds, their parents and others do not stop them but often "play" with them and convert the sounds into music. So when the potter's little girl banged on the plate, another person who was just passing by stopped to tap out a rhythm to make music.

Western education and care of children is not always so spontaneous and cooperative. However, we know that collaboration between family and early childhood staff can benefit children much more than teachers' or parents' separate efforts. It is important to have a mutual reinforcement of the home influence and the early childhood program, which can be accomplished in several ways (see Figure 9.2).

FIGURE 9.2   Ways to Collaborate with Parents to Enhance Children's Musical Development

- Parents and teachers can exchange notes, photographs, videos, and recordings of the child's interests, achievements, and progress in music and movement.
- Teachers can invite parents to observe and encourage the children when the program is in progress; parents can invite the teacher into their home to share the family's musical experiences.
- Teachers and parents can set up a joint lending library of recordings, instruments, movement props, and songbooks at the center. They can also investigate activities outside the program, in other parts of the community, such as:
  - Taking "listening" walks to focus on natural sounds (birds, crackling leaves and twigs, wind, water, small animals) or human sounds (traffic, building construction, a restaurant kitchen)
  - Visiting various places to listen to specific sounds (pet shops, the zoo, music shops, train stations)
  - Taping a wide variety of environmental sounds for use in the center later (e.g., for identification and categorization and discussion of tone quality)
  - Attending community music events (street performances, children's choir rehearsals, parades, folk festivals, Chinese New Year)
- Teachers can provide workshops for parents to share songs and to demonstrate ways to make and play instruments, to move creatively and rhythmically, and to select and play recordings.
- Parents, family members, and others in the community might volunteer to sing, play an instrument, or dance for the children, and/or to share the music of their culture.

Such strategies for collaboration should also include an acknowledgment of children's inclination to experience life openly and spontaneously and that encounters with music also should be open and spontaneous. Compared to older children or adults, young children's responses to music are often more attuned to sensory and perceptual qualities of understanding, and to *internal* rather than external reality. For example, a young child will make up songs on an occasion such as while lying in the grass, watching the pansies as they "dance" in the breeze, and hum a little tune to accompany a dance (e.g., responsively humming more quickly and loudly as the pansies move to the gusts of wind). Young children's sensory and perceptual use of music is not like adults' because they have not developed the types of abstract principles that adults use to interpret and structure their world. As a result, the way in which young children sometimes respond to their surroundings, and the spontaneous nature of their music making, may not make sense—or at least may be obscured—by the logic of older minds. To young children, music can be relevant to any moment, situation, or location, which may seem strange to adults.

Indeed, young children can teach us a great deal about music and how to include it in the natural realm of perception, emotion, and imagination. Some children regard music as the infrastructure of practical life, rather than an embellishment of it. Consequently, adults must acknowledge that they may not "hear" sounds in the same way as children. While both adults and children find *meaning* in music, this meaning may be extraordinarily different for each. Therefore, in order to be receptive to children and their responses to music, adults must tap the genius of their own childhood on behalf of the children with whom they interact. In practical terms, this means we must remain open-minded, flexible, spontaneous, curious, playful, trusting, inquisitive, and willing to learn by trial and error. In brief, we must think in terms of *pure artistic action*. Then playful musical interactions with children will emerge naturally, within a supportive learning environment that is framed by the child's frame of mind.

An Emergent Curriculum within a Supportive Musical Environment

Music should be viewed less as a subject to be taught and more as an experience to offer children, although such experiences should be more than just *laissez faire* (see Chapter 2). If an adult obviously enjoys music and actively participates in it, whether expert or not, children will respond heartily and creatively. Although it would be nice if all adults could sing with beautiful tone, stay in a key for a full song, and perhaps play a musical instrument, the odds of 100 percent of the population being able to do this are nil. As discussed earlier, although children from families with a professional-music background are advantaged musically, it would be a mistake to say to nonprofessionals, "If you can't sing, don't." The quality of the *interpersonal* interaction is also very important for establishing an appreciation and love for music, not only in children but also in ourselves. A comment attributed to Thoreau is particularly apt here: "The woods would be very silent if no birds sang except those that sang best" (Jones, 1990). Nonetheless, in cases where a teacher feels that children are being disadvantaged by his or her own lack of musical ability, or that children are not having exposure to "the best song birds," he or she should make efforts to enhance the music program through collaborative efforts with community members (e.g., music students might sing or play for the children wherever possible).

A distinction between teaching and knowing may clarify the role of the adult in the musical education of young children. "Teaching" has more to do with the teacher's perspective, objectives, and attempts to communicate, but "knowing" evolves from the learner's explorations and attempts to invent, develop, and test ideas. Perhaps the additional time needed in schools to permit understanding may be gained by reducing the time spent on teaching (Biasini et al., no date).

Early childhood music programs can be quite "teaching" rather than "learning" oriented. The traditional "group time" approach to music, for example, often centers predominantly on the teacher, with children simply

FIGURE 9.3   Singing Helps Children Learn the Culture's Musical "Grammars"

joining in; indeed, music is one of the few activities of some programs in which all children are expected to attend (see Figure 9.3). However, many young children find it difficult to tolerate large-group activities for more than a very short time and have difficulty with conformity and in not being able to respond spontaneously and creatively. On one hand, group singing is important for children (McDonald, 1979). Children experience the shared joy of singing with others and learn the rich repertoire of nursery rhymes and the standard children's song and movement literature; this is a valuable medium for passing on musical cultures from one generation to the next. On the other hand, however, such experiences should not substitute for the spontaneous exploration of sound and music. Spontaneity and opportunities for open-ended exploration (without mass oral distraction) cannot be as easily provided in large-group activities. Consequently, it is important that music also be encouraged and incorporated into naturalistic daily encounters—experiences where children can learn to interact with music originating from themselves, rather than always being initiated by an adult. The types of musical experiences initiated by children compared to those initiated by teachers are provided in Figure 9.4.

A large part of teacher-training and textbook content focuses on group-based activities. While these activities are important in the early childhood curriculum, a sole diet of these experiences has limitations, not only in relation to the amount of child input that can be provided, but also in relation to the musical role of these activities. Except for the last two of the six group-based examples in Figure 9.4, the other experiences place musical learning in a secondary role. In other words, it is all too common to use musical

FIGURE 9.4   A Comparison of Group-Based and Child-Initiated Experiences

GROUP-BASED	CHILD-INITIATED
■ Traditional and special-occasion songs ■ Activites to support other curriculum areas (e.g., social education, number) ■ Opportunities for sharing events (e.g., stories of personal/group experiences) ■ Songs and rhythmic movement for pure pleasure or for the release of emotional and physical energy ■ Making and playing instruments ■ Activities that strengthen awareness of concepts (e.g. high/low, fast/slow)	■ Individual chants, songs, or dances (while engaging in other activities or play) ■ Group chants arising spontaneosuly ■ Exploration of instruments ■ Improvised sound making with unconventional materials ■ Creation of "instruments" (sound-making resources) with play materials and objects from the environment ■ Use of props for expression of dramatic ideas and dance/movement exploration

Adapted from Stecher et al. (1978).

experiences simply to support other aspects of learning, such as learning about Halloween or how to count, or purely to release children's physical and emotional energy. When conscious of the *musical* role of teacher-initiated activities, we can draw distinctions between how an experience such as making musical instruments can be predominantly either an art activity (e.g., decorating objects), or one that focuses on the *exploration of sound and how it can be produced* (e.g., discovering the sound qualities of particular objects and various playing techniques to alter these sounds).

The focus of this chapter is on the less frequently addressed, child-initiated aspect of music—those learning experiences that emerge from the child and are process-oriented. Through child-initiated involvement, the learning sequence emerges from the creative process itself, and conceptual knowledge and skill development become a natural consequence. However, as mentioned throughout this book, such knowledge and skill cannot be acquired in a vacuum. Adults must be active participants in children's musical learning and seek opportunities for ways in which to enhance the types of understanding described in Figure 9.5.

By making the most of daily opportunities, adults can encourage children to explore and be inspired by sound and movement. This requires us being as nonintrusive as possible and resist the impulse to impose our adult ways of thinking on children. Through sensitive observation, we intuitively determine when it is appropriate to encourage from a distance, initiate without restricting, or participate without unwelcome intervention (McDonald, 1979). An alert adult can take advantage of situations in which music may play a special role (Figure 9.6).

Such natural encounters require responding to children and their music in a way that is unaffected, unguarded, spontaneous, and as musical as possible. When adults interact in this way, children will respond in kind. The atmosphere should be warm and supportive, involving mutual acceptance and respect. Under such conditions, children will feel comfortable about the process of experimentation and risk taking and will readily seek others to

FIGURE 9.5   Learning through Child-Initiated Musical Play

- The creative process itself
- The interactive and musical nature of sound production
- Involvement in the general artistic processes (e.g., discovery, self-awareness, social interaction, etc.)
- An understanding of the basic musical elements and how they can be used and combined
- The development of skills in the various modes of expression (i.e., aural discrimination, listening, singing, dancing/moving, playing instruments)
- Participation in making, presenting, and responding to music
- The enhancement of positive attitudes toward music and music participation

FIGURE 9.6 Responding to Music-Making Opportunities during Child-Adult Interactions

- When consoling a child, by rocking him or her to a steady beat of a favorite recording, or singing a soothing song
- When observing a child's rhythmic play (e.g., pounding clay or digging in dirt), improvising vocal or body-rhythm sounds to accompany the action and the sounds of the actions
- When making cookies with a small group of children, putting on a record with a catchy calypso beat and dancing fingers through the dough, or making up "cooking" words to a familiar tune
- When pushing a child on a swing, making up a chant incorporating the child's name, while using the voice expressively to mimic the high and low directions of the swing's movement (and encouraging the child to join in on the chant)
- When observing a child in a tutu swaying from side to side, accompanying the ballerina's movements with a gentle glissando on a metallophone (e.g., from top-to-bottom and bottom-to-top)
- When noticing a child putting a doll to bed, encouraging him or her to make up a lullaby
- When a small group of children are banging on a metal garbage can, encouraging them to collect other objects and find other sound-making resources (such as a fence nearby) to create a composition
- When playing outdoors, encouraging children to imitate the sound of a bird or the movement of a butterfly, while joining in with the children's sounds and movements
- When observing a child repeating a simple rhythmic pattern on a drum, selecting another instrument and playing a complementary rhythm
- When locating a child during outdoor playtime singing a familiar song (e.g., "Oh where, or where, has my little dog gone"), substituting new words: "Oh where, oh where, is our friend Jeremy?"

share their experiences. We should serve as a guide, resource, and stimulator of creative thinking, encouraging children to consider many solutions to open-ended problems.

Without interfering with the flow of a spontaneous activity, adults should aim to find an opportunity to point out to children the musical skills or concepts being explored. Drawing from the examples in Figure 9.6, this might include pointing out that new words can be used to replace the words of familiar songs to suit a particular circumstance; that chanting and creating body-percussion, vocal sounds, or instrumental accompaniments can enhance the enjoyment of an activity; that humming or singing gentle music can establish a feeling of calmness; that music can be created by using a variety of environmental and human-made sound sources; and that movement and dance are a natural part of musical play. Many examples and principles of how to socially construct children's learning were provided in Chapter 4 that can be used to aid the child to take the next step toward independence and grasp a deeper musical understanding. Specific strategies of modeling, demonstrating, providing descriptive feedback, explaining, and asking questions are provided later in this chapter to illustrate how to stimulate children's ideas and knowledge. Such strategies can enhance children's love for music, while at the same time assisting them to apply musical knowledge and skills during play encounters.

Young children's musical play usually centers on motor, imaginative, and perceptual experiences—seeing, hearing, and doing. Through these experiences, they begin to develop concepts about music. For example, when a child shows that music is slowing down by gradually moving more slowly, we can subtly introduce the terminology of fast and slow, ideally while participating in the child's movements. Similarly, when a child is using expressive qualities while playing an instrument, we can describe the effect being achieved (e.g., gentle, lively, heated) and encourage him or her to extend these expressive qualities or to explore alternative or contrasting effects. Concepts about tone (e.g., bright/dark), dynamics (e.g., loud/soft), pitch (e.g., high/low), tempo (e.g., fast/slow), melody (e.g., low to high), rhythm (e.g., short-short-long), and other musical elements will become refined as children's experience expands. (Definitions and examples of these musical elements can be found in the glossary at the back of this book.)

Finding ways to apply understanding of musical elements can emerge from children's participation in the main modes of musical expression—singing and playing musical instruments—both of which involve listening and moving. These modes of expression are discussed in the next two segments, with a particular emphasis on how to encourage children's musical knowledge, concepts, and skills through the processes of making music during play-based interactions. (It should be noted that movement, which is a significant component of music and music learning, is discussed in the chapter on dance, rather than in this chapter.)

SINGING

When extending the vocal development of very young children, early childhood programs traditionally have employed the technique of song making through imitation—children repeat each song several times until they can perform it well. This may involve breaking the song into chunks, such as teaching it phrase by phrase, then reassembling the chunks into a whole. This is valuable because it assists children to hear the bigger, inherent structure of songs (an aspect that is complementary to the brain's desire to perceive and understand pattern, as described earlier). Through singing, children have opportunities to learn the musical grammars of their culture—the characteristics of their culture's folk literature (e.g., how the musical chunks and other components of music are defined by a particular culture).

Music grammars vary from culture to culture. For example, many English-language songs are based on beat groups (i.e., meter) that feel like two or four beats per bar, whereas many traditional German or Bavarian songs feel like three, and Greek music five or seven; traditional Japanese music is based on the pentatonic scale (five notes), whereas music of Western cultures traditionally is diatonic (eight notes to the scale). Eastern-block singing style can seem dark or harsh and Chinese opera singing style can seem bright or nasal, *at first,* to the Western ear.

Hence, all children of all cultures begin to grasp the general underlying musical structures and expressive qualities of their culture's music, in a way similar to how they learn the characteristics of the mother language of the culture in which they live. They not only learn to *adapt* to these musical characteristics, but they also learn to *apply* these in their own personally created songs (Davidson, McKernon, & Gardner, 1981). Because "deep" learning involves not simply grasping knowledge, but also being able to apply it in personally meaningful ways, it is important to offer opportunities for young children not only to be *performers* of the music of others but also to be *creators* of their own songs. To do otherwise would be like expecting children to learn language by only repeating the words of others, like a scripted dialogue with only one voice.

It would be unfortunate if children believed that the only "real" or "worthy" songs were those they were taught. This belief could occur if children's own songs are treated as invisible—as unheard or ignored. It is important that we specifically reinforce and reward children's song-making behavior in the way that we do language behavior. That which may be lost by overlooking children's musical development can be recovered, but usually it is not (Weinberger, 1998). Regardless of whether children are singing their own songs or the songs they have learned from others, the underlying elements and concepts that children learn through singing are described in Figure 9.7.

FIGURE 9.7   Underlying Elements and Concepts Learned through Singing

- Pace (tempo), beat (pulse), beat groupings (meter)
- Rhythm and rhythm patterns
- Pitch (high/low and relativeness), pitch relationships (unison, skips, steps), melody (pitch contour), and staying in the same key throughout a song (adhering to the "home tone" or central tonality of the song); harmony (two or more notes sounded together) when accompanied, or if than one part is sung
- Tone quality (the characteristic qualities of individual and combined voices) and the production of tone (a gentle "head voice" rather than a husky "chest voice" sound)
- Coherence and structure (phrase, repetition, contrast, and "sections" that make up the whole song)
- Expressive/aesthetic aspects (the use of dynamics, tempo, and tone quality for particular effects, such as slowing down and becoming softer at the end of a song)

As can be seen from the list above, the mastery of song is an intricate and complex process. This is why it is important to consider the level of difficulty of the song literature that is used in group-singing contexts and the developmental capabilities of the individuals within the group. Such developmental issues include the *singing range* of the song (the lowest and highest notes and whether children can sing these pitches comfortably), the song's *rhythmic and structural complexity* (and whether children can remember the content), and the *song's tempo* (and whether children have the verbal ability to sing it at that speed). Sensitive teaching involves making subtle adaptations based on the children's vocal/verbal, cognitive, and physical abilities. For example, it is easier for three-year-old children to *sing* a song relatively slowly, because their verbal memory and articulation skills are not very advanced. However, *moving* to the same song at a slow tempo is difficult for them because their body pace is quite quick, and the coordination of slow movements can be very challenging. Such developmental principles are applicable not only to the performance of songs, but in the creation of songs.

Compared to song performance, song creation generally occurs during unstructured play, which allows much more scope for the child's own world of music, a world that is rich in spontaneous, improvised songs and chants. Entering into this world cannot involve a preset response from an adult. It is a much more spur-of-the-moment and interactive experience, generally involving only one child or perhaps a few children. This requires "going with the flow" and determining whether there may be appropriate opportunities to scaffold the learning, either directly or indirectly.

Children's spontaneous songs and chants often spring from motor activities. The sounds they produce provide a descriptive or expressive enhancement of their play experiences, a kind of musical accompaniment or additive emotional component. This might occur, for example, while digging in sand, rocking a doll, or reaching the top of a climbing frame. Some of these songs may be intimate or even private; others may be boisterous and very public. Generally children are playing with language and may use nonsense syllables or "borrow" words, rhythms, or melodies from songs they have learned. The example of a three-year-old girl's spontaneous song (see Figure 9.8) while riding in a car illustrates some of these characteristics.

Characteristics of Children's Spontaneous Songs

As mentioned earlier, babies as young as two or three months enjoy playing sound games with adults, creating a kind of musically interactive "conversation"—an interpersonal "musical babble" using gurgles and other vocal sounds. When adults engage in infant-directed speech or "baby talk" with babies, the way their speech changes includes higher and more varied pitch, the intonation is exaggerated, utterances are shorter, and pauses are sometimes twice as long as normal. The sounds have different purposes. For example, a high pitch is used to stress an important word (Adler, 1990). The

FIGURE 9.8   An Example of an Interactive Song-Creation Experience

One day during the summer holidays, a friend and I got together to work out some new arrangements and compositions for our band. His three-year-old daughter, Melanie, was with us and contentedly had been drawing pictures and playing quietly nearby. But it was becoming obvious that she was getting a bit impatient and thought it was about time to be going home (or, for that matter, *anywhere* else). So Paul threw the smallest three-year-old in the world over his shoulder, and before long she was strapped into the kid's seat in the back of his old clunker, and we were off to the beach.

We were driving along, chatting away while looking at the passing scenery of cliffs, mangroves, and hamburger joints when little, muffled song-type sounds came floating up from the back seat. Melanie was gazing out the window, thumb jammed into her mouth, while her plump little legs gently kicked to the beat of her own song. She was making up her own version of "We're Going to the Beach" to the tune of "A Hunting We Will Go." Never resisting a chance to perform, Paul and I joined in with "de **bum** bum bum, de **bum**by bum bum" type backgrounds, with harmony. I must admit, I was surprised that this little kid could hold her own part while two other loonies were adding bits all over the place.

The song probably lasted only a minute or two, and at the end of it Paul and I were in stitches, thinking we were the cleverest trio in town. We looked over our shoulders to see if Melanie agreed. Slowly, she turned away from the window and, partly extracting her soggy thumb from her mouth, gave us this cheeky grin as if to say, "So what's with you guys? I make up songs all the time." Then she turned back to the window, grinning, not saying a boo.

special musical interchanges between adults and babies are so interactive that one might indeed wonder, "Who is copying who?" Sometimes the baby makes a sound and the adult echoes; at other times the opposite occurs. Babies under six months already have such a refined ability to imitate that many researchers have been prompted to investigate the level of their skill. Kessen et al. (1979) found that after only a few brief "training sessions," babies were able to sing back specific pitches two-thirds of the time. It was also noted that the babies not only enjoyed the task, they worked hard at it.

Music and language have fundamental commonalities. The types of songs infants and toddlers create are similar to that used in infant-directed speech. Typically, infants' songs glide over several pitches, with no pitch clearly differentiated from another. By nineteen months, however, children can produce distinct pitches, are exploring rhythm patterns, and are producing melodies that show some organization. Yet these longer melodies are still quite unpredictable and difficult for a listener to repeat, even immediately afterwards.

At around two years, children begin to accommodate aspects of songs that will be recognizable to listeners of their own culture. This is aided by their developing ability to perceive and remember melodic contours and to mentally chunk sequences of sound. Their spontaneous songs, therefore, begin to incorporate the words of a familiar song into the melody or rhythm of their own personal song repertoire. This approach to song-creation is in marked contrast to that of adults, who can readily substitute any set of lyrics without destroying the musical identity of the tune, but may not be as inclined to keep the words while changing the rhythm or the melody (Davidson et al., 1981).

Most toddlers are able to grasp the basic form of songs, although their use of this structure does not always span the entire song. Instead, children tend to master brief melodic fragments, or "characteristic bits," which they sing over and over again (Davidson & Colley, 1987). For example, one child repeatedly used the descending melodic contour of the phrase "E-I-E-I-O" from "Old MacDonald" but with her own words, "Ya Ya Yo," and incorporated this musical fragment into her own song, using a new tune and new lyrics to complement her play experience (Davidson et al., 1981). As illustrated in this example, children typically select from their repertoire of fragments those that are most appropriate to a certain part of a spontaneous song. Through the blending of musical fragments, the child can produce several tunes. This process helps them master what Davidson et al. called the "outline" of a song (which is evident by about three years of age). The notion of a song outline resembles that of the "tadpole human" image found in drawings of children at around this same age. Tadpole humans depict an outline of the human form without providing other relevant details of the full body (Davidson et al., 1981; Hargreaves, 1986). Similarly, song outlines contain some organizational components, but the connections between these components do not reflect a clear, overall structure.

As their musical experience grows, children learn to fill in more musical details, such as precise pitch relationships and rhythm. By preschool, children usually can handle more than one dimension of music at once—combining, for example, the features of rhythm and pitch—and do not rely so heavily on lyrics for the basis of their songs. With age, the complexity of children's song creations increases with the addition of more phrases (i.e., larger and more musical chunks).

The issue of chunking and information structuring appears to be associated with what was described earlier as the brain's response to patterns (numerical, musical, or spatial). While responsiveness to patterns serves as a kind of prelanguage in infancy, it also seems to play an important role when children reach school age. Studies have found, for example, that music learning can assist children's reading ability. One study of first graders who had received Kodály training (which has an emphasis on folk songs and the development of music literacy) showed that these children exhibited significantly higher reading scores than children from a nonmusic control group (Lamb & Gregory, 1993). Learning of music seems to facilitate the phonemic (sounding out) stage of learning to read, which is similar to musical chunking.

Such evidence of cognitive gains through learning music can help educators advocate for the important position of music in the curriculum. However, there are many other social, emotional, aesthetic, and musical reasons for making music a core component of the curriculum, some of which are illustrated in the following sections.

Encouraging Song Improvisation

Some children seem to express their thoughts more readily through song improvisation than through normal speech. This may be because singing requires deeper breathing, which in turn makes it possible to prolong certain words, or parts of the song, while the singer thinks about the ideas to be expressed next (Stecher et al., 1978). It is a form of poetic license.

Andress (1980, p. 56) described the freely improvised songs that children create during play as random episodes about toys, pets, or the child himself or herself: "The texts are as charming as the mind of the young performer, as logical only as is the child's thinking at that point. The song may begin, 'My dolly has a pretty red dress,' and end abruptly, 'I'm hungry.' " The rhythm of such songs usually coincides with the word rhythms, and the language play is often enhanced by repetition of words, rhythms, or melodic phrases. In addition, the pitch range can be very wide, to incorporate the expressive aspect of what is being sung, such as squeals, cries, and laughter.

By comparison, the songs that are taught in a group-singing context generally have a limited range (from about D to G above middle C), which is suitable for the average three- to four-year-old (Bayless & Ramsey, 1986). If, however, such songs extend outside this average singing range, such as in "Happy Birthday" (where the high pitch on the next-to-last line is beyond the capabilities of many young children), children tend to compress the melody into a manageable but unrecognizable phrase. Yet in spontaneous songs, children often go well beyond this standard vocal range as they engage in the emotional component of music making. For example, when being pushed in a swing, a child might sing, "I'm flying *high*," and extend the voice into a high falsetto range, letting it glissando downwards while simultaneously reaching the bottom position on the swing and beginning again from low to high each time the swing is pushed. Such somatically based sound play should be encouraged because it extends the flexibility of the child's voice, making it easier to control specific pitches later and to sing more accurately in group contexts.

Children's interest in expressive word play can prompt teachers to blend music with language; in other words, what can be spoken can be sung. While letting the child take the lead, sung play episodes can evolve into delightful musical dialogues that are not so much words oriented as word-play oriented, often using nonsense syllables or rhymes simply for effect, as in Figure 9.9.

Teachers often use techniques such as these to interact with a young child, sometimes with the purpose of calming him or her. The expressive potential of words provides a logical and enjoyable starting point for vocal improvisation.

FIGURE 9.9   An Improvised Musical Conversation with a Four-Year-Old Boy

I went to visit a colleague of mine in a preschool one day, and while she was engaged with a group of children I observed a four-year-old boy who was sitting on top of a wooden table, banging on its surface while rather forcefully chanting nonsense and real words. His banging and chanting came in clusters of three, generally rhyming, words: "Fat, cat, blat" (pause), "Smat, bat, hat" (pause). Partly because he seemed a bit agitated, and partly because I couldn't resist playing along with his chant, I inserted my own three-word cluster at the end of one of his—"Pat, dat, mat." He stopped briefly to check me out, but continued again almost immediately, this time changing the vowel of his rhyming words, "Or, bore, core" (pause). I retorted with "Sore, lore, dore." Another brief pause and a look into my eyes, almost to suggest, "OK, let's get into this." "Pore, gore, shore," "Big, pig, dig," and so on. We continued along this vein for a few more minutes, and when it appeared that we were both losing the momentum of the game, I shifted the words to softer sounds and slowed the tempo down a bit: "Fun, chum, done." He responded in a similar way, and at his pause, when the stick was resting on the table, we smiled at each other and I waved as I moved on to catch up with my colleague. He watched me as I walked away, and then climbed down from the table and went to play with some of his friends.

Often the use of a puppet can be helpful, since children tend to project their ideas *through* the puppet and thus enter a realm of fantasy. They quickly focus their attention on the puppet itself, rather than on the puppet user, and talk or sing directly to it, seemingly forgetting that the puppet is not real.

One co-worker took the opportunity to interact with a four-year-old boy who had been having difficulty adjusting to the idea that there would soon be a baby brother in his family. Observing that Toby had recently regressed to baby-talk, had lost interest in many activities that once had engaged him, and instead spent time hanging around her, Ann took the opportunity to have a chat with Toby while they were waiting for him to be picked up from the center (his father was delayed by his trip to the hospital). After consoling the boy and gently explaining that his father would be arriving shortly, Ann slipped a favorite glove puppet from her pocket and invited Toby to sit on her knee. Changing her voice and demeanor, Ann began to talk to Toby through Sam.

> "I hear you have a brand new baby brother coming home to live with you today," Sam said.
>
> "Yeah," Toby gruffed, "and I don't like it one bit."
>
> "I suppose he'll be sleeping in your parents' bedroom and be using some of your toys too."
>
> Toby shifted on Ann's lap and replied in baby-talk, "I know. And I can't see why I should have to let *him* use *my* things. And he'll *cry* all the time and have to be taken *care* of."

Sam and Toby continued like this, discussing the issues that were distressing him. Toby spoke directly to Sam, got angry, and cried with him. But Ann had also made sure that Sam talked about the good aspects of having a baby brother and the ways in which Toby could be a caring and fun older friend. By the end of the conversation, Toby was visibly more relaxed and cheerful. Then, slipping the puppet off her arm, Ann resumed her normal voice and demeanor and invited Toby to help her wash the paintbrushes while waiting for his father. Toby immediately left his fantasy world and welcomed the opportunity to help.

Finger puppets, which are often easier for young children to use than hand or glove puppets, can help children develop singing conversations on their own, using more than one puppet and singing more than one part. Alternatively, a child may choose to interact with another child or adult through the finger puppets. We can extend children's ideas by using open-ended questions, such as "What happened when . . . ?" At first the conversation may be one-sided, with the adult leading. The child might mimic the teacher's phrases, such as "I'm a pretty bird," or "I have a lovely song." To shift the attention to the child's puppet, we might sing, "Where shall we fly?" so that the child no longer imitates but progresses to a creative response. During these interactions, it is important that we use the same improvised style as that of the young child. This inspires the child to take the initiative and lead the game. Once this is established, we can subtly introduce expressive components, such as singing in a high voice while moving the puppet high, "I'm flying *way* up here," and then dropping the pitch, "*Aaaaand* you are way *down* here," using a very low voice. Other musical concepts that lend themselves to such interactions include fast/slow and loud/soft, which can incorporate expressive elements such as "bouncy" rhythms, "undulating" melodies, and "dark" or "bright" tone qualities.

Through interactive song making, responses can be shaped into longer ideas, yet the complexity of the interaction should always reflect the child's level of language and musical skills. The melody and phrasing of these conversations often will mirror the rise and fall of the spoken sentence, the natural rhythm patterns of the words, and the length of the child's breath. Taking poetic license with pitch, rhythm, and expressive aspects—like holding particular words for special effect—will keep the interaction interesting and enjoyable. The child's contributions may seem rambling and loosely structured, but we should keep within this style to complement his or her thoughts and feelings and to maintain the flow of the game. When the child has had more experience, the adult can begin to introduce a bit more structure, such as rhyme, repetition, and rhythmic or melodic patterning.

In addition to using puppets, singing conversations can emerge from pictures (from a book, or poster or postcards), or while observing natural occurrences in the environment, such as a lizard scurrying across the bricks or a bird hovering above the play area. Such interaction generally will take place on a one-to-one basis, often when the child is relaxed and possibly snuggling up with an adult on a beanbag, or lying on the grass looking up at the sky. These events provide numerous opportunities for questions-comments and answers-comments. After several experiences on a one-to-one basis, we might engage a small group of children in a group singing conversation. For example, while looking at a poster depicting a range of events or a strongly expressive quality, the adult may invite participation by *singing,* "Look at this poster and *sing* what you see." Similar one-to-one and small-group improvisations also can occur with the use of musical instruments, where drumming "conversations," for example, might involve a question-answer type of interaction.

Older children also can create songs while accompanying themselves on a chorded instrument. To assist this process, ukuleles and small guitars can be tuned to a basic chord so that it is not necessary for the child to use the left hand to shape the chord. This frees the child to simply strum or pick the strings of the instrument, which can serve as a structural device for creating song. Alternatively, one child might play the instrument to accompany another child's song, which frees each child to focus on only one aspect at a time. Children will begin to learn to sing in tune with the chord and in the process develop a sense of tonality (staying within one key throughout the song).

PLAYING INSTRUMENTS

Children's first and most natural percussion instrument is their own body. Making "body sounds"—tapping their feet, patting their thighs, clapping, snapping, and making vocal sounds—can help children feel beat and rhythm as a physical experience and lead them to confident musicianship. At a very early age, young children also look for objects to satisfy their inclination to produce sound. They may use anything and everything available—the rungs of a crib, pots and pans, squeaky toys, or filing-cabinet drawers. Similarly, "authentic" instruments can enrapture children, and they will explore the various ways in which these can be used to produce different sounds. They will shake, tap, roll, or blow into them, or rub them against something or someone else, or put them up to their ear or against the ear of a friend.

At first, children are concerned solely with exploring sound effects. Consequently, free experimentation should be the starting point for musical encounters with instruments. However, it is not surprising that when several children are simultaneously exploring the sound potential of instruments, the experience can quickly turn into general pandemonium. Without opportunities to listen carefully to individual *sounds,* potentially valuable learning experiences can quickly turn into *noise,* and the process of discovering how to use musical ideas expressively will be thwarted. This is why musical instruments should be introduced into the program gradually over time and why sound exploration experiences should include only small groups of children, particularly in the beginning. With experience, children's explorations become more purposeful and controlled, and they learn to make fine discriminations between sounds and discover ways in which variations of sound can be produced on the same instrument.

While exploring the sound-making qualities of "found" and "authentic" instruments, children's natural curiosity has scope to probe the unknown, which may eventually lead toward setting predetermined goals, such as creating patterns and coordinating sounds with other players. Children often reproduce certain sounds over and over again to gain a clearer understanding of their action in relation to the sound. This leads to better control of the instrument and a greater sense of personal satisfaction. Hence, the objects presented to young children in early stages of exploration should be able to endure extreme usage, since the first musical concept that children generally comprehend and relate to emotionally is "loud and soft." To avoid breakages, instruments that are delicate and expensive should be introduced only after children have had opportunities to develop physical coordination and an understanding that instruments are special. There are several types of instruments that might be provided for young children's sound exploration (Figure 9.10).

FIGURE 9.10   Types of Musical Instruments Suitable for an Early Childhood Music Program

- *Sound-makers* can be found in the *home* (pots, graters, eggbeaters, strainers) and in the *environment* (seed pods, stones, sticks, and objects that can be created into instruments, such as "shakers").
- *Hand percussion/rhythm* instruments are *struck, hit, or tapped* (rhythm sticks, tone/wood blocks, drums, cow/agogo bells, brass tubes, tambourines, triangles, gongs); *scraped or rubbed* (ratcheted rhythm sticks, notched tone blocks, a washboard, sand blocks, guiro); *shaken* (maracas, jingle bells/sticks, ankle/wrist bells); and *"connected"* (coconut shells, cymbals, finger cymbals).
- *Melody* instruments are those on which tunes may be *struck with mallets* (melody bells, xylophones, metallophones, glockenspiels, resonator bells, tone bars, step bells, glasses of water of different depth); *played with the fingers* (autoharp, piano, synthesizer, ukulele, guitar, dulcimer, African thumb piano, rubber bands across a hollow box); and *blown or sung into* (recorders, tin whistles, slide whistles, kazoos, ocarinas, harmonicas, bamboo flutes).
- *Harmony* instruments include all of the melody instruments but these are then used for the purpose of creating *chords and accompaniments* (e.g., strumming an autoharp or ukulele, simultaneously playing more than one bar on a xylophone, playing more than one note on a piano/synthesizer or African thumb piano, or blowing or striking one or more pitched instruments at the same time).
- *Orchestral/band/folk* instruments can also be introduced to children, but because of the technical requirements involved in producing sounds and the expense of these instruments, they are generally *played for the children*, with some opportunities for the children to try the instrument under the guidance of an adult.

It is important to provide an atmosphere in which children feel free to explore the sound-making material and to discover the imaginative ideas that go with music making. It is wise to informally supervise children's first experiences, to demonstrate care and respect for the instruments, and to discourage careless use (e.g., leaving instruments where they may be accidentally damaged). Many times supervision is unnecessary, since the child may be totally engrossed in sound production and will be treating the instrumental respectfully while using it as a means for personal expression, as in the example in Figure 9.11.

Characteristics of children's *instrumental* music making are similar to those described above in relation to children's *song* creation. Examples of

FIGURE 9.11   An Example of a Three-Year-Old Girl's Composition at the Piano

While traveling overseas, I visited several early childhood centers that were noted for their arts programs. On many occasions, I withdrew into the observation booth to watch the children's spontaneous musical behavior without being intrusive. One observation booth happened to be positioned just behind the back of an upright piano, which allowed me to see the facial expressions of a three-year-old girl as she composed. Her inspiration source was the pictures of a favorite storybook, which she selected with enthusiasm and then made her way to the piano. With book held high in her right hand, Sarah climbed onto the piano stool, stomach first, chubby legs crabbing their way slowly behind. Once in position, she settled herself down, the way a concert pianist does before a performance. She breathed deeply, looked intently at the cover of the book, and began to play the picture.

One by one, Sarah turned the pages, lingering on some for perhaps a minute, or passing quickly over others. Unfortunately, I was unable to see the pictures as she played, but I was familiar with the book Sarah had selected and was able to note the movement of her eyes as she played. Sometimes they scanned the full page, almost as if to take in all the information at once; at other times, they centered on one position, as if she were creating a musical portrait of some aspect of the picture content.

Sarah's piano composition was a rambling little interlude with minimal structure. It seemed to spring from her emotional response to the visual images. Rather than personifying a particular character through a kind of story line, Sarah *became* the character. With eyes wide open, she crouched over the piano keys and created spooky, rumbling effects, which continued and were modified over several pages. Toward the end of the book Sarah sat more upright, her body language and facial expression became more relaxed and calm, and she played light and gentle music, tiptoeing her fingers across the top keys of the piano. As with her opening, her conclusion involved a deep breath and a brief bowing of the head and a downward gaze. Then she climbed off the piano stool, returned the book to its shelf, and moved on to another activity.

research studies that have explored the process that children use to create musical order in instrumental music making can be found in excellent papers, including Flohr (1985), Kratus (1991), Moorhead and Pond (1941), Reinhardt (1990), and Swanwick and Tillman (1986). Kratus described the improvisational process as being multileveled, consisting of a sequence of different, increasingly sophisticated behaviors. Children may revert to a lower level when encountering a difficult musical element, a new musical style, or a change in mood. He proposed seven developmental levels: exploration (loosely structured); process-oriented (producing cohesive patterns); product-oriented (conscious of structural principles, such as tonality and rhythm); fluid (applying relaxed and fluid technique); structural (shaping improvisations through a repertoire of strategies); stylistic (incorporating musical characteristics of a given style); and personal (transcending recognized styles to develop a new one).

Wright (1991, 1995a) found similar developmental results with kindergarten to seventh-grade children who engaged in the open-ended process of composing using a music synthesizer that provided four different sound options with contrasting characteristics (e.g., the programs were called Ice Rain, Bassoon/Oboe, Steam Cloud, and Split Bells). Results of the study suggested that, in addition to the developmental characteristics described by Kratus, children's approach to musical invention/composition seem to be linked to their individual learning style and cognitive/expressive characteristics. Some children demonstrated an analytical orientation to composition, focusing on technical or structural aspects, whereas others focused more on expressive aspects, with a greater sensitivity and responsiveness to timbral qualities and bodily-kinesthetic involvement. It is interesting that the individual children tended to manifest these analytical or expressive styles of musical expression consistently over a three-year period, which implies that these styles may be relatively stable and perhaps linked with personality and learning characteristics, such as temperament, creativity, and information-processing style (Ashman & Wright, 1997). This has implications for teaching in that children may have particular styles of responding to and creating music, and these should be taken into consideration when scaffolding children's musical learning.

Encouraging Instrumental Improvisation and Composition

Children's interests may be sparked when an adult picks up an instrument and begins to play, pointing out that other instruments are available. Restricting the number of instruments that may be used simultaneously is a useful strategy to encourage careful listening, and children soon learn to understand that such limitations are similar to that found in other activities (e.g., the availability of only a few painting easels, or only a few spaces at the collage table). By informally modeling several ways in which instruments and the voice may be used, the adult can encourage an atmosphere of adventure in the classroom or outdoor area and look for opportunities to encourage free/exploratory improvisation, which may lead to guided and musically structured improvisation. Children's processes will include:

- Manipulating objects
- Imitating sounds
- Discriminating between sounds
- Classifying sounds
- Sequencing sounds
- Organizing sounds to create musical ideas and feelings

To enhance opportunities for individual and small-group instrumental improvisation, special places in the center's or school's indoor and outdoor areas can be established as sound-making areas. In crowded and noisy centers or schools, the veranda or teacher's office may provide options for children to be able to listen with less distraction and to make sound without disturbing the others. Ideally, the space provided should be adequate to allow for dance, as this is often a stimulus or outcome of music making.

One strategy for instrumental music making is similar to that used for singing—using picture books, posters, or postcards as a visual stimulus. Slides projected onto a wall can also be powerful motivators for sound exploration. Particular instruments may be positioned in the sound-making area that, from an adults' perspective, would seem "appropriate" for the image (e.g., bright tinkling instruments to accompany an image of light rain). However, we must be careful not to be too literal in our choice of instruments, because the child may have a very different interpretation of the image. Consequently, a portable storage trolley with a range of instruments provides greater interpretive options for the children.

Nonetheless, there may be times when teachers may want to impose some limitations, perhaps to encourage a child to break set with a particular pattern of behavior (e.g., encouraging a child to play a melody instrument rather than drums all the time) or perhaps to make a complex learning task more manageable for a child. For example, a child who has an interest in playing familiar melodies, such as "Mary Had a Little Lamb," would be aided by the use of a xylophone that has all but three of the wooden bars removed (i.e., the main notes of the tune). By trial and error, the child will discover the melodic pattern of the first three chunks of this melody, using only these three notes. However, soon he or she will discover that one more note is required to play the fourth chunk of the song and will seek the missing wooden bar to add to the instrument so that the whole song might be played. The use of the pentatonic (five-note) scale is a particularly liberating structural device, because all of the five tones sound complementary regardless of how they are combined. The pentatonic scale and how it can be employed is discussed in greater detail in Chapter 12 in relation to integration.

As with encouraging singing improvisation, an adult can use several scaffolding strategies to enhance children's enjoyment and understanding. Examples of questions that a teacher may use are: "Can you play your sounds again, but this time so that they are very soft?" or "Now that you have found some different ways to play the instrument, what might you play to 'go with' this poster?" Teacher-child dialogue should include the word "sound" rather than "noise" to avoid negative connotations that are associated with the word "noise." The content in Chapter 4 that described how to help children take the next step toward independence provided a number of principles associated with scaffolding children's musical learning: modeling/demonstrating, giving descriptive feedback, explaining to help organize children's thinking, and asking questions to extend children's ideas and understanding. Figure 9.12 describes some of the key principles and strategies for scaffolding musical learning in young children.

Another strategy that can be used to encourage and enhance instrumental sound exploration is to create sound effects for stories, songs, poems, chants or nursery rhyme, such as "The Three Bears," "To Market, to Market," "Three Billy Goats Gruff," or "There Was a Pretty Princess." Character-based sounds can be created (e.g., using a drum for Papa Bear, a two-tone block for Mama Bear, and finger cymbals for Baby Bear), and simple expressive qualities or rhythmic/melodic patterns may be used as a sort of motif to depict the moods of the characters and events within the story (e.g., Goldilocks's music when she is walking through the woods, sleeping in the bears' house, or waking to discover the bears). Other children can participate by using body sounds, such as snapping their fingers, brushing their hands across the carpet, or stomping their feet at particular times in the story.

FIGURE 9.12   Strategies for Enhancing Concepts, Expression, Technique, and Imagination

Use musical language to help children develop *musical concepts* through many associated experiences: In relation to loud/soft, this might include a statement such as "That was very soft. I could hardly hear any sound at all. You played it so softly your hands were barely moving."

Use descriptive language to capture the *expressive components* in relation to musical elements—for example: "My, what spiky little sounds they were. Your mallets hit the bars of the xylophone very crisply," or "That sounded like an angry wind when you rumbled and banged that drum."

Encourage alternative approaches by focusing on *technique* (such as "You found different ways to play that maraca. Sometimes the beads rolled around inside, making a gentle hissing-type sound, and other times the beads slapped against the walls of the maraca, making a snapping-type sound"), or *imagination* (e.g., "The Wild Things are coming. How will the music sound when they discover Max hiding?").

Children should also be encouraged to create their own "sound stories," which may emerge from the sounds themselves (e.g., an association with a tinkling tambourine may stimulate a story about a brook). In addition, sound may be used in a support role for an emerging play event (e.g., deciding to make "running alongside the brook" music for a segment of play experience). Remembering the sequence of sounds, such as the order in which instruments were played, can be aided by creating simple, graphic notation (e.g., drawings of the instruments in the order in which they appear in the composition). Other forms of notation might capture rhythmic patterns (e.g., O O oo O), melodic contour (e.g., a line to illustrate the "movement" of the melody), expressive components (e.g., a large spider-type star beside a particular graphic image to illustrate its sudden, surprising loudness), and the overall structure of the musical composition (e.g., arrows to show that one segment of the composition is to be played again). Children can be helped to create their own "musical scores" using large pieces of paper or small cards that can be arranged and rearranged to help create musical meaning and purpose.

In addition, children can devise ways in which to "conduct" a musical composition. This may occur naturally from the cues that emerge from the children's play (e.g., the physical entrance or words or sounds of a particular character), or it may occur silently, through gestures similar to that used by professional conductors (e.g., pointing to a particular musical instrument or groups of instruments to indicate that they should begin playing and using expressive gestures to show rising levels of volume, a slowing down of tempo, or a lighter or heavier type of playing technique). Adults can demonstrate such cues and help children pay particular attention to the individual and combined musical inputs of the musicians by sometimes cuing only one or a couple of instruments to play. This can help children listen to similar and contrasting timbres of instruments (e.g., ringing versus sharp sounds), and to hear the effect of the different "layers" of sound, or patterns, when used in different combinations. Making these types of discriminations can help children decide what musical effects they prefer in relation to what they are trying to communicate, and they will search for words to describe what they are trying to achieve: "There are too many popping sounds all playing fast patterns," or "We need to think of some slinky, slow bits," or "That sound could be used to make loud surprises every now and then."

As children have increasing experience with playing instruments together, they begin to pay more attention not only to their own sounds, but also to the sounds of other children's playing (see Figure 9.13). They begin to hear the composition as consisting of many individual but integrated parts, and they begin to work together in a more holistic and communicative way. We can encourage children to think of group composition as a collective input, and that each part is similar to a piece in a jigsaw puzzle—each piece is important, but they all must fit together well, and it takes all of the pieces to make the complete picture.

FIGURE 9.13   Attentive Listening and Responding Using Musical Instruments

Consequently, it is important to help children listen for ways in which they can create an aesthetic overall composition, but where they all aren't playing the same type of pattern. To achieve musical variety, we can help children listen to what each child is playing and think of ways in which to complement this. One way is to help children listen for "holes" in the music —extended silences in a pattern—and to decide what to play in this silence. For example, if the xylophone and drum are playing "long-long-short (rest)," a child playing a finger cymbal might make a gentle ringing sound on the rest. Tape recording the composition will help children hear their contribution within the context of the whole, as sometimes it can be difficult for children to hear the whole when concentrating heavily on their own part.

SUMMARY

Music has deep biological and neurological roots. Babies and young children have a predisposition to process, respond to, and create musical ideas and music itself. Because the musical environment in early childhood is roughly equal to that of the linguistic environment, exposing children to music will enhance their musicianship and cognitive development. Therefore, a mutual reinforcement of the home in relation to the early childhood program can help both adults and children find meaning in music through pure artistic action, playful musical interactions, and spontaneous exploration of sound and music. Within a supportive process-oriented learning environment, we must respond to children and their music in a way that is unaffected, unguarded, spontaneous, and as musical as possible and serve as a guide, resource, and stimulator of problem solving using open-ended structures and solutions.

Young children's musical play usually centers on the motor, imaginative, and perceptual experiences of seeing, hearing, and doing, which provides opportunities for them to develop concepts about music. Song making and instrumental creation through improvisation help children perceive and understand the musical "grammars" of their culture. Children learn to adapt to these grammars and apply these to their own personally created songs and instrumental compositions. Children develop the ability to perceive and remember melodic contours, mentally chunk sequences of sound, and master brief musical fragments or "characteristic bits" that they incorporate into their own songs/compositions. Such learning is part of the cognitive process of understanding the "outline" or the structure of a musical piece.

Sensitive teaching involves making subtle adaptations based on children's vocal/verbal, cognitive, and physical abilities during children's unstructured play experiences—experiences that allow scope for children's own worlds of music, which are rich in spontaneous, improvised songs and chants and instrumental explorations. Children's musical explorations often spring from motor activities, which provide a musical accompaniment and emotional component to their play. We can enter into this play through interactive musical "conversations," either sung or played on a musical instrument. Musical improvisation provides many opportunities for poetic license by blending music with language and with bodily-kinesthetic engagement on instruments, which extend the child's vocal range, instrumental technique, and musical imagination. Such interactions lead children toward setting their own musical goals by manipulating objects, imitating sounds, discriminating, classifying and sequencing sounds, organizing sounds to create musical ideas and feelings, and coordinating sounds with other players. We can assist children's understanding by using musical language to help them develop musical concepts, expressive components, technical skill, simple forms of graphic notation, and experiences with "conducting" musical compositions. Through sensitive listening, children learn to "layer" sounds, decide what musical effects they prefer in relation to what they are trying to communicate, pay attention not only to their own sounds but also to the sounds of other children, and find ways to complement each other's sounds within the collective musical piece.

ADDITIONAL READINGS

Andress, B. (1980). *Music experiences in early childhood.* New York: Holt, Rinehart and Winston.

Aronoff, F. W. (1979). *Music and young children.* New York: Turning Wheel Press.

Bayless, K. M., & Ramsey, M. E. (1986). *Music: A way of life for young children.* Melbourne, Australia: Merrill.

Moorhead, G. E., & Pond, D. (1941). *The music of young children.* New York: Harper & Row.

Peery, J. C., Peery, I. W., & Draper, T. W. (Eds.). (1987). *Music and child development.* New York: Springer-Verlag.

PRACTICAL ACTIVITIES

1. Observe or interact with a baby engaged in "baby talk" or a young child engaged in spontaneous song. Note the *context* in which the singing took place, such as during diaper changing, while rocking a doll, while being pushed in a swing, or while dancing, painting, or participating in sociodramatic play (see Figure 9.6). Also note the *people* factors, such as whether the singing occurred independently, was influenced or stimulated by others, or was highly interactive. Consider other relevant information, such as *time-of-day* factors in relation to center/home *routines* (e.g., during bath time, the rest period, or active outdoor play) and *space/place* factors (e.g., in quiet/intimate/personal settings or in boisterous/interactive contexts).

   ▪ Capture the essence of the singing experience in relation to the context, people, time of day, and routine factors through a running record or an anecdotal record.

   ▪ "Notate" the song, using simple and crude symbols (i.e., don't worry about notating the exact pitches or rhythms, just aim to represent the essence of the song). This would include aspects such as the "words" (which may be simple syllables and vocal effects or particular words), the rhythmic nature of these "words," the inflections or pitch variations, and any emphases that may have been given to a particular part of the song.

   ▪ Discuss your examples with others who have done this activity and think about common and different characteristics of babies' and children's song-making.

2. Select posters, postcards, puppets, felt-board characters, or other resources that might stimulate children's interest in singing or instrumental "conversations" or improvisations. Refer to the sections in this chapter that describe young children's vocal/instrumental characteristics and ways to encourage musical improvisation to: (1) develop a clear rationale for how and why these materials may be used (e.g., specific musical instruments to accompany certain feltboard characters) and (2) determine teaching strategies and techniques to initiate or extend such a musical activity. Try the activity with your peers, an individual child, or small group of young children. Discuss the outcomes of your experience with others.

3. There are a number of excellent children's books that have music as a theme. Many stories invite the children to sing along in places, chime in on the chorus,

clap, or make a sound at a specific point in the narrative. This can help children think about musical sounds and rhythms. Other excellent books, in which people make their own music for pleasure or other social purposes, tell children that they also can be active participants in music. Some children's books also contain electronic chips that enable children to hear certain sounds, such as animal or nature sounds, or musical motifs to accompany a story character or event. Below is a list of books that are suitable for preschool and early elementary school children. Compile as many of these books as possible, become familiar with their content, and discuss their special merits with others.

Ackerman, Karen. (1988). *Song and Dance Man.* New York: Knopf.

Baer, Gene. (1989). *Thump, Thump, Rat-a-Tat-Tat.* New York: HarperCollins.

Bates, Katherine Lee. (1991). *America the Beautiful.* New York: Atheneum.

Brett, Jan. (1991). *Berlioz the Bear.* New York: G. P. Putnam's Sons.

Carle, Eric. (1990). *The Very Quiet Cricket.* New York: Philomel Books.

Claverie, Jean. (1990). *Little Lou.* New York: Stewart, Tabori, & Chang/Creative Education.

Cox, David. (1984). *Ayu and the Perfect Moon.* London: Bodley Head.

Diller, Harriett. (1996). *The Big Band Sound.* Honesdale, PA: Caroline House/Boyds Mill Press.

Englander, Roger. (1983). *Opera: What's All the Screaming About?* New York: Walker and Co.

Go Tell Aunt Rhody. (1974). New York: Macmillan.

Hague, Michael. (1992). *Twinkle, Twinkle, Little Star.* New York: Morrow Junior Books.

Isadora, Rachel. (1985). *I Hear.* New York: Greenwillow.

Kraus, Robert. (1990). *Musical Max.* New York: Simon & Schuster.

Lewis, Richard. (1991). *All of You Was Singing.* New York: Atheneum.

Lyon, George Ella. (1994). *Five Live Bongos.* New York: Scholastic.

Marks, Claude. (1987). *Go in and out the Window.* New York: Metropolitan Museum of Art/Henry Holt.

Martin, Bill, & Carle, Eric. (1991). *Polar Bear, Polar Bear, What Do You Hear?* New York: Henry Holt.

Martin, Bill, Jr., & Archambault, John. (1986). *Barn Dance.* New York: Henry Holt.

Medearia, Angela Shelf. (1994). *The Singing Man.* New York: Holiday.

Raschka, Christopher. (1992). *Charlie Parker Played Bebop.* New York: Orchard Books.

Seeger, Peter. (1985). *Abiyoyo.* New York: Macmillan.

Shanon, George. (1991). *Lizard's Song.* New York: Greenwillow.

Spier, Peter. (1990). *Crash, Bang, Boom!* New York: Doubleday.

Thee, Christain. (1994). *Behind the Curtain.* New York: Workman.

Walter, Mildred Pitts. (1980). *Ty's One-Man Band.* New York: Four Winds Press.

Williams, Vera B. (1984). *Music, Music for Everyone.* New York: Greenwillow.

Zelenski, Paul. (1990). *The Wheels on the Bus.* New York: Dutton Child Books.

Zemach, Margo. (1989). *All God's Critters Got a Place in the Choir.* New York: E. P. Dutton.

CHAPTER TEN

ENHANCING DRAMATIC ACTIVITIES IN THE EARLY CHILDHOOD YEARS

BY JULIE DUNN

As a child, I would sit in my classroom and yearn for the holidays to come. My yearning sprang from a keen desire for freedom, but not a freedom from learning, rather a freedom to learn. The learning I longed for took the form of play, and the play was dramatic.

Together with my older sister and a neighborhood friend, I spent every summer holiday absorbed in uninterrupted dramatic play. The long vacation offered us the chance to spend extended periods of time creating dramatic worlds and exploring the possibilities inherent within these worlds. The story lines we created were rich and exciting, improvised from the raw materials of our imaginations and the simple props and costumes we scrounged from our homes. But there were other materials on hand as well, and these were the elements of drama. We had no idea at the time that we were using them or how significant they were for ensuring that the illusions of our dramatic worlds were sustained. But present they were, for without them our play would have faltered and our enjoyment levels been reduced. Without tension, language, time, space, mood, symbol, and the other elements that make up the art form of drama, our play texts would have been meaningless for us and would have failed to satisfy the strong urges we were following. We weren't just playing, we were learning, and our learning was in drama.

Learning in drama can take many forms: (1) the *making, creating, or forming* of drama via child-structured play or within teacher-structured learning experiences; (2) the *presenting* of drama in both formal and informal contexts; and (3) the learning in and about drama by *responding* to the creations and presentations of others (ranging from peers to professional actors and theater groups). Each of these strands of learning in drama is of significance and the importance of each of these modes across all of the arts has been broadly dealt with in previous chapters. In this chapter, however, the focus will be on the learning that takes place when children are creating or making drama, especially those approaches that are child-structured or those that are designed and scaffolded to lead the children toward opportunities for self-structuring. These self-structured experiences fall broadly under the category of dramatic play, a term that can encompass all improvised experiences where the children have control over the direction of the emerging text (with the term "text" being used here in its broadest sense).

Of course there are many ways in which children can create or make drama: puppetry, playmaking, mime, movement, whole-group role play, improvisation, and story drama are just a few examples. Each approach is useful and relevant for young children, but in terms of offering opportunities for individuals to make meaning from their experiences, dramatic play is the most effective approach for many young children. Consequently, the focus of this chapter is on dramatic play and how the elements of drama can be used to enhance children's learning in this area. It begins by discussing how children intuitively use the elements of drama in their dramatic play and ways in which we can enhance their understanding by scaffolding their learning through the use of drama elements. The remainder of the chapter centers on specific drama elements—tension; symbol; role, language, and movement; and time, space, and focus—and practical ideas are provided for how these elements can be built into children's dramatic play through adult guidance.

DRAMATIC PLAY AND THE INTUITIVE USE OF THE ELEMENTS OF DRAMA

When children play dramatically, they spontaneously create texts, and many of these texts reflect a strong intuitive understanding of the elements of drama. The stories children create within these moments of play can be highly complex and rich in creativity and imagination. Working collaboratively, children build upon each other's ideas to generate fast-moving plot lines that have been cooked up using the ingredients of the art form of drama. These ingredients include tension, symbols, roles, relationships, movement, language, time, space, and focus. Highly skilled players, such as those who Creaser (1989) referred to as master dramatists, are able to mix and combine these elements in a manner that allows them to create new meanings and generate new understandings of their worlds.

Unfortunately, not all children are able to achieve these exciting and meaningful outcomes, and even master dramatist children can become frustrated by play that is repetitive, interrupted, or lacking in cohesion. At these times, an ingredient, or indeed several ingredients, are missing—the play is not "cooking up" the meanings that the children are looking for. This chapter will suggest that what is invariably missing during these times is one or more of the elements of drama.

There has been little recognition within educational contexts of the importance of these elements as the fundamental ingredients for meaningful play. Rather, the focus often is placed far more strongly on the outputs: cognition, language development, socialization, and literacy. Therefore, greater awareness is needed of how the elements of drama can be used to enhance the dramatic qualities of the texts that emerge during child-structured dramatic play and how this knowledge can enhance the outcomes desired by educators. Building knowledge of this area and then creating a framework for applying it will be the focus here, with a call made for teachers to be more actively involved in the development of play texts. In an approach closely related to that of guided learning (outlined in an earlier chapter), the teacher is called upon both to scaffold drama experiences and participate actively within them. This scaffolding and involvement are needed before, during, and after play, but must always be an involvement that values child-structuring and the process of play itself. When applied successfully, the outcome should be that teachers are able to provide the conditions for all children to become master dramatists, deriving the enjoyment and learning that only comes from play that is meaningful.

Dramatic Qualities of Child-Structured Play

Writers in the field of early childhood have used a vast array of terms to identify and describe play, and the variation in usage can be confusing. Some writers prefer the term *pretend play* (Sawyer, 1997; Wright, 1990), while others favor terms such as *imaginative play* (Singer, 1995), *fantasy play* (Davies, 1989; Fisher DiLalla & Watson, 1988), *symbolic play* (Monighan-Nourot & Van Hoorn, 1991; Yawkey & Fox, 1981), *role play* (Moyles, 1989), *creative dramatic play* (Williamson & Silvern, 1986), or *make-believe play* (Berk, 2000). These differences in terminology in many cases are reflective of the philosophies underpinning the work of these individual authors. For those who have chosen the term *dramatic*, however, it is mostly agreed that this word best represents the transformations of role, object, or situation that take place during play and that these transformations are central characteristics of all dramatic activity. Courtney (1990, p. 11), a writer from the field of drama, takes the idea of transformation further, believing that within dramatic worlds two types of transformations occur: the transformation of immediate reality and the transformation in what we know. His view is that all dramatic acts, including children's play, are inherently cognitive in nature, and hence generate new meanings for the participants. Vygotsky (1933/1976) highlighted this quality of play, describing it as a meaning-making process, capable of generating both cognitive and affective engagement—important components of the aesthetic dimension.

Another key characteristic of dramatic play is the notion that the player operates within two worlds simultaneously, a concept most clearly articulated by Vygotsky's now famous example where the child "weeps in play, but revels as a player," thus experiencing a dual affect. This dual affect is apparent even in the play of very young children, with players having full awareness of the fiction as they create it. This division between worlds in dramatic play offers the player protection, a safety not possible outside the play context. Within their dramatic worlds, children are free to experience fear, anger, adventure, danger, and other risky emotions while simultaneously being free of the consequences that might follow within the actual world. This experience is, of course, not unique to play contexts, for the dual affect is experienced by participants in almost all forms of dramatic experience.

Other authors have noted different connections between play and more mainstream drama processes. O'Neill (1991) for example, suggested that all modes of dramatic activity share a need to mask in some way the actual context. Play, like theater, has an author, a director, an actor, and an audience. However, the key difference is that, within play, these roles are combined all in one (Lindqvist, 1995). In addition, all forms of drama involving a text of some kind. During dramatic play, the texts children create are ephemeral and transient—they emerge from the improvised activity of the players and include all the negotiations that are occurring, both in and out of role. In other words, these texts are simultaneously co-authored by a number of players, and the result involves a complex process of both implicit and explicit negotiations, with children being both actors and playwrights, weaving their ideas together and striving to keep the action moving forward.

As playwrights, the children involved in play have responsibilities similar to those of professionals working to create a text to be performed on stage, and this responsibility is to use the elements of drama effectively to generate meaning. In the case of professional playwrights, this meaning is intended for the audience, but within dramatic play the players are also the audience, so the meanings being made are for an audience that consists of the players themselves. This does not mean, however, that the playwrights have any less need to use the elements of drama effectively. On the contrary, within child-structured dramatic play contexts, play that has not been effectively structured in relation to the elements of drama will eventually wither. The play will fail to offer the participants any personal meaning or enjoyment that comes with that meaning-making process.

Clearly, when young children (and even adults) play, they are almost without exception doing so without any overt understanding of the elements of drama. Instead, they are using these elements intuitively, with some players having a keener understanding of how to make the texts successful than others. As teachers, our understanding of these elements and how they can be used to enhance the play experiences for children is useful knowledge. In the following sections a number of these elements of drama will be discussed (drawn from Haseman & O'Toole's model, 1987). Examples will be provided to highlight how the ingredients of tension, symbol, role, language, movement, time, space, and focus impact upon the play progress. Suggestions also will be provided for how teachers can apply knowledge of these elements to the play contexts offered within their classrooms.

DRAMATIC TENSION

Tension is perhaps the most important element of drama. Have you ever been to a movie or watched a television program or indeed read a book that was lacking in tension? Most probably your reaction was to find the film or book dissatisfying or even boring. Dramatic play is the same, since it only works if we can answer the question "What's up?"

Haseman and O'Toole (1987) have identified *five key tensions* within dramatic action: task, relationships, surprise, mystery, and metaxis, a fifth tension that exists within the relationships between the actual world and the dramatic one. O'Toole (1992) used Ryle's metaphor of dispositional flows and eddies to describe the nature of tension as "a boulder in a stream," an intervention within the flow of dramatic text that causes that flow to be disrupted. This boulder creates emotional eddies and prevents the text from reaching resolution too rapidly.

Sometimes, within the dramatic play of very young children or of those whose dramatic structuring skills are weak, players are not placing these "boulders" into the stream and the play becomes too much like everyday life. At other times, moments of tension or challenges are introduced into the action but are too easily resolved, sometimes by magic. Children playing in this way are showing that they are not able to delay their gratification but rather are seeking immediate solutions to "problems" arising within the texts. These sudden resolutions, such as when one of the players kills the dragon rather than letting it chase them for a while, leads to play that becomes boring or repetitive. Being scared within the play is part of the enjoyment of it, and once the dragon is dead, either a new source of tension is needed or the game is over.

Master dramatists can become very frustrated during dramatic play if their play partners do not share this understanding of the need to delay gratification. Expert players use their knowledge of the element of tension to build excitement into the action, while players who are unable to understand this element of drama can lead the text back to stagnant waters when they take over the playwright function. Figure 10.1 on page 216 provides an example of a player leading a text away from eddies of interest to stagnant waters. This example is drawn from the play of preadolescent girls (Dunn, 2001).

This example highlights one of several key *playwright functions* identified in the dramatic play of preadolescent girls, namely the intervening playwright function (Dunn, 2001). The term *playwright function* is used here to highlight the player who has control of the direction of the emerging play text at any given time. This process should not be thought of as being in any way fixed or determined. Instead, the control of the direction of the text may shift from one utterance to the next. Each time a player offers an action or moment of dialogue, he or she is using a playwright function. O'Neill (1995) believed that, within all forms of improvised drama, someone must be in control of this function at any given time.

FIGURE 10.1   An Example of the Playwright Function of Intervention

The girls had built a text about a woman with powers who was threatening a small community. She was making huge demands upon them and the people of the community were growing tired of this. Arriving at her cottage, the girls (in role as people from the community) began to express their outrage at her actions. Suddenly, they joined to form a circle and began to move around her cottage in a ritualistic manner, calling her name. As the circle turned, one of the girls decided to set the woman's cottage alight, chanting, "Burn, cottage, burn; burn, cottage, burn."

The group had worked collaboratively and strongly to get their improvised text to a moment as strong as this one and they were reveling in the tension they had created. As they waited for the woman to flee her burning cottage and surrender to them, one of the group members in the circle suddenly announced, holding her palms upwards to the sky, "Oh no, and now it is raining. The fire is going out!" Everyone playing obeyed the unwritten rule of "once it's in, it stays in" and the dancing ceased.

With that single utterance the text direction had been changed and very quickly the play ground to a halt. It was clear that not only had the rain doused the fire, it had also extinguished the tension and with it, the text.

In addition to the intervening playwright function, other functions that are part of play include the narrative, reinforcing, and reviewing playwright functions. However, it is the intervening playwright's actions that are of the most importance for the survival of any play text. This playwright intervenes in the ongoing narrative with textual innovations that are aimed at either subtly or radically changing its direction. When used effectively, this playwright function takes advantage of one or more of the five tensions mentioned earlier: task, relationships, surprise, mystery, and metaxis. An intervening playwright, for example, may change the relationships by introducing a surprise or suggest a mystery. He or she may even offer something to the improvised text that touches upon the lives of the players in their actual worlds, thus injecting metaxis or the fifth tension.

These intervention changes are crucial because without them tension would be lost and the texts would become tedious and repetitive. However, there is no way of controlling the actions of this playwright. At times players, such as the one highlighted above, adopt this function without having a good understanding of how their contribution will affect the text; that is, they are intervening without an understanding of tension.

The intervening playwright function cannot operate successfully, however, without the presence of at least two of the other three functions. For example, without the *narrative* function, texts would not have a path to continue along. Consequently, this function is the one most commonly used. Here the players simply continue the planned or current line of action, offering no new directions but merely falling into line with the existing paths of the play. The *reviewing* playwright's role is to call the group together from within the text and revise the action thus far (rarely used by younger children). The *reinforcing* playwright takes up the ideas offered by the intervening playwright and builds upon them. By supporting these new developments, the reinforcing playwright is ensuring that good ideas with plenty of potential for future action are not wasted or ignored.

The process of negotiating these sequences of play using the various playwright functions is called *metacommunication*—the communication that takes place about the play itself. It involves the signals that players use collectively to "regulate and maintain their ongoing interaction in the absence of a pre-specified structure" (Sawyer, 1997, p. xxiii). This enables the integration of individual ideas within a shared text. For older children, most of these communications are in-frame (or within the dramatic world), whereas younger children's dramatic play is characterized by more out-of-frame offerings. For example, younger players tend to use more overt play proposals, such as *"Let's pretend that . . . "* or *"Let's make it that . . . "* in order to establish aspects of character, context, and plot, whereas more experienced or highly skilled players (such as master dramatists) try to avoid these more overt or explicit signals, preferring to remain within the dramatic world for as long as possible. This desire to avoid forms of communication that expose the play frame, openly reminding the players that they are only playing, is closely related to a concept called "conservation of the illusion." Giffin (1984) outlined this concept, suggesting that it was one of the most important unwritten rules of play. She suggested that the purpose of dramatic play is to "sustain and experience collaboratively a transformed definition of reality," a process that requires players collaboratively to suspend their disbelief so that the dramatic worlds created by the players are treated "as if" they are real (p. 88).

At times players are successful in their efforts, and they use the playwright functions, dramatic tension, and the process of metacommunication effectively. At other times, however, players are not able to generate the meanings they crave because one or more of these components is not operating effectively. The following descriptions of dramatic play (Figures 10.2 and 10.3 on page 218) offer an example of each of these, with both texts being built spontaneously by the input of a number of players within a Santa's workshop play space. The children involved were six- and seven-year-olds, and the play was taking place within a classroom setting that had a play space specifically set up for the children to create their own meanings about Santa, Christmas, and Santa's workshop (Dunn, 1996).

As illustrated in Figure 10.2, Sam's initial suggestion that some of the toys have disappeared is the first of three dramatic tension interventions offered in order to keep the action moving forward while at the same time slowing it down. Sam placed this first barrier or "boulder" into the flow of the simple workings of Santa's workshop, ensuring that it is not "just another day." Later, Susan took the lead in the text, suggesting that "tomorrow is

FIGURE 10.2   An Example of Children's Intuitive Use of Dramatic Tension

The children enter the play space and negotiation of roles occurs immediately. Sam adopts the role of Santa and immediately demands, "I need someone to make toys, lots of toys." The children stand back and look at the painted mural of toys on the wall and the three other players (now wearing elves hats) begin to discuss what can be taken from the shelves to fill Santa's orders. Sam declares in a shocked voice that some of the toys appear to be missing and this statement brings about a greater sense of urgency in the play, with the other players rushing to the phones to ring parents and let them know that some toys might not be available. As enthusiasm for these calls is starting to wane, Susan suddenly declares, "Santa, tomorrow is Christmas Eve, we'll have to hurry."

A flurry of activity and dialogue now begins, with Sam organizing helpers for the sleigh. The situation worsens and the pace quickens when Susan declares that there are only five toys left and lots more children to pack for. Mark is still busy on the phone, and when he hears the comment regarding the lack of toys he suggests that Santa will just have to solve that problem for himself. "We can't do everything," he complains.

FIGURE 10.3   An Example of How the Absence of Tension Can Cause the Play to Be Unfocused

The play is not proceeding well today. Jessica has not adopted a role as yet and Martin is not really leading the play from within his role as Santa. Jessica decides to step in and takes over the role of Santa herself, with Martin not putting up any resistance, choosing an elf role instead. The children eventually begin to work in role, with Adam telling Jessica, "Hurry up or I'll kill you, Santa. I want a boy's toy to work on, not a girl's one." Other children are now in role as elves and are aimlessly hammering and sawing plastic toys. The occasional "Ho, Ho, Ho" is heard, but little action develops. There is no story line to this play and the children seem to be just going through the motions. Soon the hammering becomes the only action, with the noise levels rising rapidly. At this point the teacher intervenes and suggests, "This is a noisy workshop, we can hear you from down near the South Pole. You'll give away too many secrets if you hammer loudly."

Christmas Eve" and that there are only five toys left. These problems all served to drive the action forward, giving it a direction and providing a context for the action that followed. Mark and the other elves then had a greater purpose for their telephone calls, and their roles as narrative playwrights were enhanced.

However, not all play texts are so effectively crafted and often they progress with little direction or satisfaction for the players. The description of play in Figure 10.3, occurring in the same space as that outlined in Figure 10.2, provides an example of how a group of children may struggle to create a meaningful play text.

Clearly there was little dramatic tension at work within this text illustrated in Figure 10.3. None of the six players present in the space appeared to have the skills or motivation required to accept the intervening playwright function. The result of this was that all players remained locked into the narrative function and the play broke down. The teacher's intervention, coming when and how it came, offered nothing to the players in terms of supporting their efforts to generate a viable text. It simply met the teacher's own needs for maintaining a reasonably quiet room. What was needed instead was a willingness to briefly observe the play, identify the problem (in this case the absence of tension), and then act to inject that element into the play text. Often teachers can play an important role in maintaining the tension in children's play by adopting a number of co-player roles.

Teachers Becoming Co-Players to Maintain Tension in Children's Play

By entering the action "in role" and offering the plot a new direction (one rich in inherent tension and full of possibilities for the players), the teacher can save the struggling text, such as that found in Figure 10.3. By adopting the role of the *intervening playwright,* we can model effective play for the children and demonstrate that we value the text the children have begun to create. Examples of such intervention might be for the teacher to take a role, such as one of Santa's next door neighbors, dropping in to the workshop to warn Santa that a storm was coming, that some troublemakers were on the way, or perhaps that Christmas had been cancelled. Alternately, the teacher might have adopted a role with a lower status, taking on the "one who does not know" role (Morgan & Saxton, 1987) and entering as someone lost in a snow storm who does not know anything about Santa's workshop or Christmas. With a brief intervention such as one of these, a shift in the direction of the text is easily achieved, enabling the children to continue with their play.

Co-player involvement from the teacher does not need to take very long and should not be dominating, but it does have the capacity to set the play text moving forward again. When sensitively offered, co-player involvement will enable the children to conserve the illusion of their play as "real." Unlike the intervention by the teacher described in Figure 10.3, which clearly had a negative impact upon the children's attempts to achieve realness in their play, a co-player intervention that demonstrates an awareness of the text's need for tension and the children's need for realness can be a brief but welcome intervention into children's play.

Perhaps the least understood aspects of teacher involvement in children's play is the recognition that children are creating dramatic worlds as they play and that these worlds are fragile. Teacher interventions that are not sensitive to this understanding can result in individual children's withdrawing from this form of play entirely. Children's lack of involvement may be attributed to a lack of interest, but a closer examination of their motives for avoiding dramatic play may show that these children do not consider the time spent building these worlds to be worthwhile. Given that teachers and indeed other players can so easily damage the illusions of realness they have collaboratively built, some children consider that the returns they gain are not worth the effort required.

An anecdote provided by Heaslip (1994, p. 103) offers a good example of an inappropriate teacher intervention that had this effect. He described an interaction between a teacher and two preschoolers who, up until the moment of teacher involvement, were busily and deeply engaged in dramatic play. The two children were using blocks to enact their plot line of a submarine that was about to submerge when the teacher interrupted the children, praising their construction and asking them to measure the heights of their bodies against the height of the tower they had created. This inappropriate intervention shattered the dramatic world of the players, replacing the created world of their imaginings with the actual world of the classroom context and its pedagogical demands. Heaslip suggested that what was actually needed within the described context was observation followed by the feeding in of appropriate and supportive language. Such language would aim to extend the children's thinking about the dramatic context. However, even this more sensitive intervention still fails to conserve the illusion role and would provide an interruption just as intrusive as the former one. Given that the children were deeply engaged in the play episode, with tension levels high, it would appear that the most appropriate action, from a dramatic point of view, would be just to allow the children's play to continue without adult intervention.

From a teaching perspective, perhaps the most complex of all tensions is that of metaxis—the tension that deals with the relationship between the actual world and the dramatic one. Within the context of play, children confront issues in their everyday lives that may be difficult or uncomfortable, challenging or surprising. The children in the Santa's workshop space again provide us with a useful example upon which to base a discussion relating to metaxis tension (see Figure 10.4).

Within this play sequence, the actions of the Santa in initially smacking a child and then drinking too much (forcing him to stay in just one house) provided these children with new perspectives on Santa Claus. These new ideas may have incorporated some of the ideas adults have previously shared with them (such as the need to be fast asleep when Santa comes and the Australian habit of leaving a beer out for Santa on hot Christmas evenings). The tension within the text, however, was created when a contradiction occurred between what they expected would normally happen within the actual world and what happened as they played.

FIGURE 10.4   Children Incorporating Metaxis as a Form of Tension

A new text is being created by Sam, Susan, Mark, and David (from Figure 10.2). Susan is in role as Santa and she is moving among the other three, who are lying down and pretending to be children receiving presents. Mark opens his eyes as his present is delivered. Santa notices this and gives him a hard smack on the back. This leads to some brief but surprised laughter as the children appreciate the humor of Santa smacking children. The text moves on without discussion, however, with Santa giving out toys, now prefacing each delivery with a warning for the children not to peek until the sack is empty. Once this is achieved, she announces, "Okay, it's morning!" The three children wake up and play with the toys with great excitement until Sam notices that Santa is still in the space that designates the house. Attempting to match this event to personal experience (and in a brave attempt to conserve the illusion), Sam cries, "Look, Santa is still in the house and he's drunk!"

Bateson, an important writer in the field of play (1976, first published 1955), would not have been surprised by these events because they fit quite comfortably within his theory of why children play at all. Kelly-Byrne (1989, p. 243) summarized his position in relation to everyday tensions within play experiences:

> The player plays in order to create novel frames and therefore novel thoughts for himself [sic]. In creating novel meanings, formulations are made that are clearly alternatives, reversals or amendments to the everyday.

The children within this anecdote of play have been confronted with the tension of coming to terms with a new way of looking at their previously held views and, in the process of playing, are sorting out their understandings. Just what meanings were created for these children during this play episode are difficult to determine, but clearly they were trying out some new ideas, and tension was allowing them to do this.

SYMBOL

Another important element of drama that must be kept in mind when structuring drama and play experiences for children is that of symbolism. Piaget (cited in Sawyer, 1997, p. 9) suggested that sociodramatic play should more appropriately be called collective symbolism. Boal (1995) also commented on symbolism, stating that symbols must have a plasticity about them, allowing almost anything to be possible. At first glance these two ideas may seem to be at odds with each other but, in fact, they present us with a snapshot view of the complex nature of symbols in drama and in dramatic play.

Within child-structured play texts, children select their own symbols. They choose items from their actual worlds and include these within their dramatic worlds—they transform ideas into symbols through the action of the play. Symbolic items are sometimes included at a rapid rate, and ordinary objects suddenly take on new meaning in the play space. The transformation in these items, such as a banana being used as a phone or a bean bag as a sleigh, are conveyed to the other players by the use a range of contextual clues. Particularly with younger children, these clues often are verbal ("Let's make this a phone."), but for those more confident in their use of symbolism, messages often are conveyed through actions. Actions can enable the same object to have different symbolic meaning from one child to the next. When children are playing collectively, all players within a given context must understand the use being made of any given object, at any given time.

As discussed earlier in this book, open-ended resources provide children with many opportunities to symbolize through action. Our awareness of the importance of including within the play space as many open-ended materials as possible is critical. Access to open-ended materials ensures that all children have the opportunity to flexibly transform the meaning of these items within the action. Often teachers take too much control of this element, setting up play spaces that are as "realistic" as possible, when what is actually needed are materials that the children can transform in their own ways. A play space set up with just one possibility for action will invariably become an empty space before too long. Given only one option for the play that takes place there, children will become bored with the range of action that can occur and will look for opportunities to symbolize in other contexts such as the playground, where the climbing frame can be a castle, a prison, or a tower. Figure 10.5 provides a humorous example of a teacher missing this point, by creating a shop in which the symbols are drawn from the teacher's experience rather than the children's.

Jane's error here is not a drastic one, for along with the realistic items presented in the shop, the children were also provided with open-ended construction materials that enabled them to innovate and develop their own

FIGURE 10.5   Children Favoring Open-Ended Resources

Jane, a mature-age student teacher with little experience in early childhood, decides to establish a shop in her preschool classroom in order for the children to have a lifelike experience of using money. Overnight she sets up the class shop with goods to be bought, play money, a counter, and a cash register. The children arrive and begin to play in the space, but much to Jane's surprise, the children are ignoring both the cash register and the money. She notes with a laugh that the children are scanning the purchased items over a cardboard box with a cellophane lid and making beeping sounds as the prices are tallied. At the conclusion of the purchasing, credit cards are handed over and more buttons are pressed.

space, transforming boxes into scanners and cardboard pieces into credit cards. They were able to make use of these open-ended materials and create for themselves the props that best symbolized for them their experience of the supermarket. The children from the Santa's workshop example above also symbolized freely in their space, selecting and creating equipment for the workshop that would not normally be included in an adult's view of what would be found there.

ROLE, LANGUAGE, AND MOVEMENT

Unlike an understanding of tension, which appears to be intuitive for many children, the creation of roles that are exciting and new is a challenge that most players are not always able to meet. Usually they select roles for their play that are familiar to them, and while this is seen by many researchers to be one of the most positive aspects of dramatic play, it can also be a key reason why play stalls. Children in general, but in particular boys, become bored with play spaces that constantly deal with the same domestic or occupational roles.

The standard play spaces found in early childhood classrooms are home corner, shops, hairdressers, hospitals, restaurants, and other occupational sites. The rationale for these play spaces is that these are familiar to children and offer the players a shared understanding of that particular context. However, what this approach fails to address is the need that children have for a broadening of their knowledge and for opportunities to create play texts relating to contexts that are far from familiar. These new contexts generate exciting language possibilities, with children being called upon to use registers of language and vocabulary that they might never otherwise get the chance to use, while offering additional opportunities for movement that is reflective of these roles and contexts.

Of course, the problem with this broadening of context is that children need to have a shared understanding of it in order to play collaboratively. Children cannot create shared dramatic worlds if they have no way of reaching consensus about the roles and characteristics inherent within these worlds. This is where literature, together with the scaffolding provided by teacher-structured drama, can lead children to build play texts that are rich in terms of the roles adopted and the situations explored. Play spaces can then be created that represent contexts as diverse as a dreamkeeper's kitchen, a lighthouse, or the office of a giantologist.

Figures 10.6 to 10.8 briefly outline how these three play contexts operated in real classroom situations. They illustrate the part that teacher-structured drama played in providing roles and a shared language for the play that was taking place. In each case, the roles and situations the children played out within the spaces emerged as a result of the group's exposure to literature, which was then explored and unpacked using teacher-structured drama conventions.

FIGURE 10.6   The Lighthouse Keeper Play Space

The lighthouse context emerged following the interest a group of preschoolers showed in the "Lighthouse Keeper" series of books by Ronda and David Armitage (London: Puffin, 1980). The image of the lighthouse on one side of the water and the keeper's house on the other (connected by a pulley for the delivery of lunch) captured the children's imagination, and they wanted to play out some of the ideas they had seen in the book. They subsequently created an elaborate space that reflected the images they had seen within the texts, but the play soon died. This was in spite of the best efforts of the master dramatists present and teacher injection of tension.

The problem was that the text the children were using as the basis of their play contained only two characters (the lighthouse keeper and his wife), and consequently the possibilities for text creation were limited. What the play needed was more roles. To achieve this end, the conventions of drama education were utilized, with the teacher using whole-group role play and teacher-in-role to extend and innovate on the text. Adopting a "one-who-does-not-know" or low status role, the teacher became the lighthouse keeper's nephew visiting the class to ask for help to get the lighthouse working (since the children apparently were experts in this field). His story to the children was that he had been left in charge while his Uncle Joe went on vacation but, being a forgetful fellow, had lost the instructions for running the light while he had been playing down on the beach. Unfortunately, because of Charlie's lack of knowledge, the light has not been lit for two nights and on the second morning a number of strange boxes washed ashore—boxes that Charlie was too afraid to open.

The play that followed this encounter was no longer stalled by a lack of roles or tension, but was instead exciting and dynamic, with children playing out a myriad of ideas for who might own these boxes, what might be in them, and what might happen when the owners came to claim them. The rope, lighthouse, a number of different-sized boxes, and a container of open-ended materials now became a focal point for the play. The children were no longer short of roles or situations, for the drama and indeed the written texts had provided them with a rich shared understanding of a context outside of their immediate experience, but one that offered plenty of potential for roles, language, and tension.

For a full account of this drama unit and the one below see J. O'Toole & J. Dunn (in press) *Pretending to Learn*. French's Forest: Pearson Education.

The contexts described in Figures 10.6 through 10.8, related as they are to broader teacher-structured drama experiences, highlight the important role the teacher plays in guiding and scaffolding the learning of children in drama. Previously it was noted that teachers can take a direct role in the play of children in order to inject tension into a struggling text. The next segment extends the concept of the role of the teacher.

FIGURE 10.7   The Giantologist Play Space

A group of seven-year-olds were working on a structured drama unit that revolved around a giant that was causing trouble in a small village by throwing tantrums and being a bully. Within the teacher-facilitated drama the children decided to call in an expert in giants (otherwise known as a giantologist) to help them overcome their problems. Within the drama experience the teacher took the roles of both the giantologist and the giant at various times throughout the sequence of lessons. Of course, the children were keen to share in this fun and take on these roles as well. Consequently, a play space was established that contained all the items that had been important within the drama—all the essential tools for a giantologist and all the essential belongings for a giant. Also placed within the play space were tuned and untuned percussion instruments, for during the drama the children had created a soundscape of the giant coming down the hill into the village, and many of the children wanted to explore this concept further in their play. Also included were notebooks for the giantologist, books containing stories of giants, various investigation materials such as tape recorders and cameras, and writing and drawing materials for designing traps. The space therefore became a context rich in multiliteracy tasks, with children utilizing a range of materials in their collaborative and individual responses to the drama experience.

FIGURE 10.8   The Dreamkeeper Play Space

The dreamkeeper play space was developed by a group of children in first and second grade in response to a teacher-structured drama. This drama was based on ideas that emerged from the text *The Boy and the Cloth of Dreams* by Jenny Koralek (1995). The original intention of the drama had not been to create a play space at all, but rather to focus on the teacher-structured dimensions of the experience including a number of multimodal arts activities centered on a search for a missing dreamkeeper. Initially, the children utilized drama techniques such as freeze frames, improvisation, and whole-group role play to develop their understanding of what a dreamkeeper might look like, where he or she might live, and the manner in which the dreams were made and delivered. Accompanying this drama work, a transdisciplinary approach to the arts was used, with children creating a cloth of dreams using a range of materials to construct an image of a dreamkeeper; choreographing a dance depicting the dreamkeeper delivering dreams; and composing music to accompany the delivery of dreams. In addition, the children were offered multiple opportunities for written literacy tasks relating to the notion of a dreamkeeper, and they used these opportunities to create poems, letters, missing person's posters, and recounts of experiences of dreaming.

During these teacher-facilitated experiences, the children spontaneously began to use the materials from the collage table to mix up batches of dreams. The children's involvement in this task grew until eventually it was clear that a dream kitchen play space was needed. Soon recipes were being written and complex child-structured play texts were developed that included plots relating to the delivery of dreams and searches for the missing dreamkeeper. Plenty of varied

(continued)

FIGURE 10.8   **Continued**

roles emerged, and the texts were rich in tension and creativity. A bonus of this context was that many children who had not been seen in the dramatic play space for some time became strongly engaged in this play space.

For a full account of this drama unit, see J. Dunn (1997) "The Dreamkeeper: Connecting dramatic play and process drama." *Educating Young Children, 3*(3), 16–18.

Teachers Providing Contexts for Roles, Language, and Movement

Within each of the learning experiences described in Figures 10.6 to 10.8, the teacher was providing the contextualization of role, language, and movement. By extending the repertoire of contexts for play, the children were being offered (among many other things) opportunities for the use a broader range of language registers. The language used by a giantologist, for example, is that of an expert and indeed the name itself suggests someone with great authority. Therefore, this context gave the children a chance to take on the "mantle of the expert" (Heathcote, 1984) and offered them spaces for the development of a broader range of language registers.

Movement opportunities also abounded here, with the play spaces described above providing children with the chance to gain bodily-kinesthetic awareness of these diverse roles. Playing the role of a giant offers quite different physical challenges from the demands made when playing a dreamkeeper role. In the former, the child is trying out large, heavy movements, while in the latter there is a sense of light, floating movements. These movement opportunities are not easily found in occupational or domestic play spaces.

TIME, SPACE, AND FOCUS

The final elements of drama to be considered here are those of time, space, and focus. Much has been written in other publications about the need to provide sufficient time for children to play (Moyles, 1989) and spaces that are conducive to privacy for play (Singer & Singer, 1990). However, the discussion in this section does not relate to time and space in the actual world but in the dramatic world instead. Teachers need to be aware of the distinction between these two notions of time and space, ensuring that within both child-structured and teacher-facilitated drama activities, children understand this key difference.

In relation to the element of time, drama conventions such as time jumps, framing of specific moments of action, and teacher narration can all be used fruitfully in any drama experience to ensure that the text does not become mundane, but rather focused on key or significant moments. Within drama contexts, all events do not have to be experienced. Indeed, the medium of drama works best when the energies of the participants are focused on exploring just small fragments of time rather than extended experiences.

In relation to child-structured dramatic play then, the element of time is a difficult one for children to self-manage. Skipping over periods of mundane time usually means that the action needs to be cut, with this decision being conveyed to the other players. Younger children do this regularly in their play, making announcements like, "Now it's morning," or "Let's make it that the party has finished and we're back home," but school-aged children tend to avoid such pronouncements, realizing that by doing so they will expose the play frame, acknowledging that the experiences are, after all, only pretend ones. Fortunately, the teacher can be of support here as well, with the support being addressed toward helping children focus their play episodes.

Focus is another important element of drama, but within the context of time it is useful in helping children narrow the boundaries of the "time" they will play in. Players sometimes need to be supported in their choice of a play situation, and clearly a decision to create a play text that travels across a number of time and space contexts is a problematic one. Texts that break down because of these choices can usually be restarted with teacher support.

Figure 10.9 on page 228 provides an example of such teacher support, with the play being based in this instance upon a storydrama created by the children themselves. The story is based on a fictional Australian animal known as a bunyip and an equally invented species of bird known as a golden bird.

SUMMARY

Within this chapter dramatic play has been positioned as a fundamentally dramatic activity, dependent for its success upon the elements of drama. These elements were presented as the ingredients for dramatic play, with meaning-making and a transformation in knowing seen as desirable outcomes of this form of activity.

Throughout the chapter, anecdotes drawn from children's play have been provided in order to demonstrate the importance of these elements within play contexts and to offer examples of how teachers might apply this knowledge in the support of children's play. Teacher-facilitated drama and other transdisciplinary arts experiences were also outlined, with these strategies being seen as offering additional scaffolding for learning in drama.

Key elements such as tension, symbol, role, language, movement, time, space, and focus were all explored, with tension being offered as the most important of these. The various playwright functions that children use within their collaboratively constructed texts were outlined, and processes for teachers to adopt role and utilize these functions were provided.

FIGURE 10.9   Helping Children Focus in Relation to Their Self-Devised Text

Two boys from a lower elementary school class had recently been involved in a classroom drama experience that included two key characters, a bunyip and a golden bird. Within the drama, the bunyip, a slow and cumbersome fellow, had been experiencing difficulty in finding friends, with the vain and popular golden bird making this task more difficult by poking fun at his efforts to fit in. During the classroom drama, teacher-in-role had been a key strategy, with the children working collaboratively to solve the bunyip's problem and reeducate the golden bird to be a friendlier forest dweller.

Following this experience, the two boys spent their lunch hour playtime creating a text about these characters. However, their play was not focused on resolving the conflict between these two characters. Instead, it involved a series of chasing games where the bunyip chased and attempted to eat the golden bird.

Observing this play in the context of playground duty, I noted that the play, while physically rewarding, did not develop dramatically and within a short time became repetitive and dissatisfying for the players. The boys seemed to have little idea of how to extend or transform the game from its simplistic chase and capture format, and I felt that space was a key part of the problem. I believed that the large, open space of the playground offered them little support for the development of their imagined worlds. I approached the boys and suggested that they might like to create a play space in the classroom to explore some of their ideas there. I hoped that by changing the dimension of space in the actual world, I might have an impact on their use of space in the dramatic one, and hence move them toward a play text that was more meaningful for them.

Once within the classroom, the boys spent a good deal of time creating their dramatic world, using a range of props and existing materials to create the forest. Carefully, they set out the context, and as they did so they began to discuss the possibilities for their play text. Soon other children were expressing a desire to join in, and the play text was becoming more focused.

The bunyip still managed to eat the bird, but the path to that feast was dramatically richer, involving a series of contests between the two creatures and the involvement of a number of other forest creatures whose complicity influenced the outcome.

PRACTICAL ACTIVITIES

1. Watch children play and see if you can identify the various *playwright functions* at work in their improvised texts. Remember that these functions shift rapidly from player to player and that at times they occur simultaneously.

2. Observe another sequence of play and see if you can identify the different types of *tension* present. The text you are observing may be poorly constructed and lacking in tension. It may be headed to breakdown. See if you

can think of a role you could adopt (as the intervening playwright) that might enable you to enliven the play and keep it moving without dominating the action.

3. Look in your library for a picture storybook that has possibilities for dramatic activity. See if you can think of a *role* you might take that can be used to deconstruct the text and offer exciting possibilities for play beyond the text.

4. Compare what happens when you ask children to act out a story to what occurs when you set up a *play space* and provide them with the time and resources to explore the same text through child-structured play. Establish a play space that requires children to don the "mantle of the expert." Record the language registers that you hear the children using and compare these to their everyday registers.

5. Talk with a group of young children about a play space they might like to create. Ask them what equipment they would like to include in such a space and the stories that might be played out in such a space. Look out for the "what's up" in their ideas.

6. Discuss in a small group the difference between *teacher-in-role* (as used in teacher-facilitated drama structures) and *teacher as co-player* (as used within child-structured dramatic play).

CHAPTER ELEVEN

DANCE

I was probably about five when my parents took me to my first powwow a couple of hours from my hometown. It's funny, but after all of these years, I still have strong images and emotional associations with that experience. I supposed it would be one of about twenty or so peak experiences that have stuck in my consciousness over the years—those things that you can still remember and "see" snippets of in your mind as if they were happening again. Some of the snippets from the powwow are visual, some are aural, and others bring back other sensory aspects, but with less detail.

I can still picture the majestic size of the tepee, me sitting beside my mother on a wooden bench, and how there was a fire at the center of the dirt floor, with smoke shafting up to the hole at the top of the tepee. I can hear the dancers' high-pitched, percussive, lilting singing, and see them in their tassled animal-skin clothing and feather headdresses, dancing around the fire. I watched the headdresses as they dipped and swirled in the space, and the dancers' feet pounded the earth, driving dust into the air to mix with the smoke of the fire. I so desperately wanted to join the dance and to sing with the performers, but my mother said that it wouldn't be safe because I could easily be trampled by accident.

For young children, many dance experiences will be freely improvised and based on felt thought, imagery, and self-expression—experiences that will likely occur spontaneously through play, or at least through playful or play-like encounters. As discussed in the creativity chapter, creative adults aim to retain such childlike qualities in their artworks. Isadora Duncan, for example, believed in free expression and natural form. Her philosophy and approach were what made her become seen as the matron of modern creative dance (Cecil-Fizdale, 1991). Many of her principles are particularly relevant to early childhood dance education, particularly in relation to the importance of children's movements becoming the basis for the development of dance experiences. In *The Art of the Dance* (1928), Duncan commented that the body must be taught to express itself and that such expression is through the motions that are natural to it. Her philosophy was to lead the child to move according to an inner impulse that is in accordance with nature.

Such an emphasis on natural rhythms of the body and nature are the underpinnings of a number of dance approaches used today. In the Dalcroze system of eurhythmics, for example, the rhythm of the body is used to stimulate pure movement (Findlay, 1971). In addition, the Carl Orff approach to music and movement was inspired by Mary Wigman (a student of Dalcroze who worked with Rudolf von Laban) and by Orff's extensive collaboration with the dancer Dorothee Günther (Orff, 1978). Similarly, Colby (1928), another pioneer of creative dance, believed that we should make our bodies free instruments of expression, where ideas and emotions come from within—we dance ideas, not steps.

This chapter presents a context in which the early childhood dance program can provide opportunities for young children to use their bodies as instruments of expression while at the same time learn how to control the energy of their movements for creative and bodily-kinesthetic expression. It describes ways in which early childhood educators can scaffold young children's learning through a focus on movement qualities—effort, space, and time—while developing in children an inner awareness and the ability to dance with others.

FREEDOM AND IMPROVISATION IN RELATION TO DISCIPLINE AND CONTROL

In early childhood dance, the child's ideas and personality are central to the learning process. Rather than having an emphasis on formal technique, stylized arrangements, or set forms of moving, our teaching of young children should allow them to explore and manipulate movement. Children can apply familiar movements in new forms, test their rhythmic responses, and improvise ways to move and respond to imagery and sensory and rhythmic experiences (Murray, 1975). In this way, dance involves a special interplay between spontaneity and concentration, between divergence and convergence, between free expression and control, and between creativity and discipline.

There are times, for example, when the dancer must allow the inner self to direct the body and to arrest conscious planning. In such cases, the kinesthetic sense—the moving body—inhabits the mind; it dissolves the rational or logical state (Schramm, 1971). The dancer becomes involved with the intuitive, sensory experience and the impulsive response to the moment (Alexander et al., 1969). Through dance, the child can be helped to experience what it is like to trust in such inner responses without conscious, logical interference. For example, children might be asked to respond spontaneously and instantly to a musical piece that is vibrant and joyful and to trust their intuition about how to move to this music. This liberates them to react intuitively, rather than becoming too analytical about what to do or concerned about whether their response is "correct" or is what is expected from the adult.

Dance improvisation is the freest form of movement expression, since it allows children to create their own movements and patterns of movement. Yet improvisation is also the most challenging experience, because it does not allow for planning or rehearsal. It is intuitive and spontaneous. It requires a quick reaction and an ability to be in touch with a gut response. Children can be encouraged to find their own responses, express their personal ideas and feelings, and trust their intuition. The young creator can feel a sense of joy, satisfaction, and fulfillment—suddenly everything seems integrated—and the sense of unity can be profoundly satisfying (Cecil-Fizdale, 1991).

Children's awareness of such inner states can be developed through encounters that require responding without censoring. However, children with minimal experience with inner awareness, or with open-ended dance experiences, may find too much freedom overwhelming, and this can lead to confusion or chaos. Like all learning, children's awareness of inner states through dance can be extended by systematic methods and guidance from adults. Such guidance can assist children to express movement ideas with more satisfying results. They can be helped in their imaging, feeling, and communicating expressive qualities of movement and structure without specifying the precise steps or forms that should be used. Cecil-Fizdale (p. 121) described the way in which she guides young children to become focused on a movement experience and how this can liberate and provide purpose to the dance:

> If some quiet music is played, the initial direction may be: "This is very soft music, find ways of moving softly and quietly, the way the music is telling you." In the beginning a little advice and suggestion will allow children to apply themselves more confidently and concentrate more easily. As they gain in experience, they are more able to work within a loose structure. In other words, children need a form to work around, and something specific to explore. If they are merely told to "move" or "dance," they may be confused and frustrated.

As illustrated, creativity and discipline are linked. There can be no artistic freedom without discipline and no educational value if the children's movements are merely random and performed without concentration or absorption. Through concentration and discipline, children learn to resist inward and outward distractions—they become "centered." With greater familiarity with specific musical pieces, for example, children begin to anticipate aspects of the music and might respond to sections or components of the music in specific, expressive ways, thus capturing the essence of the sounds through their bodies. This ability is linked to young children's ability to be inwardly aware of their bodies and feelings in relation to outward stimuli.

Dance as Inner Awareness

Body awareness requires inward awareness. This involves being in touch with internal feelings and the ability to be centered. When children are centered, they are conscious of the internal workings of the body—muscles stretching or relaxing, bones twisting—and can move with more alertness

and care. This awareness means that children are less likely to injure themselves by going beyond their body's physical limits.

Internal awareness is also related to emotional awareness. Children's
feelings come from within and are both a result of movement and the impetus of movement. Children integrate physical, emotional, and intellectual
aspects of themselves when they discover that joy, for example, can be
expressed by spinning with their arms outstretched, or that anger can be
expressed by stamping or by punching the air with their arms. In order to
dance expressively and creatively, children must be aware of outward stimuli
as well as inward reactions. We can help children focus on both these states so
that they center on the dance experience in concentrated ways, rather than
being distracted by external things.

Dance as a Group Experience

Creative dance and movement foster children's abilities to respond sensitively
through physical and often nonverbal means of expression and communication. Interaction and socialization are key aspects of dance/movement programs. Through movement, toddlers delight in the fun of jumping up and
falling down with other children, just for the sheer pleasure of the experience.
Likewise, four-year-old children enjoy the challenge and amusement of joining together to make an eight-legged creature and wriggling along the
ground. Six-year-olds' more extensive movement experience enables them to
respond to the shapes and movements of the group and to work together, both
individually and as a unit. Dancing with others requires sensitivity and
awareness and the ability to respond to the range of possibilities that movement can provide.

Children learn that interaction with others during dance leads to a
sense of community, a sense of belonging and moving in relation to others. It
is a sense of ensemble that is similar to that of creating music and improvising with sound in a group context. When children move with others, they
learn to give and receive physical contact. They can be assisted to understand
the importance of care and sensitivity through touch and movement and to
feel the satisfaction of such contact. This involves helping children become
aware of inner and outer sensitivity, so that they move with care and responsiveness in relation to others. As adults we must model and monitor children's interactions to avoid roughness and carelessness, which can lead to
accidents or physical discomfort. For example, in a warmup at the beginning
of a dance experience, children may be asked to sit and place their feet
together in the center of the circle. During this experience, we can encourage
children to take care that no one is pressed against, pushed, or scratched.
Instead, the aim should be to enjoy the closeness of a "hundred toes touching" (Cecil-Fizdale, 1991, p. 122). Similarly, there will be occasions in a dance
encounter when several children will create static forms that require them to
lean against one another and balance as a group. This requires not only

strength and physical control, but a sensitivity to the interactive components of working as a group.

Dancing as an ensemble gives children experience in allowing time and space for others and in contributing as a member of a group. Sometimes the child may lead; at other times he or she may follow. Yet, in beginning experiences it can be difficult for some children to participate in a simple experience of leading a movement for others to copy. For others, it may be difficult to follow—to let go of their own desires and ideas and to respond sensitively to the speed, direction, time, and energy of another. Such interactive experiences require social, emotional, and bodily-kinesthetic sensitivity. In the process of working in pairs or in groups, children learn the satisfaction of working with others. They come to appreciate how their individual participation contributes to the whole, and they learn to respect each other's contributions. As discussed in Chapter 3, learning through discovery involves a range of learning styles and potential entry points that suit these styles. Some children, for example, may lack confidence when it comes to movement, but may have a strong aesthetic sense, proficiency with dramatic or interpersonal forms of knowing, a great sense of humor, or a logical-quantitative way of reasoning. Each of the various styles of learning can be enhanced through dance and movement experiences, and children can learn from one another and become aware of other individuals' special qualities.

Because fantasy and bodily-kinesthetic skills are often united in the minds of young children, the use of imagery, association, and "acting like" something else can unleash a range of imaginative possibilities. For young children, the body is an instrument with which to discover, invent, and express relationships with the environment. Children devise their own gestures, actions, and movements to explore personal responses. With increasing control, they learn how their bodies can respond—they recognize the power of the body to produce, make, and do. Cecil-Fizdale (1991, p. 199) described a situation in which a group of two-year-old children in one dance experience used their imaginations and fantasy in relation to their movements:

> [The children] were pulling cane balls on ribbons. One child began calling the ball her "dog." The "dog" leapt and ran away, only to be chased and retrieved with exuberance, it slept cradled in a nurturing round body shape. It was rolled with and patted. Only one word had been spoken, the child then expressed this fantasy through movement and became completely absorbed and delighted in her creation.

This example illustrates how young children represent ideas in dance through association and imitation, based on personal experiences. However, such imitation is not mere copying; it involves identification with, concern for, sympathy, empathy, and seeing ourselves and other things as something or someone else. It is the activity by which children enlarge their repertoire of action and thought, not only within themselves, but also in relation to others. Appreciation of others is fostered through dance and movement. The affective aspects of relationships during dance tap into children's ability to observe another moving person, and to respond sensitively and personally. Such empathy can occur even at an early age (Preston-Dunlop, 1980). For example, when children take turns and watch one another dance, they are attentively involved. They participate with their eyes and use bodily-kinesthetic sensitivity to sense and respond to others' movements empathetically.

Hence, movement is a vital ingredient of interpersonal, nonverbal communication. It encompasses gesture, the placement of the body in space, the use of tension/relaxation and other types of energy levels, and a sense of timing. Such movement is poetic, expressive. It communicates what words often cannot express. Through dance, children learn to be aware of and responsive to the nonverbal communication of others. They develop observation skills, which in turn lead to personal and interactive physical-emotional responses. The focus of such observational and interactive responses through dance centers on children's understanding of how different qualities of movement can be applied in many different ways for expressive purposes.

MOVEMENT QUALITIES

Different qualities of movement are affected by our control of energy in relation to movement. Laban (1971) differentiated three basic qualities of movement—effort, time, and space—as the foundational components of dance. A variety of combinations of each of these qualities produces different senses of movement and different expression. These three movement qualities are described in the next segment (and in the Glossary) as foundational principles upon which the early childhood dance program may be based.

Effort

"Harmonious movement consists of an ebb and flow of effort" (Cecil-Fizdale, 1991). Through dance, children experience various levels of energy and become sensitive to the effect of physical states or moods, such as active/passive or energized/relaxed, and learn when to apply these different energy levels in different movement situations. They learn, for example, that their movement can be still while also containing energy and that this stillness can once again give rise to motion. They learn to listen and react to the moment in which the shift of mood and energy level should occur in relation to what is being expressed. In many ways, expressive movement is similar to phrasing in music, or artistic punctuation in poetry. Movement reflects the ebb and flow of the felt patterns, at times rising in energy and at other times returning to points of stillness.

Cecil-Fizdale (1991, p. 118) described how children become aware of how different energy levels can be applied when imagining that they are moving like an elephant:

> An elephant is a huge animal, its movements are large and yet it is extremely sensitive to where it places its feet. The dance of an elephant would incorporate these qualities, rather than just the repetitive swing from side to side, arm held in front of the face to represent a trunk that is often suggested by an adult.

In showing qualities of movement, as suggested above, the child learns how the energy of the body is changed by the contraction and relaxation of movements. While feeling the heaviness of the full body, the child must simultaneously lift and place his or her feet gently and carefully. Similarly, specific movement, such as a leap, can be shown with great expressive variation. It can be joyfully light, tensely explosive, or wildly exuberant (Preston-Dunlop, 1980). The dynamic or mood of these variations expresses different ideas and emotions. Hence, children need many opportunities to explore different ways in which effort or energy can be used in movement, so that they can apply this concept in many contexts, and with different feelings, effects, and results.

Movement must be understood in relation to stillness. A movement will begin and return to stillness. Just as music consists of both sound and silence, and the interplay between these, movement reflects contrasts and the interplay between action and stillness. However, stillness is not energy-less. Like a breath or the singing of a musical phrase, movement rises and falls. The completion of a movement reflects the quality being expressed in the movement itself. Figure 11.1 provides an example of a young girl's independent

FIGURE 11.1   A Four-Year-Old Girl's Expressive Use of Movement and Stillness

I watched a four-year-old girl, Julie, during a free play period, go to the dance props and select a long blue silk scarf. She also put on a calf-length flowing skirt and took her shoes and socks off. She then went to the stereo and specifically selected one of her favorite pieces of classical music. I can't recall the exact piece, but the mood was very peaceful and the tempo was relatively slow.

While she waited for the tape to begin, she stood alert but still, with the scarf hanging down from her hand and draping gently onto the floor. As soon as the music began, she started to sway her upper body from side to side, eventually shifting the weight of her feet to allow her to extend her arm movements out to the sides and upwards. As the piece continued, her arm movements became more flowing and she began to work with the scarf, undulating through the space in response to the musical patterns. As Julie twirled, her skirt billowed and whirled around her legs, with the scarf following closely behind. At the end of the piece, she returned to her original position, standing still with the scarf draped by her side and her head gently bowing forward.

dance exploration, where she sensitively expressed her ideas and feelings bodily-kinesthetically.

There are times, such as in the example above, when stillness or static shapes are part of a child's dance composition (see Figure 11.2 on page 240). A static shape may be still, but it may also be strong with a lot of energy surging through the body. In the case of Julie, her stillness at the beginning and the end of the dance composition reflected the qualities of movement expressed within the dance itself. Her movement did not drop limply away, but made its final statement in the stillness. This is an aesthetic aspect of dance composition that many children seem to feel intuitively, whereas other children may need to observe and have modeled for them. A performing musician or actor, for example, does not play the final note of a composition or say the final line of a play and then simply walk off stage. There is generally a period of coming back to reality, where the musician's hands slowly return to the player's lap, or the actor pauses and then shifts the gesture to one that implies the performance is now complete. Likewise, when assisting children to express themselves through movement, we can help them become sensitive to the ebb and flow of their effort, whether this is at the beginning and end of a dance or during the experience itself, such as showing variations in energy and illustrating the "breaths" and phrases of the music.

Relaxation is different from stillness. When children are relaxed, their muscles are soft, their breathing is easy, and their energy flow is at its minimum. We can help children relax by lying on their backs with their arms at their sides, head straight. Such opportunities help children feel their bodies at ease and appreciate revitalization without tension. Without the distraction of chatter or movement, children become aware of their emotional state and can focus their attention on abdominal breathing, the deepest kind of breathing in which the diaphragm drops and the ribcage lifts and opens to make room for the lungs to fill. Cecil-Fizdale (1991, p. 132) provides recommendations for how we can help children feel the stomach rise as the air enters and lowers as the air is expelled:

- Tell children to place their fingers lightly on the stomach and feel this natural rise and fall.
- Move from one child to the next, feeling the movement of the stomach with a gentle placement of the hand on his or her abdomen.
- Place a light object such as flower or a shell on the child's stomach, drawing his or her attention to that part of the body.
- Ask children to imagine the stomach rising like a little hill and falling like a valley.

Such relaxation experiences are important for helping children to come back to reality after a dance/movement interaction. In addition, relaxation experiences can be usefully employed at other times throughout the day to help children calm down after a period of overexcitement; to help them center their attention on music, the sounds of the environment, a story or other sensitive forms of listening; and to generally serve as a form of meditative centering. In addition, the exercise of helping children focus their attention on deep, diaphragmatic breathing is important for assisting children to sing with good technique, which helps them place their singing voices in the head register, rather than in the chest.

Space

Children enjoy discovering what their bodies can do and experimenting with moving different parts in new and varied ways. Their awareness of the capacity to move each body part provides them with a kind of movement vocabulary that widens their abilities to improvise through dance. This is why it is valuable to provide opportunities for children to focus on ways to move isolated body parts, and to discover a variety of ways to move. Arms, shoulders, backsides, legs, and a number of isolated body parts can swing, twist, sway, swirl, punch, and slice. They can also show expressive styles, such as heavy/light, wobbly/stable, rigid/loose, or strong/weak.

Through dance, children come to realize that their bodies and body parts can be propelled through space and can go around, up and down, or in and out. They can burst with great speed or be controlled in slow motion. Their bodies can exert immense energy or show restraint through lightness and gentleness. They can stretch tall and wide with tension or relax on the floor loosely and effortlessly. They can move through space in different pathways (e.g., straight, zigzagged, roundabout), creep across the floor, or leap high in the air. In addition, several parts of the body, not just the feet, can become the base for support, such as the knees, back, shoulders, and hands (Murray, 1975).

Although children delight in moving through space, they are often focused on their own feelings and responses and may not be aware of other children moving in the space with them. We can help children in their initial dance experience by making them aware of the space around them, not simply to avoid accidentally bumping into others, but also to build the foundation of awareness of group dancing. Cecil-Fizdale (1991) provides a number of recommendations for how we can help children be outwardly aware of others while dancing:

- Restrict the number of children dancing within a space to only two or three, particularly in early experiences when children have had less familiarity with moving in relation to others. When there are fewer children, there is more space for the children to move freely and a reduction in the prospect of mishaps.
- Offer side coaching, reminding the children to look for other children in relation to their own movements. Channel children's movements by moving in the space with a small group of children. Such channeling

may focus children's awareness on spatial relationships and spatial patterns within the group.

- Pay particular attention to situations in which children are moving quickly through space, since they can be highly engaged in the sheer pleasure of the movement and less aware of others at these times. By comparison, when children are moving slowly or are on the floor, there is less likelihood that they may hurt themselves or others if they make physical contact. In such cases, more children may be able to join the group and move at the same time.

While movement often goes out into space, the dancer can also remain in one place. Three types of movement that children use naturally form the basis of a movement program: locomotor, nonlocomotor, and a combination of locomotor and nonlocomotor movements (Greenberg, 1979; Stecher et al., 1978). *Locomotor* movement (that which takes the mover through space) involves moving the whole body from one place to another (e.g., walking, crawling or shuffling). *Nonlocomotor* movement (axial, stationary, static forms) is centered on the axis of the body (the feet remain stationary or other parts of the body, such as the back or stomach, form a base for movement of body parts). A *combination* of movements involves various motions that occur simultaneously, such as walking while clapping or running while rising and falling.

In nonlocomotor movement, children learn to understand that the space around each person can be restricted or expansive, and movement shapes can be formed away from or close to the body. Angles of the body, for example, can be curved/jagged, and the energy may be strong/soft. Shapes can be symmetrical or asymmetrical. When children form static shapes, their body awareness is enhanced. They discover how their bodies can be placed in space and what different parts can do (see Figure 11.2). During the stillness of the shape, children feel where their body is and where each body part is positioned in space. For example, we might invite them to make a shape using just their elbows and knees touching the floor, or to make a different shape using their toes and fingertips. Static shapes clearly express emotions—the feeling is captured in form, rather than released and dissipated in movement. In many ways, the static forms that children create are similar in concept to stopped-action frames. They are expressions that are sculpted in physical form. Such static shapes can be made individually, in pairs, or in small groups. When more than one child is working to make a static shape, each child must be aware of complementing the shape of the others to create a unified form.

Time

Movement through space or around the axis of the body can occur at different speeds. For example, children may create an axial movement while standing and moving the upper part of their bodies, such as the trunk, limbs, or

FIGURE 11.2   **Static Shapes as Part of Dance Composition**

head. The movements that are used may be the same, but at different speeds. For instance, a child might choose to sway her arms from side to side quickly in one context or slowly in another. Time or speed will be influenced by mood and feelings in relation to what is being represented either literally (e.g., the fluttering of wings, the blowing of branches in the wind) or metaphorically/symbolically (e.g., showing an abstract concept, such as heaviness, strength, or shyness). Similarly, time is used with locomotor movements when a child travels from one point in the room to another, but at different speeds. For example, he or she might walk or run from corner to corner or roll across the floor at fast or slow speeds. Again, such choices may be based on association and imagery, such as pretending to be a long-legged giant, or may be more generally expressive, such as feeling light and free.

The contrast between fast and slow can be experienced by responding to the sounds of a musical instrument, such as the tambour (a large, flat hand drum). We might ask children to listen to the sound of the drum and move fast or slow when the sound is fast or slow. It is most appropriate if specific movements are not suggested, so that children can determine their own ways of experiencing fast and slow. With very young children, obvious speed differences are more easily recognized than subtle variations of speed; they provide a secure basis for response. However, with older children or with children who have more dance experience, we can expect a more refined response to subtle difference in speed and a more controlled and responsive timing of movements through space. In addition, the use of other instruments besides the tambour and of musical excerpts from recorded works can provide numerous opportunities for children to respond to sound stimuli in different ways.

These three qualities—effort, space, and time—can be the basis for planning movement/dance experiences with children. We should consider offering a wide variety of movement experiences that are based on these movement qualities. One way to consider this is to be aware of the contrast or polarity of each movement (Cecil-Fizdale, 1991). If children have been moving softly, for example, the contrast would be strong. In this way no single aspect is emphasized or overlooked. Cecil-Fizdale (p. 129) provided a helpful list of movement polarities that might include:

Soft/hard
Strong/delicate
Big/small
Straight/curved
Expanded/contracted
Exuberant/reflective
Through space/static
Fast/slow
High/low
On the floor/in the air

Contrasts can occur during the same movement experience or at different times within the dance program. It is important to remember that a range of movement qualities provides children with a larger vocabulary with which to express their ideas and feelings. It is helpful to think of movement qualities (and polarities) in relation to the following principles:

- Direction (e.g., forward/backwards, sideways, across, and circling)
- Levels (e.g., high/low, over/under, lying down, falling, leaping)
- Dimensions (e.g., large/small motions)
- Expressiveness (e.g., smooth, quick, heavy, jerky, stiff, fluent)
- Ranges (e.g., within a large or small space, close to others, or far away from them)
- Spots (e.g., toward/away from a particular spot, while focusing on that point in space)

As with learning in all arts domains, we can help children become conscious of the movement qualities of effort, time, and space and of aspects listed above by using language that describes ideas and movement sensations. Dance employs language that crosses over into other disciplines, including spatial concepts such as over/under, in/out, up/down, wide/narrow; mathematical concepts such as groupings, or number; and musical concepts such as high/low, energetic/gentle, and tension/release. While moving and dancing, different modalities are tapped into, giving scope for children to discover through their senses as well as "through the head" (Exiner & Lloyd, 1987). The tapping into different modalities can be greatly enhanced through the use of a variety of resources as a means for stimulating movement.

THE USE OF APPROPRIATE STIMULATION

A range of stimuli can assist children to understand the principles of movement. Movement props, imagery, the voice, and hand percussion instruments can trigger ideas or pose problems for solving. Each of these stimuli is discussed in this next segment in relation to enhancing young children's movement and dance experiences.

Props

Movement props have special qualities that can reflect a particular movement quality and assist children to experience a wide range of movements. Because children tend not to think in abstract terms, they are more supported in their movement explorations of concepts when these are expressed through concrete stimuli. For example, feeling what it is like to be an autumn leaf blown in the wind is a much easier task when young children are given large leaves to toss and chase—their bodies naturally twirl, rise, and fall as they interact with the leaf. Open-ended props, which allow for improvisation, are more appropriate than those confined to specific images and associations (e.g., a cowboy, Batman, or a butterfly costume). When children are encouraged to think of ways in which to move the prop, such as a leaf, a scarf, or a hoop, their attention is centered less on themselves and more on the object itself. We can assist children to focus on the outward stimuli and thus feel less exposed. Children who tend to be shy or inhibited will feel less so if asked questions such as "What can *this* do?" (rather than "What can *you* do with this?"). Gradually, children are able to transfer the feeling of the prop into their whole body (see Figure 11.3). As illustrated in Figure 11.3, while moving with a chiffon, the whole body bends and curves in unison with the movement of the arms, reflecting the quality of the soft cloth and its movement in space. Other simple movement props that can be held in the hand and extend from the body might include scarves, crepe-paper streamers, or strips of cloth such as tulle or lace (see the integration chapter for a description of associative aspects of cloth in relation to drama and movement).

Other objects may be manipulated in various ways, such as balloons, lightweight plastic tubes, or hoops, although consideration for children's safety necessitates that only a few children use these props at the same time, since it is easy for children's concentration to center so specifically on the objects that they may become less aware of others in space.

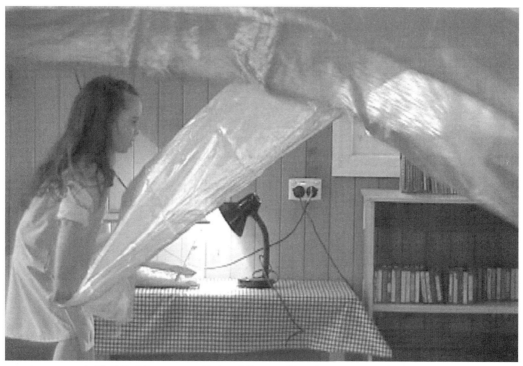

FIGURE 11.3   A Child's Movements Being Liberated by the Use of a Dance Prop

In the beginning we can support the children's desire to experiment with new and different props through statements, such as "You can have a long turn with these things because you need time to find out how they move" (Stecher et al., 1978). However, as children gain more experience, they will learn to trust their intuitive responses, will feel more attuned to their inner awareness, and will have less need for external stimuli.

Imagery

As mentioned throughout this book, the arts can convey impressions and interpretations of many aspects of our lives. Dance is particularly well linked to representations of the natural environment. For example, a waterfall, a huge mountain, a flickering fire, or the wind can be expressed through movement. In addition, a movement itself can stimulate children's ability to image. When dancing using a particular quality, for example, we might ask the children how that particular movement makes them feel, or what it reminds them of when they make the movement. Children often come up with their own images, and these can be sources of inspiration for other children's participation, creating different kinds of movement reactions and providing rich sources for making dance.

Abstract paintings can also stimulate a range of movement responses. The shapes, lines, colors, and textures of the artwork can be depicted through movement in a visual-movement, cross-modal way. Similarly, the form and expressive qualities of sculptures and carvings may inspire majestic, gentle, or vibrant dance responses and possibly inspire children to expand a concrete idea, such as creating a rain dance. As discussed in relation to vertical space, the positioning of objects within the room can also inspire movement patterns, an awareness of design concepts, and the exploration of spatial relationships, such as over/under, in/out, and around/through, as children move in relation to the placement of objects within space.

The Voice and Musical Instruments

Children's self-made sounds through the use of their voices and body percussion can be a powerful catalyst for movement. Cecil-Fizdale (1991) describes how the use of the voice is a natural part of children's expressive movement (p. 134):

> Vocalizing often has the virtue of causing the movement to come alive, especially if it is invented as the children move, so that the sounds seem to arise from the movements themselves. As a movement occurs a sound may spontaneously be released which reflects and enhances the movement. A wide-spreading expansive movement may stimulate a loud "aahhhh" sound; contracted, scurrying movements may produce chattery, gibbering sounds. Teachers should allow their playfulness to come out when producing sounds. Children find this very amusing and happily echo them or produce their own sounds.

In addition, the use of percussion instruments can stimulate movements. The long ringing of a gong, triangle, or finger cymbals can stimulate smooth, flowing, continuous movements. By contrast, the scraping sound of a guiro, the tapping of a wood block, or the shaking of maracas will suggest movements that are quick, light, and asymmetrical. Perhaps the most versatile musical instrument that a teacher may use is the tambour, because it is portable, makes many different sounds depending upon how it is played, and does not require a high level of technical skill (although this will be developed as the need for expression becomes apparent). As discussed in the music chapter, the tambour can be tapped on the edge, hit with a flat hand in the center, scraped with the back of the fingers, and tiptoed across with the tips of the fingers. Other hand percussion instruments that can be played in a variety of ways, such as a guiro, a cow bell, wood blocks, a triangle, or finger cymbals, can also provide a means for the teacher to interact with the children while playing the instrument at the same time in expressive and responsive ways. In many ways, the use of handheld instruments is better than playing the piano, unless the teacher is highly proficient on this instrument and able to watch the children and play interactively in response to their movements.

MUSIC AND MOVEMENT

Developing the ability to listen and respond to auditory stimuli is a skill separate from the principles of dance, but it is an essential component of creative dance and movement. Music is a stimulus most often used to promote expressiveness—the body reflects the mood or quality of the sound. When music is played, we can draw children's attention to its qualities by asking them to listen to how the music will help them move. For example, vibrant and joyful music will encourage expansive movements; melancholy music will provoke a feeling of turning inward, where movements may be bent downward or reduced (Cecil-Fizdale, 1991). Such emotionally based movement qualities were discussed in Chapter 7 in relation to somatic knowing and body-based metaphor. As described in Chapter 7, there can be strong associations between music and image. Music may suggest a glassy pond, a floating bubble, or a lizard scurrying in the leaves. Therefore, the types of music we provide within the dance program should be as varied as possible. The chapter on music provided many examples of the types of music that can enhance children's awareness of the grammars of different genres, and the value of having eclectic tastes.

Young children's response to music is strongly embedded in the emotional and physical self, because music is both an aural and a kinesthetic art. "The ear, the muscles and the brain are inherently related in their functions as receivers and conveyers of musical sound, and thus they play important roles in the training of musicians, and in the music learning of children" (Shehan, 1990). For young children, the body becomes an instrument of musical expression; it is a fundamental and natural way to learn. Movement is integral to a child's musical experiences. Children use movement with music for two main reasons: to satisfy an urge to explore the way their bodies move and to communicate their innermost feelings about the music they hear. Moog (1976) described learning how to control rhythmic responses to music as an important milestone in children's cognitive development, which also involves perception. Children who find their own body rhythms and acquire good motor skills usually extend their ability to express what they perceive. Because this kind of learning is such a personal experience, children should be encouraged to explore rhythmic movement in their own way, without the imposition of rigid adult standards (McDonald, 1979).

Linking the movement qualities of time, space, and effort is enhanced when we focus children's attention on musical elements and expressive aspects. Obvious links can be made between movement *levels* and *pitch* in music. For example, children may be encouraged to respond to the contours of the melody (i.e., its rising and falling pitches) by kneeling, rising up on their knees and reaching high as the melody ascends, and lowering as the melody descends. Such spatial relationships can also be shown through loco-motor movement, such as beginning a melodic phrase at one point in the room, and moving toward another spot by the conclusion of the phrase. The *range* of space used for the expression of the melodic phrases may be quite large (from one corner of the room to the other corner), or it may be close (between two designated areas, perhaps marked by pillows on the floor, or by children standing/sitting in particular places). Consequently, the timing and energy levels required to express the melodic phrases will be affected by the distance involved and other factors, such as whether the movement is forward/backward, heavy/light, or stiff/fluent.

The *tempo* of the music (i.e., its speed and variations in speed) will strongly influence children's *expressiveness* of movement, such as quick/light, or heavy/ponderous, and their use of *dimensions,* such as large or small motions. We can use techniques to help children express changes in tempo by centering on *space,* such as moving around the edges of the room when the tempo is fast, and coming together at the center of the room when the tempo is slow; or being bunched together and jiggling as a group in the fast tempo, and opening outward into larger motions when the tempo is slow.

Children's expressive responses to *dynamics* (the volume and variations of volume) and *tone quality* (the characteristic sounds of the musical instruments, such as dark and warm, or bright and vibrant) will also influence the way in which children respond to the music. As described in the music chapter, certain styles of music capture different expressive components, such as the low positioning of the body in the "grounded" feeling of African music, compared to the lilting and "upward" feeling of a jig, played on a tin whistle. Being aware of such expressive facets of music will assist us in finding words to express such qualities and by helping children find their own words and forms of nonverbal expression through the use of their bodies.

Characteristics of Children's Movement Ability in Relation to Music

Two-year-old children tend to respond actively to markedly rhythmic music, yet each in his or her own body tempo. Young children's body rhythms are often faster than the comfortable body rhythm of an adult. Therefore, to help children learn to keep in time with music, it is important that teachers adapt the tempo of the music they use to accompany a child's movement, such as while playing an accompanying musical pattern on a percussion instrument. By watching and complementing the child's rate of movement we are demonstrating to children the synchronizing between sound and movement (McDonald, 1979; Scott, 1989). In addition, while using action songs within a dance experience, simple movements such as pretending to rock a baby while singing the song "Miss Polly Had a Dolly" can help toddlers link singing with moving, without requiring a strict adherence to performing the movement exactly in time with the beat of the music. Although such action songs are often sung while seated on the floor, other songs may involve standing in one place, such as in "Dr. Knickerbocker," where a child thinks of ways to move a part of his or her body and other children imitate this movement. Action songs that require moving around in a circle, often while holding hands, usually are too challenging for toddlers, as their bodily control is not developed enough to coordinate such refined movements within a group context.

Children two to three years old tend to keep to one type of movement throughout a piece of music; they may bob up and down repeatedly in response to the rhythm. Such repetition helps them develop a perceptual understanding of the relationship between music, the beat, and movement. Perhaps the most direct and enjoyable way to encourage children's spontaneous movement is to accompany them with improvised word rhythms (e.g., bob-bob-a-dee-bob), hand-clapping or other body percussion, or instrumental accompaniment on a hand percussion instrument. Children at this age can also accompany themselves with beads or bells worn on the ankles or wrists, or by holding maracas or jingle bells.

By the age of three, children have increased physical control and have acquired some ability to synchronize their movements with music or other rhythmic stimuli for a short period of time. They enjoy the sensation of speed and of moving through space for the sheer pleasure of it. Therefore, it is advisable to limit the number of children in any movement experience and to define clearly the direction of movement and space boundaries. It is also advisable to shift the activity to a more relaxing one before children tire, to avoid unfortunate accidents.

Four-year-olds begin to take an interest in acting out and dramatizing ideas through music and in learning movement patterns, like those of singing games and simple dances (McDonald, 1979). By five, they are beginning to identify and express the beat in music, and this helps them understand more about rhythm, tempo, patterns, accent, and meter. Developing an ability to maintain the beat is very important in the early childhood years, since research suggests that this ability does not change or improve substantially after the age of nine (Zimmerman, 1971).

Music and dance content should be relevant and engaging, so that children will willingly become involved. The length of children's concentration and their ability to follow directions and take turns will affect how a dance experience is planned and what experiences are offered. For example, two- to three-year-olds have limited awareness of others in space, may find it difficult to appreciate the rights of others, may be able to follow only one or two directions at a time, and are likely to concentrate in a group only for a brief period of time before becoming distracted. They tend to learn by imitation and will copy the adult and one another. Because imitation is an important component of acquiring movement vocabularies, we can assist very young children to extend their repertoire of movements by tapping into topics and imagery that are of interest, such as objects, animals, and events of their immediate world (e.g., cheeky mice, silly rabbits, playful birds, or lazy lizards). Things of which children have had direct experience, such as rabbits as pets at the early childhood center, are the most appropriate springboards for their imagination. Such considerations should be well thought out when planning dance experiences or when deciding how to stimulate unstructured play experiences. Similarly, older children's interests and abilities should be incorporated into the program.

When movement/dance is offered as a planned group experience, it is important that the length of the session be appropriate to the developmental and concentration abilities of the children. A general rule is to continue for as long as the children are involved and responsive, which may range from ten minutes to as much as forty-five minutes. Finish the activity when children are still enjoying themselves, so they will have positive memories that will make them want to join in on future occasions. Anything that was planned but not accomplished within one session can always be used at another time.

Well-Constructed Dance Sessions

A planned session should have a clear beginning, middle, and conclusion. We should ensure that everything is well planned in advance and that all necessary props, instruments, CDs/cassettes, and equipment are ready for use. One approach to attract children to the planned session is to move through the center, playing a percussion instrument and asking children to join the line, which is moving toward the area in which the resources have been organized. Because sessions may include only a few children, preselect those who may be included on the basis of your aims and invite them to join the group. Reassure other children who are not included that they will be able to join the group at another time.

After removing shoes and socks, sit on the floor and begin with an activity that will focus children's attention, such as having them place their feet near yours in the center of the group. This will help children focus their attention of their bodies and on our voice. Cecil-Fizdale (1991, pp. 134–135) provided some examples of how to begin with a focused warmup:

- "Stretch your arms up high, quickly hide them away." (Repeat, creating an atmosphere of anticipation and surprise.)
- "Place your hands on your knees, tummies, shoulders, heads, someone else's back, someone else's feet," and so on.
- "Listen to my voice . . . big steps, big steps, big steps . . . little tiny steps, little tiny steps . . . stop!" (Repeat.)
- "Together, let's creep around the rope circle. When you hear the drum, jump into the center and make a strong shape." (Repeat with variations.)

Set the context for the middle section of the planned experience, through the use of imagery or some other means for focusing children's attention on the main body of content of the experience. This section may consist of several subsections of content all linked to the core focus, drawing on either a variety of movement qualities or focusing on one or a few qualities. As a beginning experience with children, it can be helpful to employ the use of the imagery described earlier, where the floor, wall, and ceiling can be seen as a blank piece of paper upon which children's movements may be painted (Cecil-Fizdale,

1991). Cecil-Fizdale describes how children can imagine that there are pots of paint into which they can place their hands and then spread the paint down the walls. By extending this concept to other parts of the body, children might poke their noses in the paint and put a dot on the floor, wall, window, or doorknob. Other body parts, such as the elbow, shoulder, hips, chins, top of the head, bottom, or knees can serve as other ways of making dots, blobs, streaks, swirls, and other movements that are linked to spatial awareness.

Various musical selections will enhance the types of "painting" movements that are made. For example, children can make slow and smooth movements to gentle music and explore levels, such as painting high/low, wide/narrow, or in/out, using a small part of the room (e.g., the corner) or the full space (e.g., a wavy line that goes from corner to corner). By contrast, children might respond to vibrant music by "splashing" paint throughout the room and on each other while leaping or jumping and by interacting with each other—rubbing paint on each other's toes, ears, tummies, backs, or hair in a playful, chasing manner (Cecil-Fizdale, 1991). When children have had many such experiences, the focus of the dance session may become less directive, allowing children to find their own solutions about how to apply spatial relationships (e.g., levels, direction, time, and effort/style of movement). Through self-directed experiences, children will have opportunities to generalize principles of movement in relation to their own movement vocabulary.

The conclusion of the session should be clear to children. It is helpful to give them advance warning that the session is about to end and that what they are doing will be the last example of that experience. This way, children can prepare themselves for the finish and thus avoid surprising, disappointing, or unresolved conclusions to the experience. Cecil-Fizdale (p. 136) describes ways in which this may be achieved:

> The ending can be quiet or vibrant, depending on the energy and mood of the children. The *paint* theme could end in several ways. Individually, they could run and jump in a pot of paint and then make footprints all over the room and out the door; or they could slowly roll in the paint and roll to the end of the space to put on their shoes. Direct them to their next experience, or activity, do not leave children wondering what is going to happen next.

Dance/movement sessions should be enjoyable. We should project our joy throughout the experience and model this for children—share their delight and reinforce their ideas and expression. While we may have clear ideas of what we want children to learn through well-constructed sessions, it is important not to let this dominate the agenda. The key is to be spontaneous, caring, and positive, and to encourage the children to respond in similar ways.

Linking Musical Concepts and Dance Concepts

It is important to avoid stereotyping musical pieces and associating them with only one type of movement. ("This is skipping music.") Although some music suggests certain types of movement, such as bouncing, flowing, or quick/slow, the same music can be interpreted in many ways because there are so many components within it that can be linked to different qualities of movement. The underlying bass line may be ascending and punctuated, for example, but the melody line may be liquid and shimmering. In fact, the same piece of music may be used for different movements to avoid such associations and to help children focus on particular components in the music. If we economize on the number of musical selections we use, this has the advantage of allowing children to become intimately familiar with a specific piece. Familiarity will build children's confidence and willingness to take risks and to respond sensitively to the musical and expressive aspects of their bodily-kinesthetic expression. Even as adults we are more inclined to dance to our favorites, partly because we can anticipate changes in the music and alter our movements to complement aspects such as the chorus of the song, a lead instrument's melody line, or a change in tempo or rhythmic pattern. In similar ways, this principle applies to children as well. Although there may be many occasions in which we may want children to respond spontaneously and intuitive to music on the first hearing, there are other times in which having a familiarity with the music will enhance children's responsiveness. Consequently, providing opportunities for children to become familiar with a wide variety of recorded music through short daily listening experiences, rather than longer infrequent periods, can be very valuable. Such listening may occur throughout the daily program while children are engaged in other activities, such as painting, eating lunch, or resting; however, we should be careful that music does not simply become "aural wallpaper," that children begin to block out in order to concentrate on their tasks at hand.

We can help children focus on the music to become sensitive to the expressive potential for dance. While listening, we might ask the children to move their hands and feet rhythmically while sitting to help them feel the rhythmic flow before attempting to move creatively. Brief discussion about what they hear and how their hands and feet move will assist children to become inwardly centered, which will help them express what they feel and understand in the music. Responding sensitively to the music does not stop after the initial hearing of the music. When children become engaged in moving, they can lose the aural focus and be taken away from the experience itself. In such cases, we can ask them to stop, lie down on the floor and relax (and catch their breath), close their eyes so they can hear better, and listen to what the music is saying. This can help children refocus.

In addition, listening and responding to distinctive aspects of the music provide children with an inner discipline and the ability to attend to particular components of the music. For example, we might ask children to listen for the part in the music when the tempo changes, when a different instrument takes over, or when the style shifts from smooth/gentle/flowing to separated/active/bouncing. Our use of language to describe what is happening in the music, or how children are moving in response to the music, will not only reinforce unique responses in the children, but will help them develop their musical vocabulary in relation to their dance vocabulary. The language we use can help children become aware of their emotional and rhythmic responses, their use of individual or combined body parts, and their ability to vary movement by using different levels, directions, and qualities (i.e., effort, time, and space). Such language should suggest more than define. As discussed earlier, focusing on the ebb and flow of effort in relation to time and space provides numerous opportunities and frameworks for interpretation.

GUIDANCE

Teaching and learning through dance involves a continuous interplay between the children, what they are learning, and the guidance we give them. We can provide the setting and opportunities, but children also need feedback and encouragement to succeed within their own limitations and to move to the next step of what they are ready to accomplish. The movement drive should come from within the child and must be accepted by the teacher as belonging to the child. This means that we need to be flexible, inspiring, and trustworthy. We must be sensitive, responsive, and resourceful. In addition, we need to think in pure artistic action and be aware of the nonverbal ways in which children express and communicate thoughts and feelings. This requires working within the child's framework to help him or her identify and solve movement challenges.

Some children respond readily to bodily-kinesthetic and expressive forms of working and learning. They will react immediately in natural and artistic ways through the use of the body. However, others may need time to untie inhibitions and to muster the courage to take risks that will liberate them to realize their dance potential. Patient support rather than hurried demands will express a message of acceptance of individuals' learning styles and personalities. This requires us to form a trusting and affectionate relationship with children. We must develop techniques where we can provide advice and assistance without giving an impression that the child is inferior or failing. Encouraging responses and expressions that are "appropriate," rather than self-indulgent or willful, is an important component of good dance teaching. Establishing an atmosphere of support is effected by our ability to communicate successfully with children. Cecil-Fizdale (1991, p. 125) recommended ways in which this may be achieved:

> The teacher's ability to make children relax and feel comfortable with what they have to contribute is an essential part of their communication. The teacher must be able to communicate expectations, needs and difficulties in a direct and sensitive manner and be able to accept the same level of directness from the children. It is more than just giving instructions clearly, but rather, both verbal and nonverbal communication are employed. The teacher needs to watch, listen and feel what the children need and want to express.

We must expect that children will listen. If the children do not listen to the teacher's voice, they cannot respond to prompts, nor be aware of personal and group limits. A voice that is interesting, varied, and reflective of movement qualities will attract children's attention. For example, a voice that is energetic and enthusiastic will excite and stimulate children into vibrant movements. Likewise, gentle tones will indicate soft movement. Indeed, a gentle loving voice is generally more effective than an authoritative one. When a group of children is overexcited during a dance experience, they are more likely to settle and become quiet if we drop to the floor and quietly call the children to us, rather than trying to shout louder than everyone else. One effective teaching strategy is to encourage children to move silently. Although they may be so involved in a movement experience that they might be telling you and the other children what they are doing, we should aim to lead children gradually to understand that dance is a nonverbal medium, and greater involvement can occur in silence (Cecil-Fizdale, 1991). This can be communicated through statements such as "I can see what you are doing; there is no need to tell me as well" (p. 131).

Likewise, much of the teacher's communication during dance experiences will be modeled nonverbally. Children learn the language of movement by observing the teacher, who communicates through this language. We can model respect and careful physical contact by showing children appropriate ways of coming close together. This requires us to feel comfortable with having close physical contact with young children and engaging in movements such as rolling on the floor, leaping into the air, and joining in with other movements with children. Our comfort with our own bodies, and the ways we can use them as an expressive instrument, encourages and inspires children. When we demonstrate joy in moving, we give children permission to dance. This in itself may be enough inspiration to motivate children to participate in a natural form of expression.

Children can become motivated as well by watching other children move. Their observation and appreciation of other dancers helps extend their ideas and understanding of movement. By watching, they extend their own movement vocabulary; they learn the vocabulary of other dancers and can become inspired to try out these new ideas. In situations in which there are too many dancers for the working space, children's attention can be directed to a small group of children who are dancing. We must encourage the children who are watching to try to minimize their verbal responses, however, because this can interfere with the dancers' responsiveness and attention, and can indicate disrespect for other children's creative processes.

In addition to providing verbal and nonverbal inspiration and support, we must be aware of how the physical environment may strengthen children's opportunities to participate in dance. The dance area itself should be inspirational. The space should be well prepared, with a clean floor, good-quality props, and beautiful music. The sounds and imagery used to inspire dance should be aesthetic, and our speaking voices should be appealing. The overall environment should welcome but should not be overwhelming. In fact, too much space may inhibit or overexcite children; too little space can restrict movements and create crowding, frustration, and irritation. The floor should be smooth, without unexpected levels, and the space should be free of objects projecting into the room that might be bumped into. Good ventilation and a moderate room temperature will prevent children from becoming overly tired or dehydrated. In addition, children and adults should remove their shoes and socks to prevent slipping and hurting themselves or others. All these conditions enhance the environment and inspire dance.

Problem Solving

Learning takes place through problem solving. In child-oriented creative movement experiences, children are functioning within a framework that allows them to pose questions and experiment with answers. Such problem solving demands action to fulfill a purpose and to move towards a goal. Physical, mental, social, and emotional aspects are utilized when children are asked, for example, to find as many different ways as possible of moving on the floor from one corner of the room to the opposite corner. Problem solving can be explored at a higher level as well with older children, when they are involved in making a dance that centers on movement ideas. They select movements that fit best within the dance project and learn to eliminate what is unsuitable or superfluous. Children will be asking themselves questions such as "How will I place myself in relation to the other children as I move to the other corner of the room? How can I move this streamer/cape/scarf so that it will float like the wind or ripple like the water? How can I make my body be still while showing strength? How will my stillness look if I lean against the back of a child who is on the ground?" (Cecil-Fizdale, 1991).

   We can assist children to find alternatives and to ask themselves good problem-solving questions. Prompts such as "Find your own way to do it" or "How else can you do it?" will help children focus on a variety of shapes and ways to use energy levels in relation to time and space. In the process, children will not only gain movement experience, they also will be sensing relationships, evaluating, conceptualizing, and understanding (Fleming, 1976). Our prompts help children explore tasks by suggesting possible solutions and by posing appropriate questions. Questions such as "Where else? What else? How else?" help children discover new possibilities. They realize that there are many movements that can be used to solve particular dance problems, and that there are many individual responses, all of which are "correct." In this way, children's understanding is extended rather than being confined to the repetition of previously discovered possibilities. They are stimulated to explore, and in the process have freedom to set their own goals, work in their own ways at their own pace, and influence the content of the dance.

   However, the exploration and development of problem-solving ideas and solutions can take time and may not always reach immediate or full fruition. Yet, as children develop experience and a greater vocabulary of movements, their ability to make choices and to respond both intuitively and purposefully will increase. There will be other occasions in dance experiences where there may not be sufficient time to explore the numerous movement ideas that children may have, because the impetus and dynamics may be so energized. Nonetheless, if we are aiming for creative responses from the children, we must be prepared to go with the flow and not cling too tightly to some end result that we had in mind. Spontaneous, expressive, and intuitive responses are more important than a final outcome, judged on predetermined criteria.

Likewise, there may be occasions in which we will need to use skills to redirect children's behavior constructively, such as mimimizing attention-seeking or disruptive behavior, and to handle this in ways that will protect both the group and the individual involved. Cecil-Fizdale offers a number of recommendations for how to help children release physical-emotional energy that can lead to otherwise inappropriate classroom behavior (1991, p. 123):

- Tightening and relaxing muscle groups (e.g., make a fist, now relax; squeeze your face, now relax) will help muscular tension drop away.
- Making shapes as big and strong as possible is a constructive way to handle children who are being "tough."
- Joy and laughter generated during dance experience also provide a wonderful way to release tension.

Too much discipline in a dance experience can stop children from relaxing and participating spontaneously and joyfully to the process of problem solving. By contrast, a lack of discipline can cause chaos and fear. We must aim to establish an atmosphere in which active discovery can occur within a context of respect and where concentration and focus on the learning task at hand becomes exciting and motivating. Perhaps one of the reasons that some teachers are reluctant to participate in creative dance experiences with children is that they are frightened that things might get out of control. However, we need to accept that we can take a leadership position with the children without being dogmatic or overcontrolling. Rather than being authoritarian or repressive, we should aim to be authoritative and responsive, so that children come to understand that freedom is balanced with control and responsibility. Through modeling such behavior, we demonstrate how spontaneity is balanced with trust and respect. Indeed, when an authoritative style is lacking or inconsistent, children's creativity can flounder. Their attitudes to dance within a laissez-faire approach will be that anything and everything is appropriate. Unfortunately, this also will create a belief that dance is not an important and valued art form or discipline, and many wonderful learning opportunities may be lost.

SUMMARY

Children need many opportunities to dance freely through improvisation and to develop discipline and control through inner awareness in relation to dancing with others in small groups. This chapter focused on how the three key components of dance—effort, space, and time—can provide a foundational framework for observing and interacting with children through dance. These three components are closely linked to other dance concepts, such as direction, levels, dimensions, expressiveness, ranges, and spots.

Through the use of movement props, imagery, the voice, and musical instruments, children can be assisted to expand their movement vocabulary through action, interaction, and observation. Such ability to scaffold children's learning will be assisted by our understanding of the intimate relationship between music and movement, of young children's developmental characteristics and individual movement styles, and of the employment of well-constructed dance experiences that link musical concepts with dance concepts. Our main role is to guide children's bodily-kinesthetic learning through processes of problem solving and to model joy, appreciation, and respect.

ADDITIONAL READINGS

Baily, J. (1985). Music structure and human movement. In P. Howell, I. Cross, & R. West (Eds.), *Musical structure and cognition* (pp. 237–258). London: Academic Press.

Cecil-Fizdale, S. (1991). Creative dance and movement for young children. In S. Wright (Ed.), *The arts in early childhood* (pp. 115–139). Sydney: Prentice Hall.

Exiner, H., & Lloyd, P. (1987). *Learning through dance: A guide for teachers.* Melbourne: Oxford University Press.

Laban, R. (1971). *The mastery of movement.* Boston: Plays.

Walker, M. E. (2000). Movement and metaphor: Towards an embodied theory of music cognition and hermeneutics. *Bulletin of the Council of Research in Music Education, 145,* 27–42.

PRACTICAL ACTIVITIES

1. Observe young children during spontaneous dance and think of ways in which you might provide movement props, use your voice, or play a musical instrument to extend their learning.

2. With your friends, find as many different ways to move around the room and on the ground as you can. Focus on the dance components of effort, time, and space in relation to direction, levels, dimensions, expressiveness, ranges, and spots. Can you do some of these movements while being joined to another person or a small group of people?

3. Bring some of your favorite CDs or cassette tapes to class and play them to the group. Discuss what qualities of movement might be enhanced through specific musical pieces and how young children's bodily-kinesthetic learning might be enhanced through a well-structure dance experience. What would be the specific dance quality focus that would be suitable for different musical works? How might you inspire children to interpret such qualities in relation to the music?

CHAPTER TWELVE

THE INTEGRATION
OF THE ARTS

Long ago, people made up stories to explain how things have come to be. How every-thing began. Why the seasons come and the seasons go. How the stars, rivers, and mountains were created. Why we grow old and why we die. What happens to us after death. These stories were depicted through the use of the voice and body, simple musi-cal instruments, masks, and costumes. Such forms of expression grew into rituals that represented a whole community's beliefs associated with the mysterious and sometimes hostile world around them. Through these collaborative efforts, the arts belonged to everyone.

Storytelling such as this has remained a great tradition in the East. Stories have been handed down from the distant past, passed on from generation to genera-tion. In Peking opera, for example, such stories are played out through the integration of music, word, and action, using ancient costumes and evocative masks. The per-formers mime, dance, and sing to almost continuous instrumental accompaniment, and the performance often includes some kind of audience participation. Many Chi-nese children attend specialist schools that prepare them to perform in these tradi-tional art forms.

In Africa as well, storytelling sessions combine narration, dance, music, mim-ing, and impersonation. Dance is regarded as a composite art form, embracing songs, instrumental music, costumes, makeup, props, and texts to dramatize ritual and social ideas and to bring out the meaning and significance of the occasion. In some societies today, there is no word for music as an art form by itself. Music divorced from the gestures of word and action is unknown and inconceivable. But in the West, we don't have such integrated concepts the arts. We tend to separate rather than inte-grate the arts elements, and school curricula treat the arts as separate domains.

Recently, there has been an interest in integrated, interdisciplinary, and arts-infused curricula. This is a major change from the back-to-basics, anti-arts stance that was so prominent in the 1990s. Some of this emphasis on interdis-ciplinary education has been fueled by current research on the brain and learning. In addition, the interest in Gardner's theory of multiple intelli-gences, and his stance that all intelligences are necessary for complete human development and communication, has supported the view that education without the arts is indefensible (Snyder, 2001). Research that tracks brain-wave patterns is providing new support for Gardner's theory that music, for example, is a form of intelligence.

THE BRAIN'S SEARCH FOR PATTERNS

The physicist Gordon Shaw has shown that, when the electronic intervals of brain-wave patterns are translated into sound frequency equivalents and played as notes, they sound like music (Leng & Shaw, 1991). It appears that the very act of thinking itself has some sort of musical structure (Mahlmann, 2000). Follow-up research from this work illustrated that piano training with preschool children creates long-term enhancement of their spatial-temporal reasoning ability (Graziano, Peterson, & Shaw, 1999; Rauscher et al., 1997).

Other research further shows that there are causal links between listening to music and learning to play music and the development of spatial reasoning in young children (Hetland & Winner, 2001). Scientifically, this relationship between music and spatial-temporal reasoning is interesting, because it suggests that these two areas are related psychologically (i.e., relying on some *underlying skills*) and perhaps neurologically (i.e., relying on some of the same or proximal *brain areas*). Remarkably, there now seems to be clear evidence for a Mozart Effect—the popularized term for the belief that baby's and young children's intelligence can be enhance by listening to classical music (Hetland, 2000). As a result of such research, there is increased belief that music education should be a central component of the curriculum, particularly in early childhood (Ellis & Fouts, 2001).

Leng and Shaw claim that humans are born with certain brain-cell groupings that respond to patterns, whether in numbers, musical notes, or moves on a chessboard. These researchers state that this ability to perceive structure is accessible for use from birth, without any learning. This concept of a sort of prelanguage was discussed in the chapter on music in relation to children's ability to engage in musical "babble" using complex musical patterns, even before the brain has developed verbal language skills. There seems to be an inherent structure in the brain that is devoted to music, similar to that proposed by Chomsky (1986) in relation to brain structure and language, and that learning an inherent repertoire of patterns is a necessary condition for infants to understand music. For example, studies of the brain find that the layout of the auditory cortex is similar to the keys on a piano:

> A line of neurons respond to notes in order: A neuron that responds to a certain frequency is flanked by neurons that respond to lower frequencies on one side, and higher frequencies of the other. . . . When a listener hears a chord, the notes of that chord activate the neurons that correspond to these notes, forming three peaks of activation (Azar, 1996, p. 22).

Other research also indicates that the brain seeks patterns: It resists information that is fragmented, personally meaningless, and presented in isolation (Ellis & Fouts, 2001). Much of this research has been reported in medical and psychological journals and is now making its way into popular and educational journals. In addition, educational research on learning is now turning its attention to the human ability to recognize and create meaningful patterns and to understand links between ideas (Snyder, 2001). Educators are currently discussing how knowledge is likely to be learned more quickly and remembered longer if it is constructed in meaningful contexts, contexts in which connections among ideas are made. Educators claim, for example, that teaching concepts in different contexts builds understanding and that stimulating children's creative sides fortifies logical parts of the brain (Murray, 1996).

Consequently, there is a growing interest in multidisciplinary education and the inclusion of critical, creative, higher-order thinking skills and the ability to conceptualize and generalize in the school curriculum. As discussed earlier in this book, the notion of *learning how to learn* has become a central goal of education, where process is emphasized over product. It is interesting, however, that the idea of the integrated curriculum is not new. The Consortium of National Arts Education Associations' March 1994 briefing paper stated: "The proliferation of interdisciplinary programs in the past three decades may seem to reflect a new, even revolutionary, approach to education, but the underlying motivation is as old as the ancient ideal of the unity of knowledge" (p. 1, cited in Burton, 2001).

Origins of Interdisciplinary Curricula

In the early twentieth century, interdisciplinary learning, teaching, and curricula came to the fore as part of the progressive educational movement. Today, many educators are reflecting on the progressivist theory of John Dewey and his philosophy that education should be about life experiences—it should involve interdisciplinary learning (Beane, 1997; Lehman, 2000a, b; Wiggins, 2001). Because problems outside school do not present themselves in neat packages by disciplines, helping children understand relationships between disciplines is important for helping them learn to cope with real-life situations. We need to give children a broad perspective and multiple lenses through which to view their life experiences, and authentic integration can achieve this.

It is part of the democratic nature of education to use thematic units to examine the nature of life—units that do not have subject-matter distinctions. In such units, attention should be given to the specific concepts and processes of each discipline to enable students to make interdisciplinary connections (Beane, 1997; Wiggins, 2001). Mursell (1956, p. 307) commented, "Integration has to do, not primarily with subject matter, but with people and their lives." Although Mursell viewed integration as an effort to be produced in people, not a way of organizing the curriculum, today there is a tendency to view integration as a way to organize curriculum (Burton, 2001).

Yet some school subjects that are taken for granted in today's elementary curriculum are interdisciplinary versions of several formerly separated subjects. Language arts and social studies are examples of such cross-disciplinary subjects. Current educational trends are now dedicated to crossing similar but new frontiers among school subjects (Ellis & Fouts, 2001). The area of social studies, for example, now includes history, environmental education, indigenous education, and futures studies; language arts are including grammar, declamation, literature, new technologies, and media literacy. With the information explosion and the need to include an ever-increasing amount of knowledge content in the school curriculum, it is anticipated that the trend for forging even more connections will continue.

Other educational philosophies that are currently being adopted are offshoots from previous educational movements (Smith, 2000). The 1960s, for example, called for the teaching of the basic concepts of disciplines—the structure of subjects. During this period, content was structured around a spiral curriculum, where concepts were continually revisited in progressively more complex ways, and learning was promoted through personal discovery. Then, in the 1970s, educational movements centered on forms of knowing and understanding, realms of meaning, disciplines of thought and action, and cognitive and evaluative maps. The movement known as discipline-based art education was an offshoot of this philosophy. In addition, the case study approach to teaching aesthetics, which focuses on developing a questioning and problem-solving ambience in the classroom, also has its origins in many of these earlier "best" practices.

However, some people today are critical of interdisciplinary teaching and learning and see it as nondisciplinary; they believe that it simply ignores boundaries between disciplines. Claims are made that cross-disciplinary studies can be shallow because of the mixture of methods and concepts involved and that interdisciplinary efforts can shortchange depth of subject matter and not provide adequate coverage of crucial content or the sequencing of important skills (Burton, 2001; Ellis & Fouts, 2001). Gardner (1999b) pointed out that the quality of interdisciplinary or multidisciplinary work is largely dependent upon the teachers' depth of knowledge within each of the integrated disciplines. He commented:

> I have nothing against interdisciplinary or multidisciplinary work, but I don't believe you can actually *do* those kinds of work unless you have more than one discipline. We would laugh if somebody were to say he or she were bilingual and didn't know more than one language. And yet, we often nod when people say they're doing interdisciplinary work without realizing that they haven't mastered even *one* discipline (p. 10).

There is no doubt that understanding the disciplines is essential to good teaching; "The disciplines are the key to knowledge and methods of inquiry" (Phenix, 1964, p. 316). In the arts, this requires knowledge of the four main areas: music, art, dance, and drama. Most early childhood educators recognize the importance of the arts disciplines for young children's general learning. Because young children's approach to the arts generally is integrated rather than segregated, it is difficult for early childhood educators to omit any of the arts disciplines from the curriculum. However, the requirement for early childhood teachers to assist children's learning in all of these areas can seem like a tall order—it requires being competent in all of these disciplines.

The big challenge is that cross-disciplinary studies require even greater knowledge, skill, and mastery of materials than those needed to teach a single discipline. At least within one discipline, the lines of productive thought may be kept more directly and continually in view. Consequently, designing interdisciplinary curricula can be more difficult than designing a curriculum in one discipline (Burton, 2001).

Therefore, an integrated arts program needs to be built upon an understanding of what is distinctive about each of the arts disciplines as forms of human expression (Eisner, 2001; Ellis & Fouts, 2001). The arts are a primordial way of knowing. They provide objects and experiences that are expressive of significant values and special ways of knowing—qualities of understanding that cannot be duplicated anywhere else within the curriculum (Smith, 2000). Integration requires the recognition that the arts are important, collectively as well as individually, and that there are many things that the arts have in common. When it comes to the way that young children learn, it would seem that lying underneath the distinctions among the arts are also deeper things that unify them (Best, 2000a, b).

INTEGRATING WHILE MAINTAINING DISCIPLINE INTEGRITY

A discipline is as an organized activity in culture, such as physics, gardening, computing, or playing the violin (Gardner, 1999a, b). Gardner described disciplines as our mental furniture—the ways in which we think about questions and issues that are important to human beings. We can demonstrate a range of expertise within each of these disciplines, and because of this, the word "discipline" becomes a pun: It is not only a way of thinking but also a craft, something you get better at by working at it steadily, by applying yourself and improving it over many years of practice. Gardner makes a further distinction between a discipline and an intelligence, claiming that an intelligence can be used in a variety of different disciplines, and expertise in a discipline can draw on many different intelligences.

So how do we promote young children's understanding and expertise within each of the disciplines and across the various disciplines? Most importantly, we must realize that the structure of each of the disciplines must be understood before authentic connections can be made across them. We must preserve each discipline's unique learning styles in order to maintain the integrity of the individual disciplines, while carefully thinking about the types of relationships that can be made across the disciplines that will lead to well-defined skills and knowledge (Burton, 2001; Lehman, 2000a, b; Wiggins, 2001).

One successful school-based approach to integration of curriculum structures is through a focus on the multiple intelligences. The Key School in Indianapolis, for example, organizes curriculum around process and concept connections that are addressed by teachers in all disciplines (Snyder, 2001). In such an approach, the focus is on the critical ideas that are at the heart of each of the disciplines (Wiggins, 2001). Another approach is the magnet school concept, where schools focus on one curriculum area, such as the arts. Here the trend is to schedule larger blocks of uninterrupted time so that students can become immersed in activities. Through engagement in in-depth learning, students demonstrate authentic learning and increasing understanding and skills through projects and demonstrations (Snyder, 2001).

While these school-based approaches can provide good models for early childhood education, in many cases early childhood teachers work in relatively isolated contexts, where the total curriculum can be the sole responsibility of one individual or perhaps a small handful of people. Therefore, it can be helpful to think more generally about the various approaches to integration that may be available and whether these are appropriate in early childhood contexts.

Common Approaches to Integration

A number of techniques are used by teachers to serve as a form of integration of the curriculum. Bresler (1995) described one of these types of integration as *subservient,* where the arts are used to teach other subjects to make them more interesting. Other terms for this type of integration are *connection* (Snyder, 2001) and *teaching-tool connection* (Wiggins, 2001), where, for example, a song or dance is taught to relate to some knowledge, skill, or theme within the total curriculum. In other words, materials or concepts from one discipline are used to help teach or reinforce a concept in another curricular area, such as rhymes or songs to help teach the alphabet or counting or songs to help children learn about different forms of transportation, occupations, or any number of issues. Such connection-based activities also include teacher-directed role-play experiences (e.g., being firemen or choo-choo trains), group movement/dance activities (e.g., being growing seeds or fluttering butterflies), or thematic art activities (e.g., decorating a picture of a numeral or participating in "pink day"). However, connection activities are rarely intended to develop arts-based concepts and skills. Instead, the arts are in the service of another discipline. Because the teaching and learning is *through* the arts, rather than *in* or *about* the arts, such subservient or connection approaches are not justifiable substitutions for sequential arts education. Arts activities are simply an adornment added to "dress up" other instruction.

Wiggins (2001) describes two other common but ineffective forms of integration. In the *affective approach,* music and art in particular are used to create the mood in the classroom, or the arts are seen essentially as an outlet for children's creativity. In the second, the *social integration approach,* arts performances are used to build school spirit, enhance school functions, or foster community relations. In these approaches, the integration occurs at the point at which the students produce a product, such as an end-of-year performance. However, students are seen more as producers or performers than as learners.

A fourth approach, which comes close to a truly integrated curriculum, is that of *correlation* (Snyder, 2001) or *thematic or content connections* (Wiggins, 2001). Here, a connection is made between two or more disciplines through shared materials, activities, or content. For example, two or more teachers may agree to use the same materials or address the same topics at the same time, such as using a theme that explores the various titles given to groups of animal species (e.g., schools of fish, flocks of birds, herds of cattle), and children use a variety of materials to create stuffed fish, or murals of flocks or herds, with labels to illustrate each category. Alternatively, a single teacher may correlate different aspects of one discipline, such as selecting a song and then developing lessons related to that song to address each of the National Standards for Music Education. In correlation and thematic units, the focus is usually on the use of materials rather than on content or concepts to be learned and often no plan is made to develop important ideas across disciplines to form generalizations (Snyder, 2001). Wiggins (2001) warns that care must be taken to not confuse the substance of a content area with the packaging in which it is presented.

Underpinning Principles of an Integrated Approach

In contrast to the four approaches described above, an *integrated approach* is one in which arts concepts and practices are combined in relation to broad teaching and learning goals. Making such conceptual and process connections involves unifying the disciplines while at the same time recognizing that each of the fields of knowledge is different and distinct, with its own special content. The integrity of each discipline is maintained while central concepts and processes are explored in meaningful ways. The exploration of concepts and processes occurs through the use of more than one language, such as *sound* (music), *image* (visual art), *gesture* (movement, dance, and drama), *words* (poetry or stories), and *metaphoric symbols* (which involve cross-modal or cross-domain connections).

For instance, concepts such as similarity and contrast or tension and resolution can be explored in all arts disciplines, because the arts employ these concepts as expressive, structural, communicative, and process aspects (Snyder, 2001; Wiggins, 2001). These concepts provide coherence, meaning, and affect in expression through music, art, dance, and drama. For example, explorations might include dramatic or literary representations of social tension/resolution (e.g., good versus bad "forces"), the use of expressive variation in music (e.g., aggressive versus gentle sounds), applying similar/contrasting energies in dance (e.g., various positions in space), or utilizing color, texture, or line in art to create contrast, tension, or unity. By exploring such concepts within and across the arts, the act of creating involves the use of symbol systems to express feelings through images, sounds, movements, abstractions, and impressions. A key way in which such broad concepts can be integrated is by helping children explore three forms of connection or interactive relationships through the use of structural, expressive, and process facets (Barrett, 2001; Snyder, 2001; Wiggins, 2001). These are described in Figure 12.1.

FIGURE 12.1 Using Structural, Expressive, and Process Facets of Integration

Structural Facets. Many structural concepts can be perceived in analogous ways in expressive works. For example, there is meter in poetry and music, and there is line and contour in music and art. Virtually all art forms—poetry, art, dance, sculpture, music, or architecture—include structural aspects like repetition and contrast, tension and resolution, or theme and variation. Patterning elements in language arts, such as words, phrases, sentences, and paragraphs, are similar to patterning elements in music, such as loudness, duration, pitch, and timber. For instance, structures in music include repeated melodic themes, and tension can be expressed through gradual increases in volume and speed. Structural concepts that are applicable to both music and language arts include plot, theme, subplot, mood, form, tone, meter, and dialogue. Many of these concepts are also applicable to drama and dance. Patterning elements are found, for example, in children's dramatic play, when they explore the development of characters and events; in dance, when they explore movement sequences; in art, when they develop visual prototypes of images and "stories"; and in music, when they use sound sequences.

Expressive Facets. Children can be helped to focus on the range of meanings that a work may embody—how it conveys a mood or an expressive character. Even young children are able to discuss layers of meaning and how these meanings are suggested through the creator's use of artistic elements and structure. This can include figures of speech in story; an instrument's musical timbre and expressive potential; the gradual infusion of color in painting; contrasting textures in collage; or expressive movements in dance. We can help children use perception, thought, and feeling to find complementary relationships across the arts and to participate in the arts expressively through vocal inflection, movement fluency, musical phrasing, and sensitivity to tension-relaxation and similarity-variation.

Process Facets. Many connections can be perceived and experienced by engaging with the subject matter and using the general artistic processes of the arts (e.g., discovery and pursuit, self-awareness, communication, social interaction, perception, technical skills, analysis, and critique). In addition, the three main artistic processes—making, presenting, and responding—are applicable to all arts disciplines and involve all modes of participation: as performer, composer-creator, improviser, analyzer, receiver-listener, and critic-evaluator.

These structural, expressive, and process forms of connection are based on the ways in which children process information and come to understand the various disciplines. As discussed in Chapter 3, the significant ways in which children come to understand the arts is through thinking visually, aurally, and with the body. Through all of the arts, children combine thought, emotion, and action and turn action into representation. We can help children see connections across the various arts disciplines by focusing on the ways in which children perceive, think, and respond emotionally to the structural, expressive, and process facets of each of the arts. By doing so, children are encouraged to apply and synthesize ideas from one discipline to another.

By comparing and contrasting ideas, children can be helped to develop deep understanding and critical thinking. Such learning involves a more comprehensive understanding of fewer works, rather than a shallow understanding of a number of works. Through the processes of making, presenting, and responding to their own works, children can become engaged in seeing connections across the arts. However, such learning should not be restricted to children's own works. Their understanding also can be enhanced through looking at and listening to the masterworks of professional artists.

As discussed in Chapter 4, it is preferable if the vision and resulting plan of an integrated curriculum emerges or is co-constructed with the children in collaboration with adults. It must come from within, and all players should have input into the decision-making process. Integrated learning is something that develops over time. It will require research into community resources and support and may involve parents and other community members. Snyder (2001, p. 39) gives us further insight into the emerging and collaborative nature of an integrated curriculum:

> The world of interdisciplinary and arts-infused curriculum models is rich, varied, and open to explorations large and small. It is not a set of materials, activities or strategies, but rather an opportunity for teachers to forge new relationships with students, other teachers, and the content of learning. The minute it can be "canned," it will lose the essential ingredients for integrity.

The importance of co-constructed decision making, rather than "canned" early childhood curriculum packages, is that young children are still in the process of adapting, organizing, and otherwise constructing their own schema. Consequently, the separation of academic disciplines for scholarly purposes is artificial and makes little sense (Ellis & Fouts, 2001). An interdisciplinary curriculum can help children find connections between the arts and with other disciplines. Because the arts involve such a variety of ways of knowing, it seems logical to make the arts a starting place from which other learning can evolve, particularly in early childhood, where young children's understanding often is cross-modal or cross-disciplinary.

Throughout this book, a number of examples were provided of ways in which to scaffold young children's learning by building on their ideas and events during play. Some examples were the use of recorded lizard sounds and the creation of other sounds to enhance a group's "Dinosaur Hunting

Expedition," the extension of the "Sandy Beach Fairies" play, the creation and performance of a sound story, and the class-groups' making of a movie. Such learning is authentic and relevant because it is a natural extension of children's spontaneous play, where the ideas originated from the children. The artistic objectives of the teacher can be implemented in the extension of children's play, such as suggesting that the children create music to enhance their story; to write a message to pass on to someone else; to label objects or areas of the room to represent something else; to draw pictures or maps to clarify objects, events, or places; or to create musical sound stories and "scores" to remember patterns and relationships.

There also are times when a teacher can take a more active role in initiating an integrated arts experience, or in working with other teachers on small- and large-group projects, to enable children with similar or different learning styles to collaborate. The aim of such experiences is for an integration of musical, visual, dance, and dramatic elements, while avoiding a situation in which any one of the arts domains becomes dominant. As children work together to create their own stories, music, artworks, dances, and dramatic events, they extend their imaginations and find multiple entry points for making their own contribution to the whole, working in their preferred domains and styles. Such processes bring children closer to the work of professional artists as they select and use a variety of media for the purposes of individual and group artistic expression. Reflection-in-action, collaborative interaction, and active learning and inquiry are key considerations in such projects. By engaging in "fusion" arts, children begin to understand the literal and metaphoric links between the arts domains, and use realistic and abstract symbols to communicate their meaning. The teacher's use of audio and video recording equipment is also helpful to capture both the processes and products of children's integration of:

- Music (listening, improvising, composing, learning musical literature)
- Dance (imitating, interpreting, choreographing)
- Drama (role playing, character building, miming, story building)
- Visual arts (using art media and processes to make props, masks, costumes, structures, backdrops; using lighting and projected images)

These arts domains and forms of expression create openings for a variety of lines of thoughts and feelings that can be pursued though artistic concepts and elements.We can help children identify the expressive properties of each of the arts forms, and the resources that will best support integrated meaning-making and communication. This involves helping children identify and understand a clear purpose of achievement—to know what they want to say and how they want to say it. Such expression of ideas emerges through a desire to structure thoughts and feelings in a way that tells a story through various modes of expression—visual, aural, bodily-kinesthetic, interpersonal, and intrapersonal. Here, "story" is meant as a medium for the integration of a variety of "texts" and for the exploration of the structural, expressive, and process facets described earlier.

STORYBUILDING AS A BEGINNING POINT FOR INTEGRATION

One key starting place for the integration of the arts can be through story, because this can provide a structural base from which broad concepts and expressive forms of representation can emerge via a range of texts. Through story, children have opportunities to explore historical and current events, which often lend themselves to a range of issues that embody simple and time-less truths, such as right/wrong or good/bad—the types of issues that have been the core of classical myths, legends, and folklore throughout the centuries and often are the basis for many popular children's movies today. Children seem to have an intuitive sense for working with such concepts, and they lend themselves to exploring aspects of repetition and contrast, tension and resolution, and theme and variation, as discussed earlier in relation to structural facets of integration. So omnipresent are these concepts that even college students gravitate to them when developing structural cohesion through their own sto-rylines during arts integration workshops in their teacher preparation courses.

Hence, the use of standard myths, legends, or folklore, and of children's own stories (which often include similar types of content), can be excellent starting points. As a first experience with such integration, one technique may be to tell only part of a story to the children and have small groups of children devise and enact their own ending, using all domains—visual, aural, and bodily-kinesthetic. Another approach is to use poetry, such as that found in the excellent books of Shel Silverstein, and to break the poem into parts, having each group enact one segment through movement, mime, sounds effects, and images. When all segments are assembled and presented to the full group, the completed work can provide a delightful surprise for the children and a way for them to see how the parts can be sequenced and united into the whole, larger artistic work.

Once children have had such experiences, a next step may be to "build" story with the children, to assist children's imaginations to create their own stories in collaboration with the teacher. There are a number of techniques that can be used to storybuild with children, where the use of objects, masks and costumes, enactment, and music are the stimuli for the development of open-ended ideas, leading toward structure and cohesion. Each of these are discussed in the next segments.

Techniques for Storybuilding

Objects.   Story can be built around a natural object, such as a rock fossil, or a made object, such as a goblet or a ring. In this technique, the teacher goes into role, pretending he or she has found the object, and uses a set of open-ended questions to assist the children to construct a story from their imaginations. Where do you think I found this? Who might have owned it? What was it used for? How old do you think it is? Why is it with us now? What could we use it for? How could we use it? Where could it take us? Why should we go there? As the story emerges, children add ideas based on the ideas that the other children have presented, until a coherent set of events can be synthesized and summarized by the teacher. This, then, becomes the basis for various forms of exploration, incorporating dramatization, dance, music, and art.

Masks and Costumes.   A second starting point for storybuilding can be through the use of masks that the children have made. (It should be noted that puppets that the children have made, such as glove, finger, marionette, rod, and shadow puppets with jointed limbs/waist and an opening mouth, could serve a similar purpose.) Masks can be made from paper bags, or more complex masks can be made from papier mâché molded from clay models that the children have made or plaster masks molded from the children's own faces (working in pairs, older children can create full or half masks by layering strips of plaster, wetting each strip so that it adheres and the mask eventually sets). Papier mâché and plaster masks can be made over several sessions and may include highly colorful and decorative elements, such as sequins, glitter, feathers, beads, and other details to highlight facial features and additional adornments, such as straw, strips of cloth, or pipe cleaners for hair. Masks provide an excellent starting place for the development of story, where characters and events are built based on the aesthetic qualities found in the masks.

Children take great delight in selecting clothing to wear to enhance the character of their masks or selecting things to wear from the dress-up cupboard. Teachers should also make available a range of open-ended fabrics that can be used to complement the masks' aesthetic qualities, such as a variety of lengths of cloth of various colors and textures: chiffon, burlap, satin, cotton, or felt. Such fabrics can include old drapes, dressmakers' remnants, and resources recycled from community businesses or discarded materials from parents. Headbands can be used to fasten tulle and other light fabrics to the child's head to represent a veil or long hair. Heavy black burlap or curtains can be draped across the body as a cape to make even the most innocent of children seem spooky or powerful. Rubber bands can be used to attach strips of chiffon to the wrists to free the children's hands while allowing for flowing movements of the arms.

Children can explore a variety of movements by watching themselves in mirrors to make their masks and costumes come alive and to develop belief in their character. By bringing the children back together as a full group, the teacher can develop story with the children by using open-ended questions and storybuilding techniques to define characters and to establish how these can be clustered or contrasted to create story events and sequences. As a starting point, the teacher might ask each child to show how a character can move and make sounds in a variety of ways and to discuss the impact of the character's movements and sounds. Individual children may have a particular mood and style of movement in mind to represent their characters, and we can encourage them to try different ways in which they might move—high/low, wide/narrow, and including large/small areas of the room. We can also help a child use his or her voice and body-percussive sounds to complement and enhance such movements.

By focusing the children's attention on similar and contrasting expressive qualities of each of the characters, children can be encouraged to use their own words to describe concepts, such as gentle/peaceful/timid, or strong/powerful/bold. They can also identify those characters who have similar qualities and imagine ways in which these characters might have some common idea or purpose: those who live in the cave/forest/mountains, those who have come from outer space/a small village/an ancient temple, those who are the nice/nasty ones, the queen/king, the wind/fire/rain, or any number of ideas. Such imaginative explorations lead naturally into the development of story and the sequence of events upon which a range of artistic representations can take place.

Music.   A third starting point for storybuilding can be through the use of musical ideas. Using simple percussion instruments such as a triangle, wood blocks, a guiro, maracas (shakers), drums, or melody instruments such as a xylophone, autoharp, or African thumb piano, children can discuss metaphoric associations with these sound qualities. For example, sounds can be used to enhance an already established story line (e.g., triangles are played by the gentle village folk as they enter the opening of the cave), or the sound sources themselves can be the stimulus for the development of story.

An electronic keyboard (synthesizer) is a particularly versatile instrument for storybuilding, because the full range of sound possibilities can be suggestive of a number of associations. The labels given to each of the programmed sounds are descriptive of the tone qualities and their emotional impact (e.g., "iced rain," "Milky Way," "angelic choir," "dark cave," "gospel organ," "chorused piano," "slap bass," or "symphonic orchestra"). In cases where teachers may not feel confident about playing a keyboard, there are numerous sound-producing possibilities if only the *black* keys are played. Because the keyboard consists of series of five black keys, when only a five-key series is played, that represents the pentatonic scale. In a pentatonic scale, all note combinations sound good because the half steps (the semi-tones that create the greatest dissonance) are not included. With a bit of practice, teachers can find a number of expressive pentatonic (black note) musical motifs that can be used to establish aesthetic and expressive musical ideas. Responding to the sound characteristics of a few selected settings on the keyboard, we can quickly discover a range of playing techniques to establish various musical ideas. Such explorations should involve playing on the upper, middle, and lower registers of the keyboard, using notes in various combinations to create harmony, exploring sound sequences and patterns, and experimenting with expressive qualities such as fast/slow, loud/soft, and high/low to create particular moods.

Within a relatively brief period of time, adults can develop a range of musical ideas that can be presented to children, along with open-ended questions, where children make associations between the musical sounds and images. As with storybuilding based on objects or masks/puppets/ costumes/props, children can readily discuss similar and contrasting musical qualities and use their imaginations to establish concepts of characters, events, and a storyline. For example, children might respond to the teacher's playing of a particularly majestic motif (e.g., a repeated bass note pattern with brassy notes in the top register of the instrument, similar to a trumpet heralding) by saying, "And this is where the soldiers ride into the village." A different musical motif (e.g., mellow, warm, rich sustaining sounds that melt into each other) might elicit a response such as "We could be mermaids swimming down to our underwater house." Such musical ideas can be reviewed by the teacher, and children can be helped to sequence ideas to create structure that can be enacted, such as "When the soldiers ride past the lake, the mermaids dive off the rocks and into the water."

Once a story has taken shape and children are involved in its enactment, they will be eager to take turns playing the keyboard and other musical instruments at particular points and will use the instruments as extensions of their bodies. The musicians, for example, can watch the movements of the dancers/ actors and time the playing of their music to coordinate with the dancers' speed, style, and mood, and capture the emotional and expressive components. Likewise, the dancers/actors can indicate to the musicians when they want the music to be stronger or weaker, for example, flowing or separated, extended or brief, to encompass a range of structural and expressive aspects of the process. When sound, imagery, gesture, and dance are integrated in the thoughts and actions of children, they are individually and collectively liberated to make and communicate meaning in cross-modal ways. This can be best achieved through experiences in which children's ideas emerge through integrated arts play, initially in collaboration with adults, and with increasing experience, with less participation from adults.

Integrated Arts Play Emerging from Children's Ideas

Through play-based experiences, children and adults can create imaginary worlds—learning contexts where links are made between children's ideas, using a range of thinking and feeling processes. Through collaboration, we can help children recognize and create meaningful patterns of images, events, sounds, and characters and play these out in continually evolving and emerging ways. Such thematic-oriented discovery learning allows children to examine the nature of life without subject matter distinctions. In other words, an interdisciplinary, integrated learning experience helps children make connections by drawing on the process facets discussed earlier, and using these to develop structural and expressive facets. Figure 12.2 provides a framework for how this may be achieved.

Integrated arts play also can be interpreted through music and movement alone, using vocal sounds and body percussion or simple instruments such as natural objects, hand percussion, Orff instruments (e.g., xylophones),

FIGURE 12.2   General Processes for Integrated Arts Play Emerging from Children's Ideas

1. Review the content of the told or created story and discuss the main features (characters, events, dramatic opportunities, movement/musical prospects). Contrast and find connections between structural and expressive facets that can be explored in depth.

2. Identify prime techniques and select materials with sensitivity that will support what is to be communicated and convey the essence of what is felt. The use of masks, props, costumes, and puppets need not be realistic but may merely suggest metaphoric associations. The use of these resources and the incorporation of dance, music, and art helps:
   - Build belief in the project by creating an emotional commitment
   - Contribute to the overall dramatic effect
   - Add to the total presentation

3. Explore and experiment with media simultaneously to enhance effective communication through words, actions, music/sounds, and images. Incorporate open-ended resources in many ways and in many contexts, such as:
   - Fabrics for costumes, or to represent walls, caves, tunnels, rivers, or boundaries
   - Cardboard boxes, corrugated cardboard rolls, polystyrene, and wooden blocks to serve as symbols (e.g., treasure chests, buildings, or cliffs)
   - Paper (crepe, transparent, cellophane, tissue, newspaper), paint (powder, poster, fabric), felt pens, colored pencils, and scissors to create visual contexts, such as backdrops, to enhance characters, or to serve as message-sending devices
   - Fasteners (headbands, rubber bands, staplers, tacks, pins), adhesives (paste, glue, masking tape, transparent tape), and binders (string, rope, clothesline, raffia, wire of various gauges)

4. Transform the space (the room or a section of it, or an outdoor area) to create the overall context and to develop subcontexts. The use of simple platforms (large, sturdy wooden boxes) can assist in elevating an individual and creating a symbolic meaning. A small table or a stepladder can add additional height for contexts in which a character needs to be tall or to appear from a great height; when draped with long fabric, the character receives additional impact.

5. Consider the use of scenery or visual effects to enhance the children's belief and involvement and to serve as art forms in their own right. Brainstorm ideas for artworks with children that may enhance the impression of the location (e.g., weather, buildings, rooms, alternative spaces) or to make imaginary characters such as giants or aliens more believable. Such artworks can be made into overhead transparencies and projected on to a screen as a backdrop. Colored cellophane can be used to create moods (e.g., a shift from a completely red screen to a blue one can create the context of moving from a hot or active context to a cool or subdued one). A simple cutout of a tree, window, or doorframe can also set a context. Children can dance in front or behind the screen. When shadow dancing between the overhead projector and the screen, children can move closer or further away from the light source to create variation in size and focus. By adding props, such as hats, skirts, tails, or wings, the characters take on new dimensions.

FIGURE 12.2 Continued

6. Use an inexpensive garden spotlight and position it in the space to represent changes of seasons or weather, the passage of time, journeying, coming of darkness/lightness, or a shift of context or mood. A crude gobo (a filter placed in front of the spotlight) can be made by cutting shapes, such as trees, from aluminum foil and projecting this lit shape onto a wall or screen.

7. Rely more on the power of suggestion than on theatrical realism. Aim to create an atmosphere that blends image, sound, and action while delineating objects and events carefully. For example, the impression of a garden can be acheived by children holding flowers or by placing plants in strategic places. The impression of a stream can be achieved by gently ruffling a long satin cloth at each end. The image of a boat can be created by a small group of children holding onto sections of a long piece of elastic, which they collectively shape as a boat; this allows the group to move throughout the space and create the impression of rocking, sway, or rolling.

8. Develop the work with the full group, allowing the music, art, drama, and dance to grow naturally out of the developing play. It can be helpful to assign tasks to small groups for independent work, such as focusing on the music, dance, art, or the dramatic enactment of some component, and then coming back together to share visual, aural, and movement ideas up to that point, before moving on to the development of the next segment.

or a synthesizer. The key characters can create the music themselves while dramatizing (e.g., wearing ankle bells, strumming on bamboo breast plates, or dramatically playing a gong while "journeying" from one play context to another). Other children can assist by making music and vocal or body-based sounds to accompany those who are dancing or enacting the drama. However, avoid an overemphasis on sound effects, such as the clip-clopping of horses' hooves, because in and of themselves these effects are not music; they are simply literal imitations of sounds in the real world. Instead, help children combine sounds and create musical motifs as symbols of things felt, through the use rhythmic/melodic patterns, the layering of various vocal and instrumental textures, the use of repetition and variation, and the use of expressive elements, such as dynamics (loud/soft) and tempo (fast/slow).

Assisting Children to Apply Self-Imposed Artistic Judgment

By reworking, extending, elaborating, and refining the ideas, we can guide children's learning processes through:

- Supporting (physically, socially, emotionally, intellectually)
- Clarifying (explaining, demonstrating)
- Modeling (showing alternatives through example)
- Labeling (describing literally or expressively)

By applying these scaffolding techniques, we can assist children to develop thematic ideas and processes while working with smaller, more manageable chunks of content. Figure 12.3 provides examples of the types of principles that can be applied to scaffold children's understanding and assist them to apply self-imposed standards and criteria for selecting and modifying their ideas.

From the beginning stages of the project to its final "production," the children should instinctively feel the kinds of structures they will want to develop through commitment, participation, and enactment. While the process should be undertaken with care and enthusiasm, the creative impetus should not be lost in precisely rehearsed details. There should be a natural extension from play. The story, characters, dances, music, and dramatic effects should become the children's, and their artistic objectives can be guided to help them discover connections. Connections are made when children find their own solutions and understand and apply separate and integrated knowledge and skills. Through such experiences we can assist children to establish mindsets that lead them to look for linkages and connective relationships across all areas of learning.

FIGURE 12.3   Principles for Assisting Children to Remember Previous Segments

1. Work in sections by stopping to review progress to date. When the group appears to be losing direction, go back to the beginning and work from the well-established bits to the sections that are still in an improvisatory state. Confirm new sections by repetition and then go on to create new sections. Continue until the substance and overall shape of the piece feels complete or whole. Individual judgment will tell you when this stage has been reached.

2. Assist the children to write down their ideas, using simple notation systems to represent key elements, such as a map representing the placement of objects and characters within the total space, images to capture the various styles of movement used, and symbols for the various instruments and the musical patterns that are played. Such notation acts as a means to remember, a way of "fixing" a definitive version. This can be particularly helpful when the project extends over a period of time, and the children want to remember their previous ideas so they can progress to the next stage with confidence and relative ease.

3. Videotape the process and product for discussion, reflection, and evaluation. Often this will be the first time that some of the children will be able to view their movements, hear the complete music (rather than just their part in the piece), and glean a complete picture of the full group's input. The focus of the reflection should be on the effectiveness of the depiction of events, moods, and meanings. This will include issues such as the impact of the children's movements and music; the power of the integration of sound and image; and the collaborative input and involvement of participants in the problem-solving process.

SUMMARY

When connections between disciplines are valid, the bonds between them are organic—they make sense without forcing a fit or stretching a point. Integrity across disciplines is characterized by a sense of balance, complementary relationships, and mutual illumination. Such knowledge integration occurs through emergent, arts-based play, where direct linkages across disciplines and modes of expression are established. We can assist children to find logical connections and develop structural, expressive, and process facets of integration within their artistic play. Through such experiences, children learn concepts, develop artistry and deep understanding, and value learning through interpersonal and intrapersonal collaboration.

To understand multiple dimensions of a work, children must become individual and collective participants in experiencing and appreciating the meanings that the work conveys. They take on the role of artists and begin to understand the significance of the arts in their lives. Such understanding stems from the use of artistic elements and concepts and involves reflecting on the effectiveness of how meaning is derived and communicated through the integrated modes of expression—visual, spatial, aural, and bodily-kinesthetic.

The excellence of a true, integrated experience involves depicting and describing ideas in multiple ways and from different perspectives. Each modality of expression is incomplete without the others, and hence through integrated learning experiences, ideas are developed and expressed cross-modally. Integration involves unlimited imagination partnered with purpose, structure, and discipline. It is driven by a desire to make beginning-to-end sense of ideas among ideas. Integration allows children to see the indivisibility of form and content, and of content and process. Such multidisciplinary work involves the working out of ideas, both individually and collaboratively. This kind of work evolves from inspiration, and involves intuitive, emotional, expressive, purposeful, and "spiritual" connections.

ADDITIONAL READINGS

Barrett, J. R. (2001). Interdisciplinary work and musical integrity. *Music Educators Journal, 87*(5), 27–31.

Beane, J. A. (1997). *Curriculum integration: Designing the core of democratic education.* New York: Teachers College Press.

Best, H. M. (2000a). Arts, words, intellect, emotion. Part 1: Toward artistic mindedness. *Arts Education Policy Review, 102*(6), 3–11.

Best, H. M. (2000b). Arts, words, intellect, emotion. Part 2: Toward artistic mindedness. *Arts Education Policy Review, 102*(10), 2–10.

Ellis, A. K., & Fouts, J. T. (2001). Interdisciplinary curriculum: The research base. *Music Educators Journal, 87*(5), 22–26.

Smith, R. A. (2000). Policymaking for the future: Three critical issues. *Arts Education Policy Review, 102*(2), 21–22.

Wright, S. (2001). Guiding learning processes in the integration of the arts. *Contemporary Issues in Early Childhood, 2*(2), 225–238.

PRACTICAL ACTIVITIES

1. Virtually all art forms—poetry, art, dance, sculpture, music, architecture—include structural and expressive aspects like repetition and contrast, tension and resolution, or theme and variation. Observe children during play and identify examples of how they use such aspects in their personally created artworks. These artworks may be created either individually or in a group, and often they may be rather brief (two to five minutes). Using Figure 12.1 as a guide, look for examples of how children use structural and expressive aspects in the following:

   Music, such as:

   - Repeated rhythms, the use of word repetition for musical purposes, or motor pattern while playing musical instruments (e.g., two hits on a drum followed by three shakes of maracas)
   - The use of expressive patterning over short or long passages, such as dynamic patterning "YA, YA, here I go," or singing/playing the same musical phrase loudly when one event occurs, but softly when a different event occurs (or perhaps the same melody is used in a high-pitched voice/instrument in a quick tempo at one point, and a low-pitched voice/instrument in a slow tempo at another point)

   Dramatic play and expressive movement/dance, such as:

   - The development of characters, events, plot, theme, subplot, mood, form, dialogue, gesture, and movement sequences
   - The creation of tension/relaxation through expressive facets, such as the increase/decrease in movement energy and speed/time in relation to space

   Art, such as:

   - The use of patterns in nonrepresentational images (e.g., repetition and contrast within the image) and in representational images (e.g., the use of face prototypes in people, animals, and the sun in the sky, such as in Figure 3.6 on page 57)
   - The use of expressive facets, such as the infusion of color in a painting, contrasting textures in collage, "movement" in lines and three-dimensional forms, and overall composition of a two-dimensional work

2. Refer to Figure 12.2 and discuss examples you have observed, used with children, or experienced yourself where:

   - Masks, props, costumes, puppets, open-ended resources, scenery, or visual effects were used to: (1) build belief and emotional commitment within an arts project, (2) contribute to an overall effect or presentation, or (3) transform a space to create an imaginary context
   - Sound, image, movement, and support props were used to suggest rather than depict an object or event literally
   - Segments of a project were rehearsed and refined, and then reconstructed into the whole

CHAPTER THIRTEEN

PLANNING, IMPLEMENTING, AND DOCUMENTING THE CURRICULUM

My first trip to China caused me to reflect critically on all that I knew about early childhood education and the meaning of curriculum. Several of the Chinese kindergartens I visited had over a thousand children, and the classrooms and hallways had large murals displaying the virtues of education: patriotism, loyalty to socialism, enthusiasm for manual labor, manners, politeness, discipline, spiritual beauty, friendship to classmates, respect for elders, and love of the ancestral country. A large part of Chinese education is based on roles and rituals. At recess break, for example, I watched teachers lead structured singing games, where several groups of over fifty three- to five-year-old children simultaneously practiced complex dances to music projected over loud speakers.

The kindergartens and elementary schools had specialist music and dance rooms with large-mirrored walls, ballet bars, and sprung wooden floors, and children had highly structured lessons taught by specialist teachers. At the elementary schools, groups of children wearing ornate costumes and makeup performed a range of elaborate songs and dances representing the various ethnic groups within China. In the better elementary schools, children participate in two hours of instruction in music, dance, and art per week and have opportunities to take up to twenty-two elective arts subjects, such as instrumental playing, dance, and painting, many of which begin at 7:00 A.M. and are also held every afternoon for a minimum of an hour. Since Chinese children (including preschoolers) attend school six days a week, those elementary school children who participate in two music interest groups, for example, can receive up to twelve hours of music instruction per week, provided by a range of specialist teachers (Wright, 1995b).

Prior to my visit to China, one of my colleagues had written, inviting me to attend an informal performance by the students of his early childhood teacher training institution, at which I was asked to make a short performance as well. I imagined this would be a casual, postdinner karaoke-type experience. But after dinner our Western delegation was taken to a professionally tiered performance hall, where eight hundred students gave us a standing ovation, and we were escorted to a section about a third of the way back from the stage. Throughout the one-hour performance, we were presented with what could only be equated to the performances standards of Western arts-major students. Beginning with a hundred-voice choir, resplendent in professional costuming, there were a series of high-level individual and group student performances of dance, music, theatrics, and acrobatics. This was followed by a classical duet by two stunning dance instructors, a professional-standard performance that would rival much found on contemporary Western television today. Immediately following this, I was invited to the stage to make my presentation!

Visitors to China are generally stunned by the artistic achievements of teacher trainees and very young children. The performance standards of both groups are technically far in advance of those of the West. The entrance requirements into early childhood teacher training institutions require students to pass tests that demonstrate they have some special skills, such as the ability to play the piano, dance, sing, or draw (Zhang, 1993). Students receive six to eight hours of training *per week* in dance, music, and the visual arts over their three-year degree. A significant proportion of this training involves traditional art forms, such as calligraphy, classical dance, and choral work, taught by highly competent arts specialists. Because teacher trainees live in residence, the six-story spiral-staircase tower at Wuhan Normal School, which contains a hundred practice rooms, each with an upright piano, resounds with students practicing at all times during the day and into the evening. Each student is required to demonstrate at least minimum proficiency on the piano before graduating. Several choirs and other performance groups rehearse every morning from seven until eight and again in the evening at about eight (Wright, 1995b). Music and dance in particular play a large role in tertiary student's leisure activities as well, and most competent performers are delighted to demonstrate their skills both formally and informally to visitors.

Similarly, competition for children to get into the better primary schools in big cities is high, and a child with special talent, such as the ability to play an instrument, is given extra consideration for a place in these schools. Because of the government population control regulation of one child per family, parents want their child to get ahead in the world. Consequently, many parents start their child on string or piano private lessons at a very early age, and even though the child will not play in an orchestra until he or she is about twelve years old, the child practices music daily for hours, starting from age four or five (Brahmstedt & Brahmstedt, 1997).

China has a unified national educational policy, and the curriculum and daily schedule for kindergartens and elementary schools are quite uniform throughout the country (Wu, 1992; Zhao, 1990). Full group, rather than individual or free activities, are the common means through which kindergarten and elementary school children are taught to copy the teacher. The teacher acts as a designer (deciding what, how, and when to teach), lecturer (explaining and focusing children on specific meaning), coach (demonstrating every step before the children begin), and commander (setting examples for children to follow) (Luo, 1993; Winner, 1989). All children simultaneously engage in painting the same picture, singing the same song with specific actions, folding the same shape, or creating the same block structure (Gardner, 1997; Laing & Pang, 1992; Li, 1993). Visual formulas, such as monkeys, frogs, lily pads, and baby chicks, are taught step by step and line by line before children are allowed to make personal aesthetic decisions. Such decisions might include drawing animals in different orientations, such as facing forward or in profile, or from different positions, such as from above or beside. Likewise, teacher education arts programs focus on how to teach children a range of visual schema, songs, dances, and steps. In art, for example, the students have texts that demonstrate how to teach, step by step, the painting of a chick from various positions. A new image is taught in each art lesson, and students practice the mastery of each of these schema.

In Chinese schools, comparison and appraisal are used to encourage achievement, competition, and obedience (Wu, 1992). A large part of education involves learning by rote and recitation in unison, beginning at age three. Kindergarten children, for example, are expected to recite from memory twenty-five to thirty simple poems and retell eight to ten simple stories. The evaluation of children's development is based on the number of words they know, songs they can sing, and objects they can count (Laing & Pang, 1992; Wu, 1992).

Many parts of the daily kindergarten program, including morning "free" activities, are under the teacher's direction and control. Even in play, the topics, themes, roles, and procedures are arranged, and children simply follow the teacher's lead, requirements, and regulations (Laing & Pang, 1992). There are few opportunities for children to explore materials or to create their own meaning through personal discoveries. "Play" is virtually nonexistent in kindergartens, and many Chinese teachers are puzzled by the Western concept of play. Teachers prepare all resources for the children, and the materials and toys offered almost always mean something; they literally stand for meanings and functions from the world of the adult. Consequently, there are few opportunities for adventure, wonder, or imagination; children can only identify themselves as owners or users, not inventors or creators. Open-ended outdoor equipment—such as climbing frames, sand pits, water troughs, and superstructures with movable parts, such as boards, ramps, and tires—are absent. In their place are colorful and beautifully maintained but fixed and convergent-oriented materials, such as swing sets in the shape of Chinese dragons (which accommodate a number of children at once) and large, concrete structures of shops, castles, and city walls.

This description of Chinese early childhood education illuminates the differing cultural underpinnings that can shape the arts curriculum. In China, education evolves around transmitting an appreciation of culture from past generations to succeeding generations—of preserving cultural history and continuity, passing down information and performance standards, and carefully shaping individuals to conform to societal values and practices (Gardner, 1987;Wu, 1992). Yet, compared to Western views, the arts in China are seen as restrictive because they center predominantly on technically refined performance. In the West, however, the arts are valued as dynamic agents of social change—a medium for constructing, challenging, or transforming social, cultural, political, or religious values (Gardner, 1997; Wright, 1997a).

However, influenced by the world ideas in child development and early childhood education, Chinese educational practices are shifting away from attitudes of the child as a passive recipient who respects and obeys the teacher's instruction and learns how to fit into the system. Many Asian cultures are seeking new ways to achieve a more learner-oriented approach to education and a more creative approach to the arts and learning in general (International Review of Curriculum and Assessment Frameworks Archive, 2000; Zhu, 1997). Yet, while China has learned from the West, it cannot be denied that the West has also been in awe of the artistic achievements that are possible within the Chinese context. This has challenged many of the Western definitions of developmental milestones of young children, and many Westerners wonder how Chinese children can be so technically competent at such an early age in drawing, singing, and dancing (Winner, 1989). Similarly, Westerners marvel at the artistic skills of teachers and the amount of time given to the arts in teacher preparation. However, when compared to their Western counterparts, Chinese children and teachers seem less competent in their imaginative and creative use of artistic symbol systems to represent and construct ideas, and they generally do not seem to consider these aspects of artistic expression to be as important as we do in the West (Gardner, 1987, 1997; Wright, 1997a).

This introductory section serves as a focus for a deeper reflection on the key philosophical underpinnings of an early childhood arts curriculum. It provides a radical comparison of how the West views curriculum in relation to China and provides opportunities to evaluate our meaning of an arts curriculum—how it is planned, implemented, and documented; what people, resources, time, and space are to be included; and the ways in which children's knowledge, skills, and concepts in the arts are developed. It foregrounds how education is a human exchange, involving a subcommunity in interaction. In every culture this educational community involves interacting with others, and through interaction children come to know how they must adjust accordingly to the "mutual" community and adapt to the culture's expectations (Bruner, 1996). The significance of culture is an issue that will be addressed more deeply in the final chapter, particularly in relation to how we can define the place for the arts and arts education within our future culture. Such shaping of our future in education is partly based on where we are at present.

Presently, Western ideals of the early childhood arts curriculum are that it should invite negotiation and speculation, where thoughts, ideas, and feelings are created and interpreted. While schools often involve subjects and curricula, it is the Western ideal that the emphasis in schools should be more broadly focused on modes of thinking and feeling than on subject content alone. The arts, for example, should not be taught simply as a discrete set of skills, or treated as instruction for its own sake. Rather, they are valued if they are integrated into the program via problem-solving experiences and seen as multiple languages that provide numerous avenues for learning. Particularly for young children, who are not yet very competent in conventional symbol systems such as reading and writing, the arts provide infinite opportunities for meaning-making and communication through nonverbal, cognitive/expressive symbols and symbol systems.

The ideals of a negotiated curriculum are that adults and children should enter the teaching-learning interface on an equal basis and together shape the direction of their learning, the processes undertaken, and the means for evaluating the outcomes. The mutual community of learners typically models ways of doing or knowing, provides scaffolding for understanding, and a variety of context for learning. Conceptual learning is a collaborative enterprise—it is a loan of consciousness within a framework in which the curriculum emerges through interaction (Bruner, 1996). The remainder of this chapter centers on practical aspects of how these philosophical ideas of an emergent curriculum may be put into practice in early childhood education.

THE EMERGENT CURRICULUM CYCLE

A model to illustrate the various layers that participate in a negotiated curriculum is presented in Figure 13.1. This model illustrates how the emergent curriculum cycle involves the processes of planning, implementing, and documenting. This cycle is strongly influenced by a range of support components (people, resources, space, and time). At the core of the model are the artistic components (processes, forms of expression, elements, and concepts) that overlap. At this point of intersection is the key aspect of guidance (social-constructivism and scaffolding children's artistic learning in multimodal ways).

The midlevel of the model illustrates how planning, implementation, and documentation of the curriculum evolve throughout a continuous cycle. Planning is based on documentation, which leads to implementation, followed by further documentation, and thus the cycle begins again. Though participant observation, adults engage in learning experiences *with* and *through* the child—experiences that place the child at the center of the learning, supported by adults. Adults and children enter into a type of dialogue with one another, giving prompts to guide learning.

Planning, Implementing, and Documenting

Through sensitive reflection based on what has been observed, the adult plans how to extend these experiences to assist children to climb to the next level. Once implemented, the plans become the focus for further reflection.

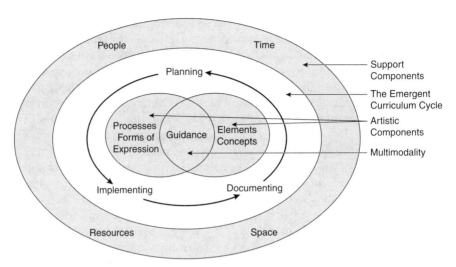

FIGURE 13.1   A Curriculum Model for Early Childhood Arts Education

The documentation of children's processes and products provides a significant resource for understanding what has been learned, what is still being learning, or what is ready to be learned. As discussed in Chapters 2 and 4, a flexible curriculum lays out general educational objectives but does not identify in advance the specific goals for each learning experience. Instead, adults formulate hypotheses of what could happen on the basis of their knowledge, and objectives are then developed and adapted to the needs and interests of the children. Such interests include those expressed by the children at any time during the learning experience, as well as those we infer from the experience as it proceeds. This knowledge forms the basis of a curriculum that emerges, where adults and children learn to cooperate and adapt, constantly accommodating.

Although this is the ideal way in which curriculum should evolve, many times in education the learning problems presented to children are artificial—they are too well structured, too well defined. In the real world, such neat packaging does not exist. If learning in schools is to be similar to that in the real world, children need experience and practice with open-ended structures rather than set, inflexible plans and strict outcomes-based assessment. The curriculum should pose challenging problems and stress approaches that require children to perceive the learning problem from diverse perspectives, so that they will eventually discover for themselves more cognitively advanced ways of understanding. A curriculum that emerges from an interactive context is based on a collective formulation of such challenging problems.

As Plummeridge (1991, p. 9) stated, "Any attempt to prescribe practice in the sense of setting out a blueprint which can be neatly applied to all situations is likely to be strictly limited . . . the reality of practice is its *particularity.*" While the National Standards for Arts Education (Consortium of National Arts Education Associations, 1994), standards and benchmarks (Kendall & Marzano, 1997), and other developmental and general guidelines (Bredekamp, 1987) can provide helpful frameworks for shaping goals in the early childhood arts curriculum, the intimate nature of teaching and learning can be overlooked if there is too much emphasis on performance and standards (Bruner, 1996). Outcomes-based uniform curricula, by their very nature of being a standard, can shift the emphasis away from *negotiation* (where the teacher is part of a community of learners) to that of *transmitting knowledge* (where the teacher is the center of the learning process, and children are passive recipients of information). Plummeridge described the National Curriculum as the great theory of our time, the original master plan that is revised on an almost daily basis. The reality is that regular revision of curricula is necessary, simply because curriculum specifications are provisional and bound to change in practice. So, too, each particular early childhood arts curriculum should be in the continuous process of change, so that it constantly provides opportunities for young children to be sensitive participants within an ever-evolving context.

Children are more actively engaged when learning experiences arouse a high degree of attention, interest, concentration, and involvement—in short, when children care about what they are doing. This is why we should make learning as interesting and exciting as possible, not just so that early childhood contexts will be pleasant places, but so that children will be active participants in learning how to learn. Consequently, the discourse of education must express stance and invite counterstance. Education should be both a mode of communication and a medium for representing the world about which it is communicating. The child at once becomes an agent of *knowledge making* as well as a recipient of *knowledge transmission*. In the process, there is a place for reflection—of objectifying in language, image, movement, and sound what one has thought and felt, and then turning around on it and rediscovering it (Bruner, 1996). Therefore, the planning, implementation, and documentation of the curriculum should involve many opportunities for children, teachers, and families to reflect on how learning is being created and communicated in the early childhood arts program. The provision of appropriate support components for such learning is a key factor in a quality early childhood arts curriculum.

SUPPORT COMPONENTS

Four components—people, resources, space, and time—are represented in the outer segment of the curriculum model (Figure 13.1). The symbolic surrounding of these support structures as an envelopment of the planning, implementation, and documentation cycle depicts the intimate relationship between these two main components of the model. Each of the four support components is discussed in greater detail below.

People

The importance of the collaborative relationship between teachers, children, and parents has been discussed earlier in this book in relation to the co-construction of the curriculum. These three groups of participants become integrated into a larger social system. In addition, other important contributors to the early childhood arts curriculum can include the involvement of artists from the community, because significant learning can occur through exposure to accomplished artists, their processes and products, and the contexts of their learning. An important feature of the Reggio Emilia programs, for example, are their *Atelierista*—competent artists in residence who work in collaboration with the teachers to enhance children's learning, particularly in the visual arts (Vecchi, 1993). The involvement of artists in residence, even if for brief periods of time, is an approach that could be more widely adopted by more early childhood programs, since it provides children with opportunities to work with those who have specialist knowledge and skills—individuals who have first-hand experience with the languages of the arts and the special meaning-making potentials that the arts can provide. In early childhood programs, where art, music, drama, and dance specialists may not be available, many parents, friends, and arts students can be invited to share their expertise with the children, to model their enjoyment and knowledge of the arts, and to serve as mentors for young learners. In addition, artists-in-residence programs, which are often provided through state and locally affiliated organizations, may provide arts specialist experiences for children for at least parts of the school year.

A number of avenues for extending the arts curriculum and enhancing young children's learning can be found through community connections. In many communities, for example, funded arts groups provide high-quality performances and hands-on learning experiences for young children in schools. Field trips to museums, galleries, and local performance sites also offer valuable experiences for children to view historical and contemporary works of art and to hear live performances of dance, drama, and music from the adult world. Many art galleries now have special installations that center on viewing and learning about art through the child's perspective, and several major cities throughout the world have arts festivals that focus on young children. Increasingly, government funding is being provided in many countries for arts centers that support the development of creative works for younger audiences.

Finally, many valuable websites, CD-ROMs, and video recordings feature the creative processes of artists, offering examples of successful cooperation between schools and artists, and providing models of exemplary early childhood arts practices. Chapters 7 and 9 mentioned a number of excellent books for young children that are designed to increase children's knowledge of visual arts and music. In addition, numerous television programs, videos, and music recordings are available that feature early childhood arts. While these resources are valuable supplements to enhance the curriculum, they should not replace the significant learning experiences that occur within the early childhood context—first-hand opportunities to encounter real-world experience through hands-on interaction with arts resources, which are supported and guided by knowledgeable teachers.

Resources

Chapters 8 through 11 gave examples of the specific types of resources appropriate for the development of each of the arts disciplines, and the role of open-ended resources has been discussed throughout this book. Materials of education are valued if they encourage imagination and offer dynamic and invented forms of learning. Resources should present opportunities for transformation where, in the process of exploration, children enter into the spirit of do-it-yourself. Therefore, resources should be open-ended—they should encourage children's meaning-making and offer opportunities for personal discovery and social interaction.

Open-endedness means that the end result can be achieved in a number of ways; there is not *one* end result that all explorers are expected to achieve. Some experiences concentrate on one answer that everyone should agree is the correct response (such as $1 + 1 = 2$); such experiences are referred to as *convergent* because the result focuses on one specific point. In contrast, open-ended experiences branch outwards to many points—they are *divergent* in orientation. Several responses and processes used to realize these are all considered to be correct. For example, a simple resource, such as a block of wood, can stand for or represent an iron in one instance, a portable telephone in another instance, or a miniature car in another. Alternatively, the block of wood might represent a potato in kitchen play or a microphone in musical play, or it might be stacked with other blocks to build a variety of structures, such as buildings, boats, or cities. With a good imagination, it is possible that many such open-ended resources can be used to represent almost anything.

However, some objects are less likely to be transformed into something else if the imagination is not readily stimulated or if the object has an established "stand for" association attached to it. A child-sized wedding veil, for example, probably will be used most regularly as just that. Because it specifically represents "bride," it is a relatively convergently oriented resource. Although some children might use the wedding veil when pretending to be a nun or a sheik, this is less likely because the shape, color, and length of the fabric suggest a specific role-play function. By comparison, a range of fabrics of a variety of shapes, lengths, colors, and weights offers opportunities for a child to discover the various ways in which these fabrics float, fall, bunch, and otherwise move when they are held, draped, looped, or tied, and how they make the child feel when they are worn. Open-ended fabrics stimulate a number of imaginative solutions when accompanied with a range of fasteners, such as scarves, belts, headbands, safety pins, rubber bands, or clips. While dress-up items such as wedding veils are valuable resources, care should be taken that they are not the only costume-based resources offered.

Because they have been shaped in specific ways (such as cut and sewn into a tutu) and are usually fixed to a specific part of the body (such as the hips), they have less potential for representation.

This example of open-ended fabrics is most applicable to dramatic play and dance, but the principle of open-endedness applies to all arts resources. In the visual arts, for example, divergent resources include the core media of drawing, painting, and clay, and other media such as collage, construction, and weaving. Through regular access to these divergent materials, children are able to fashion their own works using paper, paints, brushes, boxes, blocks, fasteners, adhesives, and a variety of utensils for cutting, shaping, molding, and otherwise transforming open-ended materials into a range of artistic products. By comparison, convergent visual arts materials include coloring books, stencils, or other forms of templates where the end results all look very similar, where processes involve step-by-step instructions, or where experiences are oriented toward random, chance-based results, such as marble painting. In convergent activities, children are not challenged to think visually—to solve visual problems, experience personal meaning making, or develop artistic techniques, knowledge, and skills.

Likewise, in music, freedom of expression and open-ended interpretation is provided through the divergent use of the voice, musical instruments, and movement experiences. Sound and the body become the media for composition, improvisation, and a variety of aural and physical thinking and problem-solving experiences. Musical and dance experiences should not simply involve children in imitation and rote memorization under the leadership of the teacher. Otherwise, children's spontaneous songs and dances may become overshadowed by set lessons, and children will begin to think that "real" music and dance occur only during such structured activities. There should be many opportunities for emergent experience, such as event-based instrumental explorations, the creation of sound stories, and singing, instrumental, and dance "conversations." Such open-ended experiences can center on physical states and aural concepts, such as light, heavy, strong, flowing, gentle, jerky, or stiff.

Children require many opportunities to freely access a wide range of quality arts resources for independent and group discovery learning. Consequently, the early childhood environment should present an atmosphere in which the children feel comfortable with taking intellectual risks. It should encourage children to experiment—to learn from both successful and unsuccessful attempts—and to be inspired to try again. In a psychologically secure atmosphere, children's learning is respected, and is supported by adults who participate in the spirit of shared discovery.

Space

Well-stocked storage cupboards that include a display of open-ended materials that are logically organized and clearly labeled will encourage free access and self-help skills in children. This will inspire children to return again and again to familiar resources so that they may explore the numerous learning experiences they offer and develop imagination, technical, and expressive potentials.

Consequently, it is important that the indoor and outdoor areas provide some secluded, quiet spaces for unself-conscious explorations, free from distraction. Resources and equipment that have been carefully selected for their flexibility will include both large-scale and small-scale demountable, stackable, and interconnecting equipment, such as frames, beams, tunnels, tires, and blocks, which can be constructed to serve multiple purposes while enhancing children's imaginations. Simultaneously, groups of children may explore a range of interests, from space-age explorations to rock concert performances to making water channels for floating objects to creating a dance in imitation of falling leaves.

In such an environment, consideration of adequate space for safe movement within and between areas should be seen in relation to the aesthetic context. Aspects such as filtered light, vegetation, mounds, and flowing water can greatly enhance children's imaginative and playful learning encounters. Many areas of the early childhood center should offer opportunities to increase children's awareness of aesthetic qualities within their environment. For example, we should always be on the alert for natural occurrences—watching and listening to birds chirping and flitting from tree to tree; appreciating the sound of rain trickling on the window; enjoying the fragrance of flowers and dirt. In addition, we should provide smell and taste experiences, such as baking and eating fresh biscuits or burning incense or taking the time to enjoy the smell of clean laundry. Parks, nearby stores and supermarkets, and other facilities within the area present many opportunities for sensory-based experiences, and we can capture these by taking "listen walks" with a tape recorder, and by observing and photographing patterns, textures, shadows, and other visual aspects of the environment.

Time

It is most critical that children have adequate time to explore each of the arts media on a regular basis so that they can master the knowledge, skills, and concepts of each of the disciplines—concepts of which children may have only minimal understanding. Sufficient time is necessary to discover the many technical and expressive properties of the various media, such as fluency of movement in dance and drama, control of the voice and musical instruments, and mastery of brushes, scissors, and other visual arts tools. With regular exposure to arts media, children learn to select particular resources with intent, become sensitive to how these materials respond, and come to control and use them for expressive and communicative purposes. Children experience what it is like to work with a variety of artistic resources and begin to notice the effects of colors, sound durations, tones, gestures, full-body movements, and a range of other artistic elements. While exploring these elements, children make perceptual judgments, and with repeated experience with each art form they begin to make finer discriminations, using their intuition and imagination. They are challenged to thinking visually, aurally, physically, spatially, and kinesthetically, and to solve problems in these nonverbal domains.

Challenging problems present themselves through the process of play. Play gives children the freedom to use self-devised symbols to create or be anything—to make their own meaning and to understand themselves and their world through first-hand experience. This is why it is so important to provide adequate time in the curriculum for children to play, so that they build knowledge and skills while representing objects and events, and expressing their thoughts and feelings. Through role play, children act *like* someone or something else, by enacting real or imaginary events. Likewise, in art, children depict themselves or others, play out events from their real or imagined worlds, and nonpictorially express aesthetic qualities such as energy, flow, pattern, or contrast. In dance and music as well, children represent thoughts and feelings both literally and metaphorically. Representation in drama, art, dance, and music involves imitation to some extent; however, imitation is not mere copying—it includes sympathy, empathy, identification with, concern for, and seeing ourselves as something or someone else. It is the activity by which we enlarge our repertoire of action and thought, not only within ourselves but also in relation to others. Such processes underpin children's artistic knowing and are as complex as other domains of learning or even more so. What the arts offer that the other domains do not is what makes them essential components of the early childhood curriculum.

Early childhood educators recognize the importance of providing time for play because, like other aspects of the arts, it enhances children's understanding through action and thought. Yet play and the arts do not seem to be understood by many parents or the general community. In fact, many high school and even elementary school teachers view early childhood education as *simply* playing with children and making pretty pictures, songs, and dances—a form of glorified baby-sitting, providing entertaining experiences to occupy young children. It would seem that a major advocacy role for early childhood is to foreground the importance of time for playful encounters through the arts and the significant role this has in helping children to come to understand themselves and their worlds. Advocating for *time for artistic knowing* should demonstrate the value of the arts in:

- Tapping into nonverbal forms of expression, meaning-making, and understanding
- Symbolizing ideas or emotions both literally and metaphorically (i.e., portraying an impression, a feeling, or a quality of experience)
- Constructing meaning through "felt thought" (i.e., experiencing patterned sound, images, and movement over time and space)
- Developing artistic knowledge, skills, and concepts through frequent and consistent participation in and exposure to the arts

It takes time and many first-hand experiences with the various arts media for children to become increasingly proficient with these forms of knowing, and to engage in felt thought. Felt thought, or body-situated knowing, is most obvious in music and dance, but it also occurs in dramatic play and the visual arts. Though play-based arts experiences, children's internal processes are created, perceived, and made meaningful through bodily experience. As discussed in Chapter 3, the arts involve a unique form of knowing—thinking with the body—and this brings together thought, emotion, and action. Through the arts, children are involved in a special kind of literacy, where they turn action into representation. Because artistic cognition involves meaning and understanding, there must be ample time in the curriculum for young children to experience the arts, their specific modes of expression, and processes that are used to develop an understanding of the artistic components: processes, discipline-based forms of expression, elements, and concepts.

ARTISTIC COMPONENTS

The central segment of Figure 13.1 graphically depicts how the artistic *processes* and *forms of expression* overlap with artistic *elements* and *concepts*. This intersection illustrates that each of the arts disciplines has unique characteristics that are not shared with the other disciplines, while at the same time there are some attributes that the arts have in common. Because music is an aural domain and art a visual domain, the ways in which children think and express themselves in these two disciplines can be quite different. In addition, the cognitive, emotional, and technical skills and processes of singing or playing a musical instrument, for example, are very different than those required for painting or drawing, or for using other visual arts modes of expression. In other words, not everything that can be expressed in art can be expressed in music, and vice versa, because the two disciplines involve different forms of knowing and communicating. Similarly, dance and drama draw on special forms of expression and symbolic domains that are not completely shared with art and music. Let us begin by looking at general components of artistic knowing that apply to all arts disciplines—processes, forms of expression, arts elements, and concepts—and then examine these in relation to those aspects that overlap more directly.

Processes

Two conceptual frameworks have been presented in this book to illustrate how children are involved in a range of cognitive, physical, affective, and "spiritual" processes while engaged in the arts. First, the *general artistic processes* described in Figure 3.5 (Chapter 3) provide a framework for how the arts engage children's interests and abilities. While these general processes apply to all arts domains, it must also be acknowledged that some of these processes are so general that they also can be applicable to learning in many disciplines, not only in the arts. Discovery learning and social interaction, for example, can occur in the teaching-learning experiences of most disciplines within quality early childhood programs. However, the special feature of the arts is that they engage children in specific forms of expression that are not found in other disciplines. Consequently, many of the subprocesses described in the general artistic processes are unique to the arts, and for this reason, Figure 3.5 should form the basis of much of the planning, implementation, and documentation of the arts curriculum.

The second conceptual framework for *understanding and applying learning processes* in the arts is through the three broad arts practices of making, presenting, and responding. These processes, which were described in Chapter 7, are key to the development of artistic literacy and should be seen in relation to the general artistic processes. Much of children's understanding emerges initially from the process of making. Through doing, children explore and come to understand arts elements, and, with repeated experience, they begin to develop concepts linked to these elements. Emerging from the process of doing, children are able to share and discuss their artistic processes and products with others and to reflect on the artworks from the adult world. The generic processes of making, presenting, and responding are imbedded in particular forms of expression that are inherent in each arts discipline, such as painting, singing, dancing, and role playing.

Discipline-Based Forms of Expression

As discussed in Chapter 7, the arts disciplines and forms of expression through which children think, feel, and express themselves in the arts include:

- The visual arts: two-dimensional (drawing, painting, printing) and three-dimensional (constructing, modeling, sculpting)
- Music: listening, singing, playing instruments, composing, notating, and conducting
- Dance: improvising, expressing, and structuring through movement
- Drama: enrolling, enacting, improvising, miming, storybuilding, and using language and props (e.g., puppets, masks, costume, lighting, scenery)

These forms of expression were discussed in greater detail in Chapters 8 through 11, along with practical examples of how we can enhance children's development in the artistic domains. Through art, music, dance, and drama, children use the various modes of expression to develop the "grammars" that are applicable to each of the arts. This grammar is linked to an understanding and ability to apply the elements of the arts that fall within each of the forms of expression.

Elements

The best way to think of arts elements is that they are the constituent parts, or simplest principles, of a subject of study. In other words, they are the substance of a specific arts domain. To review content from Figure 7.3 (Chapter 7), the arts disciplines most commonly include the following terms to describe the elements within each domain.

- Art: line, shape, color, line, texture, form, composition, and expressiveness
- Music: rhythm, melody, harmony, form, tone quality, texture, and expressive controls
- Dance: body, space, time, energy, form, mood, style, and function
- Drama: tension, symbol, roles, language, movement, time, space, focus, and metaxis

It should be reiterated that alternative and additional terminology for the arts elements might be included in this list, but these core elements are those that can be understood by young children. (For further clarification of the meaning of some of these and other arts terms, it may be helpful to refer to the definitions in the glossary at the end of this book.) Many of the terms presented above would need to be simplified for young children's initial understanding because some terminology is quite abstract and can be confusing for young children. However, once children have grasped the general meaning of a term, through numerous exposures and use of associated terminology including the children's own words, the more accurate arts terminology can be substituted. For example, children initially might understand the meaning of the *rhythm* of a song by being asked to "Clap the *way the words go*"; after several experiences with many different songs, where the children have clapped the rhythm of the words, the teacher might then introduce the more accurate musical term, saying, "Clap the *rhythm* of this song." Children will have had sufficient experiences with *the way the words go* to be able to apply the new term *rhythm* to a range of different songs. In other words, they will be able to generalize this understanding to a number of different instances—they will transfer this new knowledge and apply it to novel contexts and new songs. Such ability is related to the development of artistic concepts within each of the arts.

Concepts

Concepts are generic ideas abstracted from particular instances. In the arts, concepts are ideas in aural, visual, and bodily-kinesthetic form. In music, for example, concepts associated with the element *dynamics* involve an understanding of "loud" and "soft" and gradations between—really loud, loud, between loud and soft, soft, and really soft. Loud and soft are probably the easiest musical concepts for young children to learn, possibly because the word "loud" is used regularly in everyday language. Children know, for example, that they should not be loud in certain situations—when the baby is sleeping, when they are in a library or at a concert, or when mother has a headache. Initial understanding of the musical term "soft" can be approached through the more commonly used word "quiet." Children quickly learn to substitute the term "soft," possibly because of the metaphoric association with gentleness or peacefulness, and the physical association with singing or playing musical instruments softly.

The physical-emotional logic that young children apply to arts concepts is particularly noticeable in music. For example, it is difficult for young children to participate in a singing game when it is sung loudly without also getting faster. Children often associate loud with fast because of the energy levels required to make loud or fast music. Similarly, it is difficult for children to sing and move softly to the same musical game while keeping the energy level sufficiently high not to slow down also. The difficulty of isolating the elements of dynamics (loud/soft) and tempo (fast/slow) while also recognizing and feeling the emotional relationship between these expressive aspects of music is something that even adults must continually address when performing with musical sensitivity. Many choirs, for example, have a tendency to slow down when singing softly and, in a similar physical-emotional sense, they will also sing "flat" (i.e., below the pitch) when the music is slow. If we are receptive to our own and children's body-based, emotional involvement in the arts, we can assist children to understand and feel the dynamic relationship between arts elements, and help them respond in artistic ways.

Hence, conceptual understanding in the arts involves the interplay of many individual concepts in an infinite variety of configurations. In music, for example, the same melody can be used with different words and different rhythms. Indeed, a number of songs in the standard children's song literature deliberately incorporate the same or very similar melodies with slightly different rhythms in relation to the lyrics. Some examples (with slight variations) include:

> *London Bridge Is Falling Down* and *Mary Had a Little Lamb*
> *Eensey Weensey Spider* and *Sweetly Sings the Donkey*
> *Twinkle Twinkle Little Star* and *Baa Baa Black Sheep*

Similarly, the same rhythm may be used for the same or different melodies, with different words. The Kodály approach to music education is carefully constructed to expose children to a number of musical examples in which simple rhythms (e.g., ta ta ti-ti ta) and pitches (e.g., sol-mi or sol-la-sol-mi) are taught to help children to discover these simple concepts, such as in the songs *See Saw Up and Down* and *Blue Bells Cockle Shells*. The Kodály approach systematically focuses on treating musical tools, such as "Ta ti-ti" and "sol-mi" as a framework for teaching concepts that can be applied in a variety of ways. Teachers use questions such as "How many different ways can we show the beat to this song?" to help children understand how to apply and transfer the concept of beat to a number of instances.

Regardless of the approach used to arts education, it is important to realize that concepts can never be secured in one instance. Concepts must be rethought and reused over and over again so that new insights can evolve. As adults many of us have experienced the importance of repetition and reapplication, such as when learning a new language. Simple words such as "Hello," "Thank you," and "Excuse me" can be used in many different contexts with different effects and interpretations—they can be friendly, sarcastic, humble, or gracious. It is only through personal experience in using these words and their slight variations—via interaction within the culture's norms—that we come to understand how such words are applied and modified. In other words, we learn to understand how concepts, such as words, can be generalized or transferred to a range of instances and how this meaning can be different from culture to culture. Similarly, children learn concepts in the arts when they recognize, for example, that complementary and contrasting colors can be achieved in many combinations, that the beat of music can be felt in most songs and instrumental pieces, that levels of energy can be shown in many ways in dance, and that characters can express a specific mood, such as strength or weakness, in many different dramatic contexts.

Children's experiences with and understanding of arts concepts involve inductive, deductive, and intuitive tracks of exploration. To illustrate how concepts can be understood in these three different ways, examples are provided in the discipline of music:

Inductively. We assimilate and generalize from our experience. For example, we might know that, when we march to music, we feel "1–2." So, then, when we listen to music and it makes us feel like we want to march, we come to the conclusion that that particular piece of music has a metric grouping based on 2, or perhaps 4 (two groups of 2).

Deductively. We apply concepts to new situations. For example, we might decide that the words to a song warrant an accompaniment that is "liquid," "flowing," or "sustained." So we might select musical instruments to suit this effect, such as a metallophone, triangle, or cymbals, because they "ring" and "linger."

Intuitively. Often we make decisions about how to apply concepts based on our feelings or intuitive responses. In the inductive example above, conceptual understanding was based on a bodily-kinesthetic response to what was heard ("it *feels* like 2"); in the deductive example, musical decision making was based on an intuition of what an accompaniment to a song might sound like based on our concept of the tone quality of various instruments.

We can guide children's understanding of concepts in art, music, dance, and drama by helping them assimilate and generalize (inductive reasoning), apply concepts to new situations (deductive reasoning), and make decisions based on feelings (intuitive reasoning). This requires guidance and support—a willingness to cultivate learning rather than to impose judgments, so that children are enabled to discover through personal experience. Most importantly, this requires us to "get into the heads" of young children, and try to hear, feel, and see ideas from their perspective, so that we can "go there with them" and possibly even "take them somewhere else." Such awareness is based on how children experience and express the arts in multimodal ways.

Multimodality

This final segment of artistic components focuses on aspects of artistic expression that overlap or are shared across the arts domains. This issue is illustrated in Figure 13.1 in the most central component of the model, multimodality.

Felt thought is the first of two main components that fall within this multimodality core. As was illustrated in the musical examples above, arts concepts involve knowing through sensitivity, thought, and aesthetic judgment. Often this engages emotional logic and involves metaphoric links—associations with personal experiences in abstract ways. Many concepts that children acquire in the arts emerge through felt thought, which is often expressed as metaphor. Language is "borrowed" to describe visual domains (e.g., "hot" or "somber" paintings), movement domains ("light" or "heavy" dances/characters), and aural domains (e.g., "bright" or "dark" music). Dance, music, drama, and the visual arts all lend themselves to *cross-modal* connections. As discussed in Chapter 7, such expressive and metaphoric aspects of artistic expression involve synesthesia, where meaning in one mode can be understood in another mode. Through depicting objects and events, children symbolically express artistic knowledge and skills by making such connections, predominantly through felt thought. Thinking with the body—or somatic knowing—is key to the crossing over into each of the arts disciplines. It is the intersection of processes/forms of expression and elements/concepts.

For example, most preschool-aged children seem to be able to intuitively select "warm" from "cool" colors when presented with a range of colored paper pieces, even when they have not been taught these artistic terms (Wright & Ashman, 1991). This "borrowing" of physically felt language and applying it to arts concepts is common, not only in the visual arts, but also in drama, dance, and music. Artistic language, by necessity, is full of metaphor, largely because the arts involve abstract thought—thought that is understood through physical and sensory experience, and internal mental representations (Johnson, 1991).

The language used by musicians, for example, when teaching or talking about music includes such physical/spatial metaphors as the terms "form," "structure," "sections," "symmetry," "phrase length," "heavy rhythms," and "light tone" (Walker, 2000). When we help children understand the concept of pitch, for example, we usually connect it to *directional concepts* of up and down, higher and lower, and felt expression linked to *spatial images* and simple *movement*. Indeed, five- to seven-year-old children invent rich and articulate representations of songs by showing the rhythm of the words, such as in the line "life is but a dream" from *Row Your Boat* (e.g., O o O o O). They also show the descending pitches (Davidson & Scripp, 1988), for example, as:

lyfe

    is

        But-

      a

           Dreem.

It would seem that musical meaning based on inner representations, not only of sound but also of space, motion, and tactility, is an innate ability. This ability was discussed in relation to infant-directed speech in Chapter 3, babies' and young children's spontaneous songs and singing conversations in Chapter 9 and the brain's search for patterns in Chapter 12. So it seems natural to verbalize musical concepts in these ways and to help children make connections across the arts domains.

As Walker (2000) explained, when "objective" language is not adequate to describe music, we most frequently use metaphor, and when metaphoric language is not adequate, we are driven to gesture. For example, when illustrating the length of a musical phrase, we often "draw" a long arc with our hand, indicating the beginning and the ending of the phrase. We use expressions such as "feeling" a phrase. This is not a linguistic concept like "a phrase is a musical sentence." Instead, "feeling" is linked with space and movement and our bodily experience in it. Such forms of somatic meaning are not literal; they are poetic. Indeed, poetry itself was created to say what words alone can never say (Eisner, 2001). Poetry deliberately makes words musical, physical, visual, rhythmic, expressive, and metaphoric. Likewise, much of the language of the arts is *poetic*—it is metaphoric and somatically based.

The second component that lies within this intersection is the *common concepts* that can be understood in the arts in multimodal ways. As was discussed in the previous chapter in Figure 12.1, *structural* and *expressive* facets that may cross each of the arts disciplines include arts elements such as tension/resolution and similarity/contrast, which are achieved through related concepts such as structure/form, energy, tension, flow, interaction, space, pattern, shape, texture, rhythm, mood, and variation. Even terms like color, sound, and movement have cross-modal relevance in the arts (e.g., color in music, sound in dance, and movement in art). By working with concepts with young children (using simplified versions of these terms), we can help children find connections across the arts, by involving them in experiences where particular arts elements are explored through integrated forms of expression.

These two core components of the curriculum—felt thought and common concepts—are foundational to the content and processes used in mastering the arts *disciplines*. Such mastery is highly dependent upon the guidance children receive in learning in and through the disciplines. Therefore, the key *teaching-learning* component at the core of the curriculum is guidance and its significance in assisting children to acquire understanding of arts content and processes.

GUIDANCE

We can provide guidance for children's thoughts and feelings in their explorations of artistic forms of expression and artistic processes. Helping children to become analytical about their processes/products, to make constructive judgments, and to respond creatively can occur before, during, and after artistic experiences. In many ways, it is up to adults to determine when and how to extend children's learning. This involves sensitive observation, interaction, and guidance. The notion of guidance during play-based, open-ended experiences may appear to be in direct opposition to many early childhood teaching practices, since play is often seen as the personal, creative domain of the child. Yet, as has been discussed throughout this book, children cannot learn in a vacuum and must feel secure that they will receive respect and support from adults in their process-oriented learning.

We can encourage children to ask questions, explore ideas, and imagine new possibilities through play and project-based experiences. Such guidance assists children to experience and come to understand relationships between aural, bodily-kinesthetic, spatial, imaginative, expressive, symbolic, and technical aspects of the arts. Relationships across these aspects of the arts are imbedded in artistic processes and forms of expression. Much of children's cross-modal participation in the arts involves *feeling* the music, seeing *spatial connections* through dance, creating musical *patterns* in speech, using expressive *gesture* in dramatic play, and finding physically expressive words to *metaphorically describe* line, color, and texture in art. Feeling, seeing spatial connections, perceiving patterns, and using gesture and metaphors to describe concepts apply to all arts disciplines.

Through hands-on experiences with the various modes of expression and artistic processes, children can be assisted to understand and participate in integrated, multimodal ways. They can be helped to grasp generic ideas or concepts from particular instances, such as realizing that the blending of red and yellow makes orange; that the same dance movement can be used with different levels of energy to express different moods; that the use of various musical instruments creates different emotional effects and responses; or that a particular character can communicate different symbolic messages through the use of open-ended costumes, different positions in space, or a variety of styles of movement and speech. When children understand these concepts, they will learn to self-select knowledge and resources as needed, for personal and group expression.

Through projects that emerge from the children's interests, children and adults collectively produce works that give pride, identity, and a sense of continuity to those who participate in their making. These works are a record of mental and emotional efforts, where process and product become interwoven. The children's learning processes, as well as their development of artistic products, become a means for reflection. Documentation serves as a memory of what has been learned. It provides a springboard for further extensions and becomes the basis for the enhancement of children's understanding of artistic elements, concepts, and processes.

Having a clear picture of the various components within Figure 13.1 is critical to knowing what, how, and when to document. Each of the components in the curriculum model plays a key role in assisting young children's enjoyment, participation, appreciation, knowledge, skills, and concepts *in* and *through* the arts. We can document and reflect on the impact of each of these components in relation to the arts curriculum by using analytical, judicial, and creative reflection as a framework for thinking about each of the curriculum model components. By inserting key words of the curriculum model in the blanks below, we can analyze the impact of each of the components, judge their effectiveness, and think of creative ways in which we can enhance the curriculum.

> **Analytical**: What did I think, feel, and understand in relation to ____*?
> **Judicial**: Was an aspect of ____* used effectively/appropriately?
> **Creative**: What other possibilities in relation to ____* are available?
>
> *People, resources, time, space, planning, implementing, evaluating, forms of expression, processes, elements, and concepts

While it has been implicit that children are the focus of the curriculum, the omission of the word "children" in Figure 13.1 may be interpreted as an oversight. Hopefully, it was clear that most of the content and use of examples throughout this chapter included children at the center of the curriculum and that the meaning of curriculum was that of a shared, collaborative, and negotiated experience. The main thrust of this chapter was intentionally on unpacking the complex nature of curriculum and its many components parts, the most important one being children. If we keep children paramount in our minds as we analyze, judge, and think creatively about each aspect of the curriculum, then hopefully we are on the road to having everything else fall into place.

For many children, it is likely that early childhood may be the only time in their lives to participate in the arts in such a liberating and integrated way. If we believe that the early childhood period can have a significant impact on developing children's mindsets and desires for lifelong learning, then our role in young children's education must be seen as having an important influence on individuals who will grow to become participants in the shaping of our future cultures—in some cases, this contribution can be very significant. After all, Picasso, Mozart, and many other great people were once children whose talents were strongly influenced by the people and experiences they encountered along their life journeys.

SUMMARY

The comparison of Chinese and Western arts education illustrates extreme cultural differences and educational philosophy and practices at both the tertiary and early childhood levels. The Chinese emphasis on proficiency in arts disciplines—indeed, as benchmarks for entrance into good kindergartens, elementary schools, and teacher training institutions—is a foreign concept to many Western cultures. While China appears to be moving toward a pedagogical approach that is more learner-centered, creative in orientation, and less technically focused, the products of Chinese pedagogy cause Westerners to marvel at the artistic achievements of young children and tertiary students alike. Not only does this cause us to question our notion of typical developmental milestones, it foregrounds basic pedagogical questions: What is the main purpose of studying the arts? What is worth knowing in and about the arts? Who are considered to be expert arts educators?

In many ways, Western culture struggles with the notion of our definitions of "best" and what is achievable—it tussles with the issue that the "best" should be available to all, often to the extent of dumbing down the curriculum, and disregarding the arts as significant forms of study. As Hope (2000) described it, the more fragmented our culture, the more definitions of "best" there are. This chapter centered on the arts as highly relevant and important domains of learning, engaging special languages, grammars, structures, and compositional and design principles as a general goal—a goal to develop creative thinking, artistic meaning making, cognitively abstract reasoning through cross-domain knowledge, and emotional involvement in expressive, symbolic forms of communication.

The diagram in Figure 13.1 provides a model for an emergent curriculum in early childhood arts education. Overall, the model illustrates the big picture, and the interactive relationships between the component parts: the support components (people, resources, space, and time) that are important to the emergent curriculum cycle (planning, implementing, and documenting), its relationship to the artistic components (processes, forms of expression, elements, and concepts), and the significance of the guidance provided by adults (in the multimodal aspects of *felt thought* and *common concepts* that integrate structural, expressive, and process facets of learning). The "micro" component—guidance—centers on the nurturance and support we can provide children while learning in and through the arts. Through sensitive scaffolding, children come to understanding the unique and shared aspects of the arts, and to use the various forms of expression, processes, and elements to develop artistic concepts.

ADDITIONAL READINGS

Barrett, J. R. (2001). Interdisciplinary work and musical integrity. *Music Educators Journal, 87*(5), 27–31.

Bresler, L. (2000). The relationships of school art, national goals, and multilayered cultures. *Arts Education Policy Review, 101*(5), 3–7.

Bruner, J. (1996). *The culture of education.* Cambridge, MA: Harvard University Press.

Gardner, H. (1999). *The disciplined mind: What all students should understand.* New York: Simon & Schuster.

Ross, J. (2000). Arts education in the information age: A new place for somatic wisdom. *Arts Education Review, 101*(6), 27–32ff.

Snyder, S. (2001). Connection, correlation, and integration. *Music Educators Journal, 87*(5), 32–39.

Walker, M. E. (2000). Movement and metaphor: Towards an embodied theory of music cognition and hermeneutics. *Bulletin of the Council of Research in Music Education, 145,* 27–42.

Wiggins, R. A. (2001). Interdisciplinary curriculum: Music educator concerns. *Music Educators Journal, 87*(5), 40–44.

PRACTICAL ACTIVITIES

1. Discuss and try out the following examples of cross-domain thinking and feeling in the arts, such as:

   - Stepping from side to side and clapping your hands while singing gospel music
   - Putting on a large black velvet cape with a red satin liner and discovering flowing and undulating movements through space
   - Painting at a large easel while listening to poetry or music and capturing the structural and expressive facets of the work through imagery (and perhaps vocal sounds)
   - "Painting" music using the body only (e.g., using arm gestures to punctuate the rhythm or to shape the contour of the melodic phrase)
   - Stepping/running/swirling in response to repetition/variation of pattern and responding intuitively to expressive qualities, such as change of tempo or variation in dynamics (e.g., accented notes, dynamic levels across phrases)
   - Standing on a platform under a blue spotlight in a darkened room and improvising a character role, such as a tribal chief at the top of a mountain, describing what he or she believes are the most important values and behaviors for his or her tribe's continued existence within a modern world

2. In small groups, select and discuss one aspect of the curriculum model for early childhood arts education (Figure 13.1), such as people, documenting, concepts, or guidance. Focus on examples of how this component of the curriculum has influenced your own learning at some stage in your life or how you have observed children being affected by this component in school, through private arts lessons, or via significant interactions with arts mentors.

CHAPTER FOURTEEN

THE ARTS, CULTURE, AND SCHOOLING

It is the year 2073 B.C. A dark-skinned man eases his way between two huge rocks and enters a vast cavern. Late afternoon sunlight streams in through the fissure in the roof. He carries a small parcel. His eyes become accustomed to the darkened interior, and he waits for the detail of the cave to reveal itself to him. On the wall before him is a gallery of ancient rock paintings. He moves slowly, examining each one. He created some of them. One painted a year ago, another two years before that. There are also many painted by ancestors a thousand years before; now pale, but crafted with the same skills as his own. He chooses an apparently untouched area toward the end of the gallery and places his twig brushes and pigments carefully on a narrow ledge. Earlier that day, he had been hunting with his eldest son, only recently initiated into manhood. They had stalked a mob of kangaroos, ambushing a young male. The son had crept with great stealth and waited patiently for the kangaroo to come into range. The spear had plunged into the animal's chest. It had been his first kill as a man, and the father was about to record the hunt for future generations of his people.

Such early recordings of human beings are displayed in the art of those who lived many, many thousands of years ago. They are found in the rock paintings of the Australian Aboriginal people, can be seen in the caves of Lascaux in central western France, in the art on the burial chambers of the pharaohs in Luxor in Egypt, in ancient sites in Orkney, Scotland, and in a thousand other places around the world. Archeologists speculate about such works, believing, for example, that when European ice age cavemen [sic] were making paintings of animals, other people in Australia were painting a picture of a boat on a sandstone rock in north Kimberly (Australian Magazine, 1998). This particular rock painting of boat people shows them in ceremonial postures, wearing elaborate headdresses and tussles, using oars to propel the boat. The painting, which seems to be the first to portray ocean travel, has been dated as being at least 17,000 years old and could be as much as 30,000 years old. To create rock paintings during the last ice age would have involved building scaffolding to reach rock faces high above the ground and other collaborative commitments linked to the desire to leave an indelible mark on the landscape—a mark that has now become mineralized and bonded within the physical properties of

298

the rock. It is believed that such a wide-scale artistic endeavor must have been conducted in an environment much more conducive to survival than today's environment. The Kimberly may have been a Garden of Eden at that time, and the boat people may have migrated from the north, looking for sites of even greater antiquity. There are distinct epochs of artistic expression on these rock faces that do not seem to have a cohesive link, except for the fact that many distinct styles can sometimes be found on the same sites.

As these examples illustrate, art provides a window on the history of the human race. Since the time when humans first gathered in groups to live, life has been defined, celebrated, preserved, and rejuvenated through various forms of artistic expression, including storytelling, dance, music, and art. Throughout history, these artworks bear witness to the cultural traditions that have been handed down from one generation to the next. Through the study of art forms, we can even reconstruct long-forgotten aspects of life and culture in societies where there was no record of language, or whose history has been lost.

Such artifacts help us reflect on how the arts, throughout history, have enhanced the quality of life for people. They provide a means by which humans have expressed their customs and birthright and learn about and participate in the culture in which they live. As described throughout this book, the arts are a vehicle by which the young can express their growing awareness of themselves, their interactions with others, and the society in which they live.

Most people voluntarily experience, participate in, and enjoy the arts in a wide range of contexts and forms at any time of life, because the arts give pleasure, entertainment, meaning, and satisfaction to their lives. The importance of the arts can be shown in the extent to which art forms are supported through attendance at performances, galleries, cinemas, and community events. In fact, the arts are a major factor in a society's economic growth and stability (Boughton, 1989). But the arts provide a great deal more than entertainment. They provide a way for society to record and preserve its finest achievements—its visions, aspirations, attitudes, and values.

Although the role of the arts has been significant for the *preservation* and reconstruction of history, it is important to realize that the arts also play a significant role in the *shaping* of current and future cultures. This chapter focuses on how culture is shaped and, in the process, how it shapes individuals, groups, and institutions within it. It centers on how a culture's "reality" is collectively constructed through the use of symbols and symbol systems and how different cultural values, beliefs, and practices influence the way schools enculturate their young. The chapter concludes with the forecasts of several contemporary authors, centering on key issues that may positively shape our preferred future for early childhood arts education.

CULTURE AS CONTINUOUS CHANGE

Culture is not an established, stabilized, or irreversible way of thinking, believing, acting, or judging. Cultures are and always have been in the process of change, which is actively constructed by the people. Currently, our world is being influenced, for example, by migration, by trade, and by the rapid exchange of information. Consequently, our cultural frameworks and meanings are ongoing processes, involving an awareness of our broad goals and how we deal with abstract issues such as freedom, accountability, equality, opportunity, and responsibility (Bruner, 1996). Different cultures manage these matters differently. Our understanding of how and why there are differences across cultures requires us to take on both a broad and a focused perspective (Bresler, 2000; Bruner, 1996).

In the broadest, "macro" sense, culture involves a system of values, rights, exchanges, obligations, opportunities, and power. Cultural practices carry expectations that reflect our values, for example, about what is considered to be natural, mature, morally right, or aesthetically pleasing (Goodnow, Miller, & Kesslel, 1995; Miller & Goodnow, 1995). Such values are represented in the human components of society—our behavior patterns, historical events, symbols, and beliefs—and include issues about how we educate our young, provide social services, administer the criminal justice system, and define interpersonal relationships (Bruner, 1996). Such values are constructed as much through social and cultural interaction as through individual experience (Shore, 1996).

In the "meso" (midlevel) sense, social institutions, such as professional societies, universities, arts education bodies, and political parties, are "cultural carriers"—these groups develop their own set of values. The members of the group *learn* these values; they come to understand the practices of the group, and with time develop a sense of belonging and identity (Lave & Wenger, 1991). In a broad sense, identity groupings might be formed on a number of bases, such as ethnicity, gender, income level, religious affiliation, or national origin (Katz, 1991; Miller & Goodnow, 1995). In the case of arts education, a variety of professional bodies, for example, focus on particular arts disciplines, or specifically on the education of children. The members of these professional bodies learn the values and discourses of the arts and arts education through these groups.

Similarly, the institution of school functions in a context with its own social and political character and set of values and policies. Schools systems, for example, determine the structure and goals of education and reflect a common body of traditions—in other words, the consensus viewpoint. In countries with a federal system of government, such as in the United States, responsibility for education rests with the individual states, yet there can be great variation across schools within each state. Yet, while the policies of specific schools are based on consensus decisions, the objectives behind these decisions can be lost over time. For instance, the school's practice can become equated with the school's objectives, and the habits of a school can become the school's motives—the habits become part of a natural order. Indeed, statements such as "This is the way we have always done things" illustrate how, with time, the school's original reasons for developing a particular policy can be difficult to resurrect (Miller & Goodnow, 1995). This is why many schools provide professional development experiences for staff to collectively reflect on their school's philosophies and practices and to clarify their common aims—their consensus view of historical, current, and future directions.

Finally, in a "micro" (close-up) sense, individuals, such as teachers, learn to operate within the macro and meso contexts and adapt to a culture's expected outcomes. For example, teachers' own arts background and expertise, their ability to teach, and their personal commitment are all shaped by the macro and meso contexts. Teachers, in turn, influence what and how children learn. In a micro sense, teachers and children both live learned patterns of behaviors; they see the world in relation to how they have been socialized, or "enculturated." As Margaret Mead (1942) stated more than sixty years ago, education is an instrument for the creation of new human values; education can be used for unknown ends. Consequently, teachers' values in relation to issues such as arts education can have a significant impact on how unknown ends may, or perhaps may not, be achieved.

At all three levels—the macro, meso, and micro—culture involves an assessment of the fit between what is deemed essential for a good, useful, or worthwhile way of life, and how individuals adapt to these demands within their own lives (Bresler, 2000; Bruner, 1996; Egan, 1997). In other words, individuals, groups of people, and institutions can be aided or alternatively thwarted by the culture in which they live. Individuals and groups, for example, may have potentials that may or may not be realized (Gardner, 1999b). The realization of these potentials depends on where they live, what is valued, how these values are transmitted, and how many resources are put into particular areas, such as the arts. Consequently, our society must articulate a philosophy of education that concentrates on what we consider *worth passing on* to future generations and how we should enculturate children through the schooling process.

The educational values that have been presented throughout this book reflect a perspective that enculturation in early childhood arts education should center on the fusion of two ideals: the classical ideals of humanistic learning and contemporary ideals of neo-progressivism. Such a fusion is based on:

- Valuing child-centered learning, multiliteracies, and cross-modal knowing
- Employing democratic, play-based, and guided-learning experiences
- Using principles of social constructivism

The content has focused on the transmission of key knowledge, ideas, and beliefs associated with children's deep immersion in *arts disciplines*—immersion that involves thinking and feeling in and through art, music, dance, and drama. The underpinning belief that has been presented is that, through such processes, young children will become better able to build commitments, not just to their own communities but also to the world beyond. In other words, early childhood arts education is not only about initiating the young into the knowledge, skills, and commitments of the arts. It is about inculcating in children a valuing of the arts within the society into which they will grow—a society in which children will become active participants in shaping its development.

As discussed throughout this book, current beliefs about early childhood arts education emphasize the cultural and social nature of learning and the incorporation of principles of social constructivism within an emergent curriculum. Yet it must be recognized that social constructivism itself is *also* embedded in cultural beliefs and practices. *What* we construct and *how* we construct it is shaped by cultural perspectives on issues, such as what is seen to be "good" arts and what is considered to be "good arts learning/teaching." In other words, the interpretation of how knowledge is co-constructed is based on the particular culture's version of reality and how this reality is created.

If, for example, the culture's reality is that the "3Rs" are of primary importance in the school curriculum, it will undervalue the *artistic* modes of knowing and understanding: the visual, aural, bodily-kinesthetic/somatic forms. It would overlook the significance of the arts in activating all three modes of learning: the *enative* (blending thought, emotion, and action to portray or depict ideas by example); the use of *imagery, sound, and movement;* and the *symbolic* (the representation of something as a likeness of another thing). Within a 3Rs framework, children would learn the grammars of reading, 'riting, and 'rithmetic but would have few opportunities to understand the grammars of the arts or to use the symbol systems associated with them—the abstract nonverbal symbols that are so foundational to the creation and communication of artistic ideas and feelings. Such a cultural reality would become the reality that the children learn to adopt, a reality in which the arts have little or no importance.

Yet artistic knowing and responding are the very foundations upon which many creative cultural products are developed and are an important basis for how a culture's reality is defined. Hence, the arts must be seen in relation to the evolution of culture and how culture itself involves a process of constructing self, or personal realities, in relation to others' realities. Much is dependent upon the culture's views of how this reality should be constructed, and whether the arts are valued as an important component in the education of young children.

THE CULTURAL CONSTRUCTION OF REALITY

Psychologists view the mind as an instrument for the construction of reality. In other words, our mind helps us understand and represent our world.

Piaget talked about children constructing their understanding of a world—a world to which they fit or "accommodate." Through play, children represent social events like making a cup of tea, going to work, or bathing a baby. As their understanding of the world becomes extended, children's playing out of such social events changes, and they accommodate these new understandings into their actions and interactions with others. The process involves representing inner, private thoughts, ideas, and feelings, while at the same time learning how to identify with the outer, public world.

But what is this thing called world? Can there be a *universal* meaning, some *innate* view that is shared by all? Goodman (1984) challenged the notion of a single view of world. He stressed the active role of the mind in creating "worlds," based on the broad, social context. Using the mind for constructing worlds or realities is very much a feature of the arts and creativity. Famous artists, composers, and authors throughout history did not *find* the worlds they produced—they *invented* them. Over time, we have honored the Beethovens, Picassos, Joyces, and Einsteins who have, within their lifetime, radically altered our worldview (Gardner, 1997). Yet while the mind shapes culture, it cannot be denied that culture also shapes the minds of individuals—it is a two-way street (Bruner, 1996).

Artistic expression, in a modest or grand way, communicates and shapes our thoughts, perceptions, and feelings. It helps us represent our experiences of life, and to develop, strengthen, and transform our beliefs and values. Because the arts are shared meaning systems, they carry values, and as such have the capacity to evoke responses in others. In powerful ways, they help construct, reinforce, challenge, and transform social, cultural, political, and religious values. Hence, the arts not only reveal cultural heritage, they are also a means by which the culture is defined and evaluated.

This book has emphasized the many ways in which individual expression is captured through meaning-making and symbolizing (representing that involves "standing for" references). Various meanings are assigned to things in different settings on particular occasions. For example, a young child's use of a block of wood can serve a number of functions: a boat when floated in a stream, a mobile phone when held to the ear, or an iron when rubbed across cloth. It is only when meanings are placed in relation to some context, such as water play or domestic play, that we can know what they are about. Within the broad cultural context as well, a political cartoon, for example, has no meaning if the policies and practices of a local political party are not understood or if the politicians represented in the drawing are unknown.

So we come to understand worlds with the help of symbol systems: collections of symbols that have come to be used in an organized or systematic way through cultural practice. This is achieved through language, picturing, mathematics, science, mime, poetry, music, modern dance, and a range of other symbolic forms knowing. These symbol systems provide the tools for organizing and understanding our world and communicating within it. In other words, through symbol systems, individuals within a species adapt to the environment in terms of what things, acts, events, or signs are taken to *mean.* Human "meaning-making" has a core influence on our perceptions and thought processes in a way not to be found elsewhere in the animal kingdom, and the negotiation of meaning is at the core of culture. Consequently, all forms of meaning making should be at the core of the curriculum in the education of young children. Because the arts are a highly relevant medium for creating and communicating meaning, they should be seen as essential components of education.

The arts not only preserve and maintain tradition, they can also be dynamic agents of social change—they play a pivotal role in shaping a sense of social and cultural identity. Through the arts, we represent the world in *our own* minds, but we also come to understand and respond sensitively to the way that world is represented in the minds of *others.* In other words, the construction of reality is both a solo act and a collective experience.

Collective Construction of Reality

From birth, we seem to be guided in our responses to others. "We respond to each other's proximity by appropriate spacing, to each other's warning calls and mating releasers, but also to each other's mental states and representations of the world" (Bruner, 1996, p. 165). Through responding to the minds of others, children learn about the world *through* others. They develop the ability to interpret the thoughts, intentions, beliefs, and mental states of others, and in the process they become *enculturated* through living in communities. The school community itself involves its own networks of mutual expectation and group constructions of reality. This includes both explicit and implicit values, beliefs, ideals, and aspirations. Group decisions reflect some sort of cultural consensus, and once put into force, these decisions become *policies.* Many contemporary schools now include policies that place the arts as an important and central part of education, such as:

- Our school practices a *multiple intelligences* philosophy that provides all children with opportunities to approach the curriculum through multiple entry points.
- Our arts-centered program has a *community-based* orientation and includes artists in residence and student participation in museum, gallery, and arts festival learning.
- Our school practices *collaborative, action research* and aspires to demonstrate that our arts-centered program improves school attendance and academic achievement across the curriculum.

Such school policies reflect the importance of multiple forms of communication and the value of the arts in liberating nonverbal, symbolic forms of meaning making and communication. Increasingly, more elementary schools and early childhood programs are adopting such policies, largely as a rejection of the accountability movement of the 1990s. Motivated by studies that pointed to lagging achievement scores in United States schools, and also by politicians' desire to monitor the results of increased spending in education, the accountability movement contributed to K–12 schools' obsession with standardized tests (Schuler, 2001). But, as Schuler laments, such tests constantly drew attention and resources away from the arts and toward the narrow range of traditional academic subjects on which most of those tests focused. Consequently, there appears to be increased public backlash against this mind-numbing, narrow 3Rs approach to education, since it seems to alienate many students while only marginally improving standardized test scores. As a result, more elementary schools and early childhood programs are now centering on creativity and constructivist approaches built on arts-rich or arts-centered curricula.

In addition, current trends in research are geared toward ongoing, coordinated, site-based, and cooperative research that aims to make visible the impact of school programs built on such shared philosophical bases. Such research will have an impact on school decision making and policy development within our culture in general. Through focused action research, in collaboration with school systems, it is anticipated that we will be able to provide increased evidence for the value of a fair share of time in the curriculum for the arts, the importance of teachers well versed in arts disciplines, and the impact of quality facilities and resources for the arts. With time, it is anticipated that case studies of exemplary arts-centered schools will provide sounder evidence of the impact of such comprehensive, balanced, and sequential programs, and demonstrate the value and necessity of the arts in children's lives.

Although there is an international concern about the relative status and value accorded to arts subject in schools (International Review of Curriculum and Assessment Frameworks Archive, 2000), it must be recognized that the arts have always existed, and often thrived, even in the face of terrible social circumstances, because of humankind's irrepressible need to make and communicate meaning (Schuler, 2001). As we continue to shape our futures, our task will be to remind others that the human need for the arts and for arts education is fundamental. To return to earlier concepts presented in this book, the field of education is faced with the challenge of identifying the changing needs of education in our contemporary society. But instead of trying to project what arts education will look like in the future, based on current trends, we should formulate a vision of what we *want* it to look like and work to make that vision a reality. In other words, instead of predicting the future, we should *create* it (Lehman, 2000a, b).

CREATING OUR PREFERRED FUTURES

This chapter began with the words *It is the year 2073 B.C.* How might it conclude if the final segment began with the words *It is the year A.D. 2073?* How would our world reality look seventy or more years hence? This final segment draws on the views of a number of authors who have stated their preferred options for our world in general and the place for the arts and arts education within this world.

Hagood (2000), for example, forecasted a culture that will turn its focus toward empowering people to seek a better diet for the body and soul. He believed there will be an *intellectual, artistic, and cultural revolution*—an enlightenment for parents, their children, and communities for more tolerance for difference, tempered with considered positive outcomes. Hope (2000) also predicted society will move away from the frenetic mass culture vortex of the late twentieth century. It is believed that the overriding preference for shallowness, intellectual thinness, transiency, trendiness, and fast change will no longer serve as stand-ins for *wholeness and creative maturity* (Best, 2000a, b). Best anticipated that long-term contemplation and wisdom will replace short-term feeling, that quality will take precedence over quantity, and that deep continuity will be valued above episodic living. According to Hope (2000), the arts will become a *primary energy source* for intellectual attention and the creation of beauty. In turn, powerful new works in all art forms will demand concentrated contemplation and study on their own terms, and a larger number of citizens will have some fluency in one or more arts discipline.

The twentieth-century priority given at the national level to globalization, privatization, and capitalism is anticipated to give way to a *local civic priority* focused on quality-of-life issues (Hope, 2000). Hope envisaged that diversity and multiculturalism will be achieved more in terms of choices among approaches to culture than on racial, ethnic, or other demographic grounds. Consequently, local level rather than global education will become the mode that best supports democratic, *unified moral visions within schools.* Through local-level education programs, there will be better opportunities to promote *humanistic values,* such as responsibility and citizenship, where interpersonal qualities of children can be more of a central focus. As is currently the case in many affluent regions, niche thinking and niche marketing is developing and growing with respect to arts education, and it is anticipated that this trend will continue. For example, *specialist arts-centered, community-based schools* may become the preferred option for many families, where the types of policies that were outlined earlier will become more of the norm, such as a focus on multiple intelligences; the employment of artists in residence; learning through participation in museums, galleries, and arts festivals; and the use of arts mentors within the community.

Other authors forecasted this notion of specialist "niche" schools, and the view that increasing proportions of children's arts learning will occur *outside the school setting,* through less-formal educational venues (Reimer, 2000; Schuler, 2001). Today there are trends for expanded school days and school program choices, and it is anticipated that this trend will increase to include even further opportunities to elect arts courses through other schools and through *interlinked community sites.* Through such flexible options, children will have opportunities to develop artistic perception, knowledge, skills, and appreciation through exposure to and interaction with *arts mentors and gifted teachers* (Colwell, 2000). Consequently, authentic arts activities will increase in scope and availability, and new forms of *apprenticeship and collaboration* will emerge between artists and young people, bringing professionals into the classrooms and students out of the school (Reimer, 2000; Swanwick, 1999). The involvement of persons and institutions from the wider community will enhance the notion that the school should be an *idealized microcosm* of the larger society, where the developing minds of young children learn to adapt to, and succeed within, novel surroundings (Gardner, 1999a).

Reimer (2000) envisaged that a K–12 coordinated arts curriculum will include not only "venerable" or respected *core* subjects (which will include the visual arts, music, dance, theater, literary arts, and new arts forms) but also "outgrowths." Outgrowths will focus on teaching-learning of *new technologies,* used in new emergent combinations, which will advance our current technology-enabled forms of learning (e.g., an *Artsworld Education Network*). There are new technologies today, for example, where computers are used to provide children with possible examples of musical endings to their personally created melodies (Towsey et al., 2001). It is possible that, seventy years from now, such technologies will become even more refined, where artificial intelligence will be used in real-time interactive composition and in performance and conducting-based musical experiences.

For example, computers might be able to respond sensitively to the young composer's input and give *verbal* advice about how to improve musical and expressive aspects of compositions. The computer would also be able to tap into a huge database to provide instant examples (both aurally and through scores) of how the masters throughout history have tackled similar challenges in musical composition. Similarly, virtual conducting might be possible through the use of miniaturization, fast processors, and wireless movement sensors. By wearing headsets that allow a conductor to view and hear three-dimensional digitized visual-audio recordings of performance groups, he or she might be able to engage in real-time interaction with the virtual musicians. For example, when the conducting gestures show expressive aspects, such as slowing down or becoming more energetic, the musicians in the digitized visual-audio recording would respond accordingly. Hypothetically, in the future, such virtual conducting prospects might be available through databank choices that include musical groups of all sizes and genres: rock/jazz, full orchestra/string quartet, choir with organ, and a range of other musical combinations. Similarly, musical performance might be able to draw on "music less one" types of participation, similar to current-day karaoke (where the background music is provided and the singer is the star). However, future prospects might include drawing on a large database of "music less one" that allows performers to play the bass part in a jazz ensemble, sing the lead role in an opera, play the congas in a Latin percussion ensemble, sing in the alto section of a large choir, and a range of other performance options. In virtual fashion, it might even be possible to interact with the virtual musicians and to influence expressive and stylistic aspects, such as slowing the bass part down within a jazz ensemble and watching and hearing the results of this in relation to the virtual musician's responses.

Whether such concepts of how arts technology may develop will become reality or remain fantasy is impossible to predict. However, the very notion of such options opens our minds to new prospects—prospects that could allow children opportunities to gain not only the specialized skills and understandings of each of the arts, but also broad, inclusive insights into the shared nature of meaning-creation and cross-modal forms of thinking and doing. In addition, children's styles of learning could be supported through a huge range of entry points and options for learning. One could expect that, as generations of arts-educated children grow up and become parents and teachers, the quality and pervasiveness of arts education and new forms of artistic expression will continue to grow.

It is highly likely that the worldwide communication through media other than text will place a higher priority on children developing media literacy (Schuler, 2001). Even elementary school children might be expected to create multimedia portfolios that convey their own ideas and artistic forms of expression. Improved technology will make the collection, storage, and retrieval of multimedia work easy and affordable. Schuler adds that such course work will evolve around carefully designed *projects* that culminate in child reflection and revision, and their work will be assessed according to clear criteria that children collaboratively develop and apply. By high school, students might be expected to demonstrate basic knowledge in the four visual and performing arts and in depth mastery of one art form. For example, they might create and present an exhibit of still art, photography, or multimedia, possibly using media similar to holograms and new forms that have not even been invented yet. Similarly, children might participate in the types of virtual experiences described earlier and present a composition or performance as their assessed project, complete with layers of reflection about their learning processes in relation to their final outcome.

It is expected that scientific research will show more and more connections between the study of the arts and the development of mind/brain. Consequently, our current understanding of the languages, grammars, structures, and compositional and design principles that are unique to the arts may become part of a more general goal for developing creative and expressive thinking. One could anticipate that increased public awareness of the principles underpinning arts disciplines will influence our future research, and consequently our scientific and artistic knowledge. For example, even today, our mind/brain research shows evidence that babies and even fetuses search for patterns in music. Such evidence of mind/brain and arts-linked learning may increase the current trend of parents seeking educational advantage for their young children, including prenatal experiences and private arts tuition (Hope, 2000; Schuler, 2001).

Schuler (2001) anticipates that the solid foundation for arts learning that early childhood programs offer will have a "trickle-up" effect on the rest of education. He expects that the evidence for the benefits of arts education in child development and learning will influence the school curricula and more time and effort will be devoted to arts education in preschool, elementary, and intermediate grades. This will have an impact on teacher preparation programs, and higher education institutions will be required to train arts specialists to work with very young children. Schuler anticipates that "generalist" teacher preparation programs—such as early childhood and elementary education—will require graduates to be adept in cross-discipline studies. Social studies teachers, for example, will need to be as well versed on the history of the arts as they are on the history of politics and war, and physical education teachers will need to understand issues of lifelong fitness and happiness. Consequently, there may be a gradual decrease in competitive sports in schools and an increase in dance as an expressive medium for the discipline of the body.

It is forecasted that those with *deep knowledge* and special skills in the arts will provide models for local-level arts education, because adults with specialist arts skills will share the public's concern over *continuity of the culture* and the need for *innovation and change* (Colwell, 2000). These skilled teachers will have sufficiently deep understanding of the arts disciplines and personal experience in artistic meaning-making to be able to assist children to understand and experience artistic meaning. It could be envisaged that many teachers with such disciplinary knowledge will become active advocates for the importance of shared artistic efforts, and for the value of children creating and communicating meaning through all modes of understanding—visual, spatial, aural, and bodily-kinesthetic. Through such an appreciation of all modes, one would expect an increased respect for the artworks of children, coupled with an appreciation of the masterpieces that have been created throughout our culture's history.

As creators of meaning, children and adults alike would be active participants in this ideal, preferred option for the future. They would participate in the shared meaning systems of the arts and experience the power that the arts have in helping us to construct and transform our worlds. The arts would be valued as a significant means not only for preserving and maintaining culture, but also for being dynamic agents for social and cultural change. We would be participants in the collaborative shaping of our culture and our futures—futures in which the arts will play a significant role in shaping our world.

SUMMARY

Throughout our recorded history, the arts have played a significant role in human evolution. They have enhanced humans' quality of life, and provided a way for culture to record and preserve its finest achievements and traditions handed down from generation to generation. In addition, the arts have played a significant role in the shaping of cultures. In the macro sense, cultures have always involved a system of values, rights, exchanges, obligations, opportunities, and power; in the meso sense, social institutions and professional societies/bodies become the culture carriers of such values; and in the micro sense, individuals learn to operate and adapt to a culture's expectation of what is deemed essential for good or useful and worthwhile ways of life. In other words, institutions, groups of people, and individuals can be aided or thwarted by the culture in which they live, and opportunities for artistic expression may either be supported or unsupported, valued or disregarded.

While the mind shapes culture, culture also shapes the minds of individuals. Such construction of worlds or realities is very much a feature of the arts and creativity. The arts help construct, reinforce, challenge, and transform social, cultural, political, and religious values. They not only reveal cultural heritage, they also are a means by which the culture is defined and evaluated. Yet the construction of reality is both a solo act and a collective experience, and the philosophies and school policies reflect the value that is given to artistic forms of symbolic meaning making and communication. By necessity, our traditional cultural values associated with schooling constantly must adapt to changing times. These values are shaped by our views of human mental activity and our sense of how to enculturate children through the schooling process. Culture involves an interplay between the versions of the world that are products of individual's histories and versions that are formed as a result of institutions, such as schools. The individual teachers within these institutions have an important role to play in shaping the future direction of arts education for young children.

It could be expected that, seventy years from now, the macro, meso, and mico aspects of culture and the ways in which it is constructed will be different in many ways. Four challenges seem to encompass the essence of the content of this chapter:

- To nurture the progress of the arts and culture in an environment increasingly driven by marketplace forces, where a new emphasis is on wholeness and creative maturity and where the arts are a primary energy source for intellectual attention and creation of beauty.
- To activate public interaction with the arts by engaging a larger percentage of the population not only as arts audience members, but also as hands-on participants in making, creating, and performing artworks through local civic networks and with priorities given to quality-of-life issues and unified moral visions.
- To broaden and humanize the focus of educational reform by promoting a vision that honors the role of the arts in the curriculum, gives all forms of learning meaning, and considers learning settings to be idealized microcosms of the larger society, including interlinked community sites and interaction with arts mentors and new technologies.

■ To align teacher preparation—whether within higher education institutions or in other emerging models—both to contemporary culture and to emerging educational expectations, where deep knowledge and special skills in the arts can provide models for cultural continuity and for innovation and change.

Children, teachers, and the broader community will need to adapt to change while at the same time taking responsibility for shaping future change. Advocacy in the arts is a long-term process. It involves talking to others about values and practices and having a clear understanding and rationale of why such policies and practices are valued. Advocacy for the arts involves discussions with colleagues in the lunch room at work, with other professionals at coffee breaks at conferences, through newsletters to parents, through opinion papers in local educational journals, through showcasing children's artworks, and by using every opportunity to defend the place of the arts in the education of children—for the future of our artistic culture.

ADDITIONAL READINGS

Burton, L. H. (2001). Interdisciplinary curriculum: Retrospect and prospect. *Music Educators Journal, 87*(5), 17–25.

Colwell, R. (2000). Music education in 2050. *Arts Education Policy Review, 102*(2), 29–30.

Eisner, E. W. (1999). Getting down to basics in arts education. *Journal of Aesthetic Education, 33*(4), 145–155.

Ellis, A. K., & Fouts, J. T. (2001). Interdisciplinary curriculum: The research base. *Music Educators Journal, 87*(5), 22–26.

Gardner, H. (1999). Keynote Address. *Bulletin of the Council for Research in Music Education, 142,* 9–21.

Hope, S. (2000). Arts education in wonderland. *Arts Education Policy Review, 102*(2), 11–13.

Reimer, B. (2000). The way it will be. *Arts Education Policy Review, 102*(2), 7–8.

Schuler, S. C. (2001). Music and education in the twenty-first century: A retrospective. *Arts Education Policy Review, 102*(3), 25–36.

PRACTICAL ACTIVITIES

1. Think of very old features in nature (e.g., a thousand-year-old tree, or one of the Seven Wonders of the World), ancient artifacts (e.g., the Dead Sea Scrolls), or buildings (e.g., the Taj Mahal, a European cathedral). Try to remember your impressions of these historical objects when you first encountered them, either from photographs or through first-hand experience. Imagine what the world would be like without such historical components.

2. Try to imagine what the world will be like ten, thirty, fifty, or a hundred years from now. What do you think might have changed? Is your outlook on such changes positive, negative, pessimistic, fatalistic, or one of "what will be will be." Discuss your impressions with others.

THE VISUAL ARTS

Art is an expression, in visual form, that is concerned with concepts, feelings, intellect, and imagination and the transformation of two- and three-dimensional forms/images (abstract or realistic) using visual/tactile sensations and aesthetic values. **Craft** involves creating functional or nonfunctional objects/ works, where the purposeful outcome may be specified in advance, but the form is developed through creative problem solving and attention to skills and technique, using materials such as textiles, clay, ceramic, glass, wood, and metal. **Design** is the planning element of the visual arts that involves visualizing in the mind's eye, selecting and arranging art elements, and clarifying intentions in various graphic forms, the products of which may be either made by the creator or manufactured by others. **Media** are materials and technical means or forms of artistic expression or communication, including two-dimensional (e.g., painting, drawing, printmaking, and crafts such as weaving) and three-dimensional (e.g., sculpture, construction, and crafts such as pottery), and other media not discussed in this book (e.g., photography, television, graphic design, and computer art).

Art Creating/Making involves problem posing and solving and selecting and refining ideas and processes, while engaging with specific media and art elements, to create a symbolic form that may express and/or shape meaning.

Art Presenting/Exhibiting involves presenting artworks, either informally (through display in a center/classroom) or formally (through an exhibition, which may be open to the public).

Art Reflection/Critique involves viewing and responding to one's own and other's artworks by describing, analyzing, judging, valuing, challenging, interpreting, giving opinions and stating personal preferences, and ascribing value to the artwork based on knowledge of media, process, purpose, aesthetic merit, and other relevant criteria (e.g., history).

Elements of art are:

- **Line** is the length, direction, thickness/thinness of a drawn/painted/ engraved mark, or the edge of a three-dimensional object or group of objects.

- **Shape** is the visible or tactile form of an item, which may be a two-dimensional (e.g., circle, square, irregular, or geometric) or a three-dimensional spatial form (the contour, length, width, volume, and height of an object).
- **Color/hue** includes the primary (yellow, blue, red), secondary (orange, green, violet), and blended secondary hues (e.g., yellow-orange), the complementary or contrasting value/tone relationships between colors (e.g., light/dark, cool/warm), and tinting (adding white) or shading (adding black).
- **Texture** is the surface quality of an artwork, both tactile and as a visual illusion, such as rough/smooth, soft/hard, or irregular.
- **Form** is the relationship between length and width and depth.
- **Composition** is the arrangement of the elements of art according to organizational principles.

Other terms that can be applied to art techniques: **appliqué** (a textile technique in which separate pieces of material are sewn or otherwise attached to a larger piece of fabric), **assemblage** (the combining of unrelated materials into a new creation), **collage** (making images from pieces of colored paper and other materials pasted to a surface), **duo-prints** (completely covering an area of paper using light/bright oil pastels or wax crayons, then covering this area again by applying dark pastels or crayons, and then placing a clean sheet of paper on top and making a line drawing, which reveals the first layer of colors on the bottom sheet), **engraving** (the process of incising lines into a surface to create an image or a texture), **frottage** (holding a piece of paper against a highly textured surface, such as a tree bark or wall bricks, and rubbing the surfaces of the paper with a crayon until the texture becomes a pattern on the paper), **mono-prints** (applying paint to a nonabsorbent surface, drawing or scratching into the paint, and taking a print by placing a sheet of paper on top, rubbing lightly over its surface, and lifting it off), **mosaic** (a picture made by fitting together small tiles, stones, pieces of paper, or other materials), and **mural** (a painting on a large piece of paper or a wall, usually large in format).

DANCE

Dance is an art form that blends the body and mind in nonverbal meaning-making and communication, using movement as the medium for expressive aesthetic code. Dance is an interpretation of ideas, feelings, and sensory impressions, expressed symbolically in movement forms, through the unique use of the body. **Kinesthetic** understanding involves the development of a "muscular sense," and an awareness of the way the body moves not only in relation to one's own body parts but also in relation to space and objects in space. **Body awareness,** which is very important in developing emotive power, includes kinesthetic understanding and an awareness of the body's behavior when combined with other bodies, how the body moves/rests, and how the voice is part of the body.

Dance Creating uses the skills of improvising, forming, selecting, communicating ideas and feelings, rehearsing, and fixing (setting, firming, or stabilizing the dance, both mentally and physically). **Choreographing** utilizes the dance elements of body, space, time, and effort to form processes that organize and structure the dance and to communicate ideas, emotions, and images.

Dance Performing/Presenting is the sharing or showing of a sequence of movements or a dance to one or more people, by communicating ideas, images, and emotions through the body and movement. As in all arts disciplines, the performing/presenting of dances involves both process and product.

Dance Viewing/Critiquing involves critically observing and responding to our own and/or others' movements, as part of creating, performing, or as audience viewers. It includes discussing *how* (and *how well*) a dance or dancers expressed ideas and emotions through the use of the body, space, time, and effort, and how we respond to the dance and grasp its structures.

Elements of dance are:

- **Body** involves isolation and coordination of *body parts* (e.g., head, shoulders, arms, hands, elbows, wrists, neck, back, upper torso, ribs, hips, legs, knees, ankles, feet), *movements* (e.g., swaying, swinging, jerking, twisting, shaking, turning, lifting, tensing/relaxing, pressing, gliding, floating, flicking, slashing, punching, dabbing, becoming fluid), body *position* and relationships of the body to the ground (e.g., shape or symmetry), ways of managing body *weight* in motion and in relation to others, *momentum/collapses,* and *alignment.*
- **Space** applies to the physical and symbolic *area/range* in which one moves, *levels* (high: erect posture or in the air; middle: crawling, crouching, using four limbs, stopping; low: rolling or scooting across the floor), *direction* of movement or gaze (forward, backward, sideways), *relationships/groupings, shape/dimension* (e.g., rounded/angular, big/small), a variety of *holds, movement paths* through space (e.g., zigzaged, random, from corner to corner), and *extensions* of body parts into space.
- **Time** refers to *speed/tempo* at which the body moves and the rhythmic patterning of movements according to the individual's own *body time* (e.g., walking pace) and/or the *imposed time* (rhythm of music/sound), the *duration* of specific and combined movements, and *accent.*

- **Effort** involves the combination of space and time, developing a *force* for which the movement is produced, and drawing attention to the dynamics or *qualitative* aspects of the movement (e.g., limp/stiff, energetic/calm, light/heavy, fluid/staccato, slow/quick).

Form represents the way a dance may be divided into sections, where the harmonious balance of the dance elements are used to give a specific shape or time to a dance work and distinguish it from other dances. The defining characteristics of a dance create an appearance or impression in which an external or internal experience presents itself.

Locomotor movements propel the body to travel from one place to another through space (e.g., walking/running, crawling/rolling, creeping, cartwheeling). **Axial** movements are those in which the body stays in a stationary position in space (e.g., swaying, bending, rising/falling, stretching, opening/closing). Both locomotor and axial movements incorporate the elements of body, space, time, and effort.

Style relates to the manner in which dance elements are selected, organized, and manipulated within a particular genre, which includes various types of dances such as social, ritual (religious and other rites), folk/ethnic, modern, jazz, contact improvisation, ballet, spiritual, tap, modern, disco, ballroom, square, bush, and pop.

DRAMA

Drama is an art form that can be an extension of the self or a group of people who, through active exploration, enact realistic or fictional events through roles and situations for the purpose of exploring lifelike situations. People (their bodies and voices) are the main media of expression.

Drama Creating/Making (also called Forming) involves making and shaping shared insights, ideas, feelings, and perceptions into dramatic action, through the processes of exploring, discovering, improvising (dramatic play), re-creating dramatic texts, shaping the dramatic action, and "fixing" the action (sometimes for presenting to an audience).

Drama Performing/Presenting is the shaping and rehearsing of dramatic action to communicate the intended meaning to an audience (of one or more people) and for potentially reshaping the action for further rehearsal and performance. Presenting is process oriented whereby the product itself is an element of the process.

Drama Reflection/Critique occurs during and after a dramatic event through a form of "coming back to real life" and thinking about the character or event in the dramatic action, to understand *what* is/was being conveyed, *how* this is/was conveyed, and how *effectively* this is/was achieved. It is a process that takes children out of the action of the plot and into the action of the theme, to synthesize the experience (e.g., relationships in role, and commitment to the drama). Following reflection and critique, the dramatic action may be explored, experimented with, reshaped, fixed again, rehearsed, and perhaps performed.

Elements of drama are used to shape and express meaning through action and include human *interaction/relationships, role/character, situation, focus,* and dramatic *tension* (the "mental excitement" of relationships, dilemmas, surprises, situations, or mysteries that can be achieved through techniques such as speaking softly or limiting the time available for a task or decision), *movement/stillness, sound/silence, language/text, space* and *time, objects,* and *light/darkness, mood, contrast, symbol* (a representation of ideas and feelings and their consequences that can take the form of a sound or word, a mark, a gesture, an object, or an event, and generate a collective meaning), and *metaxis* (a tension that exists within the relationships between the actual world and the dramatic one).

Enrolling involves taking up a role, or character different from who we really are and sensitizing to relevant attitudes, points of view, and contextual factors of the new role or character. Children project into a role (feelings, looks, shape, movements, and voice) and build belief in the situation (the relevant aspects and contextual factors of the dramatic action) before participating in improvisation or role taking. Often this involves making an analogy (resembling and depicting something by comparing it to another familiar, similar thing).

Freeze Frames (also called Tableau and Still Image) are frozen actions, like a statue or still picture of a story, event, or situation, which can be used as a strategy to help the onlooker and participants understand the main thoughts and feelings of the person or group in a particular moment. A **frozen effigy** is a person dressed in role, frozen in statue form against an appropriate background. A **dream sequence** involves an in-role telling (in a few words) of what an individual is thinking or feeling at a particular moment.

Improvisation is a strategy that develops spontaneous actions and reactions, like a play without a script. This may involve *detouring* (through time, through the story, or through what the children know), and relating the children's experiences in the dramatic action to personal and immediate learning. Some participants may be *inside the action* (as key participating characters, in role), *on the edge of the action* (as characters directly associated with the situation, but removed from it in time and place), or *outside the action* (as characters quite removed from the event itself).

Mime is a sophisticated dramatic form in which nonverbal communication (thought and feeling) conveys dramatic meaning through the use of the body, gesture, and facial expression.

Narration is a strategy of using the voice to describe the situation or aspects of the dramatic context, recount the events or recap what has happened so far, establish the mood, control the plot and move the drama along, create atmosphere and build tension, span/compress time, cover sequences that are difficult to enact, provide an effective conclusion, and provide material for reflection. **Monologue,** another form of storytelling, is a dramatic sketch performed by a speaker.

MUSIC

Music is an expressive, aesthetic art form that engages our imagination and is created and communicated by using sound and silence as a medium.

Music Creating/Making: Improvisation is spontaneous individual or group musical creativity (sometimes while performing) that may involve singing, playing an instrument, or creating sound with the body/voice or with unconventional instruments (e.g., brooms, rocks, kitchen implements). **Composing** is the creation of music that involves using skills and knowledge to adapt sounds through experimenting, improvising, planning, ordering, and arranging.

Music Performing/Presenting is the act of sharing the music/sounds of voices and/or instruments (traditional or devised) with an audience. Performing is directly connected with creating and requires skill/practice (manipulating the materials of music) and, in the case of more formal performance, rehearsal.

Music Listening/Appraising. Listening is the active, sensory, and mindful attending to music that is involved in all musical skills—moving, playing, singing, creating, and later "reading." **Appraising** covers all those occasions in which we critically listen to and **respond** to our own and/or others' music, as part of composing, performing, or as audience listening. It includes talking about music and using movement as a way of responding to music and grasping its structures.

Expressive Controls: The expressive components of music include controls such as *tempo* (the speed or rate of beats—the degrees of fast and slow—

which may include abrupt or gradual changes), formally described as presto (very fast), vivace (quick and spirited), allegro (fast and lively), allegretto (moderately fast), moderato (moderate, walking pace), andante (moderately slow), lento (slow), and largo (broad and very slow); *dynamics* (the intensity of a sound, or degrees of loud and soft, which may include abrupt or gradual changes) formally described as crescendo (<, gradually increasing loudness), diminuendo/decrescendo (>, gradually decreasing loudness), pianissimo (pp, very soft), piano (p, soft), mezzo piano (mp, medium soft), mezzo forte (mf, medium loud), forte (f, loud), and fortissimo (ff, very loud). See *Tone Quality and Texture* for other examples of expressive controls.

Form refers to the scheme or framework or basic structure that organizes and gives meaning to the music. Structures include *beginnings/endings* and patterns such as *phrases* (musical "sentences" and sentence sequences), *repetition* (the same way over again), *contrast* (a different sounding part), and *themes* (recurring musical ideas). Form can be designated by letters to describe distinct *sections* (binary [AB], ternary [ABA], rondo [ABACA]), and include other simple structures, such as *verse* and *refrain* (chorus), or larger structures, such as a *symphony* (a large composition with self-contained divisions, called movements, which are large sections of music, usually each having a separate indication of speed).

Melody/Harmony: Melody is the linear succession of tones played or sung that are rhythmically controlled and perceived as a meaningful grouping. Melody includes elements such as *pitch* (high/low), *direction* (going up/down, or staying on a level), *shape* (overall up-and-down contour patterns). Melody may or may not include *harmony* (the sequence of changing or repeated tones and relationships between them—the "vertical" aspect of music). **Harmony** is used to support, enrich, and elaborate melody, to color music, and to create atmosphere. **Harmonic structure** involves *chords* (two or more tones sounded simultaneously), and *chord sequences* (e.g., the song "London Bridge Is Falling Down" has a simple I-V-I structure: London Bridge is falling down [I], falling down [V], falling down [I] . . .).

Rhythm pertains to the temporal (time-based) aspects of music—the grouping of sounds and silences of varying duration, usually controlled by a regular beat. Rhythm contains the essential elements of *beat* (regular, even pulsations), *accent* (the stress or emphasis given to a certain tone, making it stand out or seem to be a "surprise, all at one place"), *rests* (brief silences), *meter* (groups of beats, such as waltzes feeling in 3), *duration* (the length of time that a tone, chord, or rest is sustained), *pattern* (a repetition of tones within a musical passage), *ostinato* (a small musical fragment that is repeated throughout a piece to enrich the effect), *syncopation* (the emphasis/accent on normally weak beats), and *anacrusis* (the "pick up" preceding the first beat, such as in the phrase "you can dance," where the word "dance" is the emphasis).

Tone Quality and Texture: **Tone quality** (also called *timbre*) is the distinctive and variable quality or color of a sound produced by an instrument or voice that affects the characteristic *tone* and produces differing responses in the hearer. **Texture** is used to describe the result of sound/tone combinations—the vertical and horizontal elements in music that produce *effects* such as light/heavy, thick/thin, mellow/harsh, dark/bright, dense/sparse. Texture can be illustrated in relation to *styles* of composition, such as homophonic (the parts move together, with a top-melody and chords beneath, as in a hymn) and polyphonic ("layered" interplay of different melodies simultaneously, as in a fugue).

Abbs, P. (1987). *Living powers: The arts in education.* London: Falmer Press.

Adler, T. (1990). "Melody is the message" of infant-directed speech. *American Psychological Association Monitor, 21*(2), 9.

Alexander, R., et al. (1969). Development of a theatre arts and curriculum for young children. *Resources in Education.* ERIC reference ED 032 937.

Andress, B. (1980). *Music experiences in early childhood.* New York: Holt, Rinehart and Winston.

Apollinaire, G. (1949). *The Cubist painters: Aesthetic mediations.* Wienborn: Schultz.

Archambault, R. D. (Ed.). (1964). *John Dewey on education: Selected writings* (pp. 339–358). Chicago: University of Chicago Press.

Arnheim, R. (1954). *Art and visual perception.* Berkeley: University of California Press.

Arnheim, R. (1969). *Visual Thinking.* Berkeley: University of California Press.

Ashman, A., & Wright, S. (1997). Cognitive processing and the recognition of meter in music. *Journal of Cognitive Education, 5,* 217–232.

Ashton, L. (1997). Repositioning children's drawing development: From rungs to rings. *Australian Art Education, 20*(3), 3–16.

Azar, B. (1996). The brain knows the score, studies show. *American Psychological Association (APA) Monitor (April),* 22–24.

Baily, J. (1985). Music structure and human movement. In P. Howell, I. Cross, & R. West (Eds.), *Musical structure and cognition* (pp. 237–258). London: Academic Press.

Bamberger, J. S. (1991). *The mind behind the musical ear: How children develop musical intelligence.* Cambridge, MA: Harvard University Press.

Barrett, J. R. (2001). Interdisciplinary work and musical integrity. *Music Educators Journal, 87*(5), 27–31.

Barthes, R. (1972). *Mythologies* (A. Lavers, Trans.). New York: Hill and Wang.

Bateson, G. (1976). A theory of play and fantasy. In J. S. Bruner, A. Jolly, & K. Sylva (Eds.), *Play: Its role in development and evolution* (pp. 119–129). Middlesex, UK: Penguin Books.

Baumann, G. (1995). Music and dance: The royal road to affective culture. *The World of Music, 37*(2), 31–42.

Bayless, K. M., & Ramsey, M. E. (1986). *Music: A way of life for the young child.* Melbourne: Merrill.

Beane, J. A. (1997). *Curriculum integration: Designing the core of democratic education.* New York: Teachers College Press.

Becker, A. L. (1993). On Arnheim on language. *Journal of Aesthetic Education, 27*(4), 115–127.

Berk, L. (1997). *Child Development* (4th ed.). Boston: Allyn and Bacon.

Berk, L. (2000). Make-believe play and the early development of self-regulation: A Vygotskian perspective. Paper presented at a research seminar for the Centre for Applied Studies in Early Childhood, August, Queensland University of Technology, Brisbane.

Berk, L. E., & Winsler, A. (1995). *Scaffolding children's learning: Vygotsky and early childhood education.* Washington, DC: National Association for the Education of Young Children.

Best, H. M. (2000a). Arts, words, intellect, emotion. Part 1: Toward artistic mindedness. *Arts Education Policy Review, 102*(6), 3–11.

Best, H. M. (2000b). Arts, words, intellect, emotion. Part 2: Toward artistic mindedness. *Arts Education Policy Review, 102*(10), 2–10.

Biasini, A., Thomas, R., & Pogonowski, L. (no date). *MMCP interaction* (2nd ed.). Bardonia, NY: Media Materials.

Binet, A. (1905). New methods for the diagnosis of the intellectual level of subnormals. *L'Annie Psychologique, 12,* 191-244.

Blacking, J. (1990). Music in children's cognitive and affective development. In F. R. Wilson & F. L. Roehman (Eds.), *Music and child development: Proceedings of the 1987 Denver Conference* (pp. 68–78). St. Louis: MMB Music.

Bloom, B., with Sosniak, L. (1985). *Developing talent in young children.* New York: Ballantine Books.

Boal, A. (1995). *The rainbow of desire: The Boal method of theatre and therapy.* London: Routledge.

Boughton, D. (1989). The changing face of Australian art education: Past and present influences. *Studies in Art Education, 3*(4), 197–211.

Brahmstedt, H., & Brahmstedt, P. (1997). Music education in China. *Music Educators Journal (May)*, 28–29, 52ff.

Bredekamp, S. (Ed.) (1987). *Developmentally appropriate practice in early childhood programs serving children from birth through age 8.* Washington, DC: National Association for the Education of Young Children.

Bresler, L. (1994). Zooming in on the qualitative paradigm in art education: Educational criticism, ethnography, and action research. *Visual Arts Research, 20*(1), 1–19.

Bresler, L. (1995). The subservient, coequal, affective and social integration styles and their implications for the arts. *Arts Education Policy Review, 96,* 32.

Bresler, L. (2000). The relationships of school art, national goals, and multilayered cultures. *Arts Education Policy Review, 101*(5), 3–7.

Bruner, J. (1986). *Actual minds, possible worlds.* Cambridge, MA: Harvard University Press.

Bruner, J. (1996). *The culture of education.* Cambridge, MA: Harvard University Press.

Buckton, R. (1983). *Sing a song of six-year-olds.* Wellington: New Zealand Council for Educational Research.

Burton, L. H. (2001) Interdisciplinary curriculum: Retrospect and prospect. *Music Educators Journal, 87*(5), 17–25.

Carey, S., & Gelman, R. (1991). *The epigenesis of mind.* Hillsdale, NJ: Lawrence Erlbaum.

Carterette, E. C., & Kendall, R. A. (1999). Comparative music perception and cognition. In D. Deutsch (Ed.), *The psychology of music* (2nd ed.; pp. 725–782). London: Academic Press.

Cazden, C., Cope, B., Fairclough, N., Gee, J., Kalantzis, M., Kress, G., et al. (1996). A pedagogy of multiliteracies: Designing social futures. *Harvard Educational Review, 66*(1), 60–92.

Cecil-Fizdale, S. (1991). Creative dance and movement for young children. In S. Wright (Ed.), *The arts in early childhood* (pp. 115–139). Sydney: Prentice Hall.

Chomsky, N. (1986). *Knowledge of language, its nature, origin and use.* New York: Praeger.

Clemens, S. G. (1991, January). Art in the classroom: Making every day special. *Young Children, 46.*

Colby, S. (1928). *Natural rhythms and dances.* New York: A. S. Barnes and Company.

Cole, E. S., & Schaefer, C. (1990). Can young children be art critics? *Young Children, 45*(2), 33–38.

Colwell, R. (2000). Music education in 2050. *Arts Education Policy Review, 102*(2), 29–30.

Consortium of National Arts Education Associations. (1994). *Dance, music, theatre, visual arts: National Standards for Arts Education.* Reston, VA: Music Educators National Conference.

Cope, B., & Kalantzis, M. (2000). Designs for social futures. In B. Cope & M. Kalantzis (Eds.), *Multiliteracies: Literacy learning and the design of social futures* (pp. 203–234). South Yarra, Victoria: Macmillan.

Courtney, R. (1990). *Drama and intelligence: A cognitive theory.* Montreal: McGill-Queen's University Press.

Creaser, B. (1989). An examination of the four-year-old master dramatist. *International Journal of Early Childhood Education, 21,* 55–68.

Csikszentmihalyi, M. (1988). Society, culture, and person: A systems view of creativity. In R. J. Sternberg (Ed.), *The nature of creativity* (pp. 325–329). New York: Cambridge University Press.

Csikszentmihalyi, M. (1996). *Creativity: Flow and the psychology of discovery and invention.* New York: HarperCollins.

Csikszentmihalyi, M., & Rochbert-Halton, E. (1985). *The meaning of things.* Cambridge, England: Cambridge University Press.

Curtiss, D. (1987). *Introduction to visual literacy: A guide to the visual arts and communication.* Englewood Cliffs, NJ: Prentice Hall.

Dahlberg, G., Moss, P., & Pence, A. (1999). *Beyond quality in early childhood education and care: Postmodern perspectives.* London: Falmer Press.

Davidson, L., & Colley, B. (1987). Children's rhythmic development from age 5 to 7: Performance, notation, and reading of rhythmic pattern. In J. C. Peery, I. W. Peery, & T. W. Draper (Eds.), *Music and child development* (pp. 107–136). New York: Springer-Verlag.

Davidson, L., McKernon, P., & Gardner, H. (1981). The acquisition of song: A developmental approach. In *Developmental report of the Ann Arbor Symposium* (pp. 301–314). Reston, VA: Music Educators National Conference.

Davidson, L., & Scripp, L. (1988). Young children's musical representations: windows on musical cognition. In J. A. Slaboda (Ed.), *Generative processes in music* (pp. 195–230). Oxford: Clarendon.

Davies, B. (1988). *Frogs and snails and feminist tales.* Wellington, NZ: Allen and Unwin.

Davies, B. (1993). *Shards of glass: Children reading and writing beyond gendered identities.* Sydney: Allen and Unwin.

Davies, D. (1989, October). Encounters with Harpo Marx in the Wendy house. *Education 3–13, 55–59.*

Davis, G. A. (1992). *Creativity is forever.* Dubuque, IA: Kendall/Hunt.

D'Emidio, S. V. (1990, June). What makes Roger Run? *CableView Magazine, 7.*

Derham, F. (1973). *Art for the child under seven* (5th ed.). Canberra: Australian Pre-School Association.

Design Council. (2000). *Creativity in business and why we need it.* London: Design Council.

Dewey, J. (1902). *The child and the curriculum.* Chicago: University of Chicago Press.

Dewey, J. (1913). *Interest and effort in education.* Boston: Houghton-Miffin.

Dewey, J. (1916). *Democracy and education: An introduction to the philosophy of education* (1966, c. 1916 ed.). New York: Free Press.

Dissanayake, E. (1992). *Homo Aestheticus: Where art comes from and why.* New York: Free Press.

Donaldson, M. (1978). *Children's minds.* New York: W. W. Norton.

Dretske, F. (1994). Mind and brain. In R. Warner & T. Szubka (Eds.), *The mind-body problem: A guide to the current debate* (pp. 131–136). Cambridge, MA: Blackwell Publishers.

Duncan, I. (1928). *The art of the dance.* New York: Theatre Arts.

Dunn, J. (1996). Who's pretending: A study of the dramatic play of primary school children. Master's thesis. Queensland University of Technology, Brisbane.

Dunn, J. (1997). "The Dreamkeeper": Connecting dramatic play and process drama. *Educating Young Children, 3(3),* 16–18.

Dunn, J. (2001). Dramatic worlds in play: A study of the dramatic play of preadolescent girls. Doctoral dissertation. Griffith University, Brisbane.

Eckersley, R. (1992). *Youth and the challenge to change: Bringing youth, science and society together in the new millenium.* Carlton South: Australia's Commission for the Future.

Edwards, C. (1993). Partner, nurturer, and guide: The roles of the Reggio teacher in action. In C. Edwards, L. Gandini, & G. Forman (Eds.), *The hundred languages of children: The Reggio Emilia approach to early childhood education* (pp. 151–169). Norwood, NJ: Ablex.

Edwards, C., Gandini, L., & Forman, G. (1993). Introduction. In C. Edwards, L. Gandini, & G. Forman (Eds.), *The hundred languages of chil-*
dren: The Reggio Emilia approach to early childhood education (pp. 3–18). Norwood, NJ: Ablex.

Edwards, C., Gandini, L., & Forman, G. (1994). *The hundred languages of children: The Reggio Emilia approach to early childhood education* (pp. 3–18). Norwood, NJ: Ablex.

Egan, K. (1997). *The educated mind.* Chicago: University of Chicago Press.

Eisner, E. W. (Ed.). (1985). *Learning and teaching the ways of knowing.* Chicago: University of Chicago Press.

Eisner, E. W. (1988). On discipline-based art education: A conversation with Elliot Eisner. *Educational Leadership, 45(4),* 6–9.

Eisner, E. W. (1996, Fall). Qualitative research in music education: Past, present, perils, promise. *Bulletin of the Council for Research in Music Education, 130,* 8–16.

Eisner, E. W. (2001). Music education six months after the turn of the century. *Arts Education Policy Review, 102(30),* 20–24.

Elkind, D. (1987). Early childhood education on its own terms. In S. L. Kagan & E. F. Zigler (Eds.), *Early schooling: The national debate* (pp. 98–115). New Haven: Yale University Press.

Ellis, A. K., & Fouts, J. T. (2001). Interdisciplinary curriculum: The research base. *Music Educators Journal, 87(5),* 22–26.

Exiner, H., & Lloyd, P. (1987). *Learning through dance: A guide for teachers.* Melbourne: Oxford University Press.

Feldman, D. H. (1980). *Beyond universals in cognitive development.* Norwood, NJ: Ablex.

Feldman, D. H., & Goldsmith, L. T. (1990). *Nature's gambit: Child prodigies and the development of talent.* West Lafayette, IN: Purdue University.

Feldman, E. (1972). *Varieties of visual experience.* Englewood Cliffs, NJ: Prentice Hall.

Feldman, E. (1996). *Philosophy of art education.* Englewood Cliffs, NJ: Prentice Hall.

Fielding, R. (1993). The socio-cultural foundations of artistic development. *Australian Art Education, 16(3),* 4–8.

File, N. (1993). The teacher as a guide of children's competence with peers. *Child and Youth Care Forum, 22(5),* 351–360.

Findlay, E. (1971). *Rhythm and movement: Applications of Dalcroze Eurhythmics.* Evanston, IL: Summy Birchard.

Fisher DiLalla, L., & Watson, M. (1988). Differentiation of fantasy and reality: Preschoolers' reactions to interruptions in their play. *Developmental Psychology, 24(2),* 286–291.

Fleming, G. A. (1976). *Creative rhythmic movement: Boys and girls dancing.* Englewood Cliffs, NJ: Prentice Hall.

Flohr, J. (1985). Young children's improvisations: Emerging creative thought. *Creative Child and Adult Quarterly, 10,* 79–85.

Fodor, J. (1983). *The modularity of mind.* Cambridge, MA: MIT Press.

Fowler, C. (1996). *Strong arts, strong schools: The promising potential and shortsighted disregard of the arts in American schooling.* New York: Oxford University Press.

Fucigna, C., Ives, K., & Ives, W. (1982). Art for toddlers: A developmental approach. *Young Children, 37*(3), 45–51.

Gardner, H. (1973). *The arts and human development.* New York: Wiley.

Gardner, H. (1980). *Artful scribbles.* New York: Basic Books.

Gardner, H. (1982). *Art, mind and brain: A cognitive approach to creativity.* New York: Basic Books.

Gardner, H. (1983). *Frames of mind: The theory of multiple intelligences.* New York: Basic Books.

Gardner, H. (1987). *To open minds.* New York: Basic Books.

Gardner, H. (1991). *The unschooled mind.* New York: Basic Books.

Gardner, H. (1993a). *Creating minds: An anatomy of creativity seen through the lives of Freud, Einstein, Picasso, Stravinsky, Eliot, Graham, and Gandhi.* New York: Basic.

Gardner, H. (1993b). Foreword: Complementary perspectives on Reggio Emilia. In C. Edwards, L. Gandini, G. Forman (Eds.), *The hundred languages of children: The Reggio Emilia approach to early childhood education* (pp. ix–xiii). Norwood, NJ: Ablex.

Gardner, H. (1993c). *Multiple intelligences: The theory in practice.* New York: Basic.

Gardner, H. (1997). The key in the key slot: Creativity in a Chinese key. *Journal of Cognitive Education, 6*(1), 15–26.

Gardner, H. (1999a). *The disciplined mind: What all students should understand.* New York: Simon & Schuster.

Gardner, H. (1999b). Keynote address. *Bulletin of the Council for Research in Music Education, 142,* 9–21.

Gardner, H., & Wolf, D. (1982). Waves and streams of symbolisation: Notes on the development of symbolic capacities in young children. Paper presented at the International Congress on the Acquisition of Symbolic Skills, Keele, England.

Gee, J. P. (1989). Literacy, discourse and linguistics. *Journal of Education, 171,* 5–17.

Giffin, H. (1984). The co-ordination of meaning in the creation of shared make-believe reality. In I. Bretherton (Ed.), *Symbolic play: The development of social understanding* (pp. 73–100). New York: Academic.

Goldenberg, C., & Gillamore, R. (1991, April). Teaching and learning in a new key: The instructional conversation. Paper presented at the annual meeting of the American Educational Research Association, Chicago.

Goleman, D. (1995). *Emotional intelligence.* New York: Bantam.

Golomb, C. (1992). *The child's creation of a pictorial world.* Los Angeles: University of California Press.

Goodman, N. (1976). *Languages of art: An approach to a theory of symbols.* Cambridge, MA: Hackett.

Goodman, N. (1984). *Of mind and other matters.* Cambridge, MA: Harvard University Press.

Goodnow, J. (1977). *Children drawing.* Cambridge, MA: Harvard University Press.

Goodnow, J., Miller, P., & Kesslel, F. (1995). Editor's note, in cultural practices as contexts for development. *New Directions for Child Development, 68,* 1–3.

Graziano, A. B., Peterson, M., & Shaw, G. (1999). Enhanced learning of proportional math through music training and spatial-temporal training. *Neurological Research, 21,* 139–152.

Greenberg, M. (1979). *Your children need music: A guide for parents and teachers of young children.* Englewood Cliffs, NJ: Prentice Hall.

Grieshaber, S., & Ashby, G. (1997). Cognition, culture and curricula: An early childhood perspective. *Journal of Cognitive Education, 6*(1), 39–52.

Guilford, J. P. (1967). *The nature of human intelligence.* New York: McGraw-Hill.

Hagood, T. K. (2000). Popular culture and the imagined body. *Arts Education Policy Review, 102*(2), 33–34.

Hargreaves, D. J. (1986). *The developmental psychology of music.* Cambridge: Cambridge University Press.

Haseman, B., & O'Toole, J. (1987). *Dramawise.* Melbourne: Heinemann Educational.

Hausman, J. (Ed.). (1980). *Arts and the schools.* New York: McGraw-Hill.

Heaslip, P. (1994). Making play work in the classroom. In J. Moyles (Ed.), *The excellence of play* (pp. 99–109). Buckingham: OpenUniversity Press.

Heathcote, D. (1984). *Collected writings on education and drama.* Edited by Liz Johnson & Cecily O'Neill. London, UK: Hutchinson

Hepper, P. G. (1991). *Irish Journal of Psychology, 12,* 95–107.

Hetland, L. (2000). Listening to music enhances spatial-temporal reasoning: Evidence for the "Mozart Effect." *Journal of Aesthetic Education, 34,* 105–148.

Hetland, L., & Winner, E. (2001). The arts and academic achievement: What the evidence shows. *Arts Education Policy Review, 102*(5), 3–6.

Hope, S. (2000). Arts education in wonderland. *Arts Education Policy Review, 102*(2), 11–13.

International Review of Curriculum and Assessment Frameworks Archive. (2000). *The arts, creativity and cultural education: An international perspective.* http://www.inca.org.uk/thematic.as.

Itten, J. (1973). *The art of color: The subjective experience and objective rationale of color* (E. V. Haagen, Trans.). New York: Van Nostrand Reinhold.

James, A., Jenks, C., & Prout, A. (1998). *Theorizing childhood.* Cambridge, UK: Polity Press in Association with Blackwell Publishers.

Jenks, C. (1996). *Childhood.* London: Routledge.

Johnson, M. (1991). The emergence of meaning in bodily experience. In B. Ouden, & M. Moen (Eds.), *The presence of feeling in thought* (pp. 153–167). New York: Peter Long.

Jones, S. (1990). Teaching music for life. In F. R. Wilson, & F. L. Roehman (Eds.), *Music and child development: Proceedings of the 1987 Denver Conference* (pp. 389–399). St. Louis: MMB.

Katz, L. L. (1991). Cultural scripts: The home-school connection. *Early Child Development and Care, 73,* 95–102.

Katz, L. L. (1993). What can we learn from Reggio Emilia? In C. Edwards, L. Gandini, & Forman, G. (Eds.), *The hundred languages of children* (pp. 19–40). Norwood, NJ: Ablex.

Katz, L. (1996). Children as learners: A developmental approach. Paper presented at the Weaving Webs. Collaborative Teaching and Learning in the Early Years Curriculum, University of Melbourne.

Keil, F. (1989). *Concepts, kinds, and cognitive development.* Cambridge: Bradford Books/MIT Press.

Kellogg, R. (1969). *Analyzing children's art.* Palo Alto, CA: National Press Books.

Kelly, L., & Sutton-Smith, B. (1987). A study of infant musical productivity. In J. Perry, I. W. Perry, & T. W. Draper (Eds.), *Music and child development* (pp. 35–53). New York: Springer-Verlag.

Kelly-Byrne, D. (1989). *A child's play life: An ethnographic study.* New York: Teachers College Press.

Kendall, J. S., & Marzano, R. J. (1997). *Content knowledge: A compendium of standards and benchmarks for K–12 education* (2nd ed.). http://www.mcrel.org/.

Kessen, W., Levine, J., & Wendrich, K. (1979). The imitation of pitch in infants. *Infant Behavior and Development, 2,* 93–99.

Kessler, S. A. (1992). The social context of the early childhood curriculum. In S. Kessler, & B. B. Swaderer (Eds.), *Reconceptualizing the early childhood curriculum: Beginning the dialogue* (pp. 21–42). New York: Teachers College Press.

Kindler, A. M. (1992). Worship of creativity and artistic development of young children. *CSEA Journal, 23*(2), 12–17.

Kindler, A. M. (1993). Implications of research in developmental psychology to early childhood art education practice. *Visual Arts Research, 19*(1), 16–19.

Kindler, A. M. (1994). Artistic learning in early childhood: A study of social interactions. *Canadian Review of Art Education, 21*(2), 91–106.

Kindler, A. M. (1996). Myths, habits, research and policy: The four pillars of early childhood art education. *Arts Education Policy Review, 97*(4, March–April).

Kolbe, U. (1993). Co-player and co-artist: New roles for the adult in children's visual arts experiences. *Early Child Development and Care, 90,* 73–82.

Kolbe, U. (2001). *Rapunzel's supermarket: All about young children and their art.* Sydney, Australia: Peppinot Press.

Koralek, J. (1995). *The boy and the cloth of dreams.* London: Walker Books.

Koster, J. (1999). Clay for little fingers. *Young Children, 54*(2), 18–22.

Kramhansl, C. L., & Jusczyk, P. W. (1990). Infants' perception of phrase structure in music. *Psychological Science, I*(1), 70–73.

Kratus, J. (1991). Growing with improvisation. *Music Educators Journal, 78*(4), 35–40.

Kress, G. (2000a). Design and transformation: New theories of meaning. In B. Cope & M. Kalantzis (Eds.), *Multiliteracies: Literacy learning and the design of social futures* (pp. 153–161). South Yarra, Victoria: Macmillan.

Kress, G. (2000b). Multimodality. In B. Cope & M. Kalantzis (Eds.), *Multiliteracies: Literacy learn-*

ing and the design of social futures (pp. 183–202). South Yarra, Victoria: Macmillan.

Laban, R. (1971). *The mastery of movement.* Boston: Plays.

LaFuente, M. J., Grifol, R., Segarra, J., Soriano, J., & Gorba, M. A., et al. (1997). Effects of the Firstart method of prenatal stimulation on psychomotor development: The first six months. *Pre- and Peri-Natal Psychology Journal, 11*(3), 151–162.

Laing, A., & Pang, L. (1992). Early childhood education in the People's Republic of China. In G. A. Woodill, J. Bernhard, & L. Prochner (Eds.), *International handbook of early childhood education* (pp. 169–174). New York: Garland.

Lamb, S. J., & Gregory, A. H. (1993). The relationship between music and reading in beginning readers. *Educational Psychology, 13,* 19–26.

Langer, S. K. (1924/1971). *Philosophy in a new key: A study in the symbolism of reason, rite, and art.* Cambridge: Harvard University Press.

Lave, J., & Wenger, E. (1991). *Situated learning: Legitimate peripheral participation.* New York: Cambridge University Press.

Leeds, J. A. (1989). The history of attitudes toward children's art. *Studies in art education, 30*(2), 93–103.

Lehman, P. R. (2000a). A vision for the future. *Arts Education Policy Review, 102*(2), 15–16.

Lehman, P. R. (2000b). Unfinished business. *Arts Education Policy Review, 101*(3), 21–22.

Leng, Z., & Shaw, G. (1991). Toward a neural theory of higher brain function using music as a window. *Concepts in Neuroscience, 2*(2), 229–258.

Li, S. (1993). Kindergarten education in the People's Republic of China. In G. Ashby (Ed.), *Perspectives on early childhood education in the People's Republic of China* (pp. 5–14). Brisbane: Queensland University of Technology.

Lindqvist, G. (1995). The aesthetics of play—A didactic study of play and culture in preschools, Acta Universitatis Upsealiensis (doctoral dissertation at Uppsala University). Uppsala: Uppsala Studies in Education 62.

Lowenfeld, V. (1947). *Creative and mental growth* (1st ed.). New York: Macmillan.

Luke, C. (1995). Media and cultural studies. In P. Freebody & S. L. Muspratt, (Eds.), *Constructing critical literacies.* Crosskill: Hampton Press.

Luo, L. H. (1993). Arduous journey to go: Perspectives on the reform of early childhood education in China since 1989. In G. Ashby (Ed.), *Perspectives on early childhood education in the*

People's Republic of China (pp. 34–45). Brisbane: Queensland University of Technology.

MacNaughton, G., & Williams, G. (2000). *Techniques for teaching young children: Choices in theory and practice.* Sydney: Longman.

Mahlmann, J. J. (2000). Music education half a century hence. *Arts Education Policy Review, 102*(2), 23–24.

Malaguzzi, L. (1987). The hundred languages of children: Commentary. *I Cento Linguaggi Dei Bambini.* Reggio Emilia: Department of Education.

Malaguzzi, L. (1993). History, ideas, and basic philosophy. In C. Edwards, L. Gandini, & G. Forman (Eds.), *The hundred languages of children* (pp. 41–90). Norwood, NJ: Ablex.

Marzano, R. J., Brandt, R. S., Hughes, C. S., Jones, B. F., Presseisen, B. Z., et al. (1988). *Dimensions of thinking: A framework for curriculum and instruction.* Alexandria, VA: Association for Supervision and Curriculum Development.

Matthews, J. (1994a). Deep structures in children's art: Development and culture. *Visual Arts Research, 20*(2), 29–50.

Matthews, J. (1994b). Helping children to draw and paint in early childhood. *Children and visual representation 0–8 series.* England: Hodder & Stoughton.

Matthews, J. (1997). The 4-dimensional language of infancy: The interpersonal basis of art practice. *Journal of Art and Design Education, 16*(3), 285–293.

Matthews, J. (1999). *The art of childhood and adolescence. The construction of meaning.* London: Falmer Press.

McArdle, F. (2001). Art in early childhood. The discourse of "proper" teaching. Doctoral dissertation, Queensland University of Technology, Brisbane.

McDonald, D. T. (1979). *Music in our lives: The early years.* Washington, DC: National Association for the Education of Young Children.

Mead, M. (1942/1971). *And keep your powder dry: An anthropologist looks at America.* New York: Morrow.

Miller, P., & Goodnow, J. (1995). Cultural practices: Toward in integration of culture and development. In J. J. Goodnow, P. J. Miller, & F. Kessel (Eds.), *Cultural practices as contexts for development* (pp. 5–16). San Francisco: Jossey-Bass.

Moen, M. K. (1991). Introduction. In B. Ouden & M. Moen (Eds.), *The presence of feeling in thought* (pp. 1–9). New York: Peter Long.

Monighan-Nourot, P., & Van Hoorn, J. (1991, September). Symbolic play in preschool and primary settings. *Young Children*, 40–50.

Moog, H. (1976). *The musical experience of the preschool child*. London: Schott.

Moorhead, G., & Pond, D. (1941). *Music for young children*. Santa Barbara, CA: Pillsbury Foundation for the Advancement of the Arts.

Morgan, N., & Saxton, J. (1987). *Teaching drama: A mind of many wonders*. Cheltenham, UK: Stanley Thornes.

Moyles, J. (1989). *Just playing? The role and status of play in early childhood*. Milton Keynes, UK: Open University Press.

Moyles, J. (Ed.). (1994). *The excellence of play*. Buckingham, UK: Open University Press.

Murray, B. (1996, April). Students stretch beyond the "three R's." *American Psychological Association Monitor*.

Murray, R. L. (1975). *Dance in elementary education: A program for boys and girls* (3rd ed.). New York: Harper & Row.

Mursell, J. (1956). *Music education: Principles and programs*. Morristown, NJ: Silver-Burdett.

Musatti, C. (1987). The importance of looking at ourselves. *The hundred languages of children*. Reggio Emilia, Italy: Cooperative Slaughtering Company.

Nettl, V., Capwell, C., Wong., L. K. F., & Turino, T. (Eds.). (1997). *Excursions in world music* (2nd ed.). Upper Saddle River, NJ: Prentice Hall.

New, R. (1993). Cultural variations on developmentally appropriate practice: Challenges to theory and practice. In C. Edwards, L. Gandini, & G. Forman (Eds.), *The hundred languages of children* (pp. 215–231). Norwood, NJ: Ablex.

Olsho, L. S. (1984). Infant frequency discrimination. *Infant Behaviour and Development, 7*, 27–35.

O'Neill, C. (1991). Structure and spontaneity: Improvisation in theatre and education. Doctoral dissertation, University of Exeter, UK.

O'Neill, C. (1995). *Drama worlds: A framework for process drama*. Portsmouth, England: Heinemann.

Orff, C. (1978). *The schulwerk*. (M. Murray, trans.). New York: Schott Music Corp.

O'Toole, J. (1992). *The process of drama: Negotiating art and meaning*. London: Routledge.

O'Toole, J., & Dunn, J. (in press). *Pretending to learn*. French's Forest: Pearson Education.

Papõsck, M., & Papõsck, H. (1982, March). Musical elements in mother-infant dialogues. Paper presented at the International Conference on Infant Studies, Austin, Texas.

Parsons, M. J. (1987). *How we understand art: A cognitive developmental account of the aesthetic experience*. Cambridge, UK: Cambridge University Press.

Pautz, M. P. (1989). Musical thinking in the teacher education classroom. In E. Boardman (Ed.), *Dimensions of musical thinking* (pp. 101–110). Reston, VA: Music Educators National Conference.

Perry, R., & Irwin, L. (2000). *Playing with curriculum: Strategies and benefits*.

Perkins, K. (1981). *The mind's best work*. Cambridge, MA: Harvard University Press.

Petter, G. (1987). Shadowiness. In Department of Early Education, City of Reggio Emilia, Region of Emilia Romagna, *I centro linguaggi dei bambini (The hundred languages of children: Narrative of the possible)*. Catalogue of the Exhibit, Assessorato Scuole Infanzia e Asili Nido, Via Guido da Castello 12, 42100, pp. 72–76. Italy: Reggio Emilia.

Phenix, P. (1964). *Realms of meaning: A philosophy of the curriculum for general education*. New York: McGraw-Hill.

Piaget, J. (1932). *The moral judgment of the child*. New York: Harcourt Brace.

Piaget, J. (1951). *Play, dreams and imitation in childhood*. London: Routledge.

Piaget, J. (1955). *The child's construction of reality*. Sydney: Routledge-Kegan Hall.

Piscitelli, B. (1996). *Designing art programs for young children*. Brisbane: QUT.

Piscitelli, B., McArdle, F., & Weier, K. (1999). *Beyond "look and learn": Investigating, implementing and evaluating interactive learning strategies for young children in museums*. Brisbane: QUT-Industry Collaborative Research Project.

Plummeridge, C. (1991). *Music education in theory and practice*. London: Falmer.

Preston-Dunlop, V. A. (1980). *Handbook for dance in education* (2nd ed.). Extover, Plymouth, UK: Macdonald & Evans.

Qualifications and Curriculum Authority and Arts Council of England. (2000). *From policy to partnership: Developing the arts in schools*. London: Arts Council of England.

Rankin, B. (1993). Curriculum development in Reggio Emilia: A long-term curriculum project about dinosaurs. In C. Edwards, L. Gandini, & G. Forman (Eds.), *The hundred languages of children: The Reggio Emilia approach to early childhood education* (pp. 189–211). Norwood, NJ: Ablex.

Rauscher, F. H., Shaw, G. L., Levine, L. J., Wright, E. L., Dennis, W. R., and Newcomb, R. L. (1997). Music training causes long-term enhancement of preschool children's reasoning. *Neurological Research, 19*(1), 2–7.

Reid, L. A. (1983). Aesthetic knowledge in the arts. In M. Ross (Ed.), *The arts: A way of knowing* (pp. 19–42). Oxford, UK: Pergamon Press.

Reimer, B. (1989). *A philosophy of music education.* Englewood Cliffs, NJ: Prentice Hall.

Reimer, B. (2000). The way it will be. *Arts Education Policy Review, 102*(2), 7–8.

Reinhardt, D. A. (1990, Fall). Preschool children's use of rhythm in improvisation. *Contributions to Music Education, 17,* 7–19.

Reis, N. L. (1987). An analysis of the characteristics of infant-child singing expressions: Replication report. *Canadian Journal of Research in Music Education, 19,* 5–20.

Rice, D. (1990). Commentaries. *Journal of Aesthetic Education, 24*(1), 95–99.

Rinaldi, C. (1993). The emergent curriculum and social constructivism: An interview with Lela Gandini. In C. Edwards, L. Gandini, & G. Forman (Eds.), *The hundred languages of children* (pp. 101–112). Norwood, NJ: Ablex.

Rogers, S. J. (1990). Theories of child development and musical ability. In F. R. Wilson, & F. L. Roehman (Eds.), *Music and child development: Proceedings of the 1987 Denver Conference* (pp. 1–10). St. Louis: MMB Music.

Rogoff, B. (1990). *Apprenticeship in thinking: Cognitive development in social context.* New York: Oxford University Press.

Rosario, J., & Collazo, E. (1981). Aesthetic codes in context: An exploration of two preschool classrooms. *Journal of Aesthetic Education, 15*(1), 71–82.

Ross, J. (2000). Arts education in the information age: A new place for somatic wisdom. *Arts Education Review, 101*(6), 27–32.

Sadoski, M., Paivio, A., & Goetz, E. T. (1991). Commentary: A critique of schema theory in reading and a dual coding alternative. *Reading Research Quarterly, 26*(4), 463–484.

Sawyer, R. K. (1997). *Pretend play as improvisation: Conversation in the preschool classroom.* Mahwah, NJ: Lawrence Erlbaum Associates.

Schiller, M. (1995). An emergent art curriculum that fosters understanding. *Young Children, 50*(3), 33–38.

Schramm, M. (1971). A study of the process of improvisation and its role in modern dance. Master's thesis. University of Illinois, Urbana-Champaign.

Schuler, S. C. (2001). Music and education in the twenty-first century: A retrospective. *Arts Education Policy Review, 102*(3), 25–36.

Scott, C. (1989). How children grow—musically. *Music Educators Journal, 76*(2), 28–31.

Seefeldt, C. (1995). Art: A serious work. *Young Children, 50*(3), 39–45.

Seltzer, K., & Bentley, T. (1999). *The creative age: Knowledge and skills for the new economy.* London: DEMOS.

Sessions, R. (1970). *Questions about music.* New York: W. W. Norton.

Shehan, P. K. (1990). Movement in the music education of children. In F. R. Wilson, & F. L. Roehman (Eds.), *Music and child development: Proceedings of the 1987 Denver Conference* (pp. 354–365). St. Louis, MO: MMB Music.

Shetler, D. J. (1989). The inquiry into prenatal musical experience: A report of the Eastman Project 1980–1987. *Pre- and Peri-Natal Psychology, 33,* 171–189.

Shore, B. (1996). *Culture in mind: Cognition, culture and the problem of meaning.* New York: Oxford University Press.

Simpson, A. (1988). Language, literature and art. *Journal of Aesthetic Education, 22*(2), 47–53.

Singer, D. G., & Singer, J. L. (1990). *The house of make-believe children's play and the developing imagination.* Cambridge, MA: Harvard University Press.

Singer, J. L. (1995). Imaginative play in childhood: Precursor of subjunctive thought, daydreaming and adult pretending games. In A. D. Pellegrini (Ed.), *The future of play theory: A multi-disciplinary inquiry into the contributions of Brian Sutton-Smith* (pp. 187–219). New York: State University of New York Press.

Smith, N. (1993). *Experience and art: Teaching children to paint* (2nd ed.). New York: Teachers College Press.

Smith, R. A. (2000). Policymaking for the future: Three critical issues. *Arts Education Policy Review, 102*(2), 21–22.

Snyder, S. (2001). Connection, correlation, and integration. *Music Educators Journal, 87*(5), 32–39ff.

Spearman, C. (1927). *The nature of intelligence and the principles of cognition.* London: Macmillan.

Spodek, B., & Saracho, O. (Eds.). (1992). *Issues in childcare.* New York: Teachers College Press.

Stainton Rogers, R. W. (1992). *Stories of childhood: Shifting agendas of child concern.* Toronto: University of Toronto Press.

Stecher, M. B., McElheny, H., & Greenwood, M. (1978). *Joy and learning through music and movement improvisation.* New York: Macmillian.

Steele, B. (2002). *Mapping and memory.* http://www.lboro.ac.uk/departments/ac/newtracey/steele.html[20–02–02].

Stein, G. (1970). *Gertrude Stein on Picasso*/Edited by Edward Burns. New York: Liveright.

Sternberg, R. J., & Lubart, T. I. (1995). *Defying the crowd: Cultivating creativity in a culture of conformity.* New York: Free Press.

Stremmel, A. J., & Fu, V. R. (1993). Teaching in the zone of proximal development: Implications for responsive teaching practice. *Child & Youth Care Forum, 22*(5), 337–350.

Swanwick, K. (1988). *Music, mind, and education.* London: Routledge.

Swanwick, K. (1999). Music education: Closed or open? *Journal of Aesthetic Education, (33)*4, 127–138.

Swanwick, K., & Tillman, J. (1986). The sequence of musical development: A study of children's compositions. *British Journal of Music Education, 3*(3), 305–339.

Sweet, A. P. (1996). A national policy perspective on research intersections between literacy and the visual/communicative arts. In J. Flood, S. Brice Heath, & D. Lapp (Eds.), *Handbook of research on teaching literacy through the communicative and visual arts* (pp. 264–285). New York: Simon & Schuster.

Thompson, C. M. (1995). Transforming curriculum in the visual arts. In S. Bredekamp, & T. Rosengrant (Eds.), *Reaching potentials: Transforming early childhood curriculum and assessment* (Vol. 2). Washington, DC: NAEYC.

Thorpe, L. A., & Trehub, S. E. (1989). Duration illusion and auditory grouping in infancy. *Developmental Psychology, 25,* 122–127.

Thurstone, L. L. (1938). *Primary mental abilities.* Chicago: University of Chicago Press.

Thurstone, L. L. (1947). *Multiple-factor analyses: A development and expansion of "The Vectors of the Mind."* Chicago: University of Chicago Press.

Towsey, M., Brown, A., Wright, S., & Diederich, J. (2001). Towards melodic extension using genetic algorithms: Research in progress. *Educational Technology and Society, 4*(2). http://ifets.ieee.org/periodical/vol_2_2001/v_2_2001.html.

Trehub, S. E., Bull, D., & Thorpe, L. A. (1984). Infants' perception of melodies: The role of melodic contour. *Child Development, 55,* 821–830.

Trehub, S. E., & Thorpe, L. A. (1989). Infants' perception of rhythm: Categorization of auditory sequences by temporal structure. *Canadian Journal of Psychology, 43,* 217–229.

Tyler, D. (1993). Making better children. In D. Meredyth & D. Tyler (Eds.), *Child and citizen: Genealogies of schooling and subjectivity* (pp. 35–60). Brisbane: Griffith University.

Van de Carr, R. (1986). Enhancing early speech, parental bonding and infant physical development using prenatal intervention in standard obstetric practice. *Pre- and Peri-Natal Psychology, 1*(1), 20–29.

Vecchi, V. (1993). The role of the Atelierista: An interview with Lella Gandini. In C. Edwards, L. Bandini, & Forman, G. (Eds.), *The hundred languages of children* (pp. 119–31). Norwood, NJ: Ablex.

Vygotsky, L. S. (1962). *Thought and language.* Cambridge, MA: MIT.

Vygotsky, L. S. (1976). Play and its role in the mental development of the child. In J. S. Bruner, A. Jolly, K. Sylva (Eds.), *Play: Its role in development and evolution* (pp. 537–554). Harmondsworth: Penguin Books.

Vygotsky, L. S. (1978). *Mind in society: The development of higher psychological processes.* Edited by Michael Cole, Vera John-Steiner, Sylvia Scribner, & Ellen Souberman. Cambridge, MA: Harvard University Press.

Walker, M. E. (2000). Movement and metaphor: Towards an embodied theory of music cognition and hermeneutics. *Bulletin of the Council of Research in Music Education, 145,* 27–42.

Walkerdine, V. (1992). Progressive pedagogy and political struggle. In C. Luke & J. Gore (Eds.), *Feminisms and critical pedagogy* (pp. 15–24). New York: Routledge.

Walsh, D. J. (1993). Art as socially constructed narrative: Implications for early childhood education. *Arts Education Policy Review, 94*(6), 18–23.

Weier, K. (2000). Using picture books to develop art appreciation skills. *Signpost, 3,* 2–4.

Weinberger, N. M. (1998, January/February). Brain, behavior, and music: Some research findings and their implications for educational policy. *Arts Education Policy Review,* 1–11.

Wiggins, R. A. (2001). Interdisciplinary curriculum: Music educator concerns. *Music Educators Journal, 87*(5), 40–44.

Williamson, P., & Silvern, S. (1986, October). Eliciting creative dramatic play. *Childhood Education, 63,* 2–5.

Winner, E. (1986, August). Where pelican kiss seals. *Psychology Today,* 25–35.

Winner, E. (1989). How can Chinese children draw so well? *Journal of Aesthetic Education, 23,* 41–63.

Wolf, A. (1990). Art postcards: Another aspect of your aesthetics program? *Young Children, 45*(2), 39–43.

Wolf, D., & Davis Perry, M. (1988). From Endpoints to repertoires: Some new conclusions about drawing development. *Journal of Aesthetic Education, 22*(1), 17–34.

Wolf, D., & Gardner, H. (1980). Beyond playing or polishing: A developmental view of artistry. In J. J. Hausman (Ed.), *Art and the schools* (pp. 47–77). New York: McGraw-Hill.

Wong, W. (2001). Visual medium in the service and disservice of education. *Journal of Aesthetic Education, 35*(2), 25–33.

Worth, S. E. (2000). Understanding the objects of music. *Journal of Aesthetic Education, 34*(1), 102–105.

Wright, L. (1990). The social and nonsocial behaviours of precocious preschoolers during free play. *Roeper Review, 12*(4), 268–274.

Wright, S. (1985). The effect of Kodály music training on the development of meter discrimination in young children. Doctoral dissertation. University of Newcastle, NSW, Australia.

Wright, S. (1991). The relationship between meter recognition, rhythmic notation, and information processing competence. *Australian Journal of Psychology, 43,* 139–146.

Wright, S. (1993). Social and developmental influences on children's use of visual metaphors. *Australian Art Education, 17*(1), 23–29.

Wright, S. (1994a). Artistic development and learning: An integration of processes for young children. In G. Boulton-Lewis, & D. Catherwood (Eds.), *The early years* (pp. 186–221). Hawthorn: Australian Council for Educational Research.

Wright, S. (1994b). Assessment in the arts: Is it appropriate in the early childhood years? *Studies in Art Education, 36*(1), 28–43.

Wright, S. (1995a). Children's musical composition and information processing style. *Journal of Cognitive Education, 4*(2–3), 103–111.

Wright, S. (1995b). Cultural influences on children's developing artistry: What can China and Australia learn from each other. *Australian Journal of Early Childhood Education, 20*(3), 39–45.

Wright, S. (1997a). The arts and schooling: An analysis of cultural influences. *Journal of Cognitive Education, 6*(1), 53–69.

Wright, S. (1997b). Learning how to learn: The arts as core in an emergent curriculum. *Childhood Education* (M. Cohen & J. Hoot, Eds.), *73*(6), 361–365.

Wright, S. (2000). Challenging literacy perspectives. Paper presented at the Australian Association for Research in Education, University of Sydney.

Wright, S. (2001a). Guiding learning processes in the integration of the arts. *Contemporary Issues in Early Childhood, 2*(2), 225–238.

Wright, S. (2001b). Drawing and storytelling as a means for understanding children's concepts of the future. *Futures, 6*(2), 1–20.

Wright, S., & Ashman, A. (1991). The use of symbols in drawings by children, non-disabled adults and adults with an intellectual disability. *Developmental Disabilities Bulletin, 19*(2), 105–128.

Wu, D. Y. H. (1992). Early childhood education in China. In S. Feeney (Ed.), *Early childhood education in Asia and the Pacific* (pp. 1–26). New York: Garland Publishing.

Yawkey, T., & Fox, F. (1981). Evaluative intervention research in child's play. *Journal of Research and Development in Education, 14*(3), 41–57.

Zhang, B. (1993). Early childhood curriculum in China. In G. Ashby (Ed.), *Perspectives on early childhood education in the People's Republic of China* (pp. 34–45). Brisbane: Queensland University of Technology, School of Early Childhood.

Zhao, J. (1990). Early childhood education in China. In P. B. Chan (Ed.). *Early childhood toward the 21st century* (pp. 467–474). Hong Kong: Yew Chung Educational Publishing Company.

Zhu, M. (1997, April). National policy on the protection of children's rights to education. Paper presented at the First Australasian Conference on Children's Rights, Brisbane, Australia.

Zimmerman, M. (1971). *Musical characteristics of children.* Reston, VA: Music Educators National Conference.

Zohar, D., & Marshall, I. (2000). *Spiritual intelligence: The ultimate intelligence.* London: Bloomsbury.

INDEX